Working with Parents and Families of Exceptional Children and Youth

Working with Parents and Families of Exceptional Children and Youth

Techniques for Successful Conferencing and Collaboration

THIRD EDITION

Richard L. Simpson

pro·ed

8700 Shoal Creek Boulevard
Austin, Texas 78757-6897

pro·ed

© 1996, 1990 by PRO-ED, Inc.
8700 Shoal Creek Boulevard
Austin, Texas 78757-6897

Library of Congress Cataloging-in-Publication Data
Simpson, Richard L., 1945–
    Working with parents and families of exceptional children and
youth : techniques for successful conferencing collaboration /
Richard L. Simpson. — 3rd ed.
      p.   cm.
    Rev. ed. of : Conferencing parents of exceptional children. c1990.
    Includes bibliographical references and index.
    ISBN 0-89079-638-6 (pbk.)
    1. Parent-teacher conferences—United States. 2. Parents of
exceptional children—Counseling of—United States. 3. Special
education—United States. 4. Exceptional children—United States—
Family relationships. I. Simpson, Richard L., 1945–
Conferencing parents of exceptional children. II. Title.
LC225.5.S55   1996   95-20862
371.9—dc20   CIP
                                                Rev.

This book is designed in Goudy and Poetica.

Production Manager: Alan Grimes
Production Coordinator: Karen Swain
Managing Editor: Tracy Sergo
Art Director: Thomas Barkley
Reprints Buyer: Alicia Woods
Editor: Jane Doyle Guthrie
Editorial Assistant: Claudette Landry
Editorial Assistant: Martin Wilson

Printed in the United States of America

   2 3 4 5 6 7 8 9 10   00 99 98 97 96

Contents

Preface

The central theme of the third edition of *Working with Parents and Families of Exceptional Children and Youth: Techniques for Successful Conferencing and Collaboration* is that educators and related professionals, including classroom teachers, must be involved in helping parents and families to contend with the various issues they routinely confront when raising and living with a child who has an exceptionality. Suitably trained educators are the most appropriate resource for collaboratively serving the needs of parents and families of these children, and it was in an effort to provide this training that this book was undertaken.

Parent and family conferencing and collaboration is a subject area that requires both cognitive understanding and related experiences. Thus, while readers should recognize that parent and family involvement is based on a theoretical, clinical, and empirical foundation, they must also accept that the development of skills necessary for meaningful relationships with parents and families requires appropriate experiences and practice. Accordingly, readers are strongly encouraged to view the included role-playing activities and exercises as an integral and basic component of this book. Indeed, the adage that we learn best by doing presents an underlying premise of this book.

Though the training of educators and related professionals in parent and family conferencing skills has historically received limited attention, it is becoming increasingly apparent that competency in this area is necessary for professional success. Only with skill and competence in working with parents and families will educators be able to serve, collaboratively and most effectively, the needs of students with exceptionalities.

Part I

The Family of the Child with an Exceptionality

Chapter 1

Understanding and Responding to Needs of Parents and Families

How to develop and maintain meaningful and effective relationships between parents, family members, and professionals is a topic that has received widespread attention during the past decades. For example, numerous books, articles, and conferences have reflected the importance of an effective parent/family-professional relationship and suggested methods for facilitating such cooperative involvement (Barnard, Christophersen, & Wolf, 1977; Bennett, 1987; Fewell & Vadasy, 1986; Fine, 1991; Lambie & Daniels-Mohring, 1993; O'Dell, 1974; Paul & Simeonsson, 1993; Winston, 1986). However, in spite of such attention, educators and other professionals involved with children and youth with exceptionalities are often ill at ease and ineffectual when attempting to advocate, communicate, collaborate, and, in general, meet the needs of parents and family members. Even professionals with expertise in direct service to children and youth and in relating to other professional disciplines often find it difficult to extend their services to parent/family functions (Fine, 1989; Mullins, 1987).

The factors associated with this situation are multiple and complicated, yet four primary considerations emerge. First, many professionals' lack of understanding of the American family and its changing role is at least partially responsible for their deficiencies in the area of parent and family conferencing. To be able to offer appropriate, effective services to parents and families, professionals must possess an understanding of the nature of today's family, its attitudes and values, and the background against which the latter were developed.

A second factor relates to a general confusion about the relationship between educators and other professionals and parents/families. That is, there is little clarity and few guidelines regarding which professionals are responsible for meeting various parent and family needs, and how they should go about meeting these needs in an organized and orchestrated fashion. Hence it is not surprising that a lack of clarity and agreement in this respect should create service-delivery problems.

The third issue concerns how to properly identify and serve the needs of parents and families of children and youth with exceptionalities. In spite of numerous efforts, the needs of parents and families with exceptional members and the skills and procedures required of professionals to serve these needs have not been clearly identified.

Finally, widespread lack of parent/family conferencing skill can be attributed to training deficiencies. In spite of recent improvements, efficacious and appropriate curricula and training experiences in this area are still lacking, particularly in teacher education programs.

This chapter will discuss factors that are essential for improving services to parents and families of exceptional children and youth, including (a) trends in parent and family patterns, (b) educators' roles in interacting with and serving the needs of parents and families, (c) skills needed to conference with parents and families, (d) a model for parent and family involvement, and (e) development of a personalized parent/family philosophy and style.

Parent and Family
Historical Perspective

The nature and function of the American family has changed dramatically over the past decades, and with it parents' relationship to the educational institutions attended by their children. Prior to the 19th century, most day-to-day activities centered almost exclusively around the family. Parents and other members of extended families worked at or near their homes and the family functioned as the primary educational and social institution for children and youth. In fact, parents were frequently responsible for educating their own children. In the mid-17th century, for example, a provision in the Massachusetts Bay Colony stipulated that parents could be fined for failing to educate their children. Early American society was based on an agrarian economy, a way of life that required the participation of entire families, including relatively young children, to produce the basics necessary to sustain life. This lifestyle was characterized by strict role assignments and well-established family and community values. Thus, rules, policies, and values reflected the position of the family and the roles of individual family members and were compatible with the philosophy of rural America. In keeping with this tradition, schools, whenever available, were designed to both reflect and perpetuate family and community values. Consequently, close cooperation between educators and parents was a necessity (Bayles & Hood, 1966). Few of the problems experienced by present-day educators were common to that era. It is difficult, for example, to imagine debates over which reading series to use with students, whether a particular teacher-applied intervention might result in a lawsuit, or whether a pupil's IEP had sufficient parental input.

With the Industrial Revolution came the transformation of agrarian life to what eventually became modern urban society. This large-scale social and economic development brought about two profound changes: the movement of families from farms to cities, and the inclusion of women (in some instances children) in the workforce (Goode, 1971). As families moved from farms to cities, contact with extended family members often decreased and, thus, so did the opportunity for children to be exposed to a variety of adult family role models. In addition, city life resulted in exposure to families representing different attitudes and value systems. Gradually such contacts came to exert more influence on children's attitudes and values than exposure to extended family members and the more restricted beliefs of small agricultural communities. Furthermore, the induction of women into the workforce during the Industrial Revolution resulted in less contact between children, parents, and other adult family members. Hence, children and youth began to spend relatively long periods of time without parental supervision, and their peer groups came to assume a much stronger role in attitude and value formation.

During the period between the Industrial Revolution and the Civil War, American education began to exhibit many of the characteristics that are prevalent today. Children and youth were given an opportunity to attend publicly supported schools; graded schools and self-contained classrooms proliferated; formal teacher training programs in colleges and universities developed; curricular options increased; and consolidated schools staffed and operated by professional educators became the rule.

Since World War II, major technological, political, and economic events have resulted in monumental changes in the American family. Children and youth are presently a part of family units that rarely include grandparents and other extended family members; frequent moves have become commonplace; single-parent and reconstituted families are increasing in numbers; and families where both parents are employed full-time outside the home are becoming the norm. As a result of these changes, parents commonly expect the schools to fulfill roles traditionally assumed by the family.

While disagreement abounds on the nature and ultimate result of these trends (Bronfenbrenner, 1979; Hodgkinson, 1993; Vadasy, 1986; Zionts & Simpson, 1988), schools are the major social institution to feel the impact of the following statistics:

- A working father, a housewife mother, and two school-age children constitute less than 6% of U.S. households.

- Approximately 22% of the total U.S. population and 30% of school-age children are classified as minority, and it is anticipated that the minority student percentage will increase to 36% about the year 2000.

- More than 23% of children were living below the poverty line in 1993, most in inner city and rural areas.

- Over 15 million children are being reared by single mothers, whose family income in 1991 averaged about $11,400.

- Approximately 350,000 children are born each year to mothers who are addicted to cocaine during pregnancy.

- Every day in the United States approximately 2,750 teenage girls become pregnant; 6 teens commit suicide; 1,375 children drop out of school; 1,849 children are abused; and 3,300 children run away from home.

- Violent crime increased by 371% between 1960 and 1992; property crimes increased from 1,726 reported crimes per 100,000 persons in 1960 to 4,903 in 1992; and the number of guns increased from 54 million in 1950 to 210 million in 1990.

- There was a 91% increase in arrests for violent crimes by youths under 18 between 1970 and 1992.

- In 1970 there were approximately 10 births per 1,000 to unmarried women aged 15 to 19; in 1983 this figure was estimated to be approximately 18.5, an 85% increase; in 1991 about 30% of births occurred out of wedlock; and this accelerating trend continues today.

- In 1970 approximately 1 in 9 babies was born to a single mother; in 1983 this figure rose to approximately 1 baby in 5; and in 1993 the number increased to 1 baby in 3.

Without argument, the family has changed along with the other social institutions in this country. No longer is the family a self-sufficient entity where parents, children, and other extended family members jointly work together to provide for the economic security of the members, and where most educational, social, and ethical development takes place. Presently both children and parents spend increased amounts of time outside the home. In spite of irrefutable data and other signs of familial change, however, little evidence exists to indicate that the world's oldest social institution will fail to endure. The family continues to serve a major social function and will most likely persist as the major lifestyle model in the future.

For these reasons educators and other professionals involved with children and their families must recognize changing family patterns and develop responsive programs for children, youth, and families. Specifically, professionals must recognize and accept that many children and families will be impermanent community members; that current divorce and blended-family rates will likely continue; that cultural, racial, economic, and value diversity characterizes every community and school; that schools may function less as recreational and social centers of the community; and that disagreements will occur among professionals and families regarding the extent to which the education and socialization of children is the exclusive function of professional educators.

At the same time, educators must recognize that parents must be part of any instructional program—especially those designed for children and youth with exceptionalities—and that functional and efficacious models and solutions can be developed to help solve family problems and facilitate the growth and development of children and youth.

The unique and changing nature of most families as well as the complex social and economic issues affecting parents, professionals, and children make cookbook approaches to parent conferencing insufficient. Instead, today's educator needs pragmatic strategies to function effectively with parents and families. The challenge is significant; however, the procedures and technology needed for successful parent/school involvement can be acquired by those willing to develop appropriate conferencing skills.

Values and Attitudes for Effective Parent and Family Involvement

Beyond taking into consideration the values and lifestyles of others, the parent/family conferencer must also be cognizant of his or her own values and attitudes and, to the maximum extent possible, be prepared to suspend judgment on actions and lifestyles that otherwise may conflict with his or her personal preferences. Although professionals are not expected to promote or endorse lifestyles or modes of behavior with which they do not agree (e.g., raising children outside of marriage, communal living arrangements), they must recognize that they may encounter parents and families who have adopted such lifestyles. Thus, in order for educators to be maximally successful, they must possess not only appropriate professional strategies but also tolerance for modes of behavior that do not align with their own.

Major Factors Influencing Parent and Family Involvement

Over the past years unprecedented societal and educational changes have directly affected educators' and other professionals' interactions with parents and families. Several of these major changes are discussed below.

Maternal Employment

For decades the perception of the American family has been associated with images as those portrayed by television shows such as "Leave It to Beaver" and "Ozzie and Harriet." These television families presented the typical American family as comprised of a nonworking mother, a working father, and several children living together in comfortable middle-class neighborhoods, relatively free of stress and typical day-to-day problems. In contrast to these images, however, fewer and fewer family units today are represented by a working father and a stay-at-home mother. Either because of financial need or the desire to pursue a career, women with children increasingly are becoming part of the workforce (Isakson, 1979; Thurow, 1987; U.S. Department of Commerce, 1993). Indeed, trends show a number of occupations and professions becoming the domain of women (U.S. Bureau of Labor Statistics, 1991; U.S. Department of Commerce, 1993). As a result, professionals cannot expect children and youth to receive as much direct parental supervision as may be considered optimal, nor can they count on parents to be available for conferences during typical school hours. Accordingly, schools and agencies are increasingly finding it necessary to provide flexible conference schedules as well as consider alternatives to face-to-face meetings (e.g., phone conferences, written communication, computerized mail and communication systems). Without such flexibility many parents find it difficult or impossible to stay in touch with their children's teachers, let alone be active collaborators in school-related activities.

Although families in which both parents work full-time may represent a break with tradition, one cannot demonstrate that this change is in and of itself either good or bad (Copeland & White, 1991; Karpowitz, 1980; Zionts & Simpson, 1988). To date, this issue remains clouded by tremendous divergence of opinion and equivocal data. However, there are indications that the effect of maternal employment on children is directly associated with the mother's attitude towards working. Hoffman and Nye (1974) reported that children benefit most from situations where attitudes and behavior are congruent. That is, children seem to fare best when mothers desiring to work can pursue employment and when those wishing to remain in the home have that opportunity. In addition, today educators and the general public more and more recognize the benefits and necessity of employment.

Single-Parent and Blended Families

According to Dawson (1991), in 1960 three fourths of children lived with their biological parents, both of whom were in their first marriage, and only about 13% of U.S. families were headed by a single parent. In 1984 the percentage of U.S. families headed by a single parent was 22%; and in 1990 that figure had swelled to approximately 25%. While divorce rates are no longer significantly increasing, divorce and separation continue to play an important role in millions of children's lives. Moreover, ever-increasing births to unmarried women contribute to the number of children living in single-parent homes. In 1970 approximately 1 in 9 babies were born to single mothers; in 1983 this ratio had increased to 1 in 5. In 1990 approximately 1 in 5 White babies and 3 of 4 Black babies were born into female-headed households.

Not only are a significant number of individuals obtaining divorces and having children outside of marriage, remarriage is becoming more frequent. According to Hacker (1983), approximately 75% of divorced women under 30 who have children remarry, and Einstein (1982) estimated that more than 15 million children live in blended families, with approximately 500,000 annually added to that figure. More current data reveal that approximately 15% of households with children are composed of children from previous marriages (Lambie & Daniels-Mohring, 1993).

The current trend in divorce and separation has stabilized, and family reconstitution and unmarried mother rates show continued increases. Thus, professionals can expect a significant number of children and youth in their programs who are part of one-parent or blended families. Although these factors do not necessarily result in overtly negative outcomes for every child or youth, they can have a significant impact on a child's capacity to function in school (Hetherington & Cox, 1985; Hetherington & Martin, 1972; Simpson & Zionts, 1992; Wallerstein & Blakeslee, 1990). Specifically, correlates of single-parent families such as poverty and illegitimacy do not bode well for children's future (Kozol, 1991; Scherer, 1993; Yorburg, 1983), and separation, divorce, and restructuring a family can be traumatizing to children and youth (Emery, 1982; Martin, 1975; Wallerstein & Kelly, 1976; Zionts & Simpson, 1988). As noted by Kauffman (1977), "Not surprisingly, the presence of a good father or other positive male figure in the home and parental harmony in an intact family seem to bode well for children's behavior" (p. 74).

Professionals are finding it advisable to plan strategies to aid single-parent and reconstituted families. Such planning does not mean viewing every child and single-parent or reconstituted family as needing therapy, or every family that has experienced divorce, reconstitution, or those that are headed by a single adult as dysfunctional. Rather, in addition to individual differences, it is recommended that professionals recognize that single parents may have economic and time constraints beyond those of other families (Karpowitz, 1980; Schulz, 1987); that both parents and children will probably experience increased strain during periods of separation, divorce, and reconstitution (Hetherington, Arnett, & Hollier, 1985; Lambie & Daniels-Mohring, 1993; Martin, 1975); and that there may be a period when parents become so involved in their own personal matters that they may appear somewhat unconcerned and aloof about their child's school-related problems. Again, in these instances, professionals cannot allow their personal attitudes toward divorce and remarriage to interfere with effective parent/family involvement and collaboration. The success of conferencing with single-parent or blended families depends to a great extent on the professional's skills in finding ways to make parents and families a meaningful part of their child's school experience. This is particularly crucial because many parents and families undergoing a transition need close contact with school personnel.

Family Mobility

In the past teachers were often familiar with the parents and families of all the pupils in their classes. Teachers tended to be a part of a community, and families generally remained for generations in one locale. However, in pursuit of jobs, the "good life," or simply for the sake of change, families are now much more mobile. In addition, although neighborhood schools often prevail, today's professionals are much less apt to be a part of the community in which they work.

Notwithstanding arguments from certain businesses and business groups, the effects of frequent moves have not been beneficial for schools, parents, or pupils. Some parents report feeling alienated from their communities and unwilling to invest time and effort on forming new relationships for fear they would soon be transferred to another area. Similarly, some children report difficulty developing new relationships, adjusting to new schools and schedules, and becoming truly a part of changing schools or communities. One teacher reported that a newly transferred student asked that the teacher allow him to write his name in pencil in his books because his father might be transferred again before the end of the term. School personnel have also reported that frequently they cannot establish effective relationships with parents and pupils because of their transient lifestyles. In addition, school administrators and parents have voiced concern about the high turnover rate among teachers—a trend that is particularly acute in special education (Needle, Griffin, Svendsen, & Berney, 1980; Simpson, Whelan, & Zabel, 1993).

Though professionals may be unable to change or stem the mobile nature of our society, they can work to offset the problems of isolation, detachment, and fragmentation that often ensue. For example, initial attempts to establish rapport and to familiarize parents and families with their child's educational program may be significant. Such efforts may also result in bringing parents and children more closely together at a time when they are most vulnerable to stress.

Perceived Role of Schools

Along with the technological advances of the past decades has come an increased belief in the value of education and specialization. Notwithstanding frequent criticism of the public school system, Western society has become more and more wedded to the supposition that almost everybody needs specialized training. In keeping with this belief, some public school personnel and other professionals have convinced parents that professionals, not parents and families, are best qualified to train and educate children and youth. McAfee and Vergason (1979) observed that educators have been able "to convince parents that the values and expertise of the educational system is more desirable and more effective than anything the parents have to offer" (p. 2). As a result, parents have gradually allowed educators increased levels of responsibility for educating their children. For example, such topics as sex education, values, and family planning, once considered clearly within the domain of parents and the family, are now part of the public school curriculum.

As a result of the increased responsibility placed on the schools for most educational concerns, parents and other family members have in some circles become less often perceived as legitimate educators of their own children. Some parents are overly willing to relinquish all responsibility for their child's education to the school and hence are reluctant to participate cooperatively in joint programs with school personnel. Although this may not be the norm, educational personnel indeed may have undermined the basis for parental involvement by convincing the public that schools can be "all things to all people."

Although educators and other professionals must continue to play a prominent role in the welfare of parents, families, and children, they must also recognize that they cannot "be all things to all people" and that parents and families must share collaborative training and socialization responsibility. As suggested by Isakson (1979), educators must "recognize the strengths in families and capitalize on those so that they can get on with the business they were trained for—teaching" (p. 78). This collaborative division of labor will come about only through meaningful and sincere dialogue between parents and professionals. As summarized in one Gallup Poll (1979), "education in the local public schools can be achieved best when parents, the community, and the schools all work together" (p. 41).

Indeed, the recognition of parents and families as significant contributors to children's education and development is occurring. For example, in 1994 Senator Mark Hatfield of Oregon, in cooperation with Senators Nancy Kassebaum of Kansas and Kit Bond of Missouri, sponsored legislation to create a seventh national education goal, which would say: "By the year 2000, every school and home will engage in partnerships that will increase parental involvement and participation in promoting the social, emotional and academic growth of children." This proposed legislation, along with numerous other examples of cooperative parent-school programs, offers increasingly revealing recognition of the importance of combining family and professional resources to meet the needs of children and youth.

Legislation, Advocacy, and Empowerment

Parents and families, especially those with exceptional children and youth, are being urged more and more to become collaborators in their off-spring's educational programs and consequently are assuming major roles in decision making that will affect their children's future. This heightened parent-school involvement has stemmed partly from the acknowledgment by educators and other professionals of the importance of parental participation and cooperation. At the same time parents have been able to establish their position and role primarily because of legal, legislative, advocacy, and political maneuvers. Yet in spite of the importance of parents and family members in the development of their offspring, limited support and precedents exist for making them an integral part of the modern-day educational system. Historically parents were generally denied opportunities to participate as partners in the educational system. Rather, they were more commonly considered unqualified to be part of the educational decision-making process and to employ procedures in the natural environment that would facilitate their children's educational or social development. Even more inequitably, they often were looked upon as the cause of a child's problems and, thus, in need of treatment themselves.

This history of conflict has forced parents to assertively demand influence and opportunities for involvement. Specifically, through advocacy groups and other legal and legislative avenues, parents have been able to establish significant authority relative to the educational provisions for their children. These circumstances apply mostly to parents of children with disabilities. As a function of such parental action, professionals must now accommodate parents as a part of the educational team. Even though this mandated involvement has not been a panacea for all parent-professional problems, it has clearly resulted in increased home-school interaction and collaboration (Dunst & Paget, 1991; Simpson & Fiedler, 1989).

Two landmark cases in the parental struggle for educational service and involvement are *The Pennsylvania Association for Retarded Children v. the Commonwealth of Pennsylvania* (1971) and *Mills v. Board of Education, District of Columbia* (1972). In the Pennsylvania case, the state was sued for failure to provide a public education for all retarded children. The suit resulted in the issuance of an order for the implementation of educational services for retarded children in the state. Further, the decree stated that it was most desirable for these children to be educated in a program as similar to that of children without disabilities as possible. In *Mills v. Board of Education* (1972), parents filed a class action suit against the school system for failing to provide a publicly supported education for all children. As in the Pennsylvania case, the court issued a decree for educational opportunity for all children, including students with disabilities. Other particularly noteworthy court rulings are *Larry P. v. Riles* (1972), in which the court ruled that identification and/or placement in special education required a thorough and comprehensive evaluation, including consideration of students' cultural and linguistic backgrounds; and *Board of Education v. Rowley* (1982), which found that students with disabilities are entitled to an *appropriate* education as opposed to an *optimum* education.

In 1975 the Education for All Handicapped Children Act (PL 94-142) was signed into law, providing for a free and appropriate public education for all handicapped children. In 1986 PL 99-457 (Part H) amended the requirements of the previous law and mandated comprehensive multidisciplinary services for infants and toddlers and their families. PL 101-476, the Individuals with Disabilities Education Act (IDEA), amended in 1990 the Education for All Handicapped Children Act and required that school personnel provide transition services to students with disabilities. Most recently, the Americans with Disabilities Act of 1990 (ADA) reaffirmed the rights of individuals with disabilities to equal access to opportunities and facilities, including prohibition of discrimination by private sector employers against persons with disabilities. These laws, amendments to PL 93-380, the Education of the Handicapped Amendments of 1974, which in turn augmented and amended PL 89-10, the Elementary and Secondary Education Act of 1965, and PL 91-230, Education of the Handicapped Act (1969), have significantly increased the rights of persons with disabilities and the influence of their parents and guardians. In particular, four basic components of the Individuals with Disabilities Education Act (IDEA) and the Education for All Handicapped Children Act have been particularly noteworthy: assessment safeguards, due process, guarantee of placement in the "least restrictive environment," and an individualized education plan. Each allow for parental or guardian involvement and the opportunity for parents and legal custodians to function as advocates for their own children.

As a result of these efforts and programs, parent involvement has undergone significant change, and parent participation, collaboration, and influence will continue to characterize program offerings. In commenting on developments in this area over the past decades, Meyen (1978b) suggested that

> they represent changes so markedly different from the pattern estab-
> lished during the last 20 years that they will not be ignored. The conse-
> quences of these changes are so far-reaching that they affect not only the
> education of exceptional children but the future education of all chil-
> dren. (p. 3)

The legislative, legal, and advocacy transactions of recent years suggest the appropriateness of at least two basic responses by educators. First,
professionals must become familiar with educational legislation, advocacy
groups, and parent organizations; only with knowledge of local, state, and
national policies, enactments, and organizations will they be able to effectively serve the needs of parents and families. Second, and most importantly, professionals must recognize that parents and families must have an
opportunity for partnership in their children's education. History attests
to the fact that when parents are denied opportunities for participation,
collaboration, and involvement, they will seek other avenues of recourse.
When parents are forced to exercise their right to input via political, legal,
and legislative strategies, everyone suffers (Cronin, Slade, Bechtel, &
Anderson, 1992; Fiedler, 1986; McAfee & Vergason, 1979).

Indeed, parent empowerment continues to grow in terms of both its
popularity and proven utility. Rappaport (1984), who views empowerment as both a process and product, observed the following:

> Empowerment is easy to define in its absence: powerlessness, real or
> imagined; learned helplessness; alienation; loss of a sense of control over
> one's life. It is more difficult to define positively only because it takes on
> a different form in different people and contests. (p. 3)

Yet, in spite of variance in the meaning and forms of empowerment, professionals and parents increasingly agree that parents and families must be
granted opportunities to share decision-making authority and to collaborate with professionals (Dixon, 1992; Dunst & Paget, 1991).

Diverse Value Systems

Accompanying the technological changes of the past decades have been
major value changes. As reported by Kroth and Simpson (1977), "We are

not living in a valueless society; nonetheless, it is becoming increasingly difficult to generalize about group, societal, or individual values" (p. 8). Due to the variance in the values of people in this country, generalizations tend to be either incorrect or fallacious; further, values are constantly changing. Moreover, the increased presence of American families representing a variety of racial and cultural groups has intensified the educational significance of value differences (Hodgkinson, 1992).

Professionals will come into contact with children, parents, and families who represent a variety of value systems, some of which may be dramatically different from their own. Recognition of this possibility is crucial if the educational conferencer is to work effectively with children, parents, and families who present variant socioeconomic, religious, ethnic, cultural, and political persuasions (Mundschenk & Foley, 1995). As previously mentioned, educators must be able to understand their own value systems because we all tend to base our decisions and overall behavior on our own values (Raths, Harmin, & Simon, 1966). Thus, individuals unfamiliar with their personal values may find it difficult to understand their interactions or the basis of their behavior. Rutherford and Edgar (1979) observed that "behaving in a manner that is congruent with one's beliefs depends on clearly understanding one's values" (p. 41). Although clarifying one's own values is not a simple process, several sources may be consulted in this effort (Curwin & Fuhrman, 1975; Kroth, 1985; Kroth & Simpson, 1977; Raths, Harmin, & Simon, 1966; Simon, Howe, & Kirschenbaum, 1972; Smith, 1993).

In addition, conferencers must also be able to understand (and hopefully accept!) the values of the different individuals and families with whom they become associated in their professional dealings. Without such a basis the effectiveness of any interaction will be undermined. Perhaps because almost everybody has experienced school in some form, there are many self-proclaimed experts on the subject of education. The varying values of parents and families accompanied by such self-proclaimed expertise about education can potentially result in clashes. A simple acknowledgment, on the part of the conferencer, of the presence of different values and an attempt to understand these systems will frequently serve to turn conflicted encounters into meaningful and fruitful exchanges (Ivey, Ivey, & Simek-Downing, 1987; Salend & Taylor, 1993).

The educational conferencer must not only recognize that values have changed and will continue to do so, but also that personal values form the basis on which meaningful interactions and collaboration will take place (Friend & Cook, 1992).

Consideration of Family Needs

Professionals are increasingly recognizing the benefits of interacting with *families* of exceptional children and youth, not just their parents (Schulz, 1987). This change of perception and professional practice stems from the belief that all elements of a family are interconnected and that events and circumstances that affect one family member will impact others (Carter & McGoldrich, 1980; Hoffman, 1980; Minuchin, 1974; Satir, 1983). Thus, because a child or youth with an exceptionality will influence and be influenced by his or her entire family, professionals are being advised more and more to focus on others besides the parents.

Consistent with this viewpoint, a number of authorities (Lambie & Daniels-Mohring, 1993; Turnbull, Summers, & Brotherson, 1983) contend that individuals, including those with disabilities, cannot be adequately understood without analyzing how they fit into the family structure; thus they advise professionals to consider the interaction influences of each family's structure, functions, and life cycles. In this context, programs, procedures, and methodology should be based on a variety of family-related factors, as opposed to focusing exclusively on family members with exceptionalities or their parents. These factors include unique family characteristics (e.g., size, extrafamilial support, socioeconomic status), cultural styles (e.g., family values, ethnicity), ideological characteristics (parent and family attitudes), roles (e.g., unique economic, affection, education, vocational, guidance, socialization functions), and life-cycle changes (e.g., retirement-age parents, birth of a sibling, death of a parent). Failure to consider family needs in program development may result in (a) overinvolvement by parents with their exceptional children (i.e., to the exclusion of other family members' needs), (b) unrealistic expectations on the part of professionals, and (c) poor home-professional communication.

Fortunately, increased professional attention has turned to the needs of families of children and youth with exceptionalities. Increased sensitivity to these needs should enhance family-professional partnerships as well as the maximum development of children and youth with disabilities in a variety of settings (Fine, 1990; Rotheram, 1989).

Increased Poverty

Professionals, including those involved with children and youth who have exceptionalities, today are more frequently encountering families affected by poverty. *Poverty* in this context refers to a federally determined family income level needed to pay for essentials (the amount varies with family size). As poverty has increased during the past decades, American children have become poorer than any other age group. For example, according to 1983 federal statistics, more than 40% of the 13 million poor children in this country lived in families with incomes below half the federal poverty level. In 1993 almost one fourth of children in the United States lived in families with incomes below the poverty line (U.S. Department of Commerce, 1993), and other current statistics reveal that poverty conditions and their effects continue at an alarming level (Hodgkinson, 1993; Kozol, 1991; Scherer, 1993; Schorr, 1989; U.S. Department of Commerce, 1993).

Poverty conditions have particularly affected minority families (Correa & Weismantel, 1991; Hanson & Lynch, 1992). A 1985 Children's Defense Fund study, *Black and White Children in America: Key Facts*, determined that Black children, when compared to White children, are more likely to experience poverty conditions, to lack appropriate prenatal care, to suffer low birthweight, to be born prematurely, to live in a single-parent home, to drop out of school, and to be unemployed. Current statistics indicate that poverty conditions among minority groups continue to be especially high (Kozol, 1991; Scherer, 1993; U.S. Department of Commerce, 1993). Poverty conditions are not unique to minority families, however. It is presently estimated that about 25% of American children live in families meeting poverty criteria.

Poverty conditions present unique challenges for educators and other professionals. Families experiencing poverty tend also to experience multiple problems (e.g., frustration, increased stress), thus making them less apt to respond to family members' needs, including those with disabilities. These families may also require additional time and resources from professionals, and, because of a myriad social and economic concerns, may be less motivated and able to serve in a partnership role with professionals or otherwise be actively involved in their children's education. In a variety of ways, the poverty conditions that have emerged over the past years have increased the challenges and demands on professionals' ability to serve the needs of families with exceptional members.

There is no simple strategy for educators to use when responding to the needs of poor families; however, certain guidelines should be considered. First, professionals must recognize that poverty conditions will affect school performance. For example, hunger, homelessness, family frustration, and parental despair can be expected to exacerbate exceptional children's social and academic problems. Second, the multiple needs of poor families require a coordinated effort by a variety of professionals across a variety of disciplines. Thus, educators must abandon the historically narrow perception of the role of education (i.e., basic academic preparation in school settings only) in favor of a more pragmatic position and be willing to help extend nontraditional educational and social services to meet the needs of these families. Finally, professionals must abandon any stereotypic attitudes and perceptions they may have of families suffering from poverty. For example, much of the poverty of this country is a function of reduced governmental support, unemployment, low-paying positions, growth of female-headed households, and increased adolescent parenthood rather than "laziness," "poor motivation," and "the high rewards of welfare." Educators and other professionals may not be in a position to solve this country's poverty problems; however, their beliefs, attitudes, and willingness to aid the victims of poverty will offer a significant advantage to families coping with these difficult conditions.

School Reform

The 1990s have been a decade of reform, and in this spirit of change school reform efforts have had considerable impact on parents and families of school-age children. Interestingly, however, school reform advocates have focused limited attention on students with exceptionalities (Shaw et al., 1990). For example, the much heralded *America 2000: An Education Strategy* (U.S. Department of Education, 1991) gives almost no attention to children and youth with special needs. Commenting on this oversight, Ysseldyke, Algozzine, and Thurlow (1992) noted that "in a summary of the 'education reform decade' (ETS Policy Information Center, 1990), there was not a single mention of students with disabilities or even special education" (p. 140). Indeed, the National Council on Disability (1989) observed that "for the most part school reform efforts have not been directed toward addressing the special challenges that students with disabilities face" (p. 2). As a result, the Council recommended that a national commission on excellence in the education of children and youth with disabilities be established. Moreover, the Office of Special Education Programs of the U.S. Education Department has advocated for greater special education involvement in the school reform process.

Neglect of students with disabilities in school reform and restructuring initiatives has not meant that parents and families of these individuals have been unaffected by reform activities. Rather, because school reform initiatives have largely focused on such issues as identifying educational goals and outcomes, raising academic and behavioral requirements (e.g., reformers have recommended that more high school students enroll in science and math courses and that students be given more homework assignments), using normative measures to evaluate performance, making resources dependent on performance, empowering teachers and students, fostering local educational autonomy, and generally increasing both the quantity and qualtity of what is taught, parents and families of special needs students have felt the effects of school reform. As a result, many parents and families of individuals with disabilities have found themselves advocating for a restructured educational program that will address the needs of both exceptional and nonexceptional students. Similarly, educators involved in educating students with special needs have increasingly been confronted with difficult issues associated with school reform, including extended school days and extended school years, changing staff roles (e.g., more collaboration, more consultation models), adoption of more stringent accountability systems, adoption of high school core curricula, agreement on what constitutes an effective school and the accompanying programs to make sure such schools are available, open enrollment choice in education, stricter conduct policies, adoption of systems based on rewards and penalities for schools based on performance, and increased parent responsibility for student learning. Obviously these are difficult issues and acceptable solutions will require the collective efforts of both professionals and families.

Inadequate Community Support Resources

Educators and other professionals agree both that parents and families of children and youth with exceptionalities require extensive services and resources and that these should be available to every student with special needs. Moreover, there is agreement that programs and services should be available to address the needs of entire families rather than focusing exclusively on children with exceptionalities, independent of their families. Yet, in spite of this agreeement, it is clear that many needs of children with exceptionalities and their families are not being met. For example, in a U.S. Congress, Office of Technology Assessment monograph on children's mental health, Day and Roberts (1991) reported that while at least 12% of children in the United States require mental health services, only about 20% of these children received appropriate services. Knitzer, Steinberg, and Fleisch (1990) reported that over 50% of the districts they surveyed indicated that they did not provide counseling services, and that when services were provided, they occurred on a short-term basis and generally were paid for by parents. Community mental health program therapy and support resources, including crisis intervention alternatives, are also lacking; there is little continuity and limited communication among educational, legal, and mental health programs; community agencies often fail to clearly identify responsibility boundaries, comply with funding regulations, and define target populations; and limited parent involvement in mental health and community programs is the norm in many settings. Contributing to this problem is the lack of affordable health care, with over 33 million Americans estimated to be without health insurance (U.S. Bureau of the Census, 1990). Finally, overwhelming indicates evidence that students who return to public school programs from institutional, hospital, and other restrictive placements are provided limited phase-in and transfer support and resources (Paul & Epanchin, 1991).

These factors bode poorly for students with exceptionalities and have significant implications for educators. That is, educators are increasingly being confronted by parents and families of students with exceptionalities whose community support and mental health needs are being served inadequately and who thus rely on or expect educators to meet their needs. This situation requires that educators be able to provide some services in areas historically beyond the limits of education, without extending beyond the limits of their skills, time, and other resources, and that they become more competent in working and developing cooperative and collaborative partnerships with community programs.

Increased Inclusion and Integration of Students with Disabilities in General Education Settings

Without question the most significant and divisive educational issue of our time relates to the general education inclusion and integration of students with disabilities. Based on interpretations of the "free appropriate public education" (FAPE) and "least restrictive environment" (LRE) provisions of the Individuals with Disabilities Education Act (IDEA), one finds significant differences of opinion about the extent to which students with disabilities should be educated along with nondisabled students (Idstein, Gizzi, Ferrero, & Miller, 1994; Kauffman & Hallahan, 1995; Sailor, 1991). IDEA specifies that the placement decision process begin with consideration of a student with a disability being appropriate for education in a general education classroom, and that placement in an alternative setting be considered only if the general education classroom is unacceptable. Some, however, have interpreted the LRE provision to mean a general education classroom for all students with disabilities in all cases, without exception (Stainback & Stainback, 1990, 1992b).

Considerable disagreement has arisen over inclusion of students with disabilities in general classrooms. In this regard, Lieberman (1992) noted the following:

> There seem to be two different camps of full integration advocates. One group does not attempt to justify its position in logical, pragmatic, or curricular terms. When asked what has to be done in order to make full integration work successfully, they generally reply that nothing has to be done. Just do it. Just doing it will make it happen. (p. 22)

It is important to note that decisions related to inclusion have not been based on evidence generated from scientific methodology. Commenting on this fact, Kauffman (1993) observed that "empirical evidence does not indicate that we currently have effective and reliable strategies for improving and sustaining outcomes for all students in regular classrooms" (p. 8). Accordingly, debate over integration and inclusion of students with disabilities has largely come from individuals' and organizations' values related to inclusion. That is, the full inclusion debate has been characterized by arguments over who is right, who is ethical and moral, and who is a true advocate for students with special needs. Of course this situation has forced educators and parents into difficult educational placement decisions, and this challenge will likely continue as a major special education issue into the forseeable future (Kauffman, 1993; Shapiro, Loeb, & Bowermaster, 1993; Simpson & Sasso, 1992).

Technology and Communication Advances

Recent and rapid technological and communication advances make it risky to speculate on the possible future uses of technology in facilitating communication and collaboration between educators and parents. Currently a variety of audio and video equipment is used in parent and educator training, and the future development of parent and family skills and knowledge via tapes and similar modes is endless. Moreover, the increased availability of such technology as fiber optics, compressed video, satellite communications, interactive technology, and computers offers novel opportunities for parent/family and professional communication, training of parents and professionals, and home-school-agency collaboration from a distance. For example, technology allows educators and parents to communicate with one another without talking on the phone, writing in a journal, or traveling. Now parents and family members can observe ongoing programs attended by their offspring without travel and with minimal disruption of their programs. Even though the exact applications of ongoing technology and communication advances await discovery, it is safe to say this area of science will have a profound influence on the future interactions of professionals, parents, and families.

Characteristics of Families of Children with Exceptionalities

Families of children with exceptionalities have experienced the same changes as other families and exist as heterogeneously as other parents and families. Yet, traditionally, parents of children and youth with exceptionalities have been regarded as sharing so many commonalities that they present a homogeneous population—as having unique features not shared by others. However, parents and families of exceptional children are as individualized and diversified as those without "special" children; their only common denominator is at least one child who deviates from the norm to such an extent that he or she requires some type of curriculum modification, specialized educational program, or other considerations in order to function at a level commensurate with his or her ability.

In spite of their heterogeneity, parents and families of children with exceptionalities do appear to experience increased levels of frustration and certain problems not encountered by other parents and families (Miller & Hudson, 1994; Mullins, 1987; Wright, Matlock, & Matlock, 1985). Equally important, parents of children with exceptionalities may lack those feelings of accomplishment and satisfaction that are so necessary to effective parenthood. Instead, such parents experience hurt because their child may not one day be an independent adult, frustration because he or she may lack the physical capacity to respond to a parent's efforts to interact, or anger because their son or daughter is rejected by other children. As a result of such feelings, some parents perceive themselves as failures or consider their life one of shattered dreams. Whatever the particular response, it is safe to conclude that it will have significant impact and, in most instances, will intensify stress on the family (Beckman, 1983; Farber, 1968; Innocenti, Huh, & Boyce, 1992). In no way does this suggest that the presence of a child with an exceptionality precludes family harmony and parental happiness. However, it does suggest that typical parental and family pleasures may take nontraditional forms when a child or youth with a disability is involved. That is, parents and families may find themselves learning to "sign" so they can communicate more effectively with a hearing impaired child or becoming involved in a community action program designed to benefit all individuals with developmental disabilities. At the very least, the presence of an exceptional child creates unique challenges for both parents and the family (Barsh, 1968; Brinker, 1992; Fine, 1991; Ross, 1974).

The Educator's Role

The role of educators in serving the needs of parents and families can at best be described as *unresolved*. Although educators, particularly teachers, historically are considered the legitimate disseminators of *education*, they have not been perceived as primary parent counseling resources. For example, not too long ago most techniques and procedures for conferencing or counseling with parents of children with exceptionalities were developed by psychologists, psychiatrists, social workers, and counselors. Equally important, these methods were designed primarily for individuals representing these disciplines. Although some attention was focused on the application of accepted procedures by professionals working in the educational environment, especially school counselors and school psychologists, limited consideration was given to classroom teachers—the group of professionals with the greatest amount of parent contact.

This situation has changed. Along with the increase in services provided children and youth with exceptionalities has come the development of programs for parent and family involvement; thus most individuals assigned the task of interacting with parents, particularly those with special needs, have acquired some basic conferencing skills. Nevertheless, parent conferencing techniques and procedures for educational personnel have been developed and refined at a much slower pace than other educational components. Consequently, even though some advancements have been made in parent and family conferencing and counseling, this area remains one of the most neglected and underdeveloped skills in the repertoire of most educators.

Although educators have not been perceived as primary parent and family resources, evidence suggests that they can be trained to serve many parent needs effectively (Canfield & Wells, 1976; Clements & Alexander, 1975; Johnson, 1993; Miller & Hudson, 1994; Thomas, English, & Bickel, 1994; Wolf, 1982). In addition, educators represent the most economical and available resource, they tend to be in a better position than other professional groups to gain the trust of parents, and they are in the most satisfactory position to provide parent conferencing services.

Educators Represent the Most Economical and Available Resource

The concept of the "least restrictive alternative" may be extended not only to placement in environments that most closely parallel "normal" and provide no greater limitations than absolutely necessary, but also to other service dimensions. Although conclusive data do not exist yet on the specific needs and levels of need of parents and families, including those with children and youth with exceptionalities, their needs appear to be normally distributed. That is, a small percentage of parents and families require either very little or a great deal of support and attention, whereas the largest percentages fall somewhere between the extremes (Fine, 1991; Kroth, 1985). Thus, most parents and families will need opportunities to exchange information with professionals and receive information; others will be interested in seeking information on how effectively to use school resources, participate in conferences, and serve as advocates for their child. A smaller percentage of parents and families will require training in how to serve the needs of their children, such as tutoring or behavior management. An even smaller percentage of parents and families will require counseling or therapy to cope effectively or will be interested in participating in parent advisory or "parent-to-parent" groups. In the majority of cases, the families' needs can be met most expediently and effectively by the classroom teacher or other education personnel. For those parents requiring greater degrees of support or involvement, the services of psychologists, psychiatrists, counselors, and/or social workers must be made available.

Educators Are in a Good Position to Gain the Trust of Parents

Ample available evidence shows that parents and families, especially those with exceptional children, frequently experience frustration and difficulty when attempting to secure diagnostic, placement, and problem-solving services from professionals. Philip Roos, past executive director of the National Association for Retarded Citizens and himself the parent of a child with an exceptionality, recounted a number of the difficulties he and his family encountered when attempting to obtain appropriate services for their child. Roos noted that even though he was knowledgeable about the system and the procedures involved, he and his wife "embarked on a long series of catastrophic interactions with professionals which echoed the complaints . . . heard so often from other parents" (1978, p. 13).

A frequent complaint made by parents and families of children with exceptionalities regarding professionals is that they frequently fail to prop-erly communicate and listen, and then to provide necessary information or services, hence often conveying the impression that they lack a true commitment to or interest in the child or family. Although parents and families may encounter some of the same difficulties with educators, these issues are often less publicized and more amenable to change. Because there are probably no significant and consistent attitudinal and interper-sonal differences among the various professionals who come into contact with parents and families, and because each professional group conceiv-ably strives toward the best interests of children and families with whom they interact, these differences are most likely a function of other factors.

One such factor is families' opportunity for interacting and establish-ing rapport with teachers as compared to other professional groups with whom they come into contact. Frequently family members report having no opportunity to familiarize themselves with and develop a trust in the myriad professionals who are involved in the various educational and edu-cationally related processes that determine the future of their child. Con-sequently parents often express that their lack of familiarity with these individuals and their assigned roles, in combination with the infrequent contacts with these professionals, prevents them from establishing the trust and rapport necessary for an adequate conferencing relationship. In addition, family members may understandably associate shock, pain, and despair with certain professionals. McDonald (1962) noted that "when parents of handicapped children meet in small groups for counseling, it may be predicted that an early topic of discussion will be their feelings toward professional workers, particularly those with whom they first dis-cussed their child's problem" (p. 160). The educator's primary role is to serve as an advocate for children and their families and to positively influ-ence children's development—not to label, diagnose, or determine the extent of parental responsibility for a problem. It is not surprising, therefore, that teachers and other educational personnel are perceived by most parents in a relatively positive light, thereby further increasing their potential as effective conferencers.

Finally, in spite of changes in societal attitudes, most of us are threatened, to some extent, by the prospect of needing the services of certain professional groups, particularly mental health professionals. This fear is well documented in parents of children and youth with exceptionalities. For example, some parents perceive counselors as providing few relevant and functional services, while others consider the role of these professionals as exclusively one of determining the parents' responsibility for their child's problem. In addition, it is not unusual to find that families of children with exceptionalities are such victims of psychological stress that they deny their need for counseling or conferencing services. Accordingly, parents and family members may attempt to avoid contact with certain professional groups because of their perceived threat. Hence, because educators are often a less threatening and more available resource, many conferencing needs can be served effectively by this group. In instances where additional services are required, appropriately trained educators who have established a relationship with parents and families will be better able to make the necessary referrals and recommendations.

Educators Are in the Best Position to Conference with Parents and Families

Extensive evidence suggests that instructional programs are most effective when parents and families participate in supportive roles (Berkowitz & Graziano, 1972; Brinker, 1992; Calvert & McMahon, 1987; Eyberg & Robinson, 1982; Hardin & Littlejohn, 1995; Lindsley, 1966; O'Dell, 1974) and when families and professionals are able to build and maintain satisfactory lines of communication (Cronin et al., 1992; Duncan & Fitzgerald, 1969; Fiedler, 1986; Kroth, 1985; Kroth, Whelan, & Stables, 1970; Winston, 1986). One salient feature of good communication in this respect is the dissemination of accurate and current information. Although parents and families may have additional needs, the vast majority will be interested in learning about their child's classroom and school-related functioning. The individual with the closest and most consistent pupil contact will be most capable of providing information and making necessary procedural changes. Consequently, educators must again play an instrumental role in disseminating parent and family information. In addition, parents frequently report that they feel most comfortable in discussing their child with his or her classroom teacher. Thus, educators almost universally have access to the most relevant and current information about a given child. At the same time, parents often demonstrate a level of trust and openness toward them not found with many other individuals in the helping professions. It seems logical, therefore, to take advantage of their fortuitous position by training educators to serve as many parent and family needs as appropriate.

Skills Necessary for Conferencing Success

Success in this endeavor is ultimately a function of a person's attitude, skills, and conferencing philosophy. Educators must not only be proficient in a variety of both general and specific conferencing procedures, they must also recognize that to implement these skills successfully, one must develop efficacious human interaction competencies and a personal parent-conferencing philosophy. Hence, although conferencing and counseling skills can be learned (Ivey & Authier, 1978; Ivey et al., 1987; Yaffe, 1994), cookbook approaches and universally applicable solutions cannot adequately meet the varied needs of parents and families.

Interest in People

Basic to success in parent conferencing is the ability to interact successfully with others. One generic aptitude associated with successful interaction is an interest in and sensitivity to people. Thus, individuals who expect to adequately serve the needs of parents and families must possess a genuine interest in people and a willingness to invest time and energy in seeking solutions to needs and problems. Although there should not be an emphasis on "rescuing" another person, there must be an underlying core of humanism upon which to draw and build. Rogers (1942) noted the following:

> The person who is quite obtuse to the reactions of others, who does not sense the hostility or friendliness which exists between himself and others or between two of his acquaintances, is not likely to become a satisfactory counselor. There is no doubt that this quality can be developed, but unless an individual has a considerable degree of this social sensitivity, it is doubtful that counseling is his most promising field of effort. On the other hand, the individual who is naturally observant of the reac-

tions of others, who can pick out of a classroom group the unhappy child, who can sense the personal antagonism which underlies casual argu-ment, who is alert to the subtle differences in actions which show that one parent has a comfortable relationship with his child, another a rela-tionship full of tensions—such a person has a good natural foundation upon which to build counseling skills. (p. 254)

In the final analysis, an interest in and sensitivity to people may be the most basic yet significant determinant of success in the area of parent con-ferencing and family involvement.

Understanding One's Own Values

As noted previously, the educational conferencer must also have a clear understanding of his or her own values in order to develop a personal confer-encing philosophy and effectively serve a wide range of parents and families. According to Kroth and Simpson (1977), "the importance of assessing your own values or attempting to understand another's values is that ultimately you tend to act on those values you cherish the most" (p. 8). If educators are to effectively serve children, parents, and families, many from cultures and backgrounds different from their own, they must understand their own val-ues in addition to those of the individuals with whom they relate.

Conflict resolution, information sharing, cooperative planning, and most of the other activities engaged in during parent conferences are effective only to the extent that parents, families, and professionals under-stand and respect one another, including their values. Often conflicts between families and professionals arise because the two groups fail to understand each other's values and the significance of individual goals and expectations. Rutherford and Edgar (1979) suggested that "when a spe-cific school problem already exists, a misunderstanding between parents and teachers of each other's motives or actions causes the additional prob-lem of interpersonal conflict" (p. 40). The lack of value sensitivity can serve not only to increase the occurrence of conflicts but also to reduce the potential efficacy of intervention and conferencing efforts.

Ability to Attend to and Collaborate with Others

A third generic skill necessary for effective human interaction is the capac-ity to effectively attend to and collaborate with others. Thus, the ability to listen and, in turn, communicate this attention to parents and families, along with the ability to form collaborative relationships, are among the most basic attributes required for successful conferencing. According to a number of authorities (Benjamin, 1969; Kroth, 1985; Smith & Luckasson, 1992), the ability to create an effective listening environment and to accurately understand parents and families (including their nonverbal and emotional responses) is such a basic requisite that many other conferencing components and strategies hinge on this single skill.

Listening is not a passive process; it involves attention. In addition, active listening requires attention to more than manifest verbal messages; the process includes awareness of one's affect, body language, pauses, and tone as well as messages that are hinted at but not actually spoken. Although active listening is often discounted because of its elementary nature, it will most likely be one ingredient of any successful conferencing program.

Ability to Establish Trust

The successful conferencer must be able to establish initial trust and rapport with parents and families, and then maintain that relationship. Research as well as practice has documented the utility of rapport-building efforts (Duncan & Fitzgerald, 1969; Robinson & Fine, 1995; Wolf, 1982). Without a positive interpersonal relationship on which to build, it is highly unlikely that the educator could apply specific conferencing and problem-solving procedures. Hence, in addition to the professional's knowledge and skill, a basic relationship must exist on which to build. Successful conferencing programs seem to occur most frequently when parents and families feel assured that they are a necessary and valued resource and that they are working in concert with professionals in their child's behalf.

Sensitivity to Needs of the Family

Finally, successful parent and family involvement is associated with awareness and sensitivity to the unique needs and circumstances of families with exceptional members. As noted previously, these families must contend with a myriad issues, only some of them related to education (Innocenti et al., 1992; Mullins, 1987; Simpson & Carter, 1993). These issues may include social isolation and feelings of guilt and embarrassment, financial strain (e.g., medical expenses, "special baby-sitter" expenses), limitations on recreational options, pessimistic perceptions of the future, household routine delays and disruptions (e.g., additional time to feed, bathe, and dress a disabled family member), and interference with other family members' needs and gratification.

Sensitivity to the demands and stresses commonly experienced by families of exceptional children and youth will aid educators in keeping educational matters in proper perspective and in assisting families with the numerous noneducational issues with which they must contend. Without such a perspective educators lack a basic ingredient of successful parent and family involvement.

A Model for Parent and Family Involvement

Although important, basic human relations skills and an aptitude for parent and family involvement are insufficient as components of parent and family conferencing. Instead, successful parent and family involvement necessitates a comprehensive service delivery program with sufficient breadth to encompass the many individual needs experienced by families of children and youth with exceptionalities. Needs within and across families vary; needs also vary over time (Featherstone, 1980). Thus, within a comprehensive model, individualized planning is fundamental. Such a strategy allows for general planning within commonly acknowledged need areas while at the same time allowing individualization.

Parent and Family Needs

The model of parent and family involvement shown in Figure 1.1 identifies and briefly describes five major parent and family needs: information exchange; partnership and advocacy training; home and community program implementation; counseling, consultation, and support programs; and parent and family coordinated service programs. The basic premise of the model holds that these are major needs experienced by parents and families of children and youth with exceptionalities and that each element requires an appropriate and individualized professional program. Thus, educators and other professionals must be able to assess and appropriately respond to the parent and family needs listed within each of the basic components of the model.

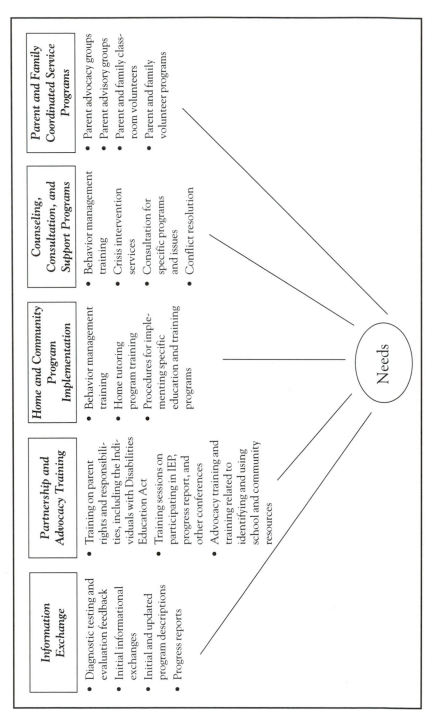

Figure 1.1. Model of parent and family involvement.

It is unlikely that every family will have needs in all five areas at any given time. However, it is likely that a group of parents and family members with children and youth with exceptionalities—as might be encountered by a special education teacher—will reflect all needs at some point. Accordingly, educators who are involved with children and youth with special needs are urged to develop basic knowledge and skills in each of the five major areas, descriptions of which follow.

Information exchange

This element of the model refers to parents' and family members' need for information as well as a basic professional need for accurate and ongoing information coming from parents and families. Thus, the educational conferencer must obtain relevant facts about children and families (e.g., developmental history, school history, family expectations) while also providing appropriate information to the parties, including progress reports.

Sharing information with parents and family members should include not only the assessment data but also a chance to discuss the findings. Even though parents and families may have received an interpretation following an assessment of their child, most likely they will benefit from a review of the information and from discussing issues associated with the assessment and subsequent recommendations.

Parents and families should also be given a description of the educational program to be provided their child, including the teacher's educational philosophy and strategy, the academic and behavioral remediation programs scheduled for use, auxiliary services to be provided, and available parent and family support programs.

Other information to be disseminated includes the procedures planned for evaluating pupil progress and the manner in which these data will be communicated. In this regard, many parents and family members prefer regularly occurring and informal contacts (e.g., phone conferences).

Effective information exchange is basic to a professional-home partnership. Educators should assume that *all* parents and families need ongoing information exchanges just as *all* professionals require accurate home and family information.

Partnership and advocacy training

Even though parents have been granted significant authority in determining what educational procedures will be used with their children (particularly those with special needs), few provisions have been made for giving them the cognizance, training, and confidence needed to serve in this participation role (Ramos, 1995). Thus, in spite of being eligible to participate in IEP conferences and other parent-teacher meetings, parents have not been trained in how to do so effectively. Indeed, historically, empowered parents and families have achieved their skills and knowledge with little or no assistance from professionals. However, parents and family members must be provided opportunities for appropriate training if they are to be expected to collaborate with professionals and to function at a level consistent with their assigned rights, needs, and personal motivation.

> In order for professionals to be willing to train parents in procedures for participation in educational conferences and other related activities, they must believe that a majority of parents, with training and encouragement, are willing to become involved with schools in generating and sharing concerns and goals for their child's education and that this participation adds to the school's ability to help the child. (Simpson & Poplin, 1981, p. 21)

Unless educators meet parents' need for sufficient information in this area, they cannot be expected to participate in parent-teacher conferences in a manner that will maximize the school's efforts.

This component of the parent and family involvement model taps several training elements, including (a) procedures for how to participate in conferences and meetings, and (b) rights and responsibilities of parents and families of children with exceptionalities. This aspect of the model also relates to how to prepare parents and families to serve as advocates for children and youth with exceptionalities and to act as effective consumers of community, school, and agency services and resources. That is, the partnership and advocacy training component of the model focuses on *empowering* parents and families to the extent that they are seeking such a role. Unlike the need for information exchange, one cannot assume that all parents and families need or desire partnership, advocacy training, collaboration, or empowerment; however, many parents and families will make use of programs designed to develop such skills and knowledge, if available (Kahne & Westheimer, 1993).

Home and community program implementation

Research has confirmed that parents and families can be effectively trained to implement educationally related services with their own children (Berkowitz & Graziano, 1972; Obiakor, Algozzine, & Ford, 1993;

O'Dell, 1974; Wielkiewicz, 1986). Both as academic tutors and agents of behavior management, parents and other family members have proven to be valuable resources for extending professional intervention and academic programs beyond the classroom setting. For example, under professional direction, parents and family members can be trained to implement individualized tutoring programs with their own child. Such tutoring serves both to involve these individuals in a child's academic program and to appropriately communicate their concern to the child. In addition, this type of activity provides a means for structuring interactions between the family and child and for bridging the gap between home and school.

Parents and families have also been trained to employ behavior management procedures with children. This approach has allowed them to effect planned behavior changes in the natural environment and thus to extend the therapeutic influence of professionals beyond the classroom.

Although some parents and families may be unmotivated or unsuited for this role, others will be highly appropriate. Training parents and families to serve in this capacity provides a vehicle for extending problem-solving efforts into noneducational environments and for coordinating parents' motivations for collaboration and participation.

Counseling, consultation, and support programs

Although only a small percentage of parents and families will need in-depth therapy and counseling, the necessary resources must be available to those who require them. In most instances, the educator's role in this area will consist of putting parents in touch with those professionals who are best equipped to serve them. The most common referrals include family counseling, psychotherapy, crisis intervention, and other clinical and social agency assistance.

Other parent and family needs within this domain are more widespread. For instance, many families will benefit from participating in support groups; at some point, a family crisis may require professional intervention; conflicts between professionals and parents/families may necessitate professional resolution programs; and many parents periodically require consultation regarding particular issues (e.g., feeding, toileting, sleeping problems) (Howe, 1993).

Parent and family coordinated service programs

Some parents and families wish to go beyond the needs of themselves and their offspring to serve the larger community of children with exceptionalities and their families. This may include serving on advisory boards, participating in community service programs, engaging in "parent-to-parent" groups, or working as volunteers in programs for children and youth with special needs.

The importance of these activities can be highlighted by noting that basically all major amendments in policies and services for children with exceptionalities have been effected through the work of parent groups. Such results, along with the need for continued progress, may motivate certain parents and families to work at local, state, and national levels to secure more and better services for all individuals with disabilities. For those parents and families who have the time, ability, and energy, opportunities for such service to the larger community of exceptional citizens should be made available.

Analysis of Parent and Family Needs

Because there are no reliable and valid standardized measures for identifying parent and family need, such needs analysis is an informal process. In this regard, the model of parent and family involvement can become a frame to identify possible parent and family requirements.

One should consider two general factors in identifying parental needs: professionals' perceptions of parent and family needs, and parents' and families' self-perceived needs. The first consideration involves professionals sharing with parents or family members their perceptions of a family's needs along with possible program and service options for addressing those needs. Although no standard formula exists for gauging parent and family needs and preferences, consideration of the following factors is recommended: (a) analysis of the family's perceived and stated needs, as per the model of parent and family involvement, including programs and services used and requested by parents and families; (b) family makeup and characteristics, including number and ages of members, and cultural, socioeconomic, and ethnic factors; (c) disabled member's exceptionality, including severity level and impact on family members; (d) human, financial, and community resources available to the family; (e) family restrictions and problems associated with the disability; (f) degree of family communication, support, and sensitivity; and (g) age of the child with a disability and the role of the child in the family. Although consideration and interpretation of these data may vary from professional to professional, these factors should serve as guidelines for how to identify parent and family needs.

Because professionals are not always able to accurately identify parent and family needs (especially if family members are not forthcoming about their concerns, circumstances, and requirements), and because parents and families may be unaware of their own needs (e.g., a parent may be unaware of advocacy training options), conferencers should apprise parents and families of potential needs they may experience. This process involves assuring parents that it is predictable that they will have various needs over the course of caring for and educating a child with an exceptionality, and that their needs can be addressed. Hence, a combination of professional analysis and solicitation of parents' self-perceived needs is recommended.

Although professionals' analyses of child and family requirements and related programs are important, parents' and families' self-perceived needs and their willingness to invest in addressing them are salient determinants of family involvement. Too frequently parents have reported encountering little or no flexibility in the manner in which their needs are perceived and the degree to which they are expected to be involved in their child's intervention and education program. Thus, professionals must be sensitive to families' self-perceived needs and their preferences for involvement and collaboration with school personnel and agencies. Although professionals must identify what they consider to be a parent or family's needs, in the final analysis these perceived requirements are acted upon only with parent and family support and endorsement. For example, a professional may observe that a parent appears to need home management training. However, home management skill training can (and should) be provided only if the parent agrees with the professional's assessment and seeks collaborative training support.

Individualization Within the Model of Parent and Family Involvement

The Individuals with Disabilities Education Act has effectively established that pupils with disabilities are to be provided an education that is based on their individual needs. Ironically, this enactment has not applied the principle of individualization to parents and families. That is, parents and families are frequently perceived as all experiencing the same needs and program requirements. Accordingly, the model of parent and family involvement is designed to accommodate individualization, based on three assumptions: (a) parents and families are unique in terms of needs,

time, resources, motivation, skills, commitment, and interests; (b) professionals should encourage a range of parent involvement matched to individual interests and needs; and (c) increased involvement by parents and
families in their children's education and development does not necessarily mean more effective involvement. In accordance with these underlying assumptions, decisions regarding the degree and type of parent and
family involvement and the most appropriate methods for satisfying parent and family needs should come from individual and family preferences
and needs (Alexander, Kroth, Simpson, & Poppelreiter, 1982; Simpson &
Carter, 1993; Turnbull et al., 1983).

The model of parent and family involvement accommodates individualization by offering parents and families various levels of participation
and collaboration options for satisfying their needs: (a) recognition and
awareness, (b) ongoing communication, (c) advocacy and skill development, and (d) partnership. The levels of involvement are not hierarchical;
that is, *advocacy and skill development* for a particular family is not necessarily better, for example, than *ongoing communication*. Rather, needs, motivation, abilities, and other factors serve as the basis for identifying the
appropriate degree of parent and family involvement. In addition, a family's level of involvement may vary over time. For instance, a family experiencing divorce or other significant changes might temporarily have
fewer resources to invest in training a disabled member. Finally, the levels
of participation apply across need components. For example, within the
counseling and consultation component, family participation may vary from
recognition and awareness of educators' ability and willingness to make
referrals to community agencies to *partnership* in conducting parent and
family support groups.

The first level of participation, *recognition and awareness*, represents
the baseline expectation for all parents and families across all needs.
Specifically, this basic level of involvement requires (a) parent and family
awareness of school and agency personnel, including their roles; (b) recognition of parent and family services available through the child's program
and community, especially those associated with parent and family needs;
and (c) basic information about the child's instructional program and the
manner in which families may obtain information and access services.

Ideally *ongoing communication* is a level of involvement that one may
achieve with all parents and families, in all areas of need expressed in the
model of parent and family involvement. This degree of collaborative
involvement entails regularly occurring information exchange between
parents/families and professionals. Included are progress reports by fami-

lies and professionals, within their respective settings; formal and informal exchanges of progress and developments potentially affecting children's performance (e.g., family crisis); progress related to parent-applied home intervention programs; and other open exchanges of information, such as expectations, attitudes, and feelings.

Advocacy and skill development refers to parents and families responding to the expressed or perceived needs of the model of parent and family involvement through various empowerment and skill application activities. For instance, involvement at an advocacy and skill development level may be appropriate for parents and families who have the need and ability to represent their child with a disability, to participate collaboratively in making relevant educational and intervention decisions, and to implement collaborative home and community programs and procedures, typically under the direction of a professional. Hence, this includes identification of IEP goals and objectives; participation in educational conference training programs; participation in advocacy and volunteer training programs, including those designed to empower parents and families; and involvement in home-based tutoring and behavior management programs.

Involvement at the *partnership* level of participation is reserved for parents and family members who demonstrate the needs, skills, motivation, time, and energy to assist children and youth with exceptionalities on an equal level (or near-equal level) with professionals. Examples of collaborative activities at the this level of participation include independent application of home-based programs; training other parents and family members to represent, advocate, or train children; and serving as leaders or co-leaders of a family support group.

Developing a Personalized Conferencing Philosophy and Style

The unique nature and needs of parents and families as well as the variant characteristics of educators necessitate the development of an individually formulated conferencing philosophy and style. Hence, although certain general aptitudes and specific skills are necesary for successful parent and family interaction, these must be applied in accord with the conferencer's strengths and weaknesses. For reasons discussed previously, ready-made approaches and universally applicable strategies are neither appropriate nor effective with all parents and families.

Consequently, conferencers must work to develop styles that are pragmatic and compatible with their individual qualities, temperaments, and predilections. Further, while recognizing that all theoretical positions may be potentially valuable and contributory to the goal of serving parents and families, conferencers must also be aware of the dangers inherent in accepting any *single* position as sufficient for meeting the needs of all parents and families. Although adherence to a single philosophy may satisfy a conferencer's need for security, it is rarely adequate for serving a wide variety of parents and families. As previously noted, the American family has undergone significant change in the past decades. Their changed and variant needs can be served most adequately by conferencers who have developed a personal style and who are flexible enough to employ different approaches to meet the unique needs of those with whom they work. If educational conferencers are truly to meet the challenges presented by today's parents and families, they must possess a repertoire of skills that align with their own character and can be individualized for a variety of parents and families.

Summary

More than ever before, the "average" American family must be considered a nonexistent entity. The needs and characteristics of families are not only varied but also in a state of constant change. Accordingly, parent and family involvement requires that professionals be familiar with the trends that impact on parents and families, the range of needs encountered by parents and families with exceptional members, the methods for individualizing parent and family involvement, and the strategies appropriate for serving their needs.

Exercises

1. Apply the model of parent and family involvement to at least one family of a child or youth with an exceptionality. As a part of your application, identify the *needs* you perceive the family to have, a brief *plan* for best serving those needs, and your perception of an appropriate *level of participation* for the family.

Chapter 2

Impact of Children and Youth with Exceptionalities on Parents and Families

hildren's social and intellectual development is greatly influenced by their parents and families. As noted by Kauffman (1977), "the earliest socialization experiences of children involve a dyadic relationship with the mother, and these initial social interactions are first extended to include other family members" (p. 73). Within these relationships, it is equally obvious that children influence the families of which they are a part. This influence becomes particularly significant when a child is exceptional (Brinker, 1992; Greer, 1975; Mullins, 1987; Paul & Simeonsson, 1993; Wright, Matlock, & Matlock, 1985). Although the degree of such an influence relates to a variety of factors, including the severity and nature of a child's exceptionality, any disability of a family member exerts a significant effect on the entire family. Madeline Will, former Assistant Secretary for Special Education and Rehabilitative Services, U.S. Department of Education, observed that "families with disabled members have many additional stresses" (1988, p. 1). Further, Buscaglia (1975) declared that "a disability is not a desirable thing and there is no reason to believe otherwise. It will, in most cases, cause pain, discomfort, embarrassment, tears, confusion and the expenditure of a great deal of time and money" (p. 11). Parents and immediate family bear this pain most directly.

Almost without exception, parents of children with disabilities report difficulties directly associated with their child's condition (Breslau, Staruch, & Mortimer, 1982; Fiedler 1986; Hancock, Wilgosh, & McDonald, 1990; Simeonsson & Simeonsson, 1993; Turnbull & Turnbull, 1990). In this regard, Gorham (1975) identified a number of problems and obstacles she and her family experienced while securing appropriate services for her child with a disability. Acknowledging that they were able to survive the ordeal, Gorham concluded that it was only after "accumulating some scars which clearly mark us parents as members of the 'lost generation'" (p. 522). She further observed:

> We are angry. We have gone to the helping profession and have received too little help.
>
> We are still in awe of specialists and intimidated by their expertise.
>
> We are unduly grateful to principals or school directors for merely accepting our children in their programs. The spectre of 24 hour a day, 7 day a week care at home, with the state institution as an alternative, has made us too humbly thankful. We demonstrate a certain indifference to the latest bandwagon on which the mental retardation experts are riding. Mixed messages have been so much a part of our history that, rather than join the parades we tend to listen politely, then do what we think best for our child. We are often, therefore, accused of apathy.
>
> Many of us have concluded that it is best not to worry about next year (or tomorrow) because things might be better then (or worse). Certainly it seems impossible to "plan for the future" as most of us are so frequently admonished to do. Generally I have found that those who wanted me to plan for Beckie's future were suggesting that I place her on the roster for permanent residence in the state institution. That is, in fact, the only option available at present. In Maryland, I cannot even provide for her future by putting money aside and setting up an inheritance. If I die, and she must enter an institution, the state's general fund becomes heir to her belongings, and the money saved could go for something as remote to her well being as highway construction. So we worry about the future, but planning for it is not yet really a fruitful activity.
>
> We are tired. We have kept our children at home and raised them ourselves, with all the extra demands on time and energy which that implies—often without much help from the community, neighborhood, professionals, friends, or relatives, and in fact commonly against their well intentioned advice. We have founded parent groups and schools, run them ourselves, held fund raising events to pay teachers and keep our little special schools afloat, organized baby sitting groups, and summer play groups. We have built and repaired special playground equipment for our children's use at home and at school. We have painted

classrooms and buildings; we have written legislators and educated them about our children's needs and rights. We have collated and stapled hundreds of newsletters, attended school board meetings, lobbied at the state legislature for better legislation for handicapped children, informed newspaper reporters about inhumane conditions in institutions, and written letters to editors. All this we have done for a decade or more.[1] (p. 522–523)

Several authors (Adelman, 1994; Gorham, Jardins, Page, Pettis, & Scheiber, 1975; Neel, Meadows, Levine, & Edgar, 1988) have observed that parents of children with disabilities frequently face the need to secure services and consideration for their children in a society that places little value on persons with exceptionalities. Gorham et al. (1975) summarized:

Society does not view their children as worthy of investment; in fact, it disdains those with certain handicaps. The parent, in turn, feels devalued and often is as he proceeds about the business of looking for help for this child. Inevitably he will feel the conflict between his quite natural desire to have "the best" for his children and the various obstacles to getting it for this child. (p. 155)

The unique challenges experienced by many families of children and youth with exceptionalities require that educators and other professionals be able to understand an atypical child's impact on the family system and be knowledgeable about procedures and strategies for aiding families with disabled members meet their needs. Without this added dimension of the role performed routinely by educators, programs for children and youth with exceptionalities will probably not adequately serve the needs of both students and their families.

Typical Responses to a Child with an Exceptionality

Family systems are characterized not only by emotional and biological ties but also by established roles and norms. Such traditions and standards

---

[1]From "A Lost Generation of Parents," by K. A. Gorham, 1975, *Exceptional Children, 41*(8), pp. 522–523. Copyright 1975 by The Council for Exceptional Children. Reprinted with permission.

structure family members' activities and the manner in which they fulfill their duties (Goldenberg & Goldenberg, 1980; Lambie & Daniels-Mohring, 1993; Rotheram, 1989; Schultz, 1987; Simpson & Fiedler, 1989). The introduction of a new child into a family system, either through birth or adoption, results in role changes for the entire family (Carter & McGoldrich, 1980; Reiss, 1971; Ronnau & Poertner, 1993). This change process is most dramatic with the birth of a child who has a disability or the discovery of a handicapping condition in a family member (Fewell, 1986). Not only can the presence of a "less-than-perfect" child threaten individual family members, it may alter the entire family system. Farber (1968) reported that a child with mental retardation disrupts the normal cycle of families. In particular, he noted that while other children in a family become more independent and accept greater amounts of responsibility, the person with the disability often remains at various levels of dependency. Farber also found that marital integration and happiness may be reduced by the presence of a child with a disability, particularly if marital difficulties existed prior to the birth. This finding has been confirmed by others (Gallagher, Beckman, & Cross, 1983; Lambie & Daniels-Mohring, 1993).

In her book, *The Child Who Never Grew* (1950), Pearl S. Buck wrote the following: "The first cry from my heart, when I knew she would never be anything but a child, was the age old cry that we all make before inevitable sorrow: 'Why must this happen to me?' To this there could be no answer and there was none" (p. 34). Buck's analysis remains relatively current. That is, in spite of the growing volume of information available on the impact of a child with an exceptionality on the family, empirically valid data on the exact nature of this impact remain scarce. Indeed, most information on the topic is based on case studies and subjective reports (Turnbull & Turnbull, 1978, 1990).

Parental Reactions

As a function of its subjective and anecdotal nature, the literature dealing with parental reactions to having a child with an exceptionality is diverse and rather inconsistent. In spite of such variance, however, parents of children with exceptionalities appear to experience some commonality of feeling (Frey, Fewell, & Vadasy, 1989; Kroth, 1985). Love (1973), for example, contended that parents go through a series of emotional reactions—shock, refusal, guilt, bitterness, envy, rejection, and, finally, adjustment—in relation to their child's handicap. Others (Cansler & Martin,

1974; Hardman, Drew, & Egan, 1984; Johnson, 1993; McDonald, 1962; Robinson, 1970; Robinson & Robinson, 1965; Weber, 1974) have identified similar stages, most focusing on shock, disbelief, anger, and stress at one extreme, and emotional and intellectual acceptance at the other.

Other researchers have described the reactions of parents of children with disabilities in terms of recurrent feelings, including chronic sorrow and inadequacy (Love, 1973; Lyon & Preis, 1983; McWhirter, McWhirter, McWhirter, & McWhirter, 1993). Perske (1973) termed the feelings of parents of children with exceptionalities as the "glooms," the "speeds," the "blocks," the "hurts," the "guilts," the "greats," the "hates," and the "give ups." These reactions are not experienced by all parents and may vary in duration and strength of response when they do occur. Some authorities interpret the reactions of parents of children with exceptionalities as ego-supportive measures and defense mechanisms, which enable them to deal with difficult circumstances (Featherstone, 1980).

Other research has suggested that parents' reactions to having a child with an exceptionality parallel reactions to death and dying. Reactions correlate with the child's age at the time of diagnosis, the severity of the handicapping condition, and a host of other factors. Thus, while it is unlikely that the parents of a child diagnosed as having a mild learning problem would respond in the same manner as the parents of a child with a severe disability, it is common for parents of children with disabilities to respond with emotions similar to those described in terminally ill patients and their families (Kübler-Ross, 1969; Zolko, 1991). In fact, Kroth (1985) observed that Kübler-Ross extracted much of her information about death and dying from interactions and observations of persons with disabilities, citing the following Kübler-Ross statement:

> You have to understand I did not learn this [death, dying, and grieving stages] from dying patients. I learned it from all my years of working with blind people and multiple-handicapped, retarded patients, first in Switzerland and then here [in the U.S.]. (p. 22)

Relative to stages of acceptance, parents and families have been observed denying their child's condition (Safford & Arbitman, 1975), going through a bereavement process (Baum, 1962), and manifesting a number of other reactions before ultimately accepting their child's condition. During particularly difficult periods, parents may manifest both psychologic and somatic symptoms, including somatic distress, preoccupation, guilt, hostility, and anxiety (Crnic, Friedrich, & Greenberg, 1983; Summers, Brotherson, &

Turnbull, 1988). These behavioral patterns appear to reduce feelings of loss, disappointment, anger, or guilt (Hancock et al., 1990).

A major topic related to parental reaction has been the manner in which they were initially apprised of their child's exceptionality. A number of authorities have reported that contact with professionals is a topic parents of children with exceptionalities frequently wish to address (Epstein, 1992; MacDonald, 1962; Simpson & Carter, 1993). Akerley (1978) articulated her concerns in this area, noting,

> We don't begin in anger. We start out the way all parents of all children do: with respect, reverence really, for the professional and his skill. The pediatrician, the teacher, the writer of books and articles on child development, they are the source of wisdom from which we must draw in order to be good parents. We believe, we consult, we do as we are told, and all goes well unless . . . one of our kids has a handicap. (p. 40)

Without attempting to recount the numerous—both positive and negative—experiences encountered by parents of children with exceptionalities in interacting with professionals, suffice it to say that the initial encounter is frequently identified as the most significant.

The well-established importance of the professional's relationship with families of children who have exceptionalities underlies a frequent criticism by parents of many educators' lack of skill in this area (Friesen & Huff, 1990; Price, 1991; Roos, 1978). Thus, parents and families have recounted instances of gross insensitivity and brusqueness at a time when they are most vulnerable. Although parents on occasion may exaggerate their negative experiences with professionals, the latter must become more skillful in their initial contacts with parents, including when such contacts involve dissemination of diagnostic and classification information. Thus, professionals must accurately *and* compassionately communicate diagnostic findings and recommendations, help families secure appropriate services, and support families through what is an extremely difficult time. As suggested, initial positive and supportive interactions between parents and families establish a basis for future effective communication and an overall effective parent-professional partnership (Hardin & Littlejohn, 1995).

Sibling Reactions

The notion that a child with a disability can have a deleterious influence on other children in the family has persisted for a long time (Farber,

1959). Klein (1972), Love (1973), and Telford and Sawrey (1977) all reported that nonexceptional siblings in a family may suffer as a function of their disabled brother's or sister's condition, particularly when they are required to assume major responsibility for the child's care. These researchers also noted that nonexceptional children frequently feel resentful and neglected because of the immoderate attention given their disabled sibling (Tew & Laurence, 1973).

Such negative influence, however, has been refuted by other authorities (Breslau, Weitzman, & Messenger, 1981; Dyson, Edgar, & Crnic, 1989; Grossman, 1972; Simeonsson & Simeonsson, 1993). Graliker, Fishler, and Koch (1962), for instance, interviewed the teenage siblings of children with mental retardation to determine the effects of having such a brother or sister on their school, social, and family life. The teenage siblings were found to lead generally "normal" lives with adequate social opportunities and peer relationships. In addition, participants reported having satisfying home relationships and that they understood and accepted their exceptional sibling's condition. Based on these results, the investigators concluded that the presence of a young child with retardation in a family did not have an adverse influence on the teenagers sampled.

Other researchers and practitioners have also observed a great variability in the impact on siblings of a child with a disability. In this regard, Powell and Ogle (1985) found that a great many factors relate to the impact of an individual with a disability on a family, including the family's socio-economic status, size, beliefs, values, and orientation and the ages of the children; in addition, such variables as the age of the individual with the disability and the severity and nature of the exceptionality are significant as well. Although work in this area has been limited, evidence does suggest that well-adjusted and supportive families are best able to accommodate and adjust to the needs of an exceptional family member (Dyson et al., 1989). Yet, in spite of equivocal findings regarding disabled children's influence on their nonhandicapped siblings, evidence indicates that the latter will be affected by an exceptionality (Schulman, 1988). Commenting on this assumption, Crnic and Leconte (1986) concluded the following:

> Although it seems clear from both research and clinical reports that the effects of having a handicapped sibling vary greatly from individual to individual, and we cannot automatically assume that the effects will be deleterious, normal siblings are at risk for any number of social, behavioral, or emotional difficulties. This at-risk status is a function of the

ongoing stress associated with the presence of a handicapped sibling, and it is likely that the nature of these risks and stress vary across the sibling's life-span. (p. 93)

Facilitating Family Adjustment to a Child with an Exceptionality

Because parents and families of children and youth with exceptionalities are clearly unique, it is difficult to draw meaningful generalizations about what they think, feel, and experience relative to living with an exceptional member. Yet, a basic element of success in interacting and working with these families is an awareness and sensitivity to their experiences and feelings. In an attempt to facilitate professionals' understanding and empathy for these families, parents have offered personal perspectives on their experiences in living with and raising a child with an exceptionality in *Exceptional Parent* and similar periodicals.

In addition to professionals' empathy and understanding, helping families accept and accommodate children and youth with exceptionalities involves identifying and responding to parent and family needs in areas such as (a) information exchange, (b) partnership and advocacy training, (c) home and community program implementation, (d) counseling and consultation, and (e) parent/family coordinated service programs. It also involves individualizing programs and services; that is, identifying and arranging appropriate levels of parent/family involvement: (a) recognition and awareness, (b) ongoing communication, (c) advocacy and skill development, and (d) partnership (see chapter 1 and Figure 1.1).

Facilitating families' acceptance and accommodation of members with exceptionalities also involves other basic considerations, such as making available appropriate educational, vocational, living, and treatment programs and resources; providing opportunities to communicate with professionals and service providers; and supporting and taking into consideration the needs of all family members.

Appropriate Educational, Vocational, Living, and Treatment Programs and Resources

Parents and families of members with exceptionalities express a great need for appropriate resources and services (Bailey, 1987; Justice, O'Connor, & Warren, 1971; Minke & Scott, 1994; Olshansky, 1966a). Though the importance of other needs cannot be denied, in most cases these will be secondary to the desire for effective educational, vocational, living, and treatment programs (Bailey, 1988). Roos (1977) observed that most parent organizations have been formed to promote educational programs for children, usually with a focus on facilitating parental involvement. More recently, parent and advocacy groups have been involved in promoting and developing vocational programs, community living opportunities, and transition services (Dixon, 1992; Dunst, Leet, & Trivette, 1988; Mundschenk & Foley, 1995).

The mother of one child with a severe disability reported that upon moving to a new community, "our entire family was consumed with getting things set up for Cindy." The mother indicated that only after having enrolled her daughter in an appropriate school program, identifying a pediatrician knowledgeable regarding special needs children, and finding acceptable after-school care was her family able to direct full attention to other matters. She also observed that "when I see Cindy's bus pick her up for school in the morning, I know my child is being provided for—then I can go about other things." Similarly, the family of an adult with a disability confided that their primary need was to know that their family member was being adequately cared for in a community program for disabled persons.

Responding to parents' and families' needs for appropriate programs and services for exceptional members is often taken for granted. Yet, professionals must recognize this basic need as a linchpin of family adjustment and accommodation, and accordingly, not underestimate it.

Having secured an appropriate educational, vocational, or community program for their child, some parents and families want to become involved in the program. Blodgett (1971) attributed this need for involvement to a desire on the part of some parents to consider their child "normal" and to a frequent parental view of their offspring as having more ability and potential than acknowledged by their teachers. In addition, some parents have reported that participation in their child's educational program and familiarity with educational procedures and protocol enable them to channel their concerns, anger, frustrations, guilt, and energies into more productive areas (Simpson & Poplin, 1981). Commenting on the need to involve interested parents in their children's programs, Fiedler (1991) noted that

> supportive and effective professionals recognize that their client responsibilities extend beyond the individual child they are serving and encompass responsibilities to that child's parents and entire family unit.

This ecological perspective is essential in realizing one's potential as an effective professional in the 1990's and beyond. (p. 331)

Opportunities to Communicate with Professionals and Service Providers

Among the most basic needs of parents and families of persons with exceptionalities is the opportunity to communicate with professionals and other persons who work with their children (Dunst & Paget, 1991; Hayden, 1976; Mundschenk & Foley, 1995; Nahmias, 1995). Frequently parents report that they lack the opportunity to be heard, recognized, and understood (Allen & Cortazzo, 1970; Fiedler, 1991). Barsh (1968) observed that most parents have a limited understanding of what goes on in their child's school, and Barnes, Eyman, and Engolz (1974) agreed, noting that most contact between parents and educators is indirect, occurring either through phone calls or notes. These researchers further reported that most parent-educator contacts take place in reference to problems, that most parents perceive the concerns of their child's teacher as different from their own, and that many parents are intimidated by school personnel. In a similar manner, parents and families of non-school-age persons with disabilities desire improved contact with the professionals and other service providers who are involved with their members (e.g., vocational counselors, group home workers).

For these reasons, professionals must be able to listen with understanding and skill to their client parents and families. Successful communication may hinge more on an individual's ability to establish conditions favorable to two-way communication than to skill in sending a message (Nahmias, 1995; Rogers, 1951; Simpson & Carter, 1993). This process should include assurances to parents and families that they are being heard and understood. Active listening, whereby the conferencer can identify and understand what a person is communicating and feeling (including the message *behind* the words), often serves as a primary vehicle for helping parents and families better understand their own feelings and frustrations about having a child with special needs. Professionals who are skillful at attending to families and whose comments are relevant to the topics under discussion are typically most effective in meeting the communication needs of parents and families (Ivey & Authier, 1978; Kysela, McDonald, Reddon, & Gobeil-Dwyer, 1988).

Effective communication also requires letting parents structure a portion of both the format and the content of parent-educator conferences. In particular, they should be invited to present specific problems and be reassured that the conferencer will provide an appropriate response. Just as importantly, the conferencer must leave the discussion open to issues and concerns that may resist a simple response. That is, one must establish an atmosphere in which parents and family members feel free to explore emotions and attitudes with an empathic listener. It is not unusual for parents of children and youth with exceptionalities to express attitudes, opinions, or feelings about the child that appear inappropriate, extravagant, or rash. Although the conferencer's natural reaction may be to correct the perception or provide a solution or answer, the parent may be seeking nothing more than to be heard. Even though it is tempting to "set the record straight," professionals should give parents an opportunity to share their perceptions and feelings regarding particular aspects of their child's exceptionality (Chinn, Winn, & Walters, 1978; Cobb & Reeve, 1991; Schlesinger & Meadow, 1976).

One mother of a child with autism revealed that she believed her daughter's condition was "God's punishment for my evil ways." She confided that she had conceived her daughter out of wedlock, much to the displeasure of her parents, and although she and the child's father married shortly after learning she was pregnant, her feelings of guilt had persisted. That her later-to-be-diagnosed-autistic daughter was born on Christmas Eve was an omen to this mother. During a conference she related that although logically she recognized that the disability was not "God's punishment," her feelings had stayed the same over the years. Obviously this mother was not seeking an answer to the question of why her child had a severe disability, but rather someone to listen and understand her situation.

Effective communication also requires giving parents the opportunity to have their messages received without distortion. Although conferencers may wish to decline support or reinforcement of a particular message, they must nonetheless extend a chance to be heard. Responses such as "I'm sure you really don't feel that way," "You don't know what you are saying," and "You couldn't possibly mean that" serve to deny and disconfirm a parent's thoughts and emotions. These responses either place parents in the position of having to deny their own perceptions ("I guess I really didn't mean that") or they create a potential conflict ("I meant exactly what I said"). In either case, responses that fail to confirm a parent's message often detract from further attempts at communicating with professionals who work with their children.

In addition to the general requirements of effective communication, the conference format must direct sufficient attention to the interpretation and reinterpretation of diagnostic information. As suggested by numerous researchers and practitioners (Dembinski & Mauser, 1977a; Love, 1973; MacDonald, 1962; Mullins, 1987; Nahmias, 1995; Seligman & Darling, 1989), this area represents a primary concern for parents. It is essential, therefore, that conferencers allot sufficient time for discussing diagnostic process issues, even when parents have previously received an interpretation. The discussion should include those issues, concerns, and problems that led to a referral; a summary of assessment procedures and findings; and further recommendations (along with the manner in which they will be implemented). Most parents receive an interpretation of their child's functioning on diagnostic measures, yet few have an opportunity to discuss the findings and/or their own feelings about them (Cobb & Reeve, 1991; Zolko, 1991).

Parents and family members also should have the chance to obtain additional information about their child's program and exceptionality. Information to disseminate during the initial parent contact (but which may need to be reviewed periodically) includes the IEP process, the teacher's educational philosophy, the academic and social intervention programs being employed, ancillary and related services provided, and program and school evaluation procedures. In addition, parents should have an opportunity to address items of specific interest or concern to them, including their child's exceptionality, its causes, and the available treatment options.

A discussion of the child's future also should comprise part of the parent conference—including prognosis, long-term school expectations, and post-school alternatives. Although both parents and professionals may be reluctant to address this topic, its significance warrants appropriate attention. Obviously professionals lack precise mechanisms for determining a child's future, but they can help parents identify and evaluate options and alternatives. In addition, they can apprise families of the post-school options available to children and youth with exceptionalities. The intent of this process is to allow parents and families to consider the future relative to their child and to begin identifying and creating options.

Finally, families of children with exceptionalities may need assurance and confirmation that it is acceptable to feel ambivalent or even negative about having a child with an exceptionality. Some parents and family members may need encouragement to pursue interests and activities other than serving and advocating for the child with a disability. That is, parents and family should be encouraged to attend to their own needs as well as those of other family members, and to recognize that being the parent or sibling of a child with a disability need not and should not be their main responsibility and pursuit. Overcommitment on the part of parents and families can sometimes be as detrimental as inattention.

Support and Consideration of All Family Members

From a family systems perspective, all elements of a family unit are inter-connected, and events affecting one member impact others (Carter & McGoldrich, 1980; Fine, 1991; Hoffman, 1980; Lambie & Daniels-Mohring, 1993; Seligman & Darling, 1989; Simmons-Martin, 1976). For example, cancellation of a family trip because vacation monies went toward therapy or medical services, or excessive child-care responsibilities that restrict siblings' participation in school activities, or increased meal-time anxiety because of implementing a language training program cannot help but affect everyone in the family. Because each family member feels the impact uniquely, individual needs must be recognized and accommodated in order for families to function effectively.

Turnbull, Summers, and Brotherson (1983) developed a family systems model for understanding and accommodating the needs of families with disabled members that consists of three major components: (a) family structure (membership characteristics, cultural style, ideological style); (b) family functions (economic, physical, rest and recuperation, socialization, self-definition, affection, guidance, education, and vocational); and (c) family life cycles (family members aging and passing through various family roles). Thus, events that affect husband/wife, parental, sibling, and extrafamilial interactions will impact all family members. As a specific example of this process, Turnbull et al. (1983) offered the following:

> Consider the example of a mother who has agreed to work on a home training program in the area of feeding with her severely retarded child. Allowing her child to feed himself triples the time involved in each meal. While the mother is working with the child on feeding, her dinner conversation with her husband and other children is substantially limited. After the other family members finish dinner, the father cleans the kitchen and the siblings proceed to their homework all feeling that some of their needs have been overlooked. Meanwhile, the mother is feeling isolated from the rest of her family and frustrated over all the tasks to which she must attend before midnight. (p. 5)

Olson, Russell, and Sprenkle (1980) contended that effective family interactions are characterized by cohesion, adaptability, and communication. *Cohesion* refers to the force that unites family members. If a family is to effectively meet the needs of all members, it must avoid becoming enmeshed (i.e., overly concerned or overly involved) or disengaged (i.e., rigid in meeting needs) in interacting with family members who have disabilities. Another determinant of effective family interactions is *adaptability*; that is, family members must be able to conform to new or changed circumstances. Functioning families also display effective *communication skills*, including receiving and sending clear messages and displaying effectual listening behaviors.

As some of the interaction elements emphasized in the preceding models may not occur naturally, professionals assisting the families of children and youth with exceptionalities must help identify strategies and procedures for facilitating such interactions.

The presence of a child with an exceptionality will inevitably exert a significant impact on a family; however, the deleterious effects may be minimized. A primary goal for the educational conferencer and other professionals must be to help parents and family members understand and plan for a child or youth with an exceptionality. Regardless of his or her stated role, the parent conferencer must work for the preservation of family unity and employ the necessary procedures to assure that the presence of a child with special needs does not destroy the family system.

Planning for Accommodation of a Child with an Exceptionality

Accommodating a child or youth with an exceptionality within his or her family usually entails a gradual process associated with a variety of factors, some of which extend beyond the control of professionals. Nevertheless, the latter must realize their potential positive influence on this process. This facilitative effect can be accomplished best through well-planned procedures and strategies, including the following:

Listen to parents and family members. As this is very frequently what they are looking for, it can become the most therapeutic offering a professional can make.

Avoid hasty attempts at problem solving, advice giving, and information dissemination. Frequently parents and family members are simply seeking an opportunity to share their concerns with someone who can understand and empathize with their situation.

Do not attempt to convince parents and family members that a child or youth with an exceptionality is good or beneficial for them and their family. Though they can be aided in accommodating the member with special needs, they should not be told that the exceptionality is advantageous.

Apprise parents and family members of the potential impact of a child or youth with an exceptionality on the family. Although obviously conferencers cannot forewarn parents and families of every eventuality, they can advise about the common problems and conditions that crop up.

Encourage parents and siblings to pursue interests and responsibilities other than those solely concerning the family member with an exceptionality. Although positive action programs can benefit the larger community of exceptional children, parents generally should be dissuaded from committing their lives to their own exceptional child or to programs for persons with exceptionalities.

Provide parents with alternatives and opportunities for working appropriately with their own child and for participating in programs designed to serve other persons with exceptionalities. Such involvement is most effective when it is individualized and compatible with individual and family needs.

Encourage parents and family members to share their feelings about having a member with an exceptionality. Make them aware of the advantages of having someone to talk with about their concerns.

Encourage parents to examine their child's future, including identifying alternatives available to both the child and the family.

Identify procedures that the parents and family can employ with their child to train and develop functional skills and accomplish agreed-upon goals. Such procedures often facilitate family communication and satisfaction of all members' needs.

Aid parents and siblings in identifying areas of growth and accomplishment shown by a family member with a disability.

Avoid responding negatively or discouragingly to lofty goals set by families for their member with an exceptionality. A certain measure of overestimation can be advantageous.

Help parents and families understand that a child with an exceptionality is only one among several members of the family and therefore should be responded to accordingly.

Be aware of value system differences between the home and school/clinic.

Do not attempt to produce or use guilt to motivate parents and family members.

Do not create a false sense of security or progress for parents and family members. Be truthful.

As necessary, review materials and issues that have previously been discussed. It is not unusual for parents and family members to periodically wish to review "old" information and share their perceptions and feelings about it.

Encourage parents to present their own agendas at conferences.

Inform parents and family members of community resources that may help them accommodate their child or youth with an exceptionality.

Remind parents that all children in the family, regardless of whether they have an exceptionality, have needs and require appropriate attention.

Apprise parents and family members that their needs, as well as the needs of their child with an exceptionality, may likely change over time.

Summary

A child or youth with an exceptionality almost always will have a significant impact on his or her parents and family. The parent conferencer can help families more adequately understand their situation and identify strategies for most successfully meeting each member's needs.

Providing for the overall well-being of a child with an exceptionality includes the availability of appropriate educational, vocational, living, and treatment programs and resources; opportunities to communicate with professionals and service providers; and support and consideration of all family members. As any experienced professional can attest, it is only with such efforts that a child or youth with an exceptionality can benefit maximally from available services and hence progress at a rate commensurate with his or her abilities while the family maintains the integrity of its structure.

Exercises

1. Develop a list of community and school resources that offer parent and family counseling services.

2. Discuss with some parents the stages they went through after learning of their child's exceptionality.

3. Discuss with some parents the impact their child with an exceptionality has had on the family. Discuss with a brother and/or sister the sibling relationship with the affected child or youth.

4. Ask some parents to suggest procedures, techniques, and services that professionals could offer to help families more effectively integrate and accommodate a child or youth with an exceptionality.

5. Invite a panel of parents of children and youth with exceptionalities to visit with a group of professionals (such as those taking a parent conferencing class, an in-service session, etc.) to discuss experiences in raising and living with an individual who has an exceptionality. As a part of the discussion, encourage the parents to identify steps that professionals could have taken to assist them in better understanding and accommodating the family member with special needs.

Chapter 3

Multicultural Issues: Accommodating Cultural and Linguistic Diversity

A t a parent-teacher conference with the mother of a recently identified student with a learning disability, the parent was encouraged to share her perceptions regarding her son and his problems and to react to the information presented by school personnel. This young African American woman readily agreed that the concerns of her son's teachers were accurate and that the same problems existed at home. In addition, she discussed several issues that she and her family were attempting to contend with. Although not the cause of her son's difficulties, these topics were at least related. This mother of four revealed that only the previous week she had received notice that a reduction in the funds available to the federal agency for which she worked, and through which she was receiving job training, would result in the elimination of her position. She confided anxiety over her ability to feed, clothe, and provide a home for her children and expressed frustration over her ability to contend with what she considered to be a severe psychological setback. She reported that not only did her ex-husband provide no financial support for the family, he was legally prohibited from having contact with his children because of alleged physical and sexual abuse.

At one point in the conference the discussion focused on the child's problem in developing and maintaining appropriate peer relationships. In response to the question whether her son interacted with children his own age at home, the mother revealed that although he had an opportunity to play daily with other children at his baby-sitter's house, she was reluctant to allow any of her children to play outside in their own neighborhood. She noted that she lived in a federally subsidized housing project "where you keep your doors locked and your kids inside." She further elaborated on various significant problems associated with confining her children to their small apartment.

This scenario pointed out the complexity of issues often surrounding the families of children with special needs. Although abundant evidence shows that no cultural, ethnic, or racial group is immune to social problems, nonetheless the parent conferencer must be sensitive to several facts: (a) culturally and linguistically diverse groups experience a great number of social and economic problems (Charleston, 1987; Flaskerud & Nguyen, 1988; Makielski, 1973; Reed & Sautter, 1990; Williams, 1992); (b) culturally and linguistically diverse children have been overly represented in special education programs (Brosnan, 1983; Dunn, 1968; Turnbull, 1993); and (c) discriminatory and otherwise biased assessment procedures represent significant concerns for culturally and linguistically diverse children experiencing school-related problems (Hammill, 1987; Walker & Fabre, 1987; Wallace & Larson, 1978; Ysseldyke, Algozzine, & Thurlow, 1992). Just as significantly, educational conferencers must recognize the need to address specific communication-related issues when interacting with culturally and linguistically diverse parents and families of children with exceptionalities (Brantlinger & Guskin, 1985; Sontag & Schacht, 1994).

The exact number of culturally and linguistically diverse students who attend public schools in the United States is unknown. However, the number is growing rapidly, and demographers estimate that by the year 2000 more than one third of school-age children will come from culturally diverse backgrounds (Hodgkinson, 1993). Hispanic and Asian Pacific American families represent the most rapidly growing groups, and estimates are that among the 25 largest cities and metropolitan areas in the United States, approximately 50% of students are culturally and linguistically diverse. In 1989 Baca and Cervantes (1989) conservatively estimated that about 9% of the U.S. population does not use English as their primary language, and currently this statistic is rapidly accelerating (Voltz, 1994). Other estimates clearly reveal that the pattern of greater diversity among school-age children and their families will continue to increase in the foreseeable future (Banks, 1994; Correra & Weismantel, 1991).

Educational Challenges Facing Culturally Diverse Students with Exceptionalities

One provision of the Federal Civil Rights Act of 1964 was that the U.S. Office of Education would conduct a study of "the lack of availability of equal educational opportunities for individuals by reason of race, color, religion or national origin in public educational institutions" (Coleman et al., 1966, p. iii). The resulting study, commonly known as the Coleman Report, was designed to assess the nature and extent of racial and ethnic public school segregation and the extent of educational inequality among minority group children, as well as to correlate academic achievement with minority status and background. This massive research effort yielded several significant findings: (a) minority children more commonly attended schools that had larger average class sizes than did nonminority children; (b) minority pupils had less access to educational facilities and experiences related to academic achievement than did nonminority children; (c) minority students were generally taught by less capable instructors; (d) minority students tended to perform more poorly on standardized achievement tests, particularly in the upper grades, than nonminority students; and, most significantly, (e) when the students' socioeconomic background was controlled, the availability of school resources (e.g., laboratories, libraries, etc.) had only a minor influence on academic achievement.

The last finding was not only a surprise to Coleman and his research team, but it also became the basis for significant debate. For example, Jencks (1966) interpreted this finding to be directly associated with familial and socioeconomic status and opportunity, noting that if children are exposed to homes and environments where verbal and other academically related skills and behaviors are accentuated, they will have a much greater chance of prospering in school. Coleman's (1968) subsequent interpretation of the data resembled that of Jencks (1966). Similarly, Bronfenbrenner (1967) also accentuated the view that a child's home and family experiences closely relate to academic achievement.

Even though the Coleman Report continues to be controversial, most professionals agree that social influences correlate closely with children's school-related performance. In particular, the report's findings further corroborate the notions that schools are limited in their capacity to influence children's performance independent of their social and family experiences, and that certain culturally and linguistically diverse students are particularly vulnerable to school-related problems. Further, the inferences and conclusions based on the 1966 study lend support to the position that unless wide-ranging social intervention programs are made available (including parent training and participation in their children's educational programs), minority group children can be expected to continue to experience severe school-related problems. As noted by a number of authorities (Kosa, 1975; Reed & Sautter, 1990; Schorr, 1989), majority status tends to be associated with a variety of privileges, including access to facilities and mechanisms for promoting healthful and productive lifestyles.

Compensatory and "special" educational provisions for culturally and linguistically diverse students with alleged handicapping conditions also represent a controversial issue. In fact, a number of special education practices have been considered discriminatory toward minority groups (Collier, 1986; Laosa, 1977; Mercer, 1973; Silberberg & Silberberg, 1974; Walker & Fabre, 1987). Jones and Wilderson (1976), for example, observed that minority group children "were over-represented in special classes, particularly for the mentally retarded" (p. 3), that discriminatory assessment methods and procedures were commonplace, and that educators tended to have negatively biased perceptions of the ability and potential of minority pupils. The authors suggested that these practices "have served to highlight for many minority parents and professionals the view that institutionalized racism is part and parcel of educational practice" (p. 3).

Johnson (1969), in a further elaboration on this point, accused special education of serving as an alternative placement when the schools failed to motivate and teach children. He specifically postulated that

> special education is helping the regular school maintain its spoiled identity when it creates special programs (whether psychodynamic or behavioral modification) for the "disruptive child" and the "slow learner," many of whom, for some strange reason, happen to be black and poor and live in the inner city. (p. 245)

In a more recent article in *U.S. News and World Report*, Shapiro, Loeb, and Bowermaster (1993) unleashed a scathing attack on special education, alleging that it discriminated against students of color and that culturally and linguistically diverse students were frequently placed in programs because teachers were unwilling or unable to deal with them.

Assessment

Assessment issues have long been significant relative to evaluation and placement of minority children into programs for students with exceptionalities (Wood, 1990). Duran (1989), for instance, questioned the reliability and validity of evaluations of minority students, citing (a) language differences or limited proficiency, (b) student lack of exposure to test item content, (c) student lack of test-taking strategies, and (d) examiner lack of sensitivity to individual social and cultural behaviors. Others (Galagan, 1985; Ysseldyke & Thurlow, 1984) contend that norm-referenced assessment measures administered to students of varying cultural backgrounds (a) fail to account for environmental factors, (b) assume cross-setting generalizability, and (c) are irrelevant to classroom settings. Purportedly these inadequate testing procedures have resulted in an overrepresentation of minority students in special education (Chinn & Hughes, 1987). In this regard, Reilly (1991) noted that school districts with lower socioeconomic status had significantly greater numbers of minority students in special education classes than did higher socioeconomic status school districts. Similarly, Chinn and Hughes (1987) reported overrepresentation of children from ethnic, racial, and cultural minority groups, and Forness (1988) reported significant problems related to under- and overrepresentation of culturally and language diverse groups, ethnic conflicts between service providers and the culture of students, limited parental involvement, and overreferral of culturally different youth to the juvenile justice system.

Evidence also exists that students from minority groups get placed in certain educational settings on the basis of their culture or language as opposed to their educational needs. Grossman (1991), for example, reported that social and ethnic factors were significant considerations in assignment of students to ability groups. Although neither ethnicity nor social class served as the sole basis for ability group assignments, educators often assigned culturally diverse and working-class students to lower ability groups than objective test scores warranted. Grossman also stated that educators maintained more prejudicial behavioral expectations for minority students than for their nonminority peers and found that when educators evaluate the severity of pupil's behavior problems, they judge the exact same behaviors as more deviant when committed by African American male students.

Academic Performance

Academic performance issues have also been significant relative to students from culturally and linguistically diverse groups. Grossman (1991), for instance, noted that minority students are overrepresented in tracks for "low potential" students, where their teachers stress concrete, repetitive drill and practice as a primary instructional method and often neglect more creative and interesting instructional approaches. In support of the notion that minority students frequently are exposed to fewer opportunities than their majority culture peers, the National Assessment of Educational Progress (1988) reported that minority high school graduates are less likely to have studied computers or to have enrolled in high-level academic courses (e.g., chemistry, physics, foreign language), and they are more likely to have taken remedial math and science classes. Further, clear evidence also points out the particular vulnerability of culturally and linguistically diverse students to leaving school prior to graduation.

A related academic policy matter relates to suspension and/or expulsion. Because PL 94-142 does not specifically address this issue, the principles used to guide such decisions in this area were developed through a series of case law interpretations. Yell (1989) summarized those findings as follows: (a) up to 10-day temporary suspensions of students with handicapping conditions are permitted; (b) expulsions/suspensions of more than 10 days constitute changes in placement under IDEA and active IDEA due process procedures; (c) trained, knowledgeable people must determine whether a causal relationship exists between the misbehavior resulting in the suspension/expulsion and the child's disability; (d) school personnel must respect students' 14th amendment due process rights during suspension/expulsion procedures; and (e) schools may transfer students with disabilities to more restrictive settings, contingent upon due process findings. Establishing fair and appropriate policies for determining when and for how long students should be excluded from attending school is quite important, given that students from diverse cultural groups are especially vulnerable to dropping out of school and experiencing out-of-school problems.

Community Services

Community services issues relative to students and families from minority culture and language groups also warrant the consideration of parent conferencers. Day and Roberts (1991) reported that while conservative estimates suggest about 12% of children in the United States require mental health services, only about 20% of these children receive appropriate mental health care. Moreover, this problem is especially significant for children who are disadvantaged and who live in poverty. Knitzer, Steinberg, and Fleisch (1990) found that over 50% of the districts they surveyed reported no counseling services, and that when services were provided, they occurred on a short-term basis and generally were paid for by parents. Community mental health program therapy and support resources, including crisis intervention alternatives, are also generally lacking (Grosenick, George, & George, 1987). These findings, in combination with research documenting a positive association between poverty and mental health concerns (Belle, 1990; Day & Roberts, 1991), present particular problems for culturally and language diverse students and their families. That is, children of multicultural ethnic backgrounds may be the most underserved, as they are at higher risk for mental health problems (Tuma, 1989) and less likely to receive necessary services (Day & Roberts, 1991).

Though many of these indictments relating to students and families from culturally diverse groups originally appeared decades ago, minority group pupils continue to be particularly vulnerable to classification as exceptional (Anderson & Anderson, 1983; Nuttall, Landurand, & Goldman, 1984; Polloway & Smith, 1983; Smith & Luckasson, 1992; Ysseldyke et al., 1992), and many of the same social, political, and economic ills identified as contributing to their educational problems remain (Berman, 1984; Rudor & Santangelo, 1979; Scherer, 1993; Smith, 1983). Accordingly, the educational conferencer must be willing and able to respond to the needs, values, and practices of culturally diverse children and their families. Specifically, such responsiveness should be manifested in (a) sensitivity to the political, economic, and educational issues that affect minorities, (b) awareness of value differences between minority and nonminority cultures, (c) knowledge of educational procedures that specifically relate to culturally and language diverse pupils, (d) awareness of legislation pertaining to minority students, (e) self-awareness, (f) awareness and acceptance of differences, and (g) conferencing strategies appropriate for particular diverse groups.

Other Challenges Confronting Culturally and Linguistically Diverse Groups

In the book *36 Children*, Herbert Kohl (1967) presented a series of dismal neighborhood descriptions written by fifth-grade students in one Harlem school. The narratives graphically depicted violence, drugs, poverty, filth, and urban decay at its worst. Similarly, Dick Gregory (1964) recalled in his autobiography that when he was a child, there was rarely enough food for his family and virtually never a regular mealtime. He, too, described the chaos, despair, and rueful conditions that seem an all-too-common part of the lives of urban minority children and their families. Coles and Piers (1969) disputed the notion that many urban minority children are experientially deprived, noting that "on the contrary, they tend to be helpless victims of a veritable onslaught on the sensorium" (p. 167), being required to suffer through overcrowded living conditions and violence.

Although these descriptions are representative of some culturally and linguistically diverse children and their families, they are not presented here as the norm. Nevertheless, the parent conferencer must recognize that the true norm, although different from the most graphic descriptions given by Gregory (1964) and Kohl (1967), may still vary significantly from typical majority culture middle-class experiences (Charleston, 1987; Chestang, 1981; Haberman, 1993; Scherer, 1993). Consider, for example, the following statistics:

- While African American citizens comprise only a fraction of the total population, they represent a significantly greater proportion of the nation's poor. Hispanic and Native American groups also contain a disproportionate number of individuals existing at a poverty level.

- African American male teens and young adults and other culturally diverse groups will experience significant unemployment and under-employment problems.

- The life expectancy for cultural minorities is significantly shorter than for the majority population. Malnutrition, infections, and respiratory diseases have in some regions existed at near epidemic levels.

- U.S. health officials report that homicide is the leading cause of death among African American men 22 to 24 years old, far surpassing disease and accidents.

- Young adults who at age 18 demonstrate the poorest academic skills are 8 times more likely to bear children outside of marriage, 9 times more likely to drop out of school before graduation, and 5 times more likely to be unemployed. Many of these persons come from minority cultures.

- In 1994 nearly a quarter of all children lived below the poverty line, up from about 14% in 1969.

- Approximately 15 million children are being reared by single mothers, whose family income in 1991 averaged about $11,400. A disproportionate number of these families are from culturally and linguistically diverse groups.

- Educational deficiencies, school failure, and dropout rates are epidemic in minority cultures.

- Alcoholism, poverty, unemployment, and economic depression are common among Native Americans, particularly those living on reservations.

- In 1990 approximately 3 out of 4 African American babies were born into a female-headed household, as compared to 1 out of 5 White babies.

- Hundreds of thousands of American children and youth are homeless, and a significant number of them belong to minority families.

- A Black baby is about 8 times more likely to be an AIDS victim than majority culture babies.

- Between 1979 and 1985, the number of Black youth placed in juvenile facilities rose approximately 40%; during the same period the number of Black youths entering college immediately after high school dropped 4%. This trend continues today.

- The United States has dropped to a tie for last place among 20 industrialized nations in infant mortality. In the District of Columbia, a city with a large minority population, a child is more likely than one born in Trinidad to die in the first year of life.

- Approximately 14% of the people in the United States speak a foreign language at home.

These and similar statistics point to the need for the educational conferencer to be cognizant of and sensitive to the factors associated with minority status and be willing to accommodate these circumstances. Coles and Piers (1969) commented on the differences in the school-related environments and activities of minority versus nonminority students. They noted that, on the way to school, the minority child frequently "finds himself in a world of alleyways and broken glass; of addicts, alcoholics, pimps; of idle, bitter men who sit about with little hope for themselves. But when the middle-class child goes to school he is welcomed by the grown-ups along his path" (p. 34). More recent reports reveal that this trend continues today (Belle, 1990; Hodgkinson, 1993).

Further, minority and nonminority pupils are often differentially perceived relative to their need for compensatory or alternative educational placement (Nuttall et al., 1984; Reilly, 1991). Forer (1970), for instance, observed that minority status is frequently in and of itself cause for "special" educational action or intervention. Similarly, Cohen, Granger, Provence, and Solnit (1975) pointed out that

> when the troubling or troubled adolescent is poor or a minority group member, he or she is more likely to be referred to the courts for help. Referrals for white, middle-class adolescents are more likely to be made to the mental health system. (p. 113)

Although the educational conferencer may be able to do little to correct the underlying conditions and inimical circumstances facing culturally and linguistically diverse families, he or she must demonstrate sensitivity to the circumstances that impact on these groups. Specifically, professionals must recognize that for some parents and families, the least of their worries will be their child's school performance; that attending school conferences may create significant logistic, economic, and child-care burdens; that trust and rapport with school personnel may be slow in developing; and that the perceived value of education as a facilitator of survival in certain environments may be minimal. Failure to demonstrate such sensitivity will likely lead to significant communication problems.

Professionals also should note that certain social and family factors may impair minority group members' ability to effectively consume available services. Accordingly, conferencers should be sensitive to strategies for strengthening entire families (rather than focusing exclusively on children with disabilities, independent of their families) and should help parents and families more effectively use available resources. Without these efforts educators may find that some culturally and language diverse families, such as those who live in poverty, are forced to choose sheer survival over the needs of a child with an educational problem (Carey, Boscardin, & Fontes, 1994).

Forming Partnerships with Culturally and Language Diverse Families

Developing effective partnerships with parents and families who have diverse cultural and/or language characteristics is a daunting task. Indeed, families from minority cultures may regard schools and school personnel with suspicion and trepidation. However, the desire for children and youth to have successful educational experiences offers sufficient motivation to pursue this task whole-heartedly. Forming collaborative partnerships with parents and families of all students, including those from minority cultures, is basic to effective education.

Accommodation and partnership formation with minority families necessitates specific strategies and procedures for establishing and maintaining rapport and cooperative relationships. Such steps include (a) developing an awareness and acceptance of cultural diversity and individual differences, value differences, and other unique issues of exceptional minority pupils and their families, (b) becoming knowledgeable about legislation pertaining to minority pupils with exceptionalities, and (c) practicing conferencing strategies appropriate to particular minorities.

Developing an Awareness and Acceptance of Cultural Diversity and Individual Differences

Increasingly educators and other professionals have reached out to improve relationships and services to children and families from diverse groups. Recognizing that these students are at risk and vulnerable to a number of problems (e.g., overidentification for special education programs), attempts have been made to better understand the unique characteristics of culturally and linguistically diverse groups and to more effectively serve the needs of minority students and their families. Basic to accomplishing these goals is the requirement that professionals remain aware and accepting of various cultures and other differences. Understanding and accepting that members of different cultures will vary in the value they attribute to certain issues (e.g., educational progress) will facilitate the professional's ability to interact more effectively with a wide range of families. Thus, for example, such awareness should aid in understanding some Hispanic families' concern over academic competitiveness and some Native American families' resistance to use of public praise in social reinforcement programs.

An important cautionary note must accompany conferencers' attempts to understand individuals of cultures different from their own. First, it is critical to invest sufficient effort in the task of learning and understanding that one can transcend stereotypical descriptions of other cultures. In this regard, Glenn (1989) notes the importance of not perceiving culture "as an occasion for reinforcing stereotypes—negative or positive—about ethnic groups" (p. 779). Thus, educators must become familiar with the day-to-day background, culture, and traditions of students and their families rather than just the popular folklore regarding a particular group.

Second, conferencers should recognize the differences among specific groups of individuals from the same general minority classification and not assume that they share common characteristics. For instance, the general term "Hispanic" includes groups such as Mexican Americans, Puerto Ricans, South Americans, and Cuban Americans, all of which have many unique characteristics. In this context, Correra and Weismantel (1991) observed that

> providing professionals with cultural profiles of ethnic groups will be effective only if the professional can affirm that the cultural pattern does indeed exist within an individual family and that it may be affecting the way the family is coping with a disabled child. (p. 86)

Developing an Awareness of Value Differences

Just as Mead (1928) observed differences in the practices and traditions of different cultures, so too can we expect members of minority groups to display a unique set of values. These values may differ significantly from those held by the majority culture, particularly regarding educational issues (Brown, 1992; Correra & Weismantel, 1991; Kroth & Simpson, 1977; McGill & Pearce, 1982; Rutherford & Edgar, 1979).

With respect to values, it is important that professionals scrutinize their own attitudes toward specific minorities. In particular, one should attempt to pinpoint personal beliefs, prejudices, fears, and concerns regarding culturally and linguistically diverse groups as well as try to better understand the nature and origin of these perceptions. The middle-class majority culture educator should be aware, for instance, that public school curricula and procedures have historically accentuated the "rightness" of the White/European tradition. While some schools have attempted to focus on the "melting pot" composition of this country and its ability to accommodate "other peoples," this traditionally has been pursued under the guise that the values, ideals, and practices of the majority culture would eventually be adopted by minority groups. As a result, we can expect that an educator reared in the tradition of the dominant culture (particularly if from a middle-class background) has developed certain beliefs and perceptions regarding minority groups as either wishing to retain their own traditions and values or as having been prevented from becoming a legitimate part of the majority culture. This should in no way be interpreted as an endorsement of biased or inappropriate attitudes and prejudices; rather, it is a position based on the premise that individuals must first understand their own values and sentiments before they can effectively communicate with persons of different beliefs (Green, 1982; Raths, Harmin, & Simon, 1966). Though individuals with particularly strong biases may need to explore strategies for modifying their attitudes, the primary benefit of self-scrutiny is better self-understanding.

As a means of gaining a clearer understanding of minority-related beliefs, readers are encouraged to complete the self-assessment survey that appears in Figure 3.1. Those who belong to culturally diverse groups themselves should complete the form on the basis of their perceptions of other minority groups. For each item, the respondent should check the column (strongly agree, mildly disagree, etc.) that most closely corresponds to his or her attitude. Respondents should base their answers on initial impressions rather than attempting to "talk themselves" into or out of certain choices. After completing and reflecting on their responses, readers are encouraged to ask a colleague to evaluate them using the same scale. Areas of discrepancy should be discussed along with attitudes that may require modification. The instrument also can serve to assess patterns of growth and change over time and to solicit feedback from minority parents and families. Although no norms are associated with this scale, it can make professionals more familiar with their diversity and minority-related values and attitudes. Such self-understanding provides the basis for more effective communication and programming efforts.

Pepper (1976) identified several value-related differences between Native Americans and the majority culture. She observed, for instance, that Native Americans tend to respect and honor their elders more, their family life more often includes extended family members, they more commonly accept and conform to Nature instead of attempting to dominate it, they put less emphasis on competition and prestige, they more frequently express themselves through actions rather than words, and they expect that adulthood will commence at an earlier stage than do members of the majority culture. Similarly, Correra and Weismantel (1991) have provided examples of cultural beliefs of Hispanic groups that may assist educators in successfully working with these families. Shown in Table 3.1, these examples extend the notion that diverse groups often hold unique beliefs that may affect educational services.

Educational conferencers must become knowledgeable regarding the particular traditions and values of the minority families with whom they work. Just as Native Americans and Hispanic groups have distinct value characteristics, as observed by Pepper (1976) and Correra and Weismantel (1991), other minority groups will have their own unique features, too. Familiarity with and acceptance of these patterns form the basic components

	Strongly Agree	Agree	Mildly Agree	Neutral	Mildly Disagree	Disagree	Strongly Disagree
1. I am uncomfortable in conferences with individuals with skin colors different from my own.	☐	☐	☐	☐	☐	☐	☐
2. I consider culturally and linguistically diverse educational problems basically to be a function of a lack of parental emphasis on doing well in school.	☐	☐	☐	☐	☐	☐	☐
3. I am intimidated by individuals from cultures that I do not fully understand.	☐	☐	☐	☐	☐	☐	☐
4. I believe that the dominant language of the home, even if not English, should be accommodated in public school.	☐	☐	☐	☐	☐	☐	☐
5. I believe that the dominant language of the home, even if not English, should be taught in public schools.	☐	☐	☐	☐	☐	☐	☐
6. I believe that certain cultural and ethnic groups are innately inferior in educational potential to the majority culture.	☐	☐	☐	☐	☐	☐	☐
7. I am uncomfortable in conferences with parents who are unable to speak standard English.	☐	☐	☐	☐	☐	☐	☐
8. I frequently become angry in conferences with parents who are unable to speak standard English.	☐	☐	☐	☐	☐	☐	☐
9. I share many similarities with the minority pupils and families with whom I am associated.	☐	☐	☐	☐	☐	☐	☐
10. I am usually as satisfied with my conferences with minority parents as with those that include nonminorities.	☐	☐	☐	☐	☐	☐	☐

(*continues*)

Figure 3.1. Minority Attitude Self-Assessment Survey.

	Strongly Agree	Agree	Mildly Agree	Neutral	Mildly Disagree	Disagree	Strongly Disagree
11. I would prefer to work in a school serving children and families from cultures and backgrounds similar to my own.	☐	☐	☐	☐	☐	☐	☐
12. I believe that most cultural and language-related social problems could be solved if groups made up their mind to improve their conditions.	☐	☐	☐	☐	☐	☐	☐
13. I do not believe that schools can solve many of the problems experienced by minorities.	☐	☐	☐	☐	☐	☐	☐
14. I am surprised when parents from culturally diverse groups show an interest in their child's school-related performance.	☐	☐	☐	☐	☐	☐	☐
15. I resent certain groups of parents calling me at home more than others.	☐	☐	☐	☐	☐	☐	☐
16. I am equally at ease in accepting a dinner invitation to the homes of my minority and nonminority students.	☐	☐	☐	☐	☐	☐	☐
17. I find it easier to empathize with parents whose background is similar to my own.	☐	☐	☐	☐	☐	☐	☐
18. I am more inclined to give advice to parents from culturally diverse groups than to parents from other groups.	☐	☐	☐	☐	☐	☐	☐
19. I find it easier to admit to a minority parent than to a nonminority that I was wrong.	☐	☐	☐	☐	☐	☐	☐
20. I am more inclined to ask minority parents to participate in home-based programs.	☐	☐	☐	☐	☐	☐	☐

Figure 3.1. *Continued*

Table 3.1. Examples of Cultural Beliefs with Implications for Services

Ethnic group	Cultural beliefs	Implication for services
Mexican American	Spiritual healing (*curanderos*)	Understand that health-related, special education, or mental health services may be secondary to the family's hope of a cure for the disabled child
Puerto Rican	*Machismo*	Respect the role of the father in family governance
		Understand that the father may be uncomfortable with the child care role
		Provide "male-oriented" activities for parent involvement
		Use male professionals when possible
		Respect the mother's need to postpone decision making until she speaks with her husband
	Compadres	Realize that the extended family system may include godparents, close friends, and neighbors
		Respect the involvement of nonfamily members in the decision-making process for the child's services
		Use extrafamilial subsystems to provide support for parents

Note. From Correra & Weismantel (1991)

of successful conferencing and culturally sensitive and appropriate interventions for families and their children.

Unique Issues of Minority Students with Exceptionalities and Their Families

Conferences with parents and families of minority pupils with exceptionalities often relate to issues of minority status and cultural diversity. In particular, one should anticipate discussions involving nondiscriminatory assessment, the effects of labeling, and strategies for how best to serve the educational needs of minority students. Due to their importance to many parents and family members, professionals must deal with these topics thoroughly and effectively.

Probably no topic in special education has received as much attention as procedures for conducting nondiscriminatory evaluations of minority pupils. Legal rulings, legislation, and mass media attention have sensitized educators and parents to these issues. In addition, professionals ethically are acknowledging the potentially harmful consequences of biased evaluations and the resulting problems of unwarranted labels and incorrect educational dispositions (Galagan, 1985; Goldstein, Arkell, Ashcroft, Hurley, & Lilly, 1975; Grossman, 1991; Reilly, 1991).

Questions regarding nondiscriminatory assessment procedures are likely to occur in conferences with parents of minority pupils. Often the evaluation procedures routinely used by schools have been devised for and standardized on nonminority populations. The potentially discriminatory influence of applying inappropriate evaluation measures to minority pupils has increasingly been recognized (Chinn & McCormick, 1986; Smith & Luckasson, 1992). As a result, increased attention has turned to the need to consider a child's culture during assessment proceedings (Bryen, 1974; Oakland, 1973) and to make his or her ethnic ties a consideration during the evaluation process (Jaramillo, 1974).

Both professionals and parents now are focusing more on factors associated with obtaining an accurate and unbiased assessment. Accordingly, some parents of minority pupils may want to discuss the assessment and classification systems that have diagnosed a disproportionate number of minority pupils as intellectually subnormal, behaviorally deviant, and educationally deficient (Hurley, 1971; Johnson, 1969; Mercer, 1973; Shapiro et al., 1993), and hence whether or not their own child's diagnosis and placement are valid. Professionals' ability to respond to such questions and demonstrate to parents and family members that the assessment procedures used with their children were nondiscriminatory, multidisciplinary, and comprehensive is closely aligned with developing and maintaining rapport, trust, and effective parental involvement.

Parents of culturally and language diverse children with exceptionalities are also concerned about issues related to labeling. In her historic "Riverside Study," Mercer (1970, 1971, 1973, 1975) reported several alarming findings associated with labeling minority groups as handicapped. In particular, she revealed (a) that public schools more commonly diagnosed and labeled individuals as "exceptional" than did other agencies; (b) that those individuals identified by schools as exceptional tended to be more mildly impaired than those identified by other social agencies; (c) that minority pupils were more likely to perform poorly on standardized intelligence tests than their nonminority peers, thus increasing their chance of being identified as having retardation; and (d) that children from minority and low socioeconomic groups were more commonly considered to have retardation only during school hours ("6-hour retardates") than White children and pupils from more prosperous homes. Although legislation (e.g., PL 94-142), court decisions (*Larry P. v. Riles*, 1972; *Diana v. California State Board of Education*, 1970), and general attention to testing and placement bias (McLoughlin & Lewis, 1986; Reilly, 1991) have helped bring about significant improvements in this area, professionals who meet with parents and families of minority children and youth with exceptionalities should anticipate that questions on this topic will continue to arise in conferences. The ability to effectively deal with these issues is likely to form the basis for future meaningful interactions.

Parents and family members of minority pupils assigned to specialized or modified programs are also interested in both the nature of the educational services that will be rendered and the manner in which their child's diversity will be accommodated. Parental concerns in this area may focus on the curriculum to be implemented and whether it will be compatible with their child's background and experiences; the cultural, ethnic, and religious mix of children with whom their child will associate; and the level of acceptance of cultural and language differences demonstrated by the nonexceptional students in a child's school. Though it has been suggested (Johnson, 1976) that the primary goal of minority education should be the achievement of academic gains rather than the accommodation of various cultures, educators must be sensitive and willing to address questions and issues pertaining to minority status. As noted by Meyen (1978a), "If teachers understand a child's uniqueness, respect the child's individuality, and are familiar with the child's cultural background, they are in a better position to make instructional decisions and to establish an environment conducive to learning" (p. 76). All parents and families are entitled to such guarantees.

Legislation Pertaining to Culturally and Language Diverse Students with Exceptionalities

Federal legislation enacted over the past three decades has clarified and fortified parents' rights to represent their children and to interact and collaborate with professionals relative to planning and programming. These enact-ment—including the Rehabilitation Act of 1973 (PL 93-112: Section 504), the Rehabilitation Act Amendments of 1986 (PL 99-555), the Fam-ily Educational Rights and Privacy Act of 1974 (PL 93-380), the Education for All Handicapped Children Act of 1975 (PL 94-142), the Education of the Handicapped Act Amendments of 1986 and 1990 (PL 9-57, PL 101-476) that changed the name of the enactment to the Individuals with Dis-abilities Education Act, and the Americans with Disabilities Act of 1990 (PL 101-336)—have particular significance and reference to individuals from minority groups. For example, the Individuals with Disabilities Edu-cation Act provides assurances that assessment procedures employed with minorities "will be selected and administered so as not to be racially or cul-turally discriminatory." Further, the mandate states that evaluative proce-dures "shall be provided and administered in the child's native language." The same type of safeguards exist for other major components of the act, including provisions for educational placement in the "least restrictive environment," rights to "due process," and guarantees of an "individualized education program." Because legislative attention has focused on issues relating to minority children with exceptionalities, it is imperative that professionals be familiar with the provisions provided through these acts. Only with such familiarity can conferencers competently interact with par-ents and family members of minority pupils within this topical area.

Developing Rapport with Families

Development of initial rapport may be particularly vulnerable to factors associated with cultural and linguistic differences. That is, during early meetings parents and professionals may be adversely influenced by the subtle (and not so subtle) characteristics associated with minority and majority interactions. In particular, professionals may find it difficult to empathize with persons who are different from themselves, and parents from minority cultures in turn may doubt the professional's ability to understand their current situation or overall heritage.

Nonetheless, as rapport builds an essential ingredient of communica-tion success, educators must identify mechanisms for developing this funda-mental trust. Accordingly, conferencers should become familiar with the effect of different rapport-building procedures on different groups. In spite of significant variance within groups, certain commonalities exist. For exam-ple, some minority groups are suspicious of "small talk" at the beginning of a conference, believing that such behavior poses a delay tactic or a strategy for avoiding an unpleasant topic rather than offering a means of establishing rapport. Conversely, other groups (e.g., Asian American and Pacific Islander) may prefer an opportunity to discuss matters unrelated to the business at hand for a few minutes before focusing on the primary agenda.

Majority culture conferencers should also recognize that some minority parents are anxious and suspicious during initial encounters. Because some minority parents may have had limited prior face-to-face contact with professional personnel, they may require special support and clarification regarding the nature of the session and their own role in the conference. For example, one Hispanic father who had been asked to attend a progress report conference about his son confided that he had punished his child prior to coming to the meeting because he assumed that it was called in response to the boy's "bad classroom behavior."

Educators must also be sensitive to language-related issues when conferencing with minority parents. In some instances, interpreters are required; however, most frequently language differences will take a more subtle form. For example, the conferencer should be aware that (a) some groups, such as Native Americans, may be parsimonious and concrete in their use of language; (b) some minority parents may fail to use standard English; (c) even bilingual educators may be unable to converse with some parents because of dialectal differences; and (d) idioms and phraseology specific to a group or region may be encountered. When language differences, albeit subtle, come up, both educators and parents must feel comfortable in asking for clarification. Failure to do so will almost certainly impede the communication process.

As a general rule, conferencers must take care not to act overly sympathetic, indulgent, or patronizing of minority parents. In a like manner, professionals should avoid attempting to convince minority parents that they "truly know" the plight of a particular group (unless, of course, this is true because they are a member of that minority, were raised in that culture, etc.) or that they are "different" from other professionals with whom the parents may have had contact. Although one hopes that such understanding and trust will develop during the course of the conferencing process, such sentiments should not be expressed in an initial overt message to parents.

Educational conferencers should also recognize the potential impact of their gender on interactions with some minority parents. Female educators, for example, should be aware that some Hispanics, for example, may be reluctant to take advice from women. Similarly, members of certain minority groups may avoid eye contact solely on the basis of gender.

Strategies Appropriate to Particular Minorities

Ideal parent-professional interactions are based on a free and accurate exchange of information and an atmosphere of trust, mutual respect, and cooperation. However, actual interactions between parents and professionals do not always meet these goals, and in particular, conferences between professionals and minority parents have tended to stumble because of misinterpretations and suspicions. Some communication problems are associated with misunderstood body language, verbalizations, or other unique expressions associated with an individual's culture. Because these and similar responses can significantly influence communication in a conference situation, professionals must become aware of their personal interaction style and its effect on specific groups of people. In addition, professionals must become familiar with the interaction styles of particular minorities and with the impact of this factor on the conferencing process. One school psychologist, for example, misinterpreted the absence of eye contact in a Native American mother to be a sign of "emotional shock" rather than the cultural manifestation that indeed it was.

Identifying all the characteristics of minority groups that warrant attention as well as the idiosyncratic habits of professionals that may impact on certain groups obviously extends beyond the scope of this work. Moreover, diversity among individuals from the same diverse groups would make such an effort inappropriate. Accordingly, conferencers must analyze their own styles and the general cultural norms of the groups with whom they relate. Awareness and sensitivity to these factors enable professionals to increase their communication effectiveness and to involve parents of minority pupils who might otherwise choose to withhold cooperation and involvement.

Above all else educational conferencers must attempt to understand culturally and linguistically diverse parents in accordance with the culture of which they are a part. They must also recognize that their own demeanor and heritage will impact on any interaction with minority families. Recognition of these significant factors should result in more productive conferences and increased parent and family involvement.

Summary

The plurality and diversity of Americans has always been a feature of this society. At the same time, however, many have assumed that the "melting pot" characteristics of the United States would eliminate the qualities that differentiate minorities from the majority culture. Most farsighted individuals, including educators, have now abandoned this naive position and recognize that the distinct qualities of all groups must be acknowledged and accommodated.

The role of educational conferencer requires the ability to deal effectively with a variety of parents, including those with different languages, cultural practices, and values. Though professionals must employ the same basic tools and procedures with all parents, these must be applied in a fashion compatible with an individual's background. One's willingness and ability to do so will increase the probability of conferencing success.

Exercises

1. Complete the Minority Attitude Self-Assessment Survey (Figure 3.1) in accordance with the directions and suggestions provided in the text.

2. Identify the various minorities in your district or region that you might be required to interact with. For each group, list particular characteristics that you should consider when providing parent and family conferencing services. Attempt to identify personal patterns of behavior that may facilitate or detract from your ability to effectively interact with particular groups.

Chapter 4

Age Considerations in Parent and Family Conferencing

Professionals have long recognized that a family member's age is a salient factor in parent and family conferencing, and the needs of parents and families vary according to the stages of a child's development (Collarusso & Kana, 1993; Edgar & Polloway, 1994; Gallagher, Beckman, & Cross, 1983; Siegel, Waxman, & Gaylord-Ross, 1992). There is of course strong evidence that parents and families play a prominent role in a child's development and, consequently, must constitute a significant component of any educational program, regardless of the child's age (Guralnick & Bennett, 1987; Szymanski, 1994). As observed by Bronfenbrenner (1974),

> evidence indicates that the family is the most effective and economical system for fostering and sustaining the development of the child. The evidence indicates further that the involvement of the child's family as an active participant is critical to the success of any intervention program. (p. 55)

The significance of the concept *any program*, including those designed for very young children, youth, and young adults, has garnered increasing recognition (Hobbs, 1978; Johnson, 1993; Minke & Scott, 1994; Peterson, 1987; Shearer & Shearer, 1972).

The growing attention to involving parents of non-elementary-age children results in large measure from legislative advances that have taken place on behalf of children and youth with disabilities. PL 99-457 (Part H), which mandated comprehensive services for infants and toddlers and their families; PL 101-476, the Individuals with Disabilities Education Act, which required schools to provide transition services to students with disabilities; and PL 101-336, the Americans with Disabilities Act, rank among the federal education policy steps that have most influenced expansion of services to individuals with disabilities. Due to efforts to comply with these regulations, the availability of parent programs and family involvement opportunities has increased significantly.

Parents' and professionals' changing expectations regarding the need for parent and family involvement have also brought about expanded services. Perhaps because the importance of parent involvement has been so widely discussed and documented (Goodman, Cecil, & Barker, 1984; Gordon, 1970; McAfee & Vergason, 1979; Miller & Hudson, 1994; O'Dell, 1974; Simpson & Carter, 1993) and because parents and professionals are becoming more accustomed to working together, the former are demanding and the latter are acknowledging that parents of children and youth with exceptionalities should become a part of their offspring's program.

The population of parents and families to whom involvement, conferencing, and counseling services are being made available has broadened and amplified the realization that a child or youth's age, to some extent, determines parental and family needs and, subsequently, the services to be rendered. A frequent need of parents of preschool children, for example, relates to information on normal child growth and development and appropriate future expectations for their offspring, as well as home- and community-based resources, programs, and training methods. Parents and families of young handicapped children may also require emotional support and information on how to interact with their child beyond that of parents of an older child.

Parents of elementary-age children in turn most often request information relating to their child's academic and social progress, strategies for developing a cooperative partnership with educational personnel, mechanisms for influencing the policies of schools and agencies, and methods for augmenting school programs through home-based efforts.

Parents and legal custodians of adolescents, particularly those with exceptionalities, most frequently request information on how to help their son or daughter make plans for the future, how to contend with issues such as sex, drugs, alcohol, and rebellious teenage behavior, and how to identify postschool options available to youth and young adults with exceptionalities.

Finally, parents of young adults frequently require information about options for facilitating independence and adjustment to the postschool world. Often these parents are more interested in community- and work-related concerns than traditional academic issues. That students with disabilities are frequently unemployed or underemployed makes this a particularly significant matter for parents and families (Wagner, D'Amico, Marder, Newman, & Blackorby, 1992).

The conferencer must recognize a child's age as a significant factor in determining parent conferencing services and then prepare to individualize accordingly. Although certain basic generic skills underlie any successful parent conference, such skills must be applied in an individualized fashion, in accordance with a child or youth's developmental stage.

Parents and Families of Young Children with Exceptionalities

A variety of reports published within the past few decades has supported the efficacy of early intervention with disabled and disadvantaged children (Barrera, Kitching, Cunningham, Doucet, & Rosenbaum, 1991; Hayden & McGinness, 1977; McDaniels, 1977; Moxley-Haegert & Serbin, 1983). In conjunction with earlier research on cognitive development (Bloom, 1964; Piaget, 1952) and the effects of early environmental experiences on school achievement (Caldwell & Yahraes, 1975), the findings of these reports have served as the basis for early childhood programs designed to stimulate intellectual development. Further, subsequent reports have identified parental support and participation as a basic ingredient in the success of these programs (Bricker & Sheehan, 1981; Dinnebeil & Rules, 1994; Holmes, Simpson, & Brittain, 1979).

Head Start, a federally supported project initially funded in 1965, is one of the first and most comprehensive early childhood models. This experimental program, designed to provide comprehensive educational, health, and social services to low-income families, has from its inception focused on parental involvement as an integral and basic component. Though some have questioned Head Start's overall impact (Westinghouse Learning Corp. & Ohio State University, 1969), its parent participation component is generally considered exemplary. Such family involvement continues to be pervasive, with parents routinely a part of developing and operating all components of the program. In particular, parents work in cooperation with

Head Start staff to select curricula, carry out daily activities, and recruit and hire staff.

Other early childhood programs, including home-based intervention projects (Gordon, 1971; Levenstein, 1970; Minke & Scott, 1994; Sandall, 1991) and preschool programs with home training and parental involvement components (Dawson et al., 1991; Gray & Klaus, 1965; Karnes, Teska, Hodgins, & Badger, 1970; Weikart, 1970), have also revealed the benefits of active parent participation. In fact, because parents present the major source of information, stimulation, and social influence for young children, their involvement is indispensable. As concluded by Honig (1975), parental involvement in early childhood programs is essential "to sustain the often considerable cognitive gains demonstrated during the child's participation in a program" (p. 10).

Efforts to involve and serve parents and families with preschool children must grow from the premise that a variety of individuals and needs must be served (Coletta, 1976; Doll & Bolger, 1991). Nonetheless, in spite of the heterogeneous nature of parents and families and the concomitant demand for individualization, needs tend to cluster in three general areas: emotional support, information exchange opportunities, and strategies for securing and utilizing services for child and family. Though these types of needs exist in every family with preschool-age children, they are most dramatic in families of children with exceptionalities.

Need for Emotional Support

The birth of a child with a disability or the later identification of an exceptionality will almost universally have a significant impact on both the parents and the ecology of the family. Considered a less-than-perfect reflection of the family, a child with a disability is typically associated not only with anxiety and strong emotion, but may also make family members more vulnerable to otherwise normal pressures and frustrations. Decades ago, Farber (1968) reported that "severely handicapped" children frequently cause their families to focus attention on problems within the family to the exclusion of community concerns. Such a reaction may serve a necessary function, since "failure to do so may lead to conflict and disturbance of family relationships" (Farber, 1968, p. 174).

Often professionals can meet the need for emotional support in parents and families with young children with disabilities most effectively by providing them an opportunity to express their perceptions, ideas, feelings, and concerns to an interested and nonjudgmental listener. In addition, one can provide support by helping them comprehend the stages they probably will go through while adjusting to and accepting their exceptional child. Karnes and Lee (1980) suggested that conferencers be "sensitive to stages of parental reaction and . . . attempt to counsel parents through each stage of adjustment" (p. 208), including denial, anger, guilt, shame, blame, overprotection, and adaptation. Although all parents and families with exceptional children routinely experience these stages, the intensity of the response is most dramatic when the child is of preschool age (Brinker, 1992; McDonald, 1962).

As part of the emotional and psychological support needed by parents and families of young children with disabilities, Hayden (1976) stressed the importance of parental acceptance of the child's condition. She noted that parents and families should be allowed to determine on their own that they require such services and then independently seek appropriate options rather than having these thrust upon them. Sullivan (1976) supported this position, adding that parents and families must be allowed to determine their own needs (including emotional support) as opposed to simply accepting those purported by professionals. One father of an infant with cerebral palsy revealed that he and his wife became extremely irritated at one professional who persisted in attempting to identify their "stages" of acceptance and in having them "share their true feelings." This parent confided that he and his wife would have enjoyed the opportunity to discuss their feelings with a supportive professional, but they were unwilling to confide in an individual who was so aggressively trying to aid them.

Although the need for emotional support in parents and families of young children with disabilities will vary, most parents and family members will experience it to some degree. Accordingly, professionals must be willing and able to develop appropriate strategies and alternatives for serving parents and families in this significant area.

Need for Information Exchange Opportunities

Probably the most common and generic need experienced by parents and families of young children with exceptionalities is for information and effective communication opportunities. Indeed, Gautt (1990) provides a model for early intervention service delivery decisions, components of which share an information exchange element. Of particular significance to many parents of young children with disabilities are opportunities to discuss the nature and etiology of their child's exceptionality. Barsch (1968) reported that a high percentage of parents of young children with disabilities first become concerned about their child's condition within 6 months following birth. Of particular concern to parents are delays in motor and speech development. All too frequently parents report insufficient opportunities to discuss their concerns with professionals and, in instances where a diagnosis has been made, to share and receive information about the demonstrated exceptionality (McDonald, 1962; Simpson, 1988).

Most parents of young children who have suspicions about their child's normality make their first professional contact with a physician. In contrast, for parents with older offspring, the most frequent contacts on their child's behalf tend to occur with school and other nonmedical professionals. Whether rightly or wrongly, physicians more than any other professional group have been criticized for their demeanor and communication style toward parents with young children who have special needs (Akerley, 1978; Farber, 1968; McDonald, 1962). Barsch (1968) reported that most parents of children with disabilities considered the time allotted by their physician to discuss the diagnosis as inadequate; over one third of the parents in his study "felt that the physician was abrupt, blunt and completely objective, showing little concern for the individuality of their problem" (p. 85). Other professionals, including educators, also have been criticized for their interaction styles (Ehly, Conoley, & Rosenthal, 1985; Paul & Simeonsson, 1993).

Children who are definitely diagnosed prior to entering school tend to have conditions that are more severe or overt than those diagnosed in the elementary grades. Barsch (1968), for example, reported that 80% of Down syndrome, 66% of cerebral palsied, 61% of blind, and 40% of deaf children are diagnosed within 12 months of birth. Accordingly, the nature of a child's condition, age at onset, and subsequent problems will at least partly determine the type and specificity of the information to disseminate to parents and families. Likewise, one can assume that parents whose children have not yet received a definitive diagnosis will also require appropriate attention, including an opportunity to exchange information. Thus, parents and families of children with unspecified developmental lags, including students at risk for school failure, may suffer through a relatively lengthy period of anxiety and uncertainty unless given adequate chances to communicate. Although information exchange opportunities may not eliminate their concerns, the process typically will help them deal more effectively with their youngster who has an exceptionality.

Parents and families of young children with exceptionalities are often interested in discussing future expectations for their child's independent functioning, available treatment and educational opportunities, and their child's performance in an intervention program. In a study conducted with parents of preschoolers with severe disabilities assigned to a transdisciplinary setting, Siladi (1980) found that parents were most interested in discussing their child's progress in the program, the teaching and intervention strategies being employed, and the educational objectives associated with future public school placement. Results also revealed that parents most preferred to meet with their child's teacher, program coordinator, physical therapist, and speech therapist, in that order.

As emphasized, parents of young children require adequate opportunities for communicating with professionals, and such opportunities most likely will form the basis of other successful parent-related program efforts.

Service and Advocacy Needs

Hayden (1979) observed that children with exceptionalities who are between the ages of birth and 3 years require not only medical intervention but also educational attention. She specifically stressed that

> while nonhandicapped young children may make acceptable progress without early educational intervention, handicapped or at risk children do not. To deny them the attention that might increase their chances for improved functioning is not only wasteful, it is ethically indefensible. (p. 510)

Other investigators (Doll & Bolger, 1991; Gautt, 1990; McDaniels, 1977; Simmons-Martin, 1976; Snyder-McLean & McLean, 1987) have also advocated appropriate educational intervention opportunities for young children with exceptionalities, noting that such services make up an indispensable component of any efficacious program.

A variety of noneducational services have also been identified as necessary for satisfying the needs of children with exceptionalities and their families (Bailey & Simeonsson, 1988; Jago, Jago, & Hart, 1984). Olshansky (1966b) recommended that the following four types of services be made available: medical, baby-sitting, respite care, and parent education. Others (Justice, O'Connor, & Warren, 1971; Kentowitz, Gallagher, & Edgar, 1977; Peterson, 1987; Simpson & Carter, 1993) have stressed the need for community-based programs and collaborative efforts (Doll & Bolger, 1991).

Professionals can expect a small percentage of parents and families of young children with exceptionalities to require counseling and therapy, and hence such services must be available. A significant percentage of parents and families will need training in the use of behavioral and educational methodology applicable in the natural environment. In both areas, parents have proven to be valuable resources and a means of extending professionally monitored intervention programs into a variety of settings. Involvement of parents in this fashion has the added advantage of establishing appropriate child advocacy expectations and training parents in strategies they can use with children at other times in their lives.

Service and advocacy needs of parents and families who have young children with exceptionalities are increasingly being met through collaborative program efforts. More than ever before, this model requires that professionals, parents, and families work together in behalf of children (Peterson, 1987; Sugai & Tindal, 1993). Although such partnerships necessitate that professionals have skills and knowledge beyond those required to implement more traditional direct service programs, the rewards of such efforts are significant. In this regard, Doll and Bolger (1991) noted the following:

> Full partnership requires considerably more effort on the part of the professional than may initially be apparent. To act as true partners, parents must be allowed to participate in the decision making and brainstorming that plan a child's intervention, as well as the implementation of already formed plans. Parental goals and parent-directed activities must be incorporated into a child's plan. To support full parental participation, professionals must be prepared to provide parents with detailed information about the child, his or her progress, and the program; to reinforce learning that occurs at home in the same way that parents reinforce what occurs at school; to offer parents training in unfamiliar information procedures; to include the parent as a participant in teaching; and to adjust their teaching and service in ways that parents advise. (p. 184)

Parents and Families of Elementary-Age Children with Exceptionalities

The needs of parents with elementary-age children are as varied and individualized as those of parents with preschoolers, yet they tend to fall within the same basic areas: emotional support and understanding, information exchange opportunities, and mechanisms for identifying, implementing, and evaluating needed services.

Emotional Support and Understanding

Identification of an elementary-age child as exceptional has a significant impact on the parents as well as the entire family structure. In some instances, identification and diagnosis confirm the family's previously undefined concerns; in other cases, the process comes as an unexpected shock. Although exceptionalities identified subsequent to infancy and preschool tend to be less severe and obvious than those found in preschoolers, one can expect their impact to be no less significant. While attempting to accept a disability condition, parents and families of exceptional children must be allowed to satisfy their own emotional needs. Coletta (1977) applied Maslow's hierarchy of needs to parents of exceptional children with exceptionalities, noting that they must have their own physical, psychologic, emotional, self-esteem, and fulfillment needs met before they can effectively accommodate and serve a child with a disability.

When parents and families become aware of a disability in a family member, they will not only confront a variety of strong emotional reactions, they may also lack the prerequisite experiences or self-confidence to accommodate and serve the child (Berger, 1995; Mullins, 1987). Thus, while few family members are trained for their respective roles as parent or sibling, they typically have the benefit of role models and direction from adult figures in the family. However, it is not unusual for families with a member who has a disability to feel overwhelmed and bewildered because they lack a frame of reference for interaction (Miller & Hudson, 1994; Stahlecker & Cohen, 1985).

Helping parents and families to understand their emotional experiences and concerns is not a simple matter. However, professionals can facilitate the process by providing opportunities to discuss affective issues and by understanding reactions such as shock, denial, fear, guilt, bereavement, anger, and depression. The mother of a recently diagnosed child with a disability reported that even though she had read and heard of the strong reactions parents sometimes experience upon hearing of their child's exceptionality, she was surprised at her own intense feelings of anger and frustration. She did note, however, that having an opportunity to discuss these feelings with her child's teachers was beneficial.

Information Exchange Needs

Parents of elementary-age children frequently observe that one of their most prominent needs relates to meeting and exchanging information with the individuals assigned the task of educating their sons and daughters. This need seems particularly acute at the time when a child is initially identified as exceptional and assigned to a "special" program (Cronin, Slade, Bechtel, & Anderson, 1992; Kroth, 1985; Simpson & Whorton, 1982). Even though parents may have received an interpretation following their child's assessment, they frequently will benefit from discussing this information with the child's teacher after having some time to ruminate over it.

Parents should also receive information about their child's educational program and have a chance to discuss it. Specifically, they should be informed about the procedures and curriculum that will implement a given program, the ancillary and related services to be rendered, and the manner in which their child will be evaluated. In addition, one should advise them of the availability of additional school and community resources that may be required. Finally, subsequent to a child's identification as exceptional, parents should receive progress report information from school personnel at regularly scheduled intervals. Such sessions should consist not only of a review of a child's academic, social, behavioral, and physical progress, but should also offer an opportunity for parents to ask specific questions, discuss problems, and suggest agenda items.

The importance of providing adequate opportunities for exchange of information between parents and educators has been highlighted by a number of professionals (Adelman, 1994; Shea & Bauer, 1985; Yoshida & Gottlieb, 1977), yet, to date, criticism of standard procedures is frequently voiced. Dembinski and Mauser (1978), for example, asked parents of gifted children to react to questions about their interactions with school personnel. The results of their survey indicated that approximately 60% of the parents sampled felt uncomfortable about asking questions of professionals. As a result, these researchers suggested that professionals create an atmosphere that encourages free discussions. Only such conditions will meet parents' information needs.

The focus of parent-professional discussions at the elementary-school-age level shifts from community to public school and from readiness and development to more traditional academic concerns. As noted, the need for information remains among the most generic parental needs; consequently, services designed to satisfy these needs will create a basis for effective program progress (Davis & Davis, 1981; Espinosa & Shearer, 1986; Mannan & Blackwell, 1992).

Needs for Service and Advocacy

Initially, one can expect parents of school-age children with exceptionalities to be most concerned about locating appropriate educational and treatment alternatives for their children. Even though federal legislation and school policy changes have produced an increased number of program options for children with exceptionalities, thus relieving many parental concerns for direct service, legitimate and meaningful involvement of parents in the child's school experiences often remains less than optimal. This issue is nowhere more apparent than at the elementary level. Here parents are frequently interested in augmenting professional services and meeting the school-related needs of their children, whereas school personnel, in some cases, may be less than totally willing to establish a partnership. According to Yoshida and Gottlieb (1977), dissatisfaction over this situation prompts many parents to search for a more equal power distribution within the school structure. Although this situation continues to improve, it remains a significant issue in many schools.

The motivation of many parents and families to be involved in the educational program of their child with a disability is matched by their ability to augment and support school-related programs and carry out independent home projects. For example, parents have demonstrated that they can systematically use educational and behavioral principles in cooperative school-home programs (Adelman, 1994; Baker, Brightman, Heifetz, & Murphy, 1973; Fox & Savelle, 1987; Walker, 1979) and facilitate their child's development under structured conditions (Barnard, Christophersen, & Wolf, 1977). Berkowitz and Graziano (1972) recommended that parents play a key role in the programs provided their children, noting that

> parents have assumed the major moral, ethical, and legal responsibility for their children, they generally have the greatest degree of contact with the children, and greatest control over the natural environment, and they are typically both willing and fully capable of assuming and carrying out detailed therapeutic measures. (p. 299)

In spite of parents' proven effectiveness in supporting school-related intervention programs, traditionally they have received only limited support and structure for doing so (Simpson & Fiedler, 1989). For example, even though parents have been granted significant authority in determining the nature of their child's program and in the subsequent implementation of intervention strategies, they have received limited training on how to exercise these privileges. Goldstein, Strickland, Turnbull, and Curry (1980) proposed training parents to participate in their children's individualized education program (IEP) conferences. Without such training, one can expect only limited parental participation and involvement. Simpson and Whorton (1982) supported this position, stating that while

> parents will want to be involved in facilitating and augmenting the educational and intervention processes employed with their handicapped children, they can be expected to do so only with appropriate training. Thus, opportunity and encouragement must be accompanied by training if parents' needs are to be met. (p. 537)

Finally, in addition to advocacy and involvement training, parents and families must be directed to appropriate counseling, therapy, and social agencies whenever appropriate. As suggested, the infrequency of this need in no way discounts its importance.

Parents and Families of Youth and Young Adults with Exceptionalities

During the past few years, attention to and availability of programs and services for youth and young adults with exceptionalities have increased greatly (Clark & Kolstoe, 1995; Rusch & Phelps, 1987). Primarily as a function of legislative mandates, litigation, and advocacy efforts, secondary-age pupils and young adults with special needs are beginning to receive greater availability of services. Although the increased availability of services for youth with exceptionalities has paralleled, to some extent, increased parent-related programs and involvement efforts, the proliferation of parent-related services has occurred relatively slowly. Siegel (1975) reported that many parents lose interest in being involved in their offspring's program after watching the child fail for an extended period of time and after determining that professionals lack a "cure" for the child's condition. Kronick (1975) supported this notion, observing that as children with exceptionalities grow older, their parents demonstrate less motivation and stamina to serve their needs. As a result, some professionals have concluded that parents of older children lack an interest in being involved in their child's program and, consequently, these professionals fail to put forth the effort necessary to encourage such participation. Indeed, a 1994 study (Zill & Nord, 1994) released by the research organization Child Trends reported that by the time they reach high school, about half of the nation's students stay away from virtually every school function. Thus, while about 75% of elementary-school parents are moderately or highly involved in their children's school lives, the numbers drop off quickly at junior high and again at high school. Nonetheless, in spite of this trend, there are signs that parents and families of youth and young adults with special needs are motivated to work with schools, agencies, and professionals in behalf of their offspring. These parents and families must be afforded the same opportunities for individualized involvement as their counterparts whose children are younger (Alexander, Kroth, Simpson, & Poppelreiter, 1982; Alley & Deshler, 1979; Rusch, Destefano, & Szymanski, 1992). In fact, their needs generally fall within the same domain. Specifically, one can expect them to experience a need for emotional support, information exchange opportunities, and appropriate service options.

Need for Emotional Support

While not as widely recognized as with young children, parents and families of adolescents and young adults with disabilities nonetheless require emotional support and attention to help them cope with the exceptionality of their family member. This need exists regardless of the time lapsed since the initial diagnosis and interpretation and the services subsequently rendered. The mother of a young adult with autism reported that when her son was of elementary-school age, she periodically would break into tears upon seeing him attempt to interact with his siblings and their friends. She noted, however, that since he has now completed school and spends most of his time at home, her concerns are much different: "Will he qualify for a community workshop if space becomes available?" "Will his behavior allow him to be maintained at home?" "What will eventually happen to our son?"

Professionals should be aware of and sensitive to parents' and siblings' needs for support even after their family member has grown up. Such sensitivity and awareness may be manifested by recognizing individual feelings and attitudes relative to living with the person who has an exceptionality, being willing to listen to concerns and perceptions, and being attentive to the issues parents and siblings must deal with. For example, the mother of an 18-year-old with Down syndrome reported that, whereas her neighbors at one time considered her son "cute," many of them now considered him a threat even though he had never shown any aggressive or antisocial inclinations. The parents of an adolescent girl with retardation and physical impairments revealed that they were revisiting emotional issues and stages they thought had been resolved years before. For instance, these parents noted that with their daughter's passage into puberty came the realization that her condition was truly permanent. Specifically, they experienced renewed feelings of anger and frustration over recognizing that she likely could never live completely independently. Other parents and family members of youth and adults with disabilities have reported problems in dealing with such issues as sex, employment, living arrangements, and marriage.

When youth and young adults classified as exceptional on the basis of school-related criteria become able to function independently in normalized settings upon leaving school, their parents generally experience a sense of relief. Conversely, parents whose children have more severe handicaps will encounter even more frustration as they see their offspring growing up. Accordingly, the educational conferencer must stay mindful that family members' emotional support needs cannot be expected to vanish once a child leaves an elementary-level program (Hobbs, 1975a; Simpson & Carter, 1993).

Need for Information Exchange Systems

Even without the side issues of an exceptionality, the nature of the psychological and developmental changes associated with adolescence and young adulthood can be highly unpredictable. The interaction between adolescence and a handicapping condition, though, can result in a period of even greater instability (Bullis, Bull, Johnson, & Johnson, 1994; Nelson & Polsgrove, 1981). Thus, while adolescence is typically a stage when peer groups replace parents as the primary social influence (Muss, 1976; Zill & Nord, 1994), an exceptionality may require the parents and families to continue to serve in a more prominent and supportive role for their adolescent or young adult member. Accordingly, parents and siblings frequently desire information relating to the changes associated with their family member's puberty and young adulthood and to the many issues associated with this period. In addition, many families seek opportunities to share information about their member who has special needs with his or her teacher and other professionals. In a report on the results of interviews conducted with mothers of children with retardation regarding their judgment of various components of a parent program, Warfield (1975) noted that parents judged as most favorable information that focused on "problems of adolescence," interpretation of test results, and planning for a child's future. McDowell (1981) listed some of the particular youth-related problems on which parents desire information: drug and alcohol abuse, juvenile delinquency, suicide, sex, and marriage. Due to the significance of these and related issues, parents and families of youth and young adults with exceptionalities, contrary to popular opinion, are often motivated to interact with professionals for the purpose of exchanging information.

In addition, based on research findings, conferencers can expect parents and family members of adolescents and young adults with exceptionalities to show interest in discussing the results of various types of assessment measures descriptive of their family member's abilities. Thus, rather than being satiated or totally familiar with their adolescent son's or daughter's strengths and weaknesses, these parents sometimes have a strong interest in more of this type of information. Perhaps because they are considering nonacademic alternatives for their children (e.g., workshops, competitive employment) or because they are more realistic about a disability, many families consider diagnostic data a topic of interest during this period of a child's life.

One of the most prominent information exchange needs involving parents/families and teachers/other professionals relates to the exceptional person's future. This discussion may focus on determining whether the person's needs can be best served in a competitive work environment, on the status and adequacy of the school district's transition services, on whether he or she is eligible or appropriate for particular types of services, and/or on the impact of an exceptionality on the youth's postschool adjustment. Because adolescents and young adults with disabilities are frequently underemployed and unemployed makes this a priority topic for discussion (Bull & Johnson, 1991; Clark & Kolstoe, 1995; Edgar & Polloway, 1994). The importance of encouraging discussions of this nature is emphasized in Clements and Alexander's report (1975), for example, which showed that "many parents believe that their children's disabilities will disappear contingent upon a number of years in special education" (p. 3).

Finally, many parents and families of children with special needs, particularly those with severe disabilities, will wish to discuss the options available to their family member upon their own deaths. Although some parents and family members may be reluctant to initiate discussions that focus on their child's future, such reticence cannot be interpreted as a lack of interest in the topic.

Service Option Needs

The historical paucity of services for adolescents and young adults with exceptionalities (Alley & Deshler, 1979; Benz & Halpern, 1987; Fredericks, Bullis, Nishioka-Evans, & Lehman, 1993; Kroth, 1981) and the notable absence of parent involvement programs at the secondary level have resulted in significant frustration and efforts on the part of parents to acquire appropriate programs for their offspring. Thus, parents who have become accustomed to a wide range of educational services often discover after their offspring's completion of public school that suitable programs and services are either unavailable or severely scarce (Clark & Kolstoe, 1995). Faced with this dilemma, one can expect many parents of youth and young adults with disabilities to focus on identifying, developing, and advocating for acceptable direct-service options for their sons and daughters.

In addition to providing direct services, educators and other professionals must be able to identify or arrange for other types of services. Alexander et al. (1982) suggested that professionals must aid parents in securing appropriate psychological, social, vocational, and academic services for youth and families. In particular, they must be prepared to serve as crisis intervention resource, community liaison, and educational referral agency. Further, these investigators emphasized that professionals must be familiar with resources outside public school settings if they are to effectively serve the needs of youth with exceptionalities and their families. Professionals must "be capable of coordinating existing community, federal and state services to meet the needs of a student and his family. These services may include welfare, medical, dental, child protection, psychological, social, psychiatric, vocational and alternatives to traditional family living" (Alexander et al., 1982, p. 8).

Parents of adolescents and young adults with exceptionalities may require the assistance of the parent conferencer in structuring their home environment and in developing behavior management strategies for their son or daughter. Some of the parent-applied procedures and consequences appropriate for managing the behavior of adolescents and young adults differ from those applicable with younger children. For example, the mother of a 200-pound teenage boy with mental retardation remarked that a time-out procedure ceased to be effective the day her son told her that he would no longer go to the time-out area.

One of the basic assumptions behind the provision of services and involvement opportunities to parents and families of youth and young adults with exceptionalities has been familial indifference. Thus, a number of educators and other professionals have judged these parents and families to be generally phlegmatic regarding their family member who has a disability and lacking in motivation to become involved in his or her education or treatment. However, Alexander et al. (1982) identified several factors related to this legacy of parental uninvolvement that were independent of motivation or interest in a youth. In particular, the following were cited as possible explanations for this pattern: (a) the history of conflict that has characterized parent-educator relationships; (b) the complexity of secondary and postschool programs and the large number of educators, support personnel, and other professionals parents must relate to in these programs; (c) the complex and changing nature of families, including the high incidence of single-parent and blended families; (d) the lack of continuity in parent education programs and the paucity of resources commensurate with parent and family needs; and, finally, (e) "parent burnout."

In spite of a purported history of uninvolvement, the importance of program participation on the part of parents and families of youth with exceptionalities was exemplified by Benz and Halpern (1987), who noted that "teachers wanted more and better parent involvement in all levels of the school program" (p. 507). In addition, professionals must recognize that parent and family uninvolvement has been associated with issues that, at least to some extent, can be abated. Accordingly, professionals must consider their role to consist in part of finding ways to facilitate cooperation behavior between parents and educators, rather than assuming an attitude of uninvolvement and lack of interest among parents of older individuals with exceptionalities.

Clear evidence shows that parents of youth with exceptionalities and the educators who instruct these students consider their relationship weak, and that the parent-professional partnership that should from the cornerstone of cooperative program efforts all too frequently does not exist. There also seems to be awareness that increased opportunities for communication between parents and school personnel could strengthen this tenuous relationship. Thus, educators must identify a variety of formal and informal ways for parents to interact with school personnel, as well as identify and eliminate barriers to parent and family involvement.

An increase in parent-professional communication opportunities must also be accompanied by changes in the nature of parent-professional interactions. In particular, professionals must strive to foster parity-based collaborative relationships that allow parents to become more broadly involved in their children's school activities instead of simply receiving information provided by professionals. Obviously such changes will not occur easily, but the advantages of pursuing such relationships appear well worth the effort.

Summary

Educators and other professionals increasingly are acknowledging that parents and families exert the most significant impact on the lives of children and youth. Accordingly, concerted efforts have been made to serve the needs of *all* parents and families of children with exceptionalities, including those of preschool age, elementary and secondary level, and young adulthood. With the increased emphasis on serving the needs of this broader spectrum of parents and families has come the realization that a child's age correlates closely with the needs of families and the types of services to be rendered. Although all of these parents and families will experience such general needs as emotional support, information, and service options, their particular needs and requirements for service delivery will vary with the age of their family member. Hence, the conferencer must be able to offer services that are consistent with various age considerations.

Exercises

1. Compare the needs of the families with whom you are most involved with those whose children are older or younger. Note areas of similarity and difference.

2. Conduct a survey of the parents/family members of students in your class or program to identify their needs for emotional support, information, service, and advocacy. Next, identify resources within your school, agency, or community for most effectively serving these needs. Finally, compare your information with that of other individuals who are involved with students of different ages.

Chapter 5

Involvement with Nontraditional Parents and Families of Children with Exceptionalities

Each family functions as a microcosm of society and as such is governed by differing rules, values, and norms, all of which are designed to perpetuate the structural integrity of the familial unit. The rules and norms for each family are products of the personalities, family histories, experiences, values, and expectations of its members. The incorporation of children into a family system, either through birth or adoption, impacts on both the child and other family members. Accordingly, infants must contend with a wholly new environment while their new parents must make time, priority, and financial adjustments. However, in spite of the significant impact a child will have on a family system—whether or not he or she is exceptional—it is the child who is expected to adapt to the rules and expectations of the family and to eventually carry on its traditions.

Traditionally, families with children have followed a set series of developmental stages, beginning with marriage, continuing with the birth of one or more children, and ending with the departure from home of the youngest offspring. However, today educational personnel are witnessing more and more deviations from this traditional progression. Indeed, a family composed of a working father, a housewife mother, and two school-age children constitutes only about 6% of current U.S. households (Hodgkinson, 1991, 1992). Thus, educators regularly interact with families of divorced parents, blended or reconstituted families, unmarried single parents, grandparents who raise their own children's offspring, and other atypical parent configurations (e.g., same-gender parents, foster parents). Regardless of one's personal perspective regarding these changes, professionals obviously must be able to communicate and interact effectively with a variety of family groups. Moreover, it is beneficial to be able to comprehend the circumstances involved in family transitions or unique situations (e.g., divorce, family reconstitution), to possess knowledge of procedures and strategies for facilitating the growth of involved family members during stressful times, and to recognize that these often difficult or stressful circumstances will likely be further complicated when a child (or children) in an involved family has an exceptionality (Gallagher, Beckman, & Cross, 1983; Johnson, 1993).

Separation and Divorce

According to 1984 census data, approximately 13% of U.S. families were headed by a single parent in 1960; the statistic rose to 22% in 1984, and then, in the 1990s, to approximately 25% (Dawson, 1991). The majority of single-parent homes result from divorce, separation, or out-of-wedlock births. According to the U.S. Department of Commerce, approximately 1.77 million divorces were granted in 1980, up more than 65% from 1970; 1984 U.S. Bureau of the Census statistics revealed that the number of single-parent families grew from 3.3 million in 1970 to 6.8 million in 1983, a 206% increase. By the 1990s the trend had leveled off, though about half of first marriages end in divorce and over 50% of divorces involve children (U.S. Bureau of the Census, 1993).

Impact on Children

Although the overall impact of separation and divorce on children remains a poorly researched area clouded by speculation and personal belief, there is good accord that the event can have a significant influence (Cashion, 1982; Coletta, 1983; Johnson, 1993; Johnson & Lobitz, 1974; Kliewer & Sandler, 1993; Thiessen, 1993). In a classic study of early latency age children, Kelly and Wallerstein (1976) reported that patterns of "pervasive sadness," denial, and fear were common. These researchers also discovered that the children's relationship to their parents changed after the separation or divorce. Those assigned to live with their mothers reported feelings of paternal abandonment and rejection, and most children considered the visitation schedule of two weekends per month insufficient for maintaining contact with their fathers. (Athough fathers may be the primary custodial parent, the vast majority of dependent children continue to primarily live with their mothers.) Kelly and Wallerstein also found that some children had feelings of anger toward their mothers, allegedly for causing the separation or driving their fathers from home. Other children report fears of antagonizing their mothers, believing that unless they appeased her they, too, would be driven from the home. Many children described conflicts in maintaining loyalty to both parents following separation and divorce. Although school progress patterns were inconsistent following the separation and divorce, few children evinced better academic progress after the exit of one of the parents.

In a similar study of children in older latency, Wallerstein and Kelly (1976) disclosed that more mature boys and girls also suffered from the divorce experience. In particular, they reported that the older children felt anger, just as did those of a younger age, but that the emotion was better organized and more object directed, usually toward one or both of the parents. In addition, a number of children experienced diminished perceptions of identity, somatic complaints, weakened school performance, and impaired peer relationships. Finally, the study revealed it is not uncommon for older children to significantly change their relationship with the custodial parent; several instances produced reports of parent-child interdependence and support. The results of the studies conducted by Kelly and Wallerstein (1976) and Wallerstein and Kelly (1976) have been supported by more recent work (Black & Pedro-Carroll, 1993; Kelly, 1993; Wallerstein, 1985; Wallerstein & Blakeslee, 1990).

The impact of separation and divorce, though significant for all children and youth, appears to exert different degrees of influence for different groups (Wolchik, West, Westover, & Sandler, 1993). Wallerstein and Kelly (1975) have suggested that preschool children are least equipped to accept and contend with divorce. Other research (Rutter, 1971; Tuchman & Regan, 1966) has found that divorce may have a more deleterious influence on boys than girls. In particular, males are more apt to demonstrate aggressive, impulsive, and antisocial behavior following a divorce than are their female counterparts.

The influence of separation and divorce on children's academic progress is also a topic clouded by equivocal results and positions. Though research has demonstrated that children from homes where fathers are absent do not function as well in school as those where fathers are present (Chapman, 1965), the contributing factors responsible for this finding are not clearly understood. Coleman (1966), for example, suggested that these differences relate more to racial and economic factors than to the absence of a paternal figure. In support of this position, Herzog and Sudia (1973) noted that "the critical element [in poorer school performance] is not father's absence itself, but rather a complex of interacting family, economic and community factors" (p. 156). In the final analysis it does not appear that parents' separation and divorce will typically serve as an academic facilitator for children; however, the complexity of the factors involved and the precise relationship of parental divorce to school achievement make this an unresolved empirical question (Hanson & Lynch, 1992).

All in all, indications are strong that separation and divorce can have a deleterious influence on children (Biller, 1970; Edelman, 1987; Johnson, 1993; Shinn, 1978; Vadasy, 1986). Yet, before definitive conclusions can be drawn, the complexity of the variables involved requires a thorough analysis of factors such as the age of the child at the time of separation, the relationship of the child and parents prior to the family disruption, the relationship of the parents at the time of the separation and divorce, and the interpersonal atmosphere of the family. As noted by Hetherington and Martin (1972),

> specific characteristics of the child such as sex, age at testing, race, socioeconomic status, and birth order influence the impact of separation and growing up in a single parent home. No studies have adequately controlled or assess the influence of all these variables. (p. 270)

Finally, conferencers should note that studies have suggested warm and effective single-parent homes are more advantageous to children than conflict-torn nuclear families (McCord, McCord, & Thurber, 1962). Although a cliché, it seems apparent that the quality of parent contact in a home is far more significant to children than the number of parents a child lives with.

Impact on Parents

The impact of separation and divorce is no less severe for parents than children. In particular, mothers, the most prominent custodial parent, seem to experience a number of problems directly associated with divorce and the resulting responsibility of raising a family without the support of a mate. Just as educators must recognize the potential impact of the family change on a child, so must they be aware of the changes that will result for parents. Without doubt this knowledge will prove indispensable in the parent and family conferencing process.

The vast majority of one-parent homes are headed by women, even though numbers of custodial male parents have increased (Brandwein, Brown, & Fox, 1974; Edelman, 1987; U.S. Bureau of the Census, 1993). Mothers who head families seem to encounter problems in three primary areas: financial, family management, and personal. For many women, resolving these issues is complicated because they not only have had to deal with problems related to divorce, but for the first time in their lives they also may be accepting sole responsibility for family matters. The degree to which they are successful in contending with these problems will not only determine whether they grow personally but also the degree to which they can develop and maintain a supportive family environment for their children.

Financial problems

A major issue facing many single parents, particularly those headed by mothers, is economic survival (DiLeonardi, 1993; Edelman, 1987; Lambie & Daniels-Mohring, 1993; Vadasy, 1986). According to Bane (1976), the 1974 mean family income of mother-headed families was less than half that of families headed by fathers; this same researcher reported that over half of the children in female-headed homes were members of families existing below the poverty level. Further, a significant percentage of fathers failed to make their agreed-upon child support payments after the first year (Brandwein et al., 1974). Current data (Corbett, 1993; U.S. Bureau of the Census, 1993) confirm that these trends continue. In some instances women must find permanent employment following their divorce or separation without the benefits of marketable skills, training, or experience (McLanahan, 1983). Even women who have worked while married may discover that, rather than working to supplement the family income, they become the sole means of support for their families. Though both men and women may have a lower standard of living after their divorce, it is the mother-headed family that seems most vulnerable to financial problems (Dore, 1993; Ruma, 1976; U.S. Bureau of the Census, 1988, 1993). Accordingly, women who head homes must concern themselves not only with the impact of personal economic change at a time when they are most vulnerable but also with the influence of this change on their children. That children may hold their mothers personally responsible for their lower standard of living can further heighten the problem.

Without question professionals must be aware of the economic issues facing divorced, separated, and other single parents and sensitive to the fact that these individuals often will have concerns that they consider far more significant than their child's performance in school (Belle, 1990). Such awareness and sensitivity will form a basic step in establishing effective communication.

One 37-year-old woman candidly revealed that a problem she had not considered when seeking a divorce from her husband of 14 years was financial. Although she had volunteered at a hospital and worked for a time as a clerk in a fabric store, she found that she was unprepared for what she considered "good jobs." Further, she discovered that even when she was able to gain full-time employment, her income fell far below what she and her children had access to when she was married. This mother was particularly distressed because, in spite of her efforts, her children held her personally responsible for their change in lifestyle.

Family management problems

Custodial parents routinely experience family management problems not shared by two-parent families (Fish, 1991; Zionts & Simpson, 1988). These concerns are attributable, at least in part, to the increased responsibility assigned the custodial parent and to the change in lifestyle that can accompany a divorce or separation. Women, for example, may find that in addition to child care, domestic responsibilities, and a full-time job, they have inherited tasks previously performed by their husbands. Single fathers may find themselves responsible for the first time for meal preparation and child care. All in all, separation and divorce are usually associated with at least short-term family disruption and disorganization (Hetherington, Cox, & Cox, 1977; Weintraub & Wolf, 1983; Werrbach, 1992).

One obvious and common concern of single parents relates to assuming total responsibility for child rearing. Mothers in particular report feeling "trapped" and unable to free themselves from the responsibilities of 24-hour-a-day child management. That there is not another parent to spell the mother must be the basic part of the issue. In a similar fashion single parents frequently voice concern that they must serve as the sole role model for their children.

Single parents may also experience problems in discipline and child management beyond those encountered in two-parent homes. Particularly vulnerable are boys in mother-headed families; they tend to be more aggressive, impulsive, and prone to delinquency than boys in two-parent families (Bath, Richey, & Haapala, 1992; Kauffman, 1977; Santrock, 1975). The factors associated with this situation are not clearly understood and may in fact not even stem primarily from a father's absence from home. Herzog and Sudia (1973), for example, noted that the issues may relate more to "stress and conflict within the home [and the] inability of the mother to exercise adequate supervision" (p. 154). Hetherington et al. (1977) suggested that this pattern has to do with changes in parent-child interactions following a divorce. In particular these investigators noted that custodial mothers tended to become more restrictive, less affectionate, and less consistent in their discipline, while noncustodial fathers tended to be overly permissive and indulgent. These patterns, which could obviously explain many of the problems identified in the literature, often tend to reverse themselves with time. In particular, mothers who head families typically become more effective as single parents after 1 or 2 years, and noncustodial fathers tend to become less indulgent and permissive.

Single parents, particularly women, must also convince their children (and sometimes themselves!) that they are in control of family-related matters. In many instances they must become successful at somewhat routine tasks that they may never have contended with before. Thus, they must be able to deal with repairmen, utility companies, a variety of agencies, and their overly aggressive children. As one seemingly bright spot in this area, Tooley (1976) observed that "while divorce is gruelingly stressful for these mothers and children, it also represents a developmental opportunity for the women involved: They could never, would never, be that helpless and overwhelmed again" (p. 40).

One mother who headed her family reported that although prior to her divorce she had been the primary disciplinarian in the family, she could rely on the support of her husband in carrying out programs. Accordingly, she noted that she could tell her three preadolescent sons that if need be their father would aid in carrying out prescribed consequences. She revealed, however, that after her divorce her sons tended to be extremely belligerent and to frequently ignore her commands. She also reported that her sons complained she was always "picking on them." She did confess that her anger toward her ex-husband and her frustration with her "plight" may have contributed to the deteriorated relationship she had with her sons.

Personal problems

The personal problems of divorced parents, particularly women, have been widely discussed in the literature (Axinn & Hirsch, 1993; Elkind, 1982; McLanahan, 1983; Newland, 1979; Wallerstein & Blakeslee, 1990). Mothers who head their homes have been described as vulnerable to economic hardships, isolation, discrimination, and anxiety over establishing new relationships. In sum, these circumstances can serve to heighten the problems associated with divorce and family change.

Employment discrimination is one commonly voiced concern of divorced women (Hausman & Hammen, 1993; Lewis, 1977). Although enactments such as the Equal Credit Opportunity Act (designed to ease credit discrimination), Title VII of the 1964 Civil Rights Act (which prohibits discrimination on the basis of race, color, religion, sex, or national origin), and the Equal Pay Act of 1963 (which requires equal pay for equal work regardless of sex) have reduced the overtness of discrimination, it allegedly continues to exist (Edelman, 1987; Weitz, 1977). As noted by Frieze, Parsons, Johnson, Ruble, and Zellman (1978), "when equal pay for equal work became the law, many employers renamed jobs and gave men slightly more to do in order to justify paying them more" (p. 286).

Single parents have further revealed that, in addition to their increased responsibilities, divorce may be associated with feelings of isolation, loss of status in their neighborhood and community, and rejection by friends, neighbors, and relatives. Although the prevalence of divorce and single-parent families has aided in instilling new attitudes, many divorced parents comment that self-esteem remains a problem. Divorced parents also report that forming new relationships, with both men and women, can be a difficult and anxiety-provoking experience (Frieze et al., 1978; Halpern, 1990; Weintraub & Wolf, 1983).

One recently divorced mother of two children indicated that she not only had far more responsibility and was working longer hours than when she was married, she also had experienced an erosion of support in her friends and neighbors. Particularly from her married friends and neighbors she felt a "coolness" following her separation and divorce. This young mother noted that, along with her other new responsibilities, she didn't have time to go out and make friends. However, she revealed that she did need someone to talk with.

Blended Families

Just as with single-parent families, the blended or reconstituted family is a symbol of the times. In fact, the blended family is nearly as common as the traditional family and is gaining in acceptance daily (Hanson & Lynch, 1992). The high divorce rate data cited previously correlate closely with the figures on blended families. That is, the majority of divorced men and women remarry, most within a few years. Hacker (1983) reported that approximately 75% of divorced women under 30 with one child remarry. This statistic is only slightly lower for divorced women under 30 with two children (74.9%) or three children (71.5%). Hacker also reported that among divorced persons of both sexes with and without children, about 73% remarry. More current statistics also support this trend (U.S. National Center for Health Statistics of the United States, 1995).

Along with the rewards of reorganizing a family will come a series of issues, all of which will impact on a child's performance in school and thus the role of the parent conferencer. Accordingly, the conferencer should be cognizant of and sensitive to such matters as previous emotional ties and children's loyalties to their noncustodial parents and other relatives, the distribution of authority within the family structure, and role development and enforcement. Each of these areas play into the effective reconstitution of a family.

Frequently, individuals assuming the role of stepparent will enter a family system with lofty, albeit somewhat unrealistic, expectations. Some may envision themselves as perfect parents who will be able to instantly love and gain the love of their stepchildren and immediately unite a new family into a closely bonded unit. Many will expect their stepchildren to automatically love and respect them, and few will consider the resentment and anger that their children may feel over the new marriage and the family reconstitution process. These negative feelings frequently heighten when both parents contribute children to a new family (Mintz & Kellogg, 1988; Visher & Visher, 1979).

Probably the most significant adjustment during reconstitution will be made by a new parent who has never had children. This adjustment will be even more prominent when the person inheriting the family is a woman, who may be expected to assume a child-care and domestic role.

The parent conferencer should be able to serve as a knowledgeable and available resource to recombined families. In particular, these professionals should familiarize themselves with the major issues that these families must face, including the clarification of lines of authority, financial concerns, loyalty to natural parents and siblings, and the need for effective communication.

Clarifying Lines of Authority

It is not at all unusual for the natural parent in a blended family to be perceived as "the parent" and the stepparent as somehow different. Children in reconstituted families may resist complying with the wishes of stepparents, natural parents may not want their spouse disciplining their children, and stepparents may feel uncomfortable assuming a parental role. These and other factors obviously will skew the communication process and subsequently the effective reconstitution process. Professionals may be asked to become involved in formulating disciplinary techniques and developing strategies for clarifying authority and communication lines. The conferencer must recognize this issue as not only common in reconstituted families but also as an area where resolution must occur if the family is to function effectively (Lambie & Daniels-Mohring, 1993; Melville, 1977; Whiteside, 1981).

Financial Issues

Just as with single-parent families, recombined families must contend with a change in the amount and distribution of money. The reconstitution of a family may sometimes include conflicts over whether or not to support a particular project and resentment because of expenditures for individuals who were not members of an original family. Thus, for example, one might anticipate more than typical animosity when the orthodontic work needed by a new child in a family takes precedence over a family vacation. Though educational conferencers are not expected to do financial counseling any more than marriage therapy, they should be aware of and sensitive to this issue (Hodgkinson, 1992; Visher & Visher, 1991).

Loyalty Issues

By its very nature the blending process involves incorporating individuals from different parentages and connections into a single familial unit.

Accordingly, one can anticipate that many children will experience conflict in remaining loyal to a natural parent while living with and relating to a stepparent or while interacting with a stepbrother or sister in the same manner as a natural sibling (Einstein, 1982; Visher & Visher, 1988).

The conferencer must be able to aid stepparents in recognizing that they can neither expect nor demand that their stepchildren respond to them as a natural parent or relinquish feelings of allegiance for their natural parents. Further, they must not expect that children brought together into a family through marriage will have the same feelings of loyalty and allegiance as those connected by blood. Finally, members of reconstituted families should be shown that there are advantages to their familial relationships. For example, stepparents should recognize that, unlike natural parents, they are not required to love their child unconditionally, and thus have the advantage of allowing a more natural relationship, based on individual characteristics, to develop.

Needs for Effective Communication

The reconstitution process will create at least short-term disorder and turmoil (Duberman, 1975; Lambie & Daniels-Mohring, 1993). Family members must adjust to the incorporation of new personalities into the unit, and with them a new set of values and expectations. Further, the reconstitution process will most likely be associated with role changes for all family members.

Although the processes associated with establishing a new family order can be anxiety provoking and formidable, they can also be exciting and rewarding if honesty and open communication prevail (Cherlin, 1992). Open communication (Berger, 1995; Fine, 1979; James & Jongeward, 1971) is not only a sine qua non for effective reconstitution, it is also an area in which most families can benefit from objective input. Hence, conferencers must not only recognize the importance of this issue but also acknowledge their role in helping reconstituted families to establish effective avenues of communication.

Other Nontraditional Families

Identification of the myriad types of families that currently compose the American landscape clearly extends beyond the scope of this work.

However, without argument, educational conferencers increasingly find themselves involved with ever-increasing numbers of nontraditional families. For example, as stated previously, in 1990 approximately 1 in 5 White babies and 3 of 4 Black babies were born into female-headed households, and current statistics reveal that millions of children are being reared by young, unmarried women, many of whom expose their children to poverty and other significant risk factors (Children's Defense Fund, 1991; Dore, 1993; U.S. Bureau of the Census, 1993). Our society also has seen significant increases in the number of relatives, especially grandparents, who raise children (Hanson & Lynch, 1992; Sonnek, 1986; U.S. Bureau of the Census, 1993). Single- and two-parent adoptive families are also increasingly familiar to educators (Groze & Rosenthal, 1991). Although any form of adoption comes with significant challenges, professionals find that adults who adopt children and youth with exceptionalities frequently encounter unique and significant issues (Glidden, 1991; Rosenthal & Grove, 1991). Finally, though not common, same-gender parents are being seen more and more by educators.

Teachers and other professionals who work with nontraditional families do not typically have available specific planning and interaction guidelines. For example, educators may not easily find suggestions for conferencing with grandparents who are raising the children of their offspring, and such resources probably will not be forthcoming. Yet, educators must sometimes plan strategies to aid such families, and the planning requires recognition of the family's unique circumstances and challenges as well as a willingness to individualize methods of addressing particular issues and needs. Because resources are often limited, professionals who work with nontraditional families should seek suggestions from their colleagues who have the appropriate experience and rely on basic effective human interaction and communication tools such as active listening. That is, rather than resorting to an "elderly grandparents conferencing style," for instance, realize that the vast majority of individuals respond to the same basic effective communication methods (i.e., the conferencing style that works for mother will most likely work with grandmother). Finally, professionals should remind themselves that their personal attitudes toward atypical families must not interfere with their commitment to support, communicate, and collaborate with them. This is particularly important because many nontraditional parents and families involved with children and youth who have disabilities will experience the need for close contact and support from school personnel.

The Role of the Educational Conferencer in Working with Nontraditional Families

Regardless of the attitude and personal position an educational conferencer assumes relative to the increased prevalence of nontraditional families, these trends do represent reality. Hence, professionals have no choice but to contend, either effectively or ineffectively, with these situations. Though educators may not be trained to provide family or marital counseling, they must nonetheless be sensitive to the issues facing single-parent and other atypical families and cognizant of their special needs. Further, professionals must recognize that the changes associated with divorce, family reconstruction, adoption, and so forth will exert significant impact on both children and adults; accordingly, the conferencer must also recognize that only with sensitivity and appropriate strategies can the special needs of these families be met. Following are considerations for educators relative to serving the special needs of nontraditional families.

Be able to suggest resources and services for single-parent, reconstituted, and other nontraditional families. Although educational conferencers must not automatically assume that single-parent, reconstituted, and other nontraditional families universally require community and professional services, they must recognize that these families will in many cases present in their most vulnerable state. Accordingly, the conferencer should keep available a list of appropriate resources to serve the various needs of such families. Included should be family counseling, mental health, and social agency contact persons; support groups for adults and children encountering particular types of change; agencies that can aid parents in such areas as establishing credit, securing child support and alimony, and understanding their various rights under the law; community recreation facilities and programs; day care programs; and various other problem-solving agencies. Even though educators may not directly provide the services needed to satisfy the multiple needs of these families, they can effectively assume the essential role of referral agent.

Be aware that the priority concerns of single-parent, recombined, and other nontraditional families may differ from those of the educator. Even though parents will be concerned about their children's progress in school, one must recognize that single unmarried, recently divorced, and separated parents—as well as those involved in reconstituting or restructuring a family—will have other concerns that they may allow to take priority. This does not imply that these parents should not be apprised or allowed to be involved in their child's educational program, but rather that the educator should be aware of the other issues that may be impinging upon these families. A recently divorced mother experiencing difficulty earning enough to feed and shelter her children may be understandably callous to learn that her daughter is having difficulty in math. Hence, the educator must be able to involve parents in their child's educational program while allowing them to put school-related concerns in proper perspective.

Be aware that some nontraditional parents may have severe time, energy, and financial restrictions. As noted previously, single-parent families are routinely beset by monetary problems and time restrictions. One recently divorced mother reported that her day started at 5:15 a.m. and ended at about 9:30 p.m. She confessed that even though she was deeply concerned about her child's school progress, she had neither the time nor energy for close involvement. Awareness of this common issue for single-parent homes should sensitize educators to the need for flexible conference schedules, alternatives to face-to-face contacts (e.g., notes, phone calls, etc.), and properly spaced contacts.

Attempt to include noncustodial parents in conferences and programs. Even though a child may be legally assigned to live with one parent or may be part of a reconstituted family, both parents and conferencers must recognize the ramifications when the child has another parent with whom he or she maintains regular contact. Accordingly, efforts must be extended to apprise both parents of their child's school-related progress and to include them, as much as appropriate, in the intervention programs. Such measures allow disrupted families not only to receive significant information but to extend therapeutic programs to a greater number of settings within the natural environment.

Recognize the importance of listening to parents. Notwithstanding the importance of entering each session with a structured agenda, the conferencer must also recognize the value of allowing all parents and family members an opportunity to be heard. The value of effective listening has been well documented (Idol, Paolucci-Whitcomb, & Nevin, 1986; Rogers, 1961; Zionts & Simpson, 1988) and must be considered a highly effective strategy for meeting a basic human needs. Although all parents must be afforded an appropriate listening environment, this need appears particularly acute in parents of families undergoing change. Hence, the educator must allow the parent an opportunity to deviate from a set agenda and to present concerns related to other matters. Individuals who chronically insist upon discussing matters only peripherally related to the purpose of the conference should be apprised of the necessity of staying on task or referred to a professional who can provide the appropriate counseling.

Though the educational conferencer may consider this expenditure of time a waste, he or she must recognize at the same time that listening is not only a basis for any human interaction but also a vehicle for establishing the rapport and trust necessary for any collaborative program to operate. Further, the conferencer should be mindful that some parents in nontraditional families have no one with whom they can discuss their problems. Consequently, the professional must initially establish an appropriate listening atmosphere for parents and then offer alternatives for allowing further interactions to occur (e.g., groups, friends, or others who can serve in a listening role).

Become familiar with your family-related values. Value familiarity in parent conferencing is important because individuals tend to act on their values (Kroth & Simpson, 1977; Schulz, 1987). Hence, the attitudes and perceptions that educators have toward marriage, divorce, family blending, and family composition will undoubtedly affect the manner in which they relate to individuals in nontraditional families. Simply becoming aware of one's values in this area can significantly improve the conferencing process.

Be able to apprise parents and family members of the potential impact of divorce, reconstitution, and other nontraditional factors on the family structure. It is not at all unusual for the educational conferencer to be a major referral and support resource for single-parent, reconstituted, and other nontraditional families. In fulfilling this role he or she must be able to apprise parents of the potential impact of the change process. In some instances this will take the form of providing reassurance that turmoil and confusion are expected by-products of divorce and family reconstitution, and that eventually more satisfying experiences will replace these problems. In other situations the conferencer may be able to direct families in procedures for facilitating the growth and stabilization of the family unit. Finally, the conferencer may find it appropriate to relate to parents that cooperation between home and school can serve to stabilize at least one significant environment for children in the face of an otherwise changing world. Regardless of the role played, the conferencer must acquire at least a basic understanding of the potential impact of divorce, family reconstitution, and other nontraditional factors on families and be able to relate this information appropriately to parents.

Aid divorced parents, stepparents, adoptive parents, and others to be effective in their respective roles. Above all, the conferencer must not provoke additional problems for nontraditional families. Accordingly, one must take care not to accuse parents of contributing to their child's problems by undergoing divorce or family reconstitution, set rigid schedules for conferences that may be difficult for single parents to meet, or insist on the use of a traditional family model in the face of familial change.

Helping parents and other family members to adequately fulfill their respective roles involves using effective listening techniques (including attention to feelings), exercising care in voicing opinions about an individual's lifestyle and behavior (e.g., "I just don't think divorced women with children should date"), avoiding taking sides in marital and family conflicts, making available appropriate intervention strategies and resources for solving particular problems, and allowing for parent/family individualization.

With support and appropriate resources, most parents and other members involved in nontraditional families can learn to effectively serve the needs of their children. It is mandatory that the educator be available to serve as a facilitator in this process.

Anticipate atypical behavior in parents and children experiencing turmoil and change. As suggested previously, parents and children involved in a divorce, family reconstitution, adoption, and so forth may experience a significant amount of pressure and family turmoil. Because frequently these influences can produce changes in behavior, the conferencer should be sensitive to deviations in the academic and social behaviors of children involved in a change process and be willing to take necessary actions to reduce their long-term injurious effects. In the same manner the conferencer must recognize that many changes in parental behavior, including even irrational actions, may be a function of the difficult situation the person is in. Hence, professionals must be cautious in drawing hasty conclusions under these circumstances.

Summary

Nontraditional families have become an increasingly common component of today's changing world and as such will impact significantly on those educators assigned the role of interacting with parents and families. Although the issues involved in divorce, reconstitution, and other traditional family circumstances are significant, the conferencer can serve as a valuable stabilizing force for families. With the cooperation of parents, the educational conferencer, and other significant individuals, the needs of nontraditional families can be addressed effectively.

Exercises

1. Identify services available through your school, agency, or community that can be used to aid parents and families contending with divorce or family reconstitution and to support other types of nontraditional families.

2. Interview parents and other members of a nontraditional family regarding their needs. Further, request that they indicate those measures that educators could employ to assist them in their effort to adjust.

Part II

Basic Skills and Strategies Needed for Successful Conferencing and Collaboration

Chapter 6

Listening to Parents and Family Members

According to Sontag and Schacht (1994), "family-centered intervention programs have become the 'best practical' model for service delivery to children with special needs and their families in the 90's" (p. 422). In accordance with this trend, educators and other professionals agree that educational and related service programs that are responsive to the needs of families and the formation of effective collaborative relationships develop most effectively in an atmosphere of mutual respect and a willingness to listen (Bailey, Buysee, Edmondson, & Smith, 1992). Indeed, listening is the sine qua non of a healthy interpersonal relationship as well as the key to effective communication. As noted by Langton and Stout (1954), "the teacher should be willing to listen as well as to talk" (p. 86). It is obvious, however, that many professional people, including educators, are far more adept at talking than listening. Kroth (1980), for example, observed that "one of the problems teachers often have is that they are quite verbal people; they abhor silence. As a result, if there is quiet during the conference the teacher is apt to step in and talk" (p. 64).

Though listening may be a skill frequently taken for granted, its importance to the successful conference is such that one cannot overestimate it (Voltz, 1994). In addition, contrary to popular belief, listening is not a natural aptitude for most people. Benjamin (1969) noted that true listening requires diligence and practice, and that the process rarely occurs spontaneously. Others (Heron & Harris, 1993; Ivey & Authier, 1978; Kroth, 1985; Larsen & Poplin, 1980) have also reported that listening is a difficult skill that requires discipline and concentration to master.

Importance of Good Listening Skills

John Dewey (1938) observed that one of man's strongest urges is to be important. Listening, and the attention that accompanies the process, offers a primary means of facilitating a feeling of acceptance and value in another person. Others have also described the impact of the attention that comes from good listening. Publilius Syrus, the poet of ancient Rome, remarked, for example, that "we are interested in others when they are interested in us," and Dale Carnegie (1936) observed that a demonstration of interest in another person is the most effective means of establishing rapport.

Though documented long ago, these observations are by no means out of step with current parent and family conferencing goals and practices (Berger, 1995; Fine, 1990; Galen, 1991). Without question the ability to communicate interest and attention will largely depend on the professional's ability to follow the parent's topics and to communicate an accurate understanding of what he or she is saying and feeling. In the words of Carl Rogers, "I believe the quality of my encounter is more important in the long run than is my scholarly knowledge, my professional training, my counseling orientation, the techniques I use in the interview" (1962, p. 416). Accordingly, educators should remember that one of their most important assets is the ability to effectively attend and listen to parents.

Developing Listening Skills

Although not an easy task, the capacity to listen can be learned (Brammer, 1985; Paul & Simeonsson, 1993; Voltz, 1994). Though perhaps an oversimplification, at its core this skill just allows another person the opportunity to talk, with assurance that what he or she is communicating is important enough to capture the full attention.

Ivey, Normington, Miller, Morrill, and Hease (1968) successfully employed a video training procedure to instruct students in basic counseling skills, including listening. This training program, which was later clarified and expanded (Ivey & Authier, 1978), focused on developing such skills as "attending behaviors" and reflecting and summarizing the feelings of others. Ivey and his colleagues reported that they were able to develop basic counseling skills, and thus to more effectively serve the needs of individuals with whom the counselors dealt, using this strategy.

According to Kroth (1985) there are two varieties of listeners: passive and active. The passive listener allows another individual the opportunity to talk without playing an overly intense role and without making numerous responses. Passive listeners are frequently sought out by others because they offer speakers the opportunity to hear themselves. This type of listener, although perhaps not appropriate in all situations, offers parents and family members of children with exceptionalities what they may need most—the chance to talk about their attitudes and feelings relative to the child with an interested, yet quietly accepting professional person. Carnegie (1936) provides the following historic example of passive listening: Abraham Lincoln sought out a friend during the Civil War to discuss the issue of slavery. As the story was related, President Lincoln spent a great deal of time verbalizing the pro's and con's of abolishing slavery. After going on for hours about the situation without asking the friend's opinion, Lincoln thanked his listener for "talking" with him. Carnegie noted that "Lincoln hadn't wanted advice. He had wanted merely a friendly, sympathetic listener to whom he could unburden himself. That's what we all want when we are in trouble" (p. 113).

Parents and family members of children with exceptionalities frequently desire *and require* nothing more than the opportunity to be listened to. Though educators must be able to disseminate information and respond to questions when answers or guidance is truly being requested, they must also allow parents and families the opportunity to derive the benefits of a good listening atmosphere. As observed by Johnson (1956), an attentive listener is the most effective physician.

Active listeners, as opposed to the passive variety, will assume a far more vigorous and enthusiastic role in the parent conference (Kroth, 1985). This intensity will take the form of increased levels of responding, body animation, and question asking. Active listening also implies a well-established degree of rapport between respondent and listener. Zionts and Simpson (1988) noted that effective communication is associated with acceptance and interpersonal security. Fine (1979) revealed similar beliefs, noting that in instances of effective communication, "you seem to understand what your friend is attempting to communicate, and your friend seems to understand you" (p. 103).

Gordon (1970) identified active listening as a basic means of communicating with another person. He observed that the process takes the form of attempting to relate to

what it is the sender is feeling or what his message means. Then he puts his understanding into his own words (code) and feeds it back for the

sender's verification. The receiver does not send a message of his own
—such as an evaluation, opinion, advice, logic, analysis, or question.
(p. 53)

Davis (1977) offered several suggestions for facilitating the listening
process, including (a) giving another individual an opportunity to talk,
(b) establishing an environment in which the person feels comfortable
speaking, (c) demonstrating interest in the person and his or her subject,
(d) removing distracting stimuli, (e) being empathic, (f) allowing sufficient time in each session for the respondent to complete his or her
agenda, (g) avoiding becoming angry, argumentative, or critical, and
(h) demonstrating interest by asking appropriate questions.

As noted previously, effective communication between parents/family
members and professionals will not occur without an adequate listening
environment. Listening is a learned behavior, one that must be con-
sciously developed and practiced. Consequently, the listening process
must include a willingness to listen to parents and their points of view.
The professional who attempts to respond to parents prior to listening to
them, or the educator who too hastily assumes the position of "telling"
parents what to do or "answering" their questions when they simply desire
the opportunity to talk, will rarely offer the most satisfactory conferencing
relationship. Parents have repeatedly observed that educators routinely
fail to meet their listening needs (Kupper, 1993), noting the following listening traits of some professionals:

1. Some professionals listen with one ear, waiting for the parent to fin-
   ish speaking so that they can make their point or explain the way it
   "really is."

2. Some professionals merely tolerate the parents' talking without really
   listening.

3. Some professionals reduce and analyze the content of the parents'
   messages without really listening to what they are saying.

4. Some professionals seem preoccupied while parents and family members are talking; they obviously have something else on their minds.

5. Some professionals seem to go through the mechanics of listening,
   but their responses make it apparent that they do not understand.

6. Some professionals respond critically to things related by parents and
   family members or attempt to provide suggestions when all that is
   wanted (or needed) is an opportunity to talk.

Developing the Listening Environment

In order for effective communication to occur, one must create an appropriate listening atmosphere. This atmosphere will include both external factors and components internal to the parent and professional. Kroth and Simpson (1977) identified several external factors that should be evaluated, including assurances of privacy and suggestions for arranging the physical environment. These authors suggested that "it is possible that negative environmental variables may neutralize other efforts that may be employed by the interviewer to communicate interest and sensitivity" (p. 77).

In addition to providing an acceptable external setting, the parent/family conferencer must also strive to create an acceptable interpersonal setting. This should include establishing a psychological atmosphere that will impart a sense of well-being and security for parents of children with exceptionalities. In particular, one should attempt to achieve a professional, yet relaxed, atmosphere. Although few would argue with the latter's importance, the mechanism for achieving it may not be readily apparent. However, there are a variety of steps counselors may take to produce the most desirable conferencing conditions:

Acknowledge parents' and family members' role as collaborators and active participants. Acknowledgment of parents' and family members' potential collaborative contributions, personal investment in their offspring, and need for involvement in the communication process will go a long way toward facilitating an appropriate listening environment. That is, professionals must recognize and believe that listening to parents facilitates collaborative relationships and the realization of mutual goals because parents know a good deal about their children that professionals have no way of knowing, and because parents care about their children and have every right to be involved in program development. Such a mind set is important because it serves to remind us that parents and families have significant contributions to make if professionals allow them to be heard.

Strive to achieve relationship parity with parents and family members. There is no question that professionals typically enter counseling relationships with more experience and training than the parents involved. Nonetheless, parents bring information and resources to these relationships that can significantly facilitate children's growth and development. Maximally capitalizing on such contributions requires that professionals view parents and family members as equals in the interaction and decision-making process. Relative to listening, this translates into perceiving parents as individuals who should be listened to because their input is valuable rather than because they are legally permitted to be involved, because listening to them is the appropriate or humanistic thing to do, and so forth.

Strive to understand the parents' frame of reference. A suitable listening environment includes a true effort on the part of professionals to understand and appreciate a family's frame of reference. This not only helps professionals remove themselves from situations and issues, but it also assists them in generating understanding and in clarifying parents' genuine concern for their children, which are basic components of an effective listening environment.

Be prepared. No single measure will facilitate the desired psychological climate of the conference as much as solid preparation. Both parents and professionals tend to report feeling qualified, confident, and relaxed when they are well prepared for a conference. Accordingly, a thorough review of a child's folder and an assessment of progress and problems experienced, together with an outline of agenda items to be pursued, will typically aid in creating the conditions necessary for a meaningful interaction to occur.

Arrange a private, professional setting for the conference. Attention to the physical setting may not always enhance the overall success of the parent-professional conference, but failure to attend to this important feature may significantly interfere. Consequently, it is important to arrange for a professional setting where privacy and confidentiality can be assured. A classroom may or may not serve this purpose.

Arrange for appropriate furniture. In order to create an atmosphere conducive to discussing parent-educator matters, all parties should be provided comfortable, adult-sized seating. Not only will such physical considerations facilitate an adult-to-adult conversation, but failure to attend to this factor may significantly impair the parent's and/or professional's capacity to pay attention.

Identify anxiety-reduction measures. Conferences scheduled back-to-back, which prohibit professionals from taking a short break, frequently serve to increase the anxiety of a conference. Though some administrators may consider breaks between sessions a luxury, their overall importance should serve to make them a mandate. Some individuals have taken the few minutes prior to a parent conference to jog in place, breathe deeply, engage in passive mental imagery (visualizing a relaxing scene), and practice deep-muscle relaxation exercises. Although the means for best achieving a relaxed state will vary from person to person, the parent conferencer must remember that these efforts will aid in creating an appropriate conferencing climate. Professionals should also keep in mind that productive interactions with parents will depend at least in part on one's capacity to put them at ease. Consequently, it is essential in preparation for the conference that professionals attempt to reduce parents' anxiety. This process will consist to some extent of reducing uncertainty for the parents. That is, parents should be informed of the time of the conference, the amount of time allotted, the location of the school and meeting room, the purpose of the session, and the information that they should be prepared to receive or share.

Maintain a natural demeanor in the conference. During the conference, the educational counselor should attempt to act as natural as possible. Rather than adopting a contrived manner simply to simulate an ideal "counselor style," the professional is far wiser to assume as natural a posture as possible. Such a strategy will serve to put all parties at ease.

Recognize that eye contact is a basic component of good listening. In an attempt to identify the characteristics of a male "10," one popular magazine suggested that the perfect man "listens with his eyes." In addition, others (Ehly, Conoley, & Rosenthal, 1985; Harrison, 1974; Schulz, 1987) have identified eye contact as a necessary and basic means of creating and maintaining an appropriate listening atmosphere. Hence, educational counselors should concentrate on communicating that they are listening via the attention of their eyes.

Be sensitive to the emotions of parents. Beyond attending to the manifest content of parents' verbalizations, the conferencer should also be aware of the tone, gestures, expressions, and other affective responses made. As observed by Ekman (1964), individuals should listen not only with their ears but also their eyes, minds, and hearts. Accordingly, the professional must be sensitive to feelings as well as to content.

Empathy: A Basis for Listening

Effective communication appears to be most feasible in situations where professionals can listen empathically. *Empathy,* from a Greek term that literally means "suffering in," describes an attitude of understanding that goes beyond the surface. To empathize is to attempt to experience and understand another person's world and situation in a fashion similar to what he or she is experiencing. Although obviously one can never totally achieve true empathy, the climate created by attempting to understand another person's view can establish an attitude of acceptance that will facilitate the conferencing process.

Empathy facilitates the listening process by increasing one's acceptance of the parents' or families' situation and position. The empathic listener is able, within obvious limits, to relate to another individual's frame
of reference as if it were his or her own. By relating to and understanding
the internal world of the parent or family member, the professional can
better create an accepting and supportive listening environment.
Although empathic relationships are achievable, the parent conferencer
must appreciate that they occur only with significant effort; ordinarily,
attempts to truly understand the position and perception of parents are
less common than attempts to analyze situations or arrive at solutions to
problems. Although these strategies are not necessarily incorrect, they are
frequently incompatible with true understanding and effective listening.
According to Benjamin (1969),

> The empathic interviewer so cares for the self of the interviewee and so
> wants him to learn to care that he is willing to abandon temporarily his
> own life space and try to think and act and feel as if the life space of the
> other were his very own. (p. 48)

Once this atmosphere has been achieved, the parent conferencer should
have in place the basic ingredient for an effective relationship and thus be
able to more effectively meet parents' and families' needs.

Empathy also involves understanding and relating to the emotions
being experienced by the parent or family member. Carkhuff and Berenson
(1967) suggested that the empathic counselor must be able "to allow himself to experience or merge in the experience of the client, reflect upon this
experience while suspending his own judgements, tolerating his own anxiety, and communicating this understanding to the client" (p. 27). Accordingly, empathy goes beyond the mere cognitive level to connect to the
emotions and feelings of the parent or other family member.

Specific Listening Techniques

The effective listener, in addition to demonstrating the skills of attention,
acceptance, and empathy, must also possess specific listening strategies for
facilitating the communication process. This armamentarium includes
door-opening statements, clarifying responses, restatements, reflecting,
silence, and summarization.

Door-Opening Statements

Door-opening statements (and questions) are designed to demonstrate an interest in the parent or family member and thus indicate a willingness to listen. These efforts at stimulating the interaction process are not aggressive attempts to interrogate or analyze a situation, nor are they necessarily intended to obtain information or to establish a routine of questions and answers. Rather, these remarks should set an appropriate interaction tone. Implicit in the use of door-opening statements is the message that the professional does not intend to do all of the questioning and have the parent do all the answering. In addition, these remarks are designed to discourage an interaction set whereby the professional is the expert who will be able to solve all the family's problems. Rather, door-opening statements function to stimulate parents and family members to talk about a particular issue or situation.

Questions or comments such as "Can you tell me about how you see the matter?" "How do you feel about having a child with a disability?" "Can we talk about that?" "Tell me about that," and "That's interesting" illustrate door-opening statements. In addition, there are door-opening responses one can make to specific parent-initiated comments, such as in the examples provided below:

PARENT: Nothing seems to go right at home anymore.

EDUCATIONAL CONFERENCER: Oh, tell me more.

PARENT: Parent-teacher conferences always upset me.

EDUCATIONAL CONFERENCER: Sounds frustrating.

Clarifying Statements

Clarifying statements serve to focus information that requires additional elaboration or that the listener could not understand. In situations where, for whatever reason, the conferencer is unable to follow or understand the parent, it is best to ask directly for clarification. Statements such as "I'm not sure exactly what you mean" or "Could you state that again?" present requests for clarification. This same strategy can also apply in situations where professionals desire feedback regarding whether or not they have been understood correctly. "What is your understanding of all of this?" illustrates of this type of clarifying statement.

Perhaps most commonly, clarifying responses can serve to prompt parent and family members to elaborate on a point. In addition to providing clarification, these responses indicate that the conferencer is attentive and interested. Examples of this type of clarifying statement would include "You mentioned feeling guilty about not giving as much attention to your nonhandicapped kids. What do you mean?" and "Can you describe more fully how you felt when you learned your child was mentally retarded?"

Restating Content

Listening can also be conveyed by restating (paraphrasing) that which was presented, and the intent of the technique is threefold. First, this process serves to demonstrate to the parent or family member that the conferencer is, in fact, listening and is requesting further information and elaboration. Second, the process allows parents and family members an opportunity to hear themselves through the conferencer. As parents may be more able to absorb and understand their own thoughts and motivations when echoed through another person, this process can prove highly beneficial.

Finally, the restatement process can help secure agreement between what is said and what is perceived. That is, content restatement allows others to hear what we believe we are hearing and thus affords them the opportunity to clarify our understanding. Consensus and understanding in the conferencing and counseling process comprise a basic component without which little progress and rapport can take place. The restatement of content process frequently transpires through statements such as "You seem to be saying that you don't understand the nature of your son's special education program" or "If I understand correctly, you would like to see more emphasis put on vocational training for Jennifer."

Reflecting Affect

Along with attention to the manifest content of a parent's message the professional should show sensitivity to the feelings and emotions being expressed. To be in a position to accurately reflect, the listener must be able to empathically follow the parents. Empathy, as noted by a number of authorities (Carkhuff & Berenson, 1967; Cobb & Reeve, 1991; Ivey, Ivey, & Simek-Downing, 1987; Rogers, 1951), is so integral a component of accurately responding to affect that one can legitimately undertake the process only after this basic listening condition has been achieved. The reflection process, just as with restating content, is undertaken for three reasons. First, these responses communicate to the parent or family member that the professional is listening to more than the expressed content of the message; that is, the person's feelings are also being followed and understood. This act serves to legitimize his or her feelings and to communicate that it is acceptable to have such emotions. This simple acknowledging of feelings' acceptability can serve to greatly enhance the communication and rapport-building process. Failure to acknowledge or adequately respond to the feelings of parents is frequently interpreted as an indication that emotions are not an acceptable component of the conference and that the conferencer is either uninterested or unable to respond to affect. Either situation can impair the conferencing process. Although educators may consider themselves most qualified to deal with agenda items unrelated to affect, the nature of the needs of many parents and families with exceptional members dictates that the professional has no alternative but to respond appropriately to emotion.

The reflection process also allows parents and family members an opportunity to hear their own feelings expressed through a concerned and involved professional. As emotions may or may not be evident to a parent or family member, this mirroring process can play an insightful role. In this way, for example, parents could respond to observations that they appear to have been "extremely hurt" by the insensitivity of the professional who provided the initial diagnosis or by their child's lack of acceptance by neighborhood peers.

Finally, reflection of feelings serves to confirm the accuracy of the conferencer's perceptions. Although parents may not always acknowledge their feelings (even when correctly identified by the conferencer), this process nonetheless does communicate the sensitivity and attentiveness of the professional and gives parents an opportunity to clarify the professional's perception. The mother of a child with a learning disability, for instance, was told by his teacher during a conference that she seemed very angry and frustrated. Subsequent to this response the mother revealed she was unaware of her pervasive anger, although she noted, "I knew something was going on with me." These feelings associated with her son's disability had probably been impeding previous parent-educator progress and communication.

As suggested, the reflecting process takes the form of accurately understanding and expressing for the parent or family member those feelings that are present. According to Benjamin (1969), "reflection consists of bringing to the surface and expressing in words those feelings and attitudes that lie behind the interviewee's words" (p. 117). Thus, the educational conferencer plays the role of a mirror, reflecting both those feelings expressed by the parent and those observed by the professional but not directly stated.

Ivey et al. (1968) identified three major components of the reflecting process, the first of which is one's sensitivity to the emotions of another person. To fulfill the second component, the conferencer must be able to appropriately time the reflecting comments. Ivey and his colleagues suggested that professionals not attempt to respond to every comment, but rather wait for those fortuitous occasions when the response will be most meaningful and when it will facilitate rather than interfere with the interaction process. The third component of the reflecting process, according to these investigators, is to restate for the other person the emotion that he or she originally expressed.

Though conceptually valid, the reflection process has been criticized in recent years, primarily because of inappropriate and rigid use. In instances where counselors attempt to rely on this procedure in the absence of other established listening and conferencing techniques, and when the reflecting response takes on a hackneyed and routine format, its efficiency will be greatly diminished. Many individuals have encountered at least one aspiring therapeutic agent whose entire counseling repertoire consisted of an overused phrase like "It appears that you feel . . ." or "I hear you saying you feel . . . ." In instances of following this strategy rigidly, one can expect minimal success. This is particularly true in educational settings, where parents and family members are typically not seeking therapy for themselves.

It should be apparent at this point that reflecting affect or any other single listening strategy or tool will prove inadequate and inappropriate if relied upon exclusively. Relative to interactions with educators who serve children with exceptionalities, parents and families have multiple needs; hence, it is logical that they will be inadequately served by overreliance on any single method. Nonetheless, it is important for conferencers to remember that they must have strategies for responding to affect. When emotional content is the most salient feature of a session, the educational conferencer must respond appropriately. To fail to do so will undoubtedly undermine other aspects of the parent-teacher interaction and the future goals of the relationship. Thus, the conferencer must concentrate on developing an authentic and spontaneous style compatible with his or her personality but also appropriately responsive to the emotions of the parent. Examples of reflecting affect follow below:

PARENT: It's just heartbreaking to see Tommy flounder in school and not be able to do anything to help.

EDUCATIONAL CONFERENCER: It's really frustrating.

PARENT: We could have just shot the psychologist who told us our son was retarded. He was so cold.

EDUCATIONAL CONFERENCER: You feel like he wasn't very sensitive to your feelings.

Silence

Periods of silence may also serve to facilitate listening and interactive processes. Though some individuals may view the absence of conversation as "wasted opportunities" or times of discomfort, counseling authorities and researchers have identified silence as a valuable listening and attending tool (Benjamin, 1969; Matarazzo & Wiens, 1977).

The value of silence is in part a function of the listening opportunities associated with this response. That is, during absences of conversation professionals can concentrate on listening and attending rather than talking. Silence may also communicate a willingness to listen. Thus, silence may cue parents and family members that the professional is interested in listening to and understanding them rather than expecting them always to concentrate on what he or she has to say. Silence may also draw out taciturn parents and family members. That is, the psychological vacuum created by silence may sometimes serve to stimulate conversation, thus giving parents and family members opportunities to be heard and understood. Finally, silence allows professionals opportunities to attend to nonverbal signs. Thus, periods of quiet allow one time to attend to body language and other nonverbal cues as opposed to concentrating on what is said.

It should be obvious that parents and family members expect professionals to talk and interact. It is equally obvious, however, that professionals' prudent use of silence can facilitate an effective listening environment.

Summarizing

A final listening technique is to summarize for parents or family members, at periodic intervals, the information and affect that have been generated or observed. Summarizing statements can thus occur at points in the conference other than at the close and can be designed to respond to both manifest content and affect. Again, the intent of these comments is to communicate to parents that the professional is interested and sensitive to what they are saying and that he or she is attempting to understand them.

Summarization statements can also serve to clarify perceptions of parents and family members and to sensitize and integrate affect. Examples of these types of statements include "Can we say, then, that you felt most uncomfortable about special education placement because you didn't understand the diagnostic testing and because you felt powerless to help your son?" and "To summarize, it appears that you have identified three major concerns."

Summary

The ability to accurately listen and to communicate this interest to parents and family members is one of the most basic attributes of the successful conferencer and a primary basis for obtaining and disseminating information. Successful parent and family conferencers have clearly established that the ability to create an appropriate listening environment is so germane to the parent-educator communication network that other conferencing components will depend on the mastery of this single skill.

Exercises

1. Identify an individual (preferably a friend, relative, or classmate rather than a parent) to relate a topic of interest to you. Practice the following:

   a. Putting yourself and the person with whom you are relating at ease.

   b. Maintaining good eye contact.

   c. Being an empathic listener.

   d. Making use of specific listening behaviors, including door-opening statements, clarifying students, restatements of content, reflecting affect, silence, and summarization statements.

Discuss with the person the reactions that you both had to the various procedures. This can be an in-class or out-of-class exercise.

2. Observe other people, including the students in your class, as they manifest different emotions and feelings. Pay particular attention to the way in which their nonverbal cues (e.g., posture, expressions, etc.) serve to communicate the way they feel.

3. Attend to individuals whom you consider good and poor listeners. Identify the particular characteristics that lead you to categorize them as you do.

hapter 7

Development of Trust in the Family–Professional Relationship

A basic concept of effective parent and family conferencing is that the process is not something applied to parents and family members by the professional but rather involves the joint participation of both groups; it is *collaborative*. The cooperative participation of parents and professionals, however, will depend largely on the latter's capacity to establish conditions conducive to a cooperative and collaborative effort. Paramount among the factors associated with the development of the environment will be the educator's skill in establishing a relationship based on trust. Without trust, the ability of parents and professionals to effectively communicate and collaborate will be significantly impaired. As suggested by Rutherford and Edgar (1979), "when teachers and parents find themselves in adversary roles, distrusting each other, children suffer" (p. 20). Others (Benjamin, 1974; Hammond, Hepworth, & Smith, 1977; Schulz, 1987; Voltz, 1994) have also identified trust as essential to any therapeutic and collaborative relationship.

Although trust in the counseling and collaborative relationship is typically thought of as an atmosphere created for parents and family members, it is equally important for the professional to have trust in parents and family members. As the conferencer is not an unfeeling technician, simply programmed to disseminate and interpret information, but rather an individual who is profoundly affected by the attitudes and responses of parents and families, educators must be able to both create and receive trust. It is simply unrealistic to attempt to establish a collaborative relationship in which parents are expected to trust the professional without a reciprocating response. Unfortunately this futile strategy has sometimes been pursued and may explain somewhat why the parent-professional relationship has not been noted for its high levels of mutual trust.

The Nature of Trust Relative to Collaboration

Trust, as used in the context of the parent-professional collaborative relationship, forms the foundation on which the conditions for achieving objectives grow. In fact, in both professional and business affairs, little can be accomplished without an acceptable level of trust. Even though definitions of this rather nebulous term may fail to describe its precise characteristics, professionals are in agreement as to its significance (Adelman, 1994; Friend & Cook, 1992; Moeller, 1986; Rogers, 1969; Truax & Carkhuff, 1967).

Kroth and Simpson (1977) defined trust as "the belief that another person will act honestly or perform reliably and, therefore, can be depended upon" (p. 34). Others have identified trust as a necessary condition for change and growth to occur. In keeping with this notion, Combs, Avila, and Purky (1971) noted that "an atmosphere which makes exploration possible must be established" (p. 210) if one individual is to help another.

Although the characteristics and distinct features of trusting associations will vary from situation to situation, certain qualities typify these relationships (Hardin & Littlejohn, 1995). One particular aspect of individuals in a trusting relationship is a heightened willingness to take interpersonal risks and to reveal elements of themselves to the other person. Risk taking, in this context, is a willingness to make oneself vulnerable. That is, parents, family members, and educators involved in trusting collaborative relationships display confidence that agreed-upon patterns of behavior will prevail. Although similar in some respects to gambling, trusting is more a faith in or reliance on the recurrence of previously agreed-upon standards. Whereas gambling involves a situation where one ventures a small risk to possibly secure a large gain, interpersonal risk taking is more aligned with confidence in a previously identified outcome. In gambling, an individual does not expect to be consistently reinforced; by contrast, interpersonal risk taking, and the trust upon which it is based, requires confidence that what one anticipates will in fact occur.

It should be apparent that collaboration will be little more than a hollow pretense without assurances from both parents and educators that mutually agreed-upon roles and arrangements will occur. Thus, for example, when parents confide in a teacher, taking the risk that their confidence will be maintained, they expect (and trust) that this assurance will be upheld. Accordingly, the willingness to venture, which is a direct manifestation of a trusting and collaborative relationship, must not be associated with uncertainty. That parents and families of children with exceptionalities are often vulnerable to uncertainties and self-doubt underscores the importance of working to establish trusting relationships.

The trusting relationship, upon which the conditions of collaboration, change, and growth are based, involves three basic components. First, professionals must create, with the aid of parents and family members, an atmosphere in which a shared feeling of safety exists. Second, the professional must provide reassurance and a model for risk taking. Finally, both the professional and the parent must reinforce one another for their risk-taking and collaborative efforts.

Creating the Conditions of Safety

One of the primary ways that educational conferencers can establish the safe, trusting, and secure atmosphere needed for collaboration is through a display of warmth for the parents with whom they work. Rogers (1962) suggested that counselors who are authentically warm and positive in this way are more likely to produce desired outcomes. Rogers termed this attitude "positive regard." This researcher, along with others (Kroth, 1985; Sicley, 1993; Truax & Carkhuff, 1967), has convincingly articulated the need and value of establishing a supportive atmosphere for individuals involved in a conferencing relationship.

An atmosphere of safety will also be facilitated when parents and family conferencers are comfortable with themselves and willing to enter the collaborative relationship without a facade. Truax and Mitchell (1971) suggested that the ability to display nonpossessive therapeutic warmth depends on the "ability to feel a receptivity and warmth for our own self— an openness to both the good and bad that lives within us" (p. 317).

One mother of an adolescent with a severe behavior disorder revealed to the program staff serving her son that she was able to put her trust in them only after "doing some testing." In particular, this involved assessing the extent to which staff members were willing to follow through with her requests and with what they said they would do. Although in previous programs the mother had been promised numerous things, little follow-through was provided. After the program staff had convinced her that they were willing to make good on their promises, this mother was more willing to enter into a trusting relationship.

Providing Reassurance and a Model for Interpersonal Risk Taking

In addition to developing the atmosphere of trust and safety, the educational conferencer must also be willing to provide cues and reassurances for parent and family risk taking and a model for this behavior. Hence, in spite of the degree of safety and rapport developed, parents and family members must have reassurance that the educational conferencer will maintain their trust even under vulnerable conditions. In addition, the professional must not expect parents and family members to display a willingness to venture in their interpersonal relationships until he or she has set the stage for this response. Although professionals need not display vulnerability in order to secure a reciprocal response, they must nonetheless demonstrate a willingness to show their humanness and to suggest that they may not have all the answers. Such conditions form the basic elements of effective collaboration (Christenson & Cleary, 1990; Fine, 1990). For example, the mother of an elementary-age boy with a learning disability confided it was only after a teacher acknowledged she didn't have all the solutions to the boy's problems that the mother felt willing to share information and collaborate. She noted, in particular, that she had been exposed to a series of professionals who gave the impression that her child's behavior could be easily managed if the right techniques were used, implying that she was not using the right approach. Only after being asked to jointly develop a cooperative and collaborative plan was she willing to candidly provide the information needed to develop the intervention strategy.

The willingness to expose oneself in a parent-educator relationship must also be based on a feeling of security and a belief in joint responsibility and solutions. Though professionals may agree that a relationship exists between an educator's attitudes and the development of security with parents, consensus regarding the methodology for identifying the precise nature of these attitudes may be much more difficult to secure.

The Risk-Taking Questionnaire shown in Figure 7.1 serves as one means for educational professionals to gain feedback relative to their

How comfortable are you in . . .	Very Comfortable	Somewhat Comfortable	Neutral	Somewhat Uncomfortable	Very Uncomfortable
1. telling parents that you don't know?	☐	☐	☐	☐	☐
2. telling parents that you made a mistake?	☐	☐	☐	☐	☐
3. suggesting to parents that another professional made an error?	☐	☐	☐	☐	☐
4. suggesting to parents that they should consider therapy for themselves?	☐	☐	☐	☐	☐
5. telling parents that there are behaviors displayed by their children that you dislike?	☐	☐	☐	☐	☐
6. displaying your emotions in a parent-educator conference?	☐	☐	☐	☐	☐
7. confronting parents with their failure to follow through on agreed-upon plans?	☐	☐	☐	☐	☐
8. talking about your own problems in a parent-educator conference?	☐	☐	☐	☐	☐
9. praising parents for things they do well?	☐	☐	☐	☐	☐
10. having parents take notes during conferences?	☐	☐	☐	☐	☐
11. allowing parents to observe in your class while you are teaching?	☐	☐	☐	☐	☐
12. allowing parents to tutor their own child at home?	☐	☐	☐	☐	☐
13. allowing parents to use behavior modification procedures with their own child at home?	☐	☐	☐	☐	☐

(*continues*)

Figure 7.1. Risk-Taking Questionnaire.

	Very Comfortable	Somewhat Comfortable	Neutral	Somewhat Uncomfortable	Very Uncomfortable
14. telling parents their "rights"?	☐	☐	☐	☐	☐
15. having parents assume an active role during IEP conferences?	☐	☐	☐	☐	☐
16. having parents ask you to defend your teaching strategies?	☐	☐	☐	☐	☐
17. having parents bring a friend to IEP conferences?	☐	☐	☐	☐	☐
18. having parents call you at home about a problem their child is having at school?	☐	☐	☐	☐	☐
19. having parents recommend a specific curriculum for use with their child?	☐	☐	☐	☐	☐
20. having parents review school records on their child?	☐	☐	☐	☐	☐
21. having parents collaborate on various problems and issues?	☐	☐	☐	☐	☐
22. maintaining relationship parity with parents?	☐	☐	☐	☐	☐

Figure 7.1. *Continued*
©1996 by PRO-ED, Inc.

capacity to create conditions of safety for parents and family members, and thus to facilitate a collaborative problem-solving relationship. Use of the instrument is simple. Respondents place a check mark in the column that most accurately describes their degree of comfort for each item (i.e., very comfortable, somewhat uncomfortable, etc.). This measure also can be completed again at a later time to assess changes that have occurred. Finally, a co-worker or supervisor who knows the respondent well can also complete the rating. Comparing personal perceptions with those held by colleagues can offer interesting insights.

Providing Reinforcement

An amendment to the adage, "Behold the turtle, he makes progress only when he sticks his neck out," might be that he is willing to stick his neck out only because that behavior was followed by a positive consequence. Accordingly, parents/families and professionals alike must be reinforced by their honesty, sincerity, willingness to share relative information, and collaborative efforts. Though a safe atmosphere in and of itself will provide the means and opportunity to secure positive *internal* feedback for risk taking and collaborative behavior, this willingness can be greatly augmented by appropriate positive *external* feedback. One parent related that a teacher's positive feedback regarding the parent's openness was of tremendous personal value. Although ordinarily positive reinforcement may be considered applicable only with children in classroom settings, one should remember that there are ample demonstrations of the efficacy of operant conditioning on adult behavior, too (Skinner, 1948). With specific regard to counseling and conferencing situations, Siegman and Pope (1972) found a reduction in interviewer feedback directly associated with a reduction in verbal productivity. Again, overwhelming evidence supports the contention that positive verbal feedback will facilitate the rapport-building and general communicative process (Ivey, Ivey, & Simek-Downing, 1987).

Development of a Trusting and Collaborative Relationship

Although one could argue that the foremost requirement for professional status is technical competence, an equally compelling argument would contend that in the area of parent and family conferencing, the professional must be equally skilled in gaining trust and establishing a collaborative relationship. Regardless of conferencers' technical competence, they must first be able to secure the confidence of parents and families, and only where this trust and rapport have been developed can they utilize whatever technical skills they have. Thus, the efficacy of essentially every strategy and technique of the educational professional will be intricately tied to the relationship developed with the parents.

Even though a great deal has been said about the erosion of trust in parent-educator relationships, it is significant to note that good and trusting such relationships do exist. An analysis of factors associated with the development or dissolution of confidence, trust, and a willingness to collaborate reveals several elements that should be given close scrutiny.

Parents and teachers must be willing to give if trust and a collaborative relationship is to develop. In the trusting relationship, both families and professionals are willing and comfortable in contributing to a common cause. One father of a child with a severe disability reported that he enjoyed contributing time and energy to community programs for children and adults with disabilities. When asked about his efforts for all individuals with disabilities, he commented that he made these contributions because doing so was personally gratifying. Likewise, educators who have successfully conducted collaborative parent-oriented programs have commented that they are willing to invest the necessary time and effort in these endeavors because they enjoy the results or recognize the ultimate benefits as worthwhile. In virtually every instance the trusting and collaborative relationship stems from a willingness to give that is not motivated by a hope for reciprocation. These individuals do not need to keep score ("If I do this for you, what will you do for me?"), nor are they motivated by a need to think of themselves as martyrs making a sacrifice. They fulfill their own needs by responding to the needs of others.

Both parents and educators must acknowledge that they have a commitment to children. It is not uncommon to hear parents say that professionals can never truly understand the plight of families because they are with the child for only a few hours daily and because they are paid for their services. Professionals, on the other hand, have been heard to say that parents fail to take responsibility for their children or that the child's problems relate directly to the parents' problems. Unfortunately, such attitudes will almost universally impede the development of a trusting and collaborative relationship. Parents and professionals must acknowledge that they are both actively committed to the child and that only through their mutual concerted efforts will progress take place.

Both parents and educators must assertively serve as advocates for children. Although cooperation and collaboration provide an obvious component of the successful parent-educator relationship, so does the need for strong advocacy. The two roles are not opposing, and, in fact, many indications suggest that respect and trust most likely prevail when both parties can candidly share their perceptions and positions. In the case of children and youth with exceptionalities, advocacy means that children's interests receive priority status. Although this may lead parents and family members to perceive matters differently from professionals, it does not mean that they should distrust or otherwise oppose cooperating and collaborating with educators and other professionals involved. Conversely, parents should not automatically accept all recommendations without considering child and family needs as well as alternative suggestions. Parents, families, and professionals must strive for a relationship wherein all parties can voice their opinions and disagree. Such an open relationship strengthens the family-professional partnership and facilitates the growth and maintenance of a collaborative and trusting relationship. Openness and directness also promote boundary clarity, thus reducing opportunities for confusion and frustration to develop.

Following one conference, a mother revealed to a teacher that she was elated at the teacher's willingness to strongly argue a point. This mother, who had gained the reputation of being somewhat disagreeable, indicated it was a pleasure not to be patronized. She further revealed that she felt the teacher's willingness to stand up for her beliefs indicated her commitment to the child.

A positive outlook is essential to the development of trust and collaboration. Inevitably these relationships will undergo periods of difficulty for both parents/families and educators of children and youth with disabilities. However, when both parties firmly believe that the situation will improve and when they are willing to actively work together to accomplish this goal, the relationship will survive the ups and downs of the child. Without doubt, a willingness to collaborate and trust will grow when every change in a child's behavior or progress is not viewed as an opportunity to determine what the parents (or the teacher) did to create the situation.

Professionals and parents must be willing to both reinforce and confront one another. A goal for both parents and teachers of children with exceptionalities is to acknowledge that they are equally committed to their respective roles. Accordingly, neither parents nor teachers must become so immersed in the "collaborative relationship" that they lose their independent perspective. Only when parents, family members, and educators can independently analyze and respond to particular situations will trust and an effective collaborative relationship develop. Thus, both groups must be able and willing to selectively and appropriately praise the other for things that are done well and to confront or disagree on matters where a difference of opinion exists. According to Hoover-Dempsey, Bassler, and Brissie (1992), such a perspective facilitates feelings of efficacy, which promotes confidence and other protective interpersonal conditions.

Parents and professionals must maintain a sensitivity to the needs of one another. A fundamental component of a trusting and collaborative relationship is the ability to demonstrate sensitivity to the needs of another person.

This skill requires that parents, family, and professionals concentrate on recognizing one another's positions and feelings. For professionals, this will involve attempting to truly understand the parent and family frame of reference rather than analyzing the appropriateness or logic of their needs or positions. Further, this process will involve the ability to listen and respond to the affective elements of the family's world. Thus, while assertively advocating their own position for a child, the parent, family member, or professional must also stay sensitive to the positions of the others.

Parents and professionals must want to trust one another. Rather than waiting to be "shown," parents and teachers must actively want to trust and collaborate. Although trust must be earned, it is counterproductive to adopt an attitude of distrust until reasonable evidence to the contrary has emerged. That is, parents, family members, and professionals must avoid restricting trust only to situations in which another person has been manipulated into responding in an acceptable manner or when trust-related responses have been observed. Rather, a willingness to trust and collaborate must be pervasive and relatively contingency free.

As a further component of this concept, the educator and parent must be willing and able to understand and accept themselves. Only through the demonstration of this attitude can they expect others to trust them.

Be willing to promote parity-based relationships. In this regard, parity refers to professionals' perceptions of parents and families as equal partners in the educational and development process of children and youth with exceptionalities. Thus, in spite of differing perspectives and background, both professionals and parents must assume that both parties have important skills and knowledge related to serving children and that the contributions of both groups are valued.

Professionals and parents should have opportunities for identification of goals and outcomes. Ideally the goals and outcomes identified by parents and professionals should be shared and mutual. Yet, even if this turns out not to be the case, an important element of developing a trusting and collaborative relationship involves opportunities for all parties to promote their individual perceptions of the goals and outcomes to pursue. Such conditions facilitate not only development of mutual goals, but also a willingness to consider novel and innovative perspectives.

Honesty is an essential ingredient of trust and collaboration. Regardless of whatever other positive characteristics professionals may have, they must be honest if they are to earn the trust of parents and families. Although there is a difference between honesty and outspoken candor, there is no excuse for dishonesty in the parent-educator conference. If, for example, educators are not able to promise complete confidentiality, they must make that clear to the parents. McDonald (1962) noted that a "willingness to supply correct information about the nature of a child's handicapping condition will help create a climate of acceptance" (p. 48). Langton and Stout (1954) also suggested the salient nature of honesty in parent-educator conferences, noting the positive effects that are derived when parents know they can "get an honest answer, to know that they will be told truthfully how their youngster is doing in school, to know that whatever the teacher says can be depended upon to be honestly spoken" (p. 296).

Honesty is also demonstrated through conferencer authenticity. The professional must strive to be as genuine as possible and to avoid the temptation of setting a tone or creating a facade that may create barriers. Carl Rogers (1969), in commenting on the need for authenticity, noted that "when the facilitator is a real person, being what he is, entering into a relationship with the learner without a front or facade, he is more likely to be effective" (p. 106).

Attempt to use a solution-oriented, noncompetitive problem-solving process. Robinson and Fine (1995) recommend that conferencers view most problems and issues involving parents and families of individuals with exceptionalities as having a number of possible solutions. Accordingly, they suggest that focusing on problems and solutions alternatives orients professionals and parents away from less productive behaviors (e.g., blaming, challenging ideas). Further, presenting ideas and solutions in a noncompetitive fashion encourages a sense of working together, and thus a collaborative spirit.

Be aware of some basic do's and don'ts for parent-educator collaboration enhancement and relationship building. Although lists seldom provide a comprehensive statement of desired outcomes, they can serve to remind us of certain basic elements that should be considered. This also applies to the creation of trust and a collaborative relationship between parents and educators.

Do's

1. Maintain a sense of humor.

2. Be accepting of yourself and the parents and family members with whom you work.

3. Demonstrate warmth and sensitivity.

4. Be positive.

5. Demonstrate respect for the parents and families with whom you work.

6. Be sincere.

7. Listen.

8. Use language that parents and family members can understand.

9. Attend to the emotions and body language of parents and family members.

10. Reinforce parents when it is appropriate.

11. Recognize that parents and families can be effective collaborators who are able to make unique informational and problem-solving contributions.

Don'ts

1. Don't attempt to be a sage who has all the answers.

2. Don't make premature judgments.

3. Don't be overly critical.

4. Don't threaten, ridicule, or blame parents and families.

5. Avoid arguing with parents and family members.

6. Avoid strong expressions of surprise and concern.

7. Avoid making promises and agreements that you may not be able to keep.

8. Don't patronize parents and family members.

9. Avoid making moralistic judgments.

10. Don't minimize what parents and family members have to say about their child.

11. Don't attempt to exclude parents in decision making regarding their child.

Values and the Development of Trust and a Willingness to Collaborate

There is currently tremendous concern with value issues, particularly regarding those differences that exist among students and their parents/families; students and educators; and parents, family members, and professionals (Sontag & Schacht, 1994). Because values hold the very beliefs, convictions, and other persuasions through which individuals structure their lives, they will exist as a paramount factor in establishing and maintaining a trusting and collaborative conferencing relationship. Given the salient nature of values, it is obvious that conflicts and dissonance can arise when professionals and educators are unaware of their own values or those of others. That is, failure to recognize one's own values or the importance of another's may facilitate a severe breakdown in the communication process.

Although the significance of values to the communication process may be somewhat disconcerting, it is not difficult to understand. The technological advances of the past decades combined with the ever-changing divergent and contradictory values of our society serve to obscure the validity of even the most basic convictions and principles. In fact, more than ever before, individuals (including parents and educators) are questioning the existence of any universal values in our multicultural and diverse society. In addition, an individual's values are not rigidly maintained but are dynamic and constantly changing. And yet, despite the tenuous and ethereal nature of values, they exist as a basic determinant of the parent/family-educator conferencing relationship and thus are an aspect that must be understood and dealt with if trust and collaboration are to result.

The need for the educational conferencer to understand the nature of values comes primarily from the role of values in decision making. In particular, both parents and professionals tend to utilize their personal value systems in making educationally related decisions. As noted by Kroth and Simpson (1977), "The importance of assessing your own values or attempting to understand another's values is that ultimately you tend to act on those values you cherish the most" (p. 8). That is, individuals, contrary to what they may believe or have people think, tend to respond on the basis of their values rather than on logic or empirical facts. Values, for example, frequently form the basis for a professional's choice of one therapeutic approach over another. In addition, many times conferencing goals are more an extension of a professional's values than of the counselee's needs (Robinson & Fine, 1995; Wiener & Ehrlich, 1960). Finally, the efficacy of a particular strategy will often relate to the extent to which certain desired outcomes align with a particular value system. Thus, for example, an educational conferencer may consider that a particular parent has made significant strides if the family spends additional time together, when in fact the parent's relationship with his or her child has not changed. Hence, it is undeniable that values in a parent-educator relationship become a primary factor in the communication and collaboration process.

The goal of value clarification and assessment is typically not to change individuals' values, but rather to make them aware of their own patterns and the values of other people. An acknowledgment of the differences in individuals' values will conceivably make educational conferencers more empathic and knowledgeable of the basis for parent-professional conflicts (Heron & Harris, 1993; Mundschenk & Foley, 1995).

The task of clarifying personal values and becoming sensitized to others' has been undertaken by several different researchers (Raths, Harmin, & Simon, 1966; Simon, 1974). Simon, Howe, and Kirschenbaum (1972) developed an entire book of activities for aiding in the clarification of values. Kroth and Simpson (1977) also adapted a number of value clarification activities for training teachers to work with parents. In all instances, these procedures are not designed to instill a particular set of values or change a person's value system, but rather to sensitize one to his or her own values and to those of others. The accomplishment of this goal will, without question, be closely tied to the development of a trusting and secure interpersonal relationship.

Summary

Without trust as a basis on which to build, the collaborative relationship among parents, families, and educators so important to successful programs will at best be impaired. Strategies and procedures for establishing and maintaining trust and collaboration exist and professionals must actively pursue them. Although trust may be considered so elementary as to defy attention, its importance to the communication and collaboration process demands it be assigned a prominent position by professionals who aspire to effectively meet the needs of parents and families.

Exercises

1. Identify the characteristics of a friend or relative that you trust and find friendly to collaboration. Translate these behaviors into procedures that you can use to increase the trust level and collaborative relationships of the parents and families with whom you work.

2. Recall and analyze the feelings you have had in instances when you felt trusted or untrusted and where your collaborative input was wanted and unwanted. Attempt to identify situations where you felt parents or

family members displayed these attitudes. Are there particular conditions or behaviors you can identify that resulted in these attitudes?

3. Obtain a copy of Simon, Howe, and Kirschenbaum's (1972) book, Kroth and Simpson's (1977) text, or another resource containing values clarification activities and complete some of the exercises. Note the manner in which a sensitivity to this factor can improve your relationship with parents and family members.

# Part 3

Regularly
Occurring and
Ongoing
Conferencing and
Collaboration
Activities

Chapter 8

Initial Contact
Conferences: Forming
the Foundation
for Successful
Collaboration

Plato's creed that "the beginning is the most important part" seems particularly well suited to describing the initial contact between parents, family members, and professionals. In most instances this preliminary conference will establish the tenor for future contacts and, as such, should be considered among the most significant of all parent-school sessions. Because the nature and timing of the initial session are dictated by a number of factors, it can take several forms. However, regardless of its specific nature, the classroom teacher should always be involved in the initial contact process.

Inclusive Nature of the Initial Conference

Initial contacts between parents and professionals are rarely limited to a single meeting or a single professional. Rather, initial parent/family contacts with school and community professionals occur over a period of time, in a number of different settings, and with a variety of professionals.

Consider, for example, a typical parent-contact scenario for a child believed to have a significant educational problem. Prior to involvement by special services personnel, the student's regular classroom teachers will usually have contacted his or her parents on several occasions in an effort to obtain and/or provide information and to identify problem-solving strategies. Much of the information gathered in this fashion, whether in written or oral report form, will influence future parent-professional communication exchanges.

If a child continues to experience significant educational problems, additional diagnostic and remedial actions are likely. An initial step may involve *preassessment*, whereby an attempt is made to obtain informal evaluation data and apply regular classroom setting problem-solving strategies. Preassessment may involve a variety of professionals (e.g., counselors, special educators, psychologists, administrators) and a number of different activities, including information exchange with parents and family members. Thus, it is common for parents and family members to have significant contact—sometimes initial contacts—with professionals prior to the identification of a student as having an exceptionality.

Additional professional-parent contacts may result from preassessment recommendations for comprehensive and multidisciplinary evaluation. At this point social workers and psychologists may attempt to secure family history, while physical therapists and medical personnel may inquire about the child's developmental history. After the evaluations have taken place, these same professionals may provide parents and family members with interpretations of testing results. Thus, parents and family members may have opportunities for numerous professional contacts—many of them initial-type—during the evaluation period.

If the team ultimately agrees that a child needs specialized services, additional parent-professional contact will occur during the IEP conference. In addition to developing a student's individualized program, parents and professionals may engage in other activities construed to be a part of an initial contact conference. At a later stage, concurrent with or following program implementation, parents and family members may again meet with their child's teachers and/or direct service personnel. During such conferences one would expect additional information exchanges, rapport building, and collaboration.

This overview of parent and family involvement in evaluation, planning, and service delivery activities illustrates the comprehensive and lasting nature of initial parent-educator contacts. Thus, various elements of the initial contact conference will be carried out by various individuals at different times. The segmented nature of the initial contact conference underscores the importance of organizing and orchestrating parent and family contacts with school personnel. Parents and families must be spared from having to provide the same information to different professionals and at the same time guaranteed adequate opportunities to meet with those who can best respond to their specific questions and concerns (e.g, school psychologist, class-within-a-class teacher, inclusion coordinator). In this regard, classroom personnel play a prominent role. Specifically, teachers and other direct service professionals often see parents and family members subsequent to preassessment and evaluation, thereby being in a unique position to determine which initial contact activities must be emphasized. They also have a significant part in establishing and maintaining parent and family rapport and developing the foundation for collaboration—*primary* initial conference activities. Finally, teachers and other direct service persons are uniquely qualified to discuss individual students' specialized methods and procedures, information most parents and family members find particularly useful.

Purposes of the Initial Conference

The initial conference is first and foremost designed to establish rapport and a foundation for collaboration with parents and families. In addition, this first session should solicit information and history from parents that may be pertinent for the accurate assessment and educational programming. A third purpose for this contact entails providing parents with information regarding their son or daughter's exceptionality and the educational strategy to be employed. Finally, the initial conference provides educators an opportunity to evaluate and better understand parents and families. This is imperative for ensuring that the school, agency, or organization successfully orchestrates cooperative efforts between home and school. The following sections will discuss the initial conference with regard to each of these purposes.

Establishing Rapport

A basic reason for initial contact conferences is that they can facilitate a positive and collaborative working relationship. Positive initial contact with parents has not only been shown to serve as a vehicle for increasing the probability of success with students, but also as the basis for other types of parent-school interaction (Schulz, 1987). Early on, Duncan and Fitzgerald (1969) investigated the effects of establishing a positive parent-school relationship with individual parents prior to pupils' entrance into junior high school. Initial positive parent contacts significantly increased not only the amount of parental interest in the school, but also the attendance, grade-point average, dropout rate, and number of disciplinary referrals of those pupils whose parents participated in the program.

More recently, Christenson and Cleary (1990) described a correlation between parent involvement and a variety of positive outcomes, including student learning. Christenson and Cleary also documented that parents who are actively involved in their children's education tend to perceive teachers as having better teaching skills than less involved parents. More importantly, these investigators noted that there was a positive relationship between parents' involvement and school effectiveness ratings, and that parents who are most involved in their children's education have an enhanced sense of personal efficacy. Accordingly, professionals should attempt to make initial contact with the parents of each student referred for a exceptionality-related issue. Even when other professionals have had prior contact with the parents, the teacher should attempt to facilitate future positive contact and a collaborative spirit by meeting with parents and family members.

An additional argument in favor of conducting initial interviews to establish rapport is that such contact can facilitate parental and family member cooperation, participation, and collaboration, including in the development of their son or daughter's Individualized Education Plan (IEP). As a function of the Individuals with Disabilities Education Act (IDEA), each pupil with an exceptionality must have an individualized program that outlines the goals and strategies to employ in the educational process. This document is jointly developed by a representative of the school or agency (other than the teacher), the teacher(s), the parents or legal custodians, the student (when appropriate), and other individuals chosen at the discretion of the parents or school/agency. The enactment specifies that the IEP must be in effect prior to the time a student receives services as an individual with an exceptionality.

Although the concept of an Individualized Education Plan represents a monumental step toward ensuring that children and youth with exceptionalities receive needed services, the participation of parents in this process is not automatically guaranteed. That is, even though parents are theoretically equal partners in the IEP development process, their initial face-to-face contact with professional staff frequently takes place at the IEP conference. Also, this conference often is the time when they receive interpretative test information and learn about the IEP process. Many parents and family members will be intimidated, emotionally upset over the diagnosis of their child as exceptional, or simply unfamiliar with the myriad professionals in attendance at IEP meetings. In such circumstances, they probably cannot serve as contributing and functioning members of the IEP team. If the goal is to secure meaningful participation and collaboration from parents in this significant conference (and other conferences as well), one must take special measures. The most efficient means of reaching this goal is to meet with and establish a working and collaborative relationship with parents and families prior to the IEP conference. Once this step has been accomplished, the process of educating a pupil has the potential to become a truly cooperative and collaborative endeavor between home and school.

Professionals should not underestimate the importance of a positive parent-educator relationship from the outset; it is the primary purpose for conducting the initial parent session. As noted by Conant (1971),

> If schools do not acknowledge this responsibility in their [parents] role as the formal educational agents of society, they will find themselves reacting rather than acting—and not always constructively—to the demands of the parents for more information, more involvement, and more control of school policies and practices. (p. 114)

Obtaining Information from Parents and Families

As previously suggested, each of the reasons for conducting the initial parent conference relates to the dual supposition that parents have a significant impact on a child or adolescent's ability to function in educational settings, and that parent-professional contact should not begin when problems arise. Therefore, an open and ongoing collaborative relationship between home and school is crucial. One of the most obvious reasons for obtaining background information from parents and family members early in the educational planning process is that it may lead to data not previously discovered. Historically, a high percentage of programs for students with disabilities and at risk have served children and adolescents from minority and lower socioeconomic groups. Thus educators and related school personnel often have been the single professional group to come into contact with all school-age children identified as exceptional. For these reasons, it is apparent that to base the assessment or educational planning process on a pupil's individual history requires that the educational community secure that information necessary for maintaining a child advocacy role and for guaranteeing appropriate services. Professionals must obtain relevant information consistent with optimal educational planning, and as noted previously, it may be acquired over time by a variety of professionals.

Most educational interviewers find an interview outline beneficial when conducting the initial session. However, with experience, many find that they can obtain the needed information in an organized fashion without rigidly adhering to a set format. The format proposed in the following section allows for the solicitation of information most commonly of value to the educator; however, because each initial session will have its own unique emphasis and purposes, users should adapt the format accordingly. For example, the interviewer should be highly sensitive to not duplicating previous efforts. With great regularity, parents report that they are irritated by multiple interviewers from the same school system or agency asking the same questions.

Format for Obtaining Initial Information

The following sections describe specific information to obtain as well as a format for conducting the initial session. As noted previously, the requisite information may be gathered by a variety of individuals over a period of time rather than during a single initial interview conference.

Parents' statement of issues

Even though the interviewer may have access to detailed diagnostic information regarding a child's school-related exceptionality, the initial interview should commence with a request for the parents to discuss their perception of the presenting problem or issues. This type of information is dealt with first in the session for four basic reasons. First, even though educators and other diagnosticians may have conducted a thorough multidisciplinary evaluation of a child, because no one will possess more information about the child than his or her parents or guardian they should always be asked to supply what they know. A second reason for beginning the initial session in this manner is that it offers the most effective way of getting the parents to talk. In addition, once the parents have begun to discuss the issues, the interviewer can direct the session, based on information they have provided, into those areas that appear to warrant further pursuit.

A third reason for beginning the initial session with a discussion of the issues or problems is that the interviewer can thereby determine whether parents and family members have received accurate diagnostic information and also fully understand it.

Finally, requesting that the parents state the issues in their own words helps determine if their perception of the exceptionality jibes with that of the professionals who have assessed the child. In cases of discrepancy, the educator will need to clarify the nature of the incongruence as well as plan a strategy for bringing about greater insight. In instances where a significant discrepancy exists, the interviewer should attempt to determine whether the parents' statement reflects inaccurate information provided during an interpretation, whether they have misinterpreted or denied information conveyed in an earlier interpretation, or whether they are presenting accurate information that should alter professionals' diagnostic information and inferences. Although the interviewer may choose to avoid dealing indepth with a discrepancy issue during the initial interview, it must be explored.

Developmental history

Although the developmental history of a child or a youth with an exceptionality is of significance when developing an educational program, the educational interviewer may not need to obtain that information directly. That is, if it is apparent that another professional, such as a school nurse, physician, social worker, or psychologist, has previously obtained and recorded the child's developmental history, the educator may skip this area. However, in situations where it is doubtful that the history has been obtained, such information should be sought at this session. Because school personnel are sometimes the only professionals to have sustained contact with children with exceptionalities, they must assure that students are not denied appropriate services because of a lack of background knowledge.

A child's developmental history will consist of those significant events that have occurred since the time of conception. Consequently, the interviewer must be sensitive to unusual events during the pregnancy, birth, newborn, or childhood periods. Specifically, the following should be explored: emotional stress or unusual circumstances that occurred during the pregnancy; complications or difficulties during delivery; and complications, illnesses, or serious accidents that took place during the infant or childhood stages. Because parents tend to respond that "nothing" of significance occurred, even in describing unusual situations, one should design discussions in this area to require more than simple "yes" or "no" responses. Thus, the interviewer should ask parents to elaborate and provide specific data such as the age at which specific major developmental landmarks were reached—for example, the age at which the child talked, walked, and developed bowel and bladder control, and when he or she had specific illnesses, accidents, and behavioral manifestations. When possible, a developmental history questionnaire should be sent to the parents prior to the session; then, during the conference, attention can be directed at following up on areas in need of clarification. A sample developmental history form appears in Figure 8.1. This particular questionnaire serves well either when completed by parents ahead of time or when used as a format for obtaining developmental information at the time of the conference.

It must be emphasized that the information generated from a developmental history may not be directly translatable into educationally related recommendations. For that reason, educators having to solicit developmental information must be willing to make referrals to professionals who have more expertise in applying this type of data.

Parents' analysis of child's attitudes

This section of the interview allows parents (or family members) to comment on their son's or daughter's attitudes toward school, home, and friends, and it provides them an opportunity to discuss the child's likes and dislikes, hobbies, and leisure-time activities. It is also a vehicle for discussions of behavioral and social traits and tendencies. The interviewer should be sensitive to such behavioral traits as antisocial or withdrawn behavior, temper tantrums, aberrant sleeping patterns, enuresis or encopresis, hyperactivity, and destructive or overaggressive responses.

Discussions of a child's attitudes and personality not only help gather information for use in educational planning, but also provide the parents an opportunity to comment on the child's areas of strengths. Because the initial parent interview often focuses on a child's problems (at least with regard to children and youth who have disabilities), it is important to encourage parents to also talk about their youngster's strengths. Indeed, if the parents are unable to provide such information, this very observation is valuable for the educator.

THE CHILD DEVELOPMENT UNIT
A University Affiliated Program
University of Kansas Medical Center

Name of Child _____ Date of Birth _____

Address_____

Father's Name _____ Birthdate _____

   Occupation _____ SSN _____

   Phone Number - Home _____ Work _____

   Address_____

Mother's Maiden Name _____ Birthdate _____

   Occupation_____ SSN_____

   Phone Number - Home _____ Work _____

   Address_____

Legal Relationship of Parents to Patient (please check):

Natural Parent:	Mother ☐	Father ☐
Adoptive Parent:	Mother ☐	Father ☐
Step-Parent:	Mother ☐	Father ☐
Foster Parent:	Mother ☐	Father ☐

Relative: _____

(continues)

Figure 8.1. Patient Information Form. (Copyright © 1994 by The University of Kansas. Reprinted with permission from The Child Development Unit, A University Affiliated Program, University of Kansas Medical Center.)

All persons living in the home:

Name	Age	Relation to Patient	Present School Grade or Highest Grade Completed
_____	____	_____	_____
_____	____	_____	_____
_____	____	_____	_____
_____	____	_____	_____
_____	____	_____	_____
_____	____	_____	_____

Parental Concerns

Please describe the major concerns you have in seeking help for your child. List your concerns in order of their importance to you.

1. (Most Important)_____

_____

2. _____

_____

3. _____

_____

4. _____

_____

5. _____

_____

(*continues*)

Figure 8.1. *Continued*

How can the Child Development Unit/University Affiliated Program help you
most with these concerns? _____

_____

_____

Medical History

Pregnancy

While pregnant did child's mother have any of the following:

	Yes	No		Yes	No
German measles	☐	☐	Vaginal infection or bleeding	☐	☐
Anemia (low iron)	☐	☐	Have a high fever	☐	☐
Diabetes	☐	☐	Smoke cigarettes	☐	☐
Kidney problems	☐	☐	Use alcohol	☐	☐
High blood pressure	☐	☐	Use drugs	☐	☐
Any severe emotional problems	☐	☐			

What medications did child's mother take during pregnancy? (Include vitamins
and iron) _____

Birth

Was the child born: early _____ late _____ on time _____

Was child born by C-section? Yes _____ No _____ If yes, please give reason for C-section: _____

_____

About how long was mother in labor? _____

What was baby's birth weight? _____ length? _____

What was baby's condition at birth _____

_____

(continues)

Figure 8.1. *Continued*

Has child ever had the following:

	Yes	No		Yes	No
Eye or vision problems	☐	☐	Anemia	☐	☐
Ear or hearing problems	☐	☐	Vomiting spells	☐	☐
Allergies	☐	☐	Frequent diarrhea	☐	☐
Asthma	☐	☐	Frequent colds	☐	☐
Convulsions or "spells"	☐	☐	Kidney or urine problems	☐	☐
Head injury	☐	☐	Meningitis	☐	☐

Has child had any other health problems not listed above? (Describe) _____

_____

_____

_____

Does child take medication on a regular basis? Yes _____　No _____

Please list medications taken and amount:

_____

_____

Development & School History

Development

At what age did child first:

Sit alone	_____	Feed self finger foods	_____
Crawl (hands & knees)	_____	Speak first real words	_____
Stand alone	_____	Speak first real sentences	_____
Walk well	_____	Become completely toilet trained	_____

(*continues*)

Figure 8.1. *Continued*

School History

Is your child currently enrolled in a school program?   Yes _____   No _____

If yes, please answer the following:

School Name: _____

Address: _____

Grade (if applicable): _____

Has child been evaluated by school diagnostic team?   Yes _____   No _____

If yes, when was evaluation completed? _____

Please describe child's performance at school. What subjects does he/she do well in;

what subjects does he/she have difficulty with?

_____

_____

_____

_____

Does child receive any special services to help him/her at school?   Yes ____   No ____

If yes, please describe _____

_____

_____

Social-Emotional Development

Does child exhibit behaviors at home or school that concern you? Yes _____   No _____

(*continues*)

Figure 8.1. *Continued*

If yes, please describe the behaviors that concern you:_____

_____

_____

What methods are used to discipline child?_____

_____

_____

Are these methods effective?   Yes _____   No _____

What does child like to do to occupy his/her time? _____

_____

Does child have regular playmates or friends?   Yes _____   No _____

Person completing application   _____

Relation to child _____   Date _____

Parent/Guardian Signature _____

Please enclose a recent picture of your child if available.

Return Form to

Patient Services Coordinator
Child Development Unit
3901 Rainbow Blvd.
Kansas City, KS 66160-7340

Figure 8.1. *Continued*

History of past school performance

Although the educational interviewer usually has access to information about the child's school-related history, it is nonetheless important that the parents and family members comment on this area. Specifically, the focus should be on parental perceptions of school success and failure and their causes, academic performance as compared to the child's peer group, and those academic and social areas in which the parents would like to see the greatest investment of effort. In addition, the parents should have a chance to discuss previous relationships they and their child have had with school personnel. This area has frequently been reported as among the most beneficial for educators to explore.

Finally, the interviewer should discuss with the parents any measures they have employed to deal with the child's problems. For example, it is not uncommon for parents of children with mild disabilities to have had prior contact with a number of professionals. Knowledge of past evaluation results and remediation strategies not only aids in planning for the pupil in the classroom, but a discussion of these procedures can function as an invitation for parents and family members to discuss issues associated with gaining an evaluation of their child.

Parental goals and expectations

Parents' and family members' goals and expectations for their child with an exceptionality, including the role educators play, will exert a significant impact on the relationship between the family and the school. Consequently, this significant variable element must be carefully analyzed. First, of course, one must determine what these goals are and whether or not they are commensurate with the child's abilities.

Conferencers should also solicit information from parents regarding their expectations regarding the educator, the school (or agency), and the community. For example, parents may assume that identification of a student as disabled and eligible for special education support services will result in significant curriculum modifications and immediate academic and social improvements. Although some of these expectation issues may be resolved at IEP conferences, the educator needs to obtain parents' perceptions relative to their goals if a specific strategy for reducing discrepancies is to be planned.

Sociological information

Another area of significant educational interest, and thus a topic for the initial conference, concerns the ecological and sociological aspects of the child's environment. An understanding of the child's family and home/community environment will enable educators to more adequately understand and plan for the pupil.

Items of specific interest in this area include (a) the socioeconomic status of the family, (b) the individuals living in the home, (c) the physical and mental health of those residing in the home, (d) the ethnic, cultural, or religious backgrounds and beliefs of the family that may have an influence on the parents' attitudes toward educational planning, (e) the languages other than English spoken in the home, (f) the child-rearing practices and attitudes of the parents and family members, and (g) the type of supervision provided the child or adolescent before and after school, including whom to contact regarding implementation of out-of-school programs.

Although interviewers agree on the importance of avoiding "personal" questions, it is necessary to address those issues that will provide an adequate understanding of the family. Though no simple strategy exists for securing this sometimes sensitive material, most frequently it will emerge through a positive interpersonal relationship with the parents.

Providing Parents and Families with Information

Although some might argue that families have ample opportunity to gain information about the educational program their child with an exceptionality will receive through the various preliminary contacts that occur (i.e., meetings prior to or concurrent with assessment and diagnostic decision making), these sessions, including diagnostic feedback and IEP meetings, often fail to provide all the information in which parents and family members are interested. One obvious explanation for this lack of information is that the classroom teacher, the individual most knowledgeable about the educational program, often has only marginal involvement in these early meetings with parents and families. Likewise, those professionals who have the most involvement with the parents initially may be unable to provide basic information about the classroom operation. As noted by one father following an interpretation conference, "Those may have been smart people, but they never did tell me what time school started and ended, what supplies he would need, and how the class would be different from his other one." It is absolutely mandatory, therefore, that parents have an opportunity to meet individually with the classroom teacher— the one person most capable of satisfying families' information needs and of specifically describing collaborative opportunities and expectations.

Just as educators expect parents to be able to provide basic information about their child, parents and families should be able to expect educators to inform them regarding the procedures to be employed with the child. Although a logical expectation, it historically has not been the norm. Rather, teachers and other educational personnel have sometimes been more concerned with obtaining information from parents than with providing information to them.

Although the specific information to disseminate depends on the unique needs of parents and family members, the condition of the pupil, and the educational program to be utilized, certain generic elements should be covered, including (a) a discussion of assessment and diagnostic procedures and findings, (b) a description of the educational program to be employed with the pupil, (c) a rundown of the methodology for evaluating pupil progress and the manner in which such information will be communicated, and (d) a discussion of problem-solving alternatives and other resources available to the parents and family through school and community.

Assessment and diagnostic information

The heavy emphasis on formal assessment procedures with children and adolescents who have exceptionalities has been criticized by a number of authorities (Hammill, 1987; Salvia & Ysseldyke, 1985). Nonetheless, testing results—both formal and informal—continue to serve not only as a major means of drawing diagnostic inferences but, more importantly, as the basis for making educational programming decisions. Consequently, the importance of assessment in any diagnostic and remediation program must not be underestimated.

Along these lines, parents (and family members) frequently relate that one of their strongest and most immediate needs is for interpretative information about their son or daughter. Even in instances where interpretative data have been shared previously, many parents and family members indicate they want more information. Although the reasons for this situation may vary, there appear to be several basic considerations.

First, though parents may have been involved in the interpretation process, even one skillfully conducted, they perhaps were intellectually and emotionally detached from the conference. It is not uncommon to find that parents are overwhelmed by the quantity and sophistication of material covered in a conference or that they are in a state of emotional shock over the diagnostic classification or the finality of the educational disposition (Kroth, 1985). Parents have frequently reported that they were only able to "hear" information presented up to the point that the term "mentally retarded," "emotionally disturbed," "brain damaged," or whatever was used. Consequently, even though some parents and family members may appear attentive and involved, they may actually comprehend little of the information coming at them.

Second, many parents and family members seem more comfortable receiving information from teachers than from other professionals whose role, identity, mission, and commitment they may understand less clearly. Teachers have been the brunt of much recent criticism, yet, as a group, they remain among the most respected and endeared of all professionals.

Third, parents and family members frequently relate that the initial interpretation of testing results was so muddled by esoteric language and terminology, anachronisms, and other confusing information that they could not benefit. Although teachers are not immune to this type of error, as a group they tend to engage less in this kind of nonfunctional behavior than other professional groups. In addition, classroom teachers and other direct service providers (e.g., speech pathologists, occupational therapists) usually have more samples of behavior on which to base their inferences and, hopefully, are in a position to augment standardized testing results with informal measures and observations that are more closely aligned with remediation or enhancement programs.

As implied, parents of exceptional offspring frequently experience a number of concerns at the time of their child's evaluation and program alteration. Such concerns can take a number of forms, but frequently they are expressed as questions. Kanner (1957) listed a series of questions frequently asked by parents of children with mental retardation and other developmental delays, many of which surface at the time of the initial parent teacher conference. These questions included the following:

- What is the cause of our child's condition?

- Have we personally contributed to his (or her) condition?

- Why did this have to happen to us?

- What about heredity? Is it safe to have another child?

- Is there any danger that our normally developing and achieving children's offspring will be similarly affected?

- How is his (or her) presence in the home likely to affect our other children?

- How shall we explain him (or her) to our friends and neighbors?

- How shall we explain him (or her) to our other children?

- Is there anything we can do to brighten him (or her) up?

- Is there an operation that might help?

- What about vitamins?

- Will our child ever talk?

- What will our child be like when he (or she) grows up?

- Can we expect graduation from high school?

- Would you advise a private tutor?

- Should we keep our child at home or place him (or her) in a residential school? If so, how long will he (or she) have to remain there?

- What specific school do you recommend?

- Will our child become alienated from us if placed in a residential school?

- Will our child ever be mature enough to marry?

- Do you think our child should be sterilized and, if so, at what age?

These difficult questions, many of which lack answers, frequently serve as a vehicle through which parents and families vent anger, fear, and frustration. Hence, they most typically come out in follow-up conferences. That is, while such inquiries may surface only periodically during the initial interpretation session, they may occur on a regular basis in ensuing contacts. Many parents and family members may not reach a point where they can make such emotionally laden comments during the initial interpretation, but they seem to have less difficulty doing so during conferences that follow.

In brief, the reinterpretation process should focus on (a) offering a clarification of the purpose of the evaluation and the expectations for the assessment, (b) providing an opportunity for parents and family members to ask questions about the assessment procedures, (c) presenting the evaluation findings in summarized form, (d) encouraging parents and family members to raise questions about or discuss the findings, (e) restating the recommendations; (f) allowing an opportunity for parents and family members to raise questions about or discuss the recommendations, (g) discussing the manner in which the recommendations are to be implemented, and (h) identifying those individuals who are responsible for implementation. Though some parents/family members may need only a brief review of this information, others will require a more thorough discussion; hence, the person who conducts the meeting must adapt the following format accordingly.

CLARIFY THE PURPOSE AND EXPECTATIONS FOR THE EVALUATION. Although more and more professionals are acknowledging the limitations of tests, the public still attributes powers to these instruments that often outweigh their capabilities. Consequently, the purpose of the testing, the capabilities of the instruments used, and the expectations of the diagnostic team should be shared with parents.

DISCUSS THE ASSESSMENT PROCEDURES. As diagnosticians often assume either that parents understand or that they do not really need to understand the nature of the assessment procedures used, there has been a tendency to provide test results without an explanation of what the tests involve. For example, if parents are informed that their son or daughter has a perceptual motor deficit, an emotional disturbance, or a specific learning disability, they should also be apprised of the manner in which the condition was identified. Although one need not enter into discussions regarding the validity of particular tests, it is necessary to inform parents of the nature of a particular exceptionality. In addition, parents can frequently augment specific findings once informed of the types of behaviors sampled. Without this discussion parents cannot be expected either to understand the evaluation process or to serve as a collaborative member of the team.

SUMMARIZE THE FINDINGS. Assessment results should be given to parents and family members in abbreviated form, with attention turned to those areas considered most significant. Because most assessment techniques yield data in the intellectual, educational (achievement), emotional/personality, physical/sensory, or ecological areas, the interpretation summary should follow this outline.

ALLOW OPPORTUNITIES FOR QUESTIONS. As noted previously, parents and family members may be far more able to ask questions after the initial interpretative session. Consequently, the reinterpretative process, perhaps even more so than the initial sequence, must allow parents and family members to address areas of concern or confusion. The interpreter should be prepared to entertain difficult questions related to the diagnostic and placement process. Questions such as "Is he mental?", "Will he be able to marry?", "Did we cause this?", and "Will his offspring have the same problems?" are not uncommon. To help parents deal with these complex issues, the following guidelines may be useful: (a) have the parents and family members define what they mean by their terms (e.g., *mental, hyper*); (b) determine whether parents and families are looking for an answer or structuring an opportunity to offer their own views (frequently parents who ask this type of question are merely looking for an opportunity to talk); (c) allow the parents and family members an opportunity to discuss their feeling and perceptions; and (d) attempt to candidly answer questions when the questioner is sincerely looking for an answer. Throughout, it is important to keep in mind that "I don't know" may be the most appropriate response at times.

RESTATE RECOMMENDATIONS. Not only must recommendations be reviewed, especially those specifics the teacher can best address and clarify, but the parents must have an opportunity to raise questions about the remediation strategies. Because this is probably the most frequently glossed over component in the initial interpretation (and obviously a major need for parents), the conferencer should plan for it very carefully.

The educational program to be employed

Although individuals who routinely conduct interpretation and disposition conferences may be proficient at meeting many of parents' and families' basic needs, they may be unable to offer specific information about the operation and nature of the educational program and the enrichment and adaptation strategies to be provided. Consequently, even though descriptors such as "low pupil-teacher ratio," "individualized program," "structured classroom," "class-within-a-class," and so forth may suffice for indicating what type of model will be provided, this area requires further clarification for parents and families. Thus, topics that should be discussed are (a) classroom and school schedules, (b) classroom and school philosophy and administration, (c) academic adaptation and enrichment programs (goals and objectives for the pupil and the manner in which the school personnel and program will be able to satisfy these needs), (d) classroom management and emotional-social intervention strategies, (e) ancillary personnel and programs to which the pupil will be exposed, and (f) availability of parent/family programs.

CLASSROOM AND SCHOOL SCHEDULES. Parents and family members will be interested in the educational and treatment schedule and routine their son or daughter will follow, including the bus schedule, school starting and stopping times, the pupil's activity schedule (including in general and/or special programs), lunch, recess, and break periods, the school calendar (including vacations, special events, and so forth), and a listing of those activities that the pupil will be exposed to in a special program, or if special activities are provided as a part of an inclusion program. Both day-to-day and longer-term schedules should be shared with the parents.

CLASSROOM AND SCHOOL PHILOSOPHY AND ADMINISTRATION. Because the philosophy of the teacher and the administration will dictate the general educational approach, the conferencer must provide this information to parents and family members. For example, inclusion program philosophies and interpretations vary widely from system to system, and educational programs serving the emotionally disturbed can follow any one of a number of orientations, including behavioral, psychoeducational, or ecological. Consequently, in language they can understand, parents and family members should be oriented to the philosophy of the program.

REMEDIATION, ADAPTATION, AND ENRICHMENT PROGRAMS. As noted, individuals who interpret test information and make program recommendations for parents and family members may have limited information regarding the specific academic programs to be employed for a particular child. Thus, even though a strength or deficit area may have been identified, the precise manner in which it will be dealt with may receive little attention. Program components such as degree of structure, curricula, specific procedures and equipment, and teaching strategies should be outlined. Attention should also focus on the goals and objectives identified in the IEP as well as on any other areas that the teacher thinks need further clarification or about which parents and family members raise questions.

CLASSROOM MANAGEMENT AND EMOTIONAL/SOCIAL INTERVENTION. Emotional/social intervention strategies to be applied should receive the same attention as the specifics of the academic intervention programs. This orientation will include both the manner in which IEP goals and objectives will be accomplished and overall classroom management. The conferencer should give special attention to procedures that may be considered controversial or that are based on reward systems or consequences. Token economy systems, time-out, and making certain class activities contingent upon classroom productivity or behavior should be discussed.

ANCILLARY PERSONNEL AND RELATED SERVICES. Related services, or those resources needed by a pupil with an exceptionality, include

> transportation and such development, corrective, and other supportive services as are required to assist the handicapped child to benefit from special education, and includes speech pathology and audiology, psychological services, physical and occupational therapy, recreation, early identification and assessment of disabilities in children, counseling services, and medical services for diagnostic and evaluation purposes. The term also includes school health services, social work services, and parent counseling and training. (Implementation of Part B of the Individuals with Disabilities Education Act, 1990)

Because related services frequently involve resources and personnel that are unfamiliar to the parents, they will require careful explanation. The example offered below, taken from a booklet entitled *Who Can Help?* (1977), describes the role of the physical therapist in language that parents can understand. Similar descriptions may be developed for each ancillary role.

> *The Physical Therapist:* If your child has a certain type of physical disability, he may benefit from the assistance of a physical therapist. The physical therapist is concerned with developing the strength and endurance of the body parts and in developing normal motor patterns, and in helping your child move easily so he becomes as independent as possible. The physical therapist has completed a program of training in the therapeutic use of movement and physical activity. He holds either the Bachelor's degree (B.A., B.S.) or Master's degree (M.S.) in the specialty of physical therapy. The Licensed Physical Therapist (L.P.T.) has also completed a state examination and is licensed to practice in the state. The physical therapist is usually affiliated with an agency, clinic, or school which offers a team approach for the treatment of children [with disabilities]. He will see your child only upon the referral of a licensed physician. The referring physician may be a pediatrician, neurologist, or orthopedist. The physical therapist will often train you, as parents, in daily treatment procedures to help your child [with a disability] at home. You may be taught to assist your child in a program of exercises or you may be asked to participate in certain play activities at home that will help your child build physical strength and endurance. (p. 21)

PARENT/FAMILY PROGRAMS. As many special education programs involve parents and families, the teacher should review for the parents the schedules, expectations, and procedures associated with their component. Individual and group conference dates, workshop schedules, and resources available to the parents and family (both in school and in the community) should be reviewed. In addition, because some parents and family members are interested in augmenting classroom academic programs through home tutoring, the teacher should structure or provide input and/or material for parental teaching activities. Finally, parents and family members should be informed about procedures for visiting the classroom, general expectations for their role, materials/equipment they should supply, and other related items.

To ensure that the information deemed important for parents continues to be readily available to them, a handbook may prove to be an excellent resource, both for the parent and the teacher. According to Kroth

(1985) a handbook should be succinct, attractive, inclusive, and written on a level parents can understand. With regard to its content, this same author suggested that anything that all parents of students in that classroom need to know should be included. An example of part of one teacher's handbook appears in Figure 8.2.

Evaluating pupil progress and disseminating this information to families

Assessing the progress of students and communicating such information to parents and family members forms a basic and necessary element of any good educational program, and provides a necessary component of any collaborative effort. Accordingly, the initial conference should include a discussion of the manner in which students are evaluated and how parents will be kept up to date.

The Individuals with Disabilities Education Act mandates that students' progress be assessed, but the requirement for just an annual accounting makes it of rather dubious utility for parents and families. Therefore, to make evaluation and communication of progress to parents an ongoing activity, educators need to develop alternative evaluation procedures. Alternatives (in addition to parent-teacher conferences) appropriate for this purpose include (a) telephone contacts, (b) daily or weekly report cards, (c) letters/notes, and (d) technology communication (e.g., computer mail systems). Evidence that parents prefer regular, informal contact (Sicley, 1993; Simpson, 1988) underscores the need for appropriate planning in this area. Thus, these parent-educator communication procedures should be used on a regular basis and designed to focus on progress rather than problem areas.

Telephone contacts are most appropriate as a means of providing parents with reinforcement and feedback, scheduling conferences, providing progress reports, and obtaining information on changes in behavior or performance. Besides being convenient and time-saving, the phone also can serve to overcome some parents' inability or unwillingness to attend face-to-face conferences. However, in spite of the advantages, telephone contacts pose several potential problems. First, whether or not a call is scheduled at a mutually convenient time, some parents do not wish to be telephoned at home. Second, although a convenient means of communicating, telephone contacts must never be thought of as substitutes for ongoing person-to-person conferences. Finally, the telephone should typically not be used to confront parents or to discuss any sensitive material that should be dealt with in a face-to-face fashion.

General information about autism

Children who have been diagnosed as having *autism* and *pervasive developmental disorders* vary widely in terms of their characteristics, behavior and learning abilities. Thus, some children with autism (or pervasive developmental disorder) may have minimal symptoms of the disorder, experience few learning and other educational problems, and require few educational supports. Other students with autism are more severely affected, and will need a greater degree of support. While the specific patterns of autism will vary from child to child, persons with the disorder tend to have (a) problems in relating normally to people and situations; (b) speech and language problems; (c) developmental delays; (d) problems in reacting to environmental changes; and (e) stereotypic, repetitive actions, self-stimulatory, and other peculiar motor movements.

Problems in relating normally to people and situations refers to children preferring to spend time in isolation or giving the appearance of having little awareness or interest in others. Some children with autism may attempt to interact with others in unacceptable or abnormal ways. For instance, a child may repeatedly ask the same question over and over, ignoring the answer. . . .

Classroom and school philosophy

Students with autism can and do benefit from educational experiences. While curriculum and procedures will vary depending on individual needs, all children and youth diagnosed as having autism require and benefit from education. Parents and professionals jointly make decisions regarding what programs are best suited for individual children. Some children with autism are educated in general or regular classrooms. Indeed, the general philosophy of the faculty and staff who work with your child is to have students with disabilities (including those with autism) spend as much time with regular class students as possible, including being in the same classes and having opportunities for the same experiences, whenever possible. Students placed in regular classrooms are expected to do the same work and otherwise be involved in the same activities as the other students, although they are often given specialized assistance. For example, your child's IEP may indicate that a teaching assistant will be available to help your child, or that your child's teacher will make teaching modifications to assist your son or daughter learn most efficiently and effectively.

Some children with autism will require intensive special education programs. For such students, a variety of options are available, including special education classes where a student may spend all or most of his time in a classroom for boys and girls with autism. . . .

(*continues*)

Figure 8.2. Samples of a school district information handbook for parents of elementary-age students with autism. (*Note.* Reprinted from *START Program Information Manual*, by R. Simpson, 1995 (pp. 3–5). Copyright 1995 by The University of Kansas.)

Parent/family programs

There is overwhelming evidence that children with autism tend to make their greatest progress when their families are supportive of them, including their educational and treatment programs. To the extent to which you are interested and able, you and your family will be encouraged to be involved in your child's education and development. In this regard, your child's program has staff available to assist you in a variety of ways, including being a collaborative support agent or a case manager. The role of *collaborative support agent* involves parents and professionals cooperating and supporting agreed-upon plans. . . .

Figure 8.2. *Continued*

Relative to daily or weekly report cards, Rutherford and Edgar (1979) observed "of all written methods, report cards are used most frequently" (p. 6). To be most effective, these reports should be sent home on a regular basis and both the family members and child should have a positive orientation. Examples of reporting systems used to communicate with parents are provided in Figure 8.3.

Letters and notes to parents can also become useful communication tools. Specifically, they are most appropriate for reinforcing parents, family members, and/or the child as well as for routine information exchange. Just as with the telephone, however, letters and notes should not be used as a means of sharing sensitive information, criticizing parents or children, or handling other types of communication best exchanged in person.

More and more educators today rely on communication via computer modems and other technology such as fax machines, and there is every reason to believe that such options will become increasingly popular in the future. For example, electronic mail allows parents/family members and professionals to exchange information conveniently and efficiently. As is the case with telephone and written communication, technology-based mail systems are best reserved for routine information exchanges such as progress reports rather than for problem solving.

Problem-solving alternatives

Some parents and families of children with exceptionalities will have needs that require tapping certain community agencies or school district support services. Accordingly, the educator should be able to provide information on how and where to secure the necessary services, including those for the parents or family as opposed to just for the child with an exceptionality.

	Reading	Math	Language Arts	Science	Social Studies	Health
Leroy had satisfactory social behavior						
Leroy completed his work independently						
Leroy participated in group activities						

U WERE THE 🍎

OF MY 👁 TODAY!

_____

HAD GOOD BEHAVIOR.

_____

TEACHER

Figure 8.3. Sample parent reports.

The educator should be familiar with available social and welfare services, respite care programs, baby-sitting services for children and youth with exceptionalities, psychiatric, psychological, and counseling services, social agencies, and so forth. Finally, the educational conferencer should be aware of crisis intervention programs that serve the immediate needs of parents and families. Though many will not require access to this type of information, those that do should be assured that educators can make appropriate referrals to assist them in meeting their needs (Epstein, 1992).

Evaluating Parents and Families

A fourth major purpose for conducting the initial conference is to identify the characteristics, including strengths and weaknesses, of parents and families. This process stems from the supposition that in order for an educator to collaborate and most effectively make use of the resources within parents and families, these must first be understood. Both popular and professional literature reflect abundant interest in the influence of parents and families on the development of their offspring (Epstein, 1995; Martin, 1975; Turnbull, Summers, & Brotherson, 1983), and as empirically illustrated, parents and families can exert a profound influence on children's development and school-related performance. However, whereas attention in this area focused at one time almost totally on parental influence as the cause of certain problems, today more and more consideration goes to procedures for collaborating and enlisting the aid of parents and families in accomplishing specified goals, responding to family needs, and in better understanding the impact of the family on the pupil. Thus, rather than being held responsible for certain types of educationally related problems, parents and family are viewed instead as partners in the educational process. Although the process in general has been demonstrated as logical and efficacious, the strengths and weaknesses of parents and families—including their needs and participation preferences (see chapter 1 for a discussion of this issue)—must be carefully evaluated to assure an effective parent-educator program. In the same manner that a teacher implements an educational program only after determining a student's abilities and needs, he or she must also take careful stock of parent and family strengths, weaknesses, and needs.

Each of us constantly evaluates the individuals and families with whom we work using criteria that are consistent with our own value structure and needs. However, parent and family assessment methods must be tempered by use of more objective criteria, including (a) parents' strengths and weaknesses, (b) family structure, (c) family interactions, (d) family functions, and (e) family life cycles.

Parents' strengths and weaknesses

However intimidating it may sound, this role is carried out very effectively by many educators. Particular areas of attention include parents' cognitive, educational, physical/health, and personality/emotional characteristics.

Some educators may not consider themselves qualified to estimate the cognitive capabilities of another person—especially in the absence of formal testing. Yet, it is possible to make reasonably accurate *general* estimates of intelligence based exclusively on verbal interactions, at least to arrive at such general estimates as whether or not an individual is functioning at or near an average intellectual level. Beyond that, this gross procedure is not valid or useful. However, based on the information the parent provides, especially as it relates to occupation and education, as well as his or her verbal fluency, memory, and demeanor, it is frequently possible to draw reasonably accurate intellectual inferences. The rationale for undertaking this analysis is simply that different parents will need different programs; it cannot serve as a basis of etiology for a pupil's exceptionality or as a discriminator for services. Moreover, because racial, ethnic, language, and other diversity-related factors may influence one individual's perceptions of another, educators must be extremely cautious in making inferences.

Parents' educational level is also significant when considering needs and appropriate levels of participation. In many instances parents will volunteer the extent to which they have been formally educated. At other times such information can be inferred from their occupation, vocation, or behavior. Just as when making intellectual judgments, the intent here is simply to determine whether the parents are literate and, if so, the extent to which they will be capable of utilizing self-directed programs, participating as tutors with their own child, and so forth. Although this process may appear to be an invasion of privacy, the success of many collaborative programs is founded on such information. Consequently, the conferencer would be remiss by neglecting this area.

Physical and health considerations include the age of the parents and family members, plus their health, physical limitations, sensory deficits, and other related factors. Although a particular program might be effective under normal circumstances, modifications may be needed for a parent or family member with a physical or health-related disability.

Personality factors are probably the most significant variables in determining the success or failure of collaborative and home-school programs, yet they are also the most elusive. Although educators frequently report that they feel unprepared to "analyze" the personality of another adult, simple observations of the parents' style and strategies often help one arrive at estimates in this regard. Of course educators need to closely monitor their own values and biases in this area. Under these conditions, information relating to parents' personality and attitudes can be extremely helpful to educators.

One mother, for example, repeatedly referred to herself in a conference as highly dependent on other individuals for providing care for her son with mental retardation. She revealed that she relied heavily on friends and relatives for making even minor parenting decisions and reported feeling overwhelmed at the prospect of making independent decisions and assuming total responsibility for the child's care. Though the educational conferencer identified independent functioning as a goal for this mother, she also wisely adopted the strategy of initially collaborating with the mother in conjunction with someone from her circle of support.

Although information regarding parents' characteristics is important, it is usually not formally recorded. In fact, because such information stems from subjective judgments, the educator is advised not to make a written record of it (e.g., parents' estimated intellectual abilities, emotional stability).

Family structure

Diverse family structures must be considered when evaluating parents and families. In particular, one should assess families' membership characteristics, cultural style, and ideology (Lambie & Daniels-Mohring, 1993; Simpson & Fiedler, 1989; Turnbull et al., 1983).

Family membership characteristics include the family's size, individual member factors, and extrafamilial support. Membership characteristics, in turn, determine the needs and resources of a given family. For example, the needs of a divorced mother with six children will likely differ from those of a two-parent family. Furthermore, extrafamilial support, such as close friends or relatives, can have a significant impact on the availability of parents to participate in school meetings and other education-related activities.

Families are also influenced by cultural and ideological factors, which affect their values and their perceptions of the needs of their child with an exceptionality. Thus, parents and family members react differently to the stress of coping with a child with an exceptionality. Some become immersed in their child's education and development, while others may distance themselves from the school program. Obviously these factors must be evaluated and accommodated on an individual basis.

A family's socioeconomic status should also be assessed as a part of determining their educational involvement. For instance, a family experiencing financial strain perhaps cannot afford to become actively involved in their child's treatment or education.

Family interactions

An anlysis of family interactions involves consideration of the interplay among individual family members. The traditional nuclear family consists of four subsystems: (a) husband/wife, (b) parent/child, (c) child/child, and

(d) interactions of family members with others (e.g., neighbors, friends). Consideration of the aforementioned factors is called for because events that affect any of the four subsystems are felt by all family members. For example, in discussing the proposition that parents should assist in teaching their children at home, Turnbull et al. (1983) described the following:

> Consider the example of a mother who has agreed to work on a home training program in the area of feeding with her severely retarded child. Allowing her child to feed himself triples the time involved in each meal. While the mother is working with the child on feeding, her dinner conversation with her husband and other children is substantially limited. After the other family members finish dinner, the father cleans the kitchen and the siblings proceed to their homework all feeling that some of their needs have been overlooked. Meanwhile, the mother is feeling isolated from the rest of her family and frustrated over all the tasks to which she must attend before midnight. (p. 5)

According to Olson, Russell, and Sprenkle (1980) and other investigators (Lambie & Daniels-Mohring, 1993), the interaction among the four family subsystems is based on cohesion, adaptability, and communication. Knowledge of these factors will assist educators in effectively meeting the needs of all family members and in selecting an appropriate level for their participation in the educational program of the child with an exceptionality.

Family functions

Turnbull et al. (1983) noted that families serve the needs of their members through the following nine functions: economic, physical, rest and recuperation, socialization, self-definition, affection, guidance, education, and vocational. It is important to note that education is but one of the functions with which a family must be concerned. Overemphasis in one area may reduce the family's ability to effectively respond to needs in others (MacMillan & Turnbull, 1983). Educators should understand family functioning in order to secure appropriate levels of parent and family involvement and collaboration, and to plan in accordance with prevailing needs and capabilities.

Family life cycles

Goldenberg and Goldenberg (1980) described family life cycles as "successive patterns within the continuity of family living over the years of its existence—with members aging and passing through a succession of family roles" (p. 14). Educators should be aware of the life cycle events that impact upon families of exceptional children and youth for two reasons (Benson & Turnbull, 1985). First, life cycle events clarify the changing nature of a family's needs and characteristics. For instance, a recently widowed parent might have less time and energy to be involved in his or her child's education. Second, awareness of a family's life cycle events heightens educators' sensitivity to the sources of stress that impact upon the family. Again, parents experiencing stressful times will undoubtedly expend their personal resources in the area(s) causing them the most stress.

A significant family life cycle issue to which educators should be particularly sensitive relates to developmental changes. Such changes include a family's progression from one stage to another, including couples without children, families with preschool children, families with school-age children, families with youth, families with adults and their children who reenter families, post-parental families, and aging. Movement from one stage to another is frequently accompanied by stress, as is transition failure associated with accommodating a child or adolescent with an exceptionality. For example, parents may need support and help in planning for adequate care of their child with an exceptionality once they themselves are no longer capable of doing so (e.g., through death, disability). Awareness of such factors has obvious implications for understanding, collaborating, and planning for parent and family needs.

Summary

Initial contacts between parents and professionals must be considered a basic and essential component of an effective parent-educator relationship. The four major elements of this conference—establishing rapport and a collaborative relationship, obtaining information, providing information, and evaluating parents and families—can facilitate the pupil's educational process as well as the positive working relationship between parents and professionals.

Exercises

1. Conduct a simulation conference using the role-playing materials in Appendix A. Materials are provided for the exceptionalities of behav-

ior disorder, giftedness, learning disability, physical handicap, and mental retardation. Use those materials most closely aligned with the pupils you are associated with or plan to educate.

In conducting the simulation exercise, one individual should assume the part of the parent, using the materials labeled "Parent Role." Another person, taking the part of the teacher, should structure his or her responses around the teacher materials. A third individual should assume the role of the evaluator, using the evaluation form provided.

In disseminating the information about "your program" to the person playing the part of the parent, talk about an actual program you would employ with this pupil.

Change roles after completing the exercise.

2. Conduct an analysis of a parent and family with whom you have contact. In particular, comment on the parents' strengths and weaknesses and the family's structure, interactions, functions, and life cycles.

Chapter 9

Legal and Legislative Considerations, Including Individualized Education Program Conferences

A basic prerequisite to effective functioning as an educational conferencer and as an advocate for children and their parents is familiarity with legal and legislative information. With respect to parents of children and youth with exceptionalities, this translates into cognizance and insight into the Individuals with Disabilities Education Act (IDEA), including skill in developing effective individualized education plans (IEPs), as well as an understanding of other related legislation and legal rulings.

The Individuals with Disabilities Education Act

Without argument, the most comprehensive and significant legislation yet proposed and enacted for meeting the educational needs of children and youth with exceptionalities has been the Individuals with Disabilities Education Act (IDEA), previously called the Education for All Handicapped Children Act. Up until the enactment of PL 94-142 in 1975, students with disabilities were frequently excluded from public school attendance. In an attempt to put this problem into historical perspective, Smith and Luckasson (1992) noted that prior to passage of PL 94-142,

> In most states, even those children with the mildest levels of disabilities were not allowed to attend school. Children with more severe disabilities were routinely excluded even until the 1970's. While children without handicaps were required to attend school under compulsory school attendance laws, children *with* handicaps were *prevented* from attending school. (p. 21)

The Individuals with Disabilities Education Act was an amendment to the Education for All Handicapped Children Act (PL 94-142). PL 94-142 had been a modification of the Education of the Handicapped Amendments of 1974 (PL 93-380), which in turn had clarified, expanded, and amended the Elementary and Secondary Education Act of 1965 (PL 89-10). At the time of its passage, PL 94-142 was so significant and far-reaching that it dominated every prior piece of legislation enacted for children and youth with disabilities. In 1986, PL 99-457 extended the requirements of PL 94-142 to infants and toddlers and required Individualized Family Service Plans (IFSPs), thus even further expanding the significance of this monumental legislation.

In 1990, an additional amendment, PL 101-476, resulted in the following: (a) the name of the enactment was changed from the Education for All Handicapped Children Act to the Individuals with Disabilities Education Act; (b) the term "children with disabilities" supplanted "handicapped children"; (c) traumatic brain injury and autism were added to the list of disabilities recognized under the enactment; (d) transition plans were added for youth with disabilities; and (e) states could be sued in federal court for violations of the enactment. More recently, the Americans with Disabilities Act (ADA; PL 101-336) affirmed the rights of individuals with disabilities to equal access to facilities and opportunities. This historic legislation, which complemented and augmented Section 504 of the Rehabilitation Act of 1973 (Section 504 prohibits discrimination against otherwise qualified persons with disabilities, including rights to a free and appropriate public education), was composed of several significant components: (a) employers may not discriminate against an individual with a disability in hiring or promoting if the person is otherwise qualified for the job; (b) employers are excluded from asking whether someone has a disability and cannot administer tests that are designed to screen out persons with disabilities; and (c) employers are required to make "reasonable accommodations" for persons with disabilities (e.g., equipment modification, job restructuring).

The Education for All Handicapped Children Act of 1975 was designed to ensure a free and appropriate public education for all children and youth with disabilities. This law, signed into effect by President Gerald Ford on November 29, 1975, following nearly 4 years of legislative proceedings, provided initial guidelines for states and individual agencies in offering suitable educational experiences to children and youth with disabilities and in ensuring that the rights of these individuals and their families were protected. Many of the specific procedures involved in PL 94-142 were outlined in individual "state plans," which were documents explaining the precise manner in which each state was to provide educational provisions and alternatives for students with exceptionalities. Amendments to this original legislation, including the Individuals with Disabilities Education Act and the Americans with Disabilities Act, have significantly clarified and expanded attempts to serve the needs of persons with exceptionalities and their families.

Although the discussion that will follow is not intended to offer a comprehensive review of the Individuals with Disabilities Education Act, the relationship this enactment has with parental and family issues is so significant that to fail to examine at least its most basic concepts would constitute a significant deficiency for any work claiming to address the issues of parent and family involvement. However, because the present chapter is not intended to provide a comprehensive and in-depth analysis, the reader is directed toward the appropriate documents that contain this detailed information.

The Individuals with Disabilities Education Act (PL 101-476) is designed to provide for the following: (a) free and appropriate education (FAPE), including identification of and provision of service to all children, (b) individualized, nondiscriminatory assessment, (c) due process rights, which protect children and youth from erroneous classification and denial of equal education and protection, (d) placement of students with exceptionalities in the least restrictive educational environment (LRE), (e) Individualized Education Plans (IEPs), which ensure an appropriate education, and (f) parental opportunity for involvement in their children's education.

As previously suggested, the participation of parents in the various activities associated with identifying and programming for children and youth with exceptionalities is extremely significant. Thus, parents and family members cannot be considered an unimportant appendage to the system or process, but rather must be made a collaborative component and effectively integrated with other stakeholders in the process. Although future reference will be made only to parents, the reader will remember that the same principles apply to other legal custodians as well.

Free and Appropriate Education (FAPE)

This fundamental element of the Individuals with Disabilities Education Act assures that children and youth with disabilities receive suitable services at public expense. Accordingly, special education for a student with an identified educational disability is to be provided at no cost to the pupil or the family. Moreover, special education services must be *appropriate;* that is, individualized for the unique needs of each pupil. After establishing an appropriate program, the team identifies an educational setting that is least restrictive.

As an important element of a free and appropriate education, children and youth with exceptionalities are entitled to *appropriate related services,* or support measures, such as speech pathology, occupational therapy, physical therapy, psychological and counseling services, recreation services, certain types of medical services, and similar types of resources. Thus, the Individuals with Disabilities Education Act includes provisions for related services and support resources that will permit students to benefit maximally from their educational programs. Such measures are used to support students in both integrated and more restrictive settings.

Individualized and Nondiscriminatory Assessment

The Individuals with Disabilities Education Act requires that the assessment materials and procedures utilized for evaluation and program planning be selected and administered so as to avoid racial, cultural, or other forms of discrimination. Whenever feasible, evaluation instruments, materials, and procedures should be compatible with and administered in the child's native language or mode of communication (e.g., nonverbal for a child with a severe hearing loss), and no single procedure can become the sole criterion for determining an appropriate educational program.

Identification and diagnostic procedures are given a good deal of attention in the Individuals with Disabilities Education Act because accurate adherence to effective evaluation methodology assures that students with exceptionalities receive appropriate services. That is, unless screening, diagnostic, and evaluation processes effectively and reliably identify and provide utilitarian programming information, pupils with significant educational exceptionalities will probably not be exposed to functional intervention strategies and programs.

In a related IDEA provision, states are required to conduct public information campaigns and related programs to identify children and adolescents who require services because of an exceptionality. This initial identification step is intended to assure that all children with special needs come to the attention of schools and agencies in order to receive appropriate services.

Obtaining permission of parents

The role of parents in the diagnostic process is so significant that the procedures themselves hinge on the ability of the diagnostic team to secure permission to conduct the evaluation. Specifically, parents of those children or youth considered potential beneficiaries of further investigation must be notified and apprised of the need for evaluation prior to the initiation of any assessment procedures. The notification, which can and should be given orally but which must also appear in written form, should provide a rationale for the proposed evaluation and a description of the tests and procedures to be employed. In addition, the notice should indicate the approximate duration of the evaluation and the anticipated benefits to the pupil. This information must be presented in a fashion that parents can understand.

Upon receipt of the request for permission to evaluate, parents can make one of three possible responses. First, they can grant permission for the child to be evaluated. Once permission is extended, the evaluation can commence immediately. Second, parents can choose to deny permission to have their son or daughter evaluated. In fact, they must be informed of their right to deny permission for their offspring to be assessed. In the event that parents choose to exercise their denial privileges, and school district or agency personnel are not successful in convincing them of the need for the assessment, the district or agency can either accept the parents' position or, if they believe the pupil's best interests demand the evaluation, they can seek permission to conduct the assessment via a due process hearing. (Due process procedures will be discussed in a later section.)

Finally, parents can choose not to respond to the request to permit an evaluation. If follow-up contacts do not produce a response from the parents, the district or agency must interpret the failure to reply as an indication that they oppose the evaluation. Accordingly, the same procedures applicable to a "no" response apply to a failure to respond.

For example, a mother and father were both angry and frightened when they received a request from the school district to conduct an evaluation on their first-grade daughter. The notice from the school and a follow-up conversation with the child's teacher indicated that their daughter was having "difficulty keeping up with the rest of the class." Although the district's school psychologist attempted to assure the parents that the evaluation would be "routine" and that it would not necessarily lead to special education placement (but rather to "a better understanding so that more appropriate educational provisions can be made"), they remained suspicious. Their 14-year-old nephew had been tested and subsequently placed in a "special education class" when he was 8, which, according to his parents, produced "nothing but problems." The mother's sister and brother-in-law had, on numerous occasions, expressed the belief that their son began to have "problems" only after being placed in special education. After learning that these parents had received a request for permission to evaluate, their relatives strongly recommended that they "fight."

Fortunately, however, a single session with the school psychologist and classroom teacher convinced these parents that the best interests of their daughter would be served by allowing the evaluation to take place. In addition, the parents learned that their prior approval would be required before any change in their child's educational program could be initiated.

Requests by parents for assessment

Requests for evaluation can come not only from schools but also from parents. The latter, in fact, can request an evaluation or reevaluation of their offspring at any time they deem appropriate. However, the school district has the choice of conducting or not conducting the evaluation. In the event the district concedes to the request for an evaluation, it must still obtain written permission from the parents prior to actually conducting the assessment. If the district takes the position that an evaluation is not needed, it must notify the parents, in writing, of this decision. The notice must also inform the parents that if they desire, they can request a due process hearing to arbitrate differences of opinion between the school and themselves regarding the need for an evaluation.

One mother believed strongly that her 12-year-old son was "learning disabled" and should be provided special programming assistance. Even though he already had been evaluated twice in 6 years by the school district's diagnostic team and once by an educational psychologist in private practice at her request, and even in spite of the fact that each of the evaluations failed to indicate learning or behavior problems, she requested an additional assessment session. Because classroom reports and observations did not justify the need for another evaluation, the request was denied. Although the mother initially filed for a due process hearing, she later decided to move to a neighboring district in order to obtain "the right program."

Language of the request

Candidly explicit in the Individuals with Disabilities Education Act is the directive that requests for permission to evaluate must be in a language understandable to the child's parents. If the parents' primary language is not English, the notice must be provided in the major language of the home. In the event that the parents' primary language or mode of communication is nonwritten, or if they cannot interpret written materials, the school district must take whatever steps necessary to ensure that the parents understand the content of the notice. Professionals should also be sensitive to dialectal, regional, and other cultural and linguistic variables when selecting appropriate communication modes for seeking permission to evaluate.

The parents of an 11-year-old boy had both been profoundly deaf since infancy. They had met while students at a state school for the deaf and had married shortly after completing their programs at the institution. Although both were gainfully employed and had been for over 8 years, neither could communicate effectively orally. In addition, neither had more than the most minimal academic survival skills. They were able to sign manually, however, and essentially all of the communication that took place between these parents and the "hearing world" occurred via manual signing. When the school district made contact to solicit permission to evaluate their son because of alleged "learning and behavior problems," it not only sent a letter to the parents explaining the procedure but also sent an individual to their home to "sign" the contents of the letter and to further elaborate on the need for the evaluation.

Requirement for a comprehensive and multidisciplinary assessment

Historically, evaluation efforts have accentuated procedures associated with labeling and justifying the placement of children and youth with disabilities in special education programs (Wallace & Larsen, 1978). However, this emphasis has occurred at the expense of generating information that will serve to formulate an appropriate individualized teaching strategy. This pattern has specifically been characterized by an overreliance on a limited number of procedures with dubious levels of utility and by evaluations conducted by individuals with somewhat narrow perceptions of the needs of children and youth with exceptionalities. These evaluative shortcomings have been positively modified, at least to some extent, by the implementation of PL 94-142 and PL 101-476, which directly require a comprehensive evaluation by a multidisciplinary staff. A comprehensive and multidisciplinary evaluation, just as the concepts suggest, involves a complete assessment prior to the initiation of any program modification. In order for an evaluation to meet the spirit of comprehensiveness, it should involve not only consideration of the child's ability to function on standardized and teacher-made instruments but also an analysis of relevant home, school, and community variables that appear to exert an impact on the ability to function. Consequently, the evaluation must provide data relating to the physical, psychological, sociological, and educational status of each pupil being evaluated.

Furthermore, these evaluations must be made by a variety of knowledgeable professionals representing their respective disciplines as opposed to a single diagnostician. That is, in addition to informal assessment procedures, direct observations, and related techniques commonly employed by classroom teachers, the input of individuals representing other disciplines must also be considered. Even though the roles of the individuals involved will vary with the diagnostic questions under consideration, the team will commonly represent the disciplines of school psychology, social work, physical and occupational therapy, speech pathology, audiology, medicine, nursing, counseling, and school administration. Input from these professional groups will, of course, be considered along with that provided by the parents or legal custodians.

Each individual involved in the assessment process is charged with utilizing his or her expertise and the technology associated with the respective discipline to provide relevant information. The importance of accuracy in this function was underscored by Turnbull and Turnbull (1978):

> Misclassifying children as handicapped when they are not, or classifying them inaccurately with respect to their handicaps, can result not only in denying them their rights to an educational opportunity (not to mention their rights to an appropriate education), but also in unjustifiably stigmatizing them. (p. 85)

Requirement for a fair assessment

Implicit in the above discussion and expressly a component of the Individuals with Disabilities Education Act is the mandate that pupils under evaluation not be discriminated against in the assessment process, as a function either of the alleged disability itself or of racial, language, or cultural factors. With regard to the latter, the Individuals with Disabilities Education Act requires that the following assessment procedures be followed prior to any program modification:

(a) Tests and other evaluation materials

    (1) Are provided and administered in the child's native language or other mode of communication, unless it is clearly not feasible to do so;

    (2) Have been validated for the specific purpose for which they are used;

    (3) Are administered by trained personnel in conformance with instructions from the producer;

(b) Tests and other evaluation materials include those tailored to assess specific areas of educational need and not merely those which are designed to provide a single general intelligence quotient;

(c) Tests are selected and administered so as best to insure that when a test is administered to a child with impaired sensory, manual, or speaking skills, the test results accurately reflect the child's aptitude or achievement level or whatever other factor the test purports to measure, rather than reflecting the child's sensory, manual, or speaking skills (except where those skills are the factors which the test purports to measure);

(d) No single procedure is used as the sole criterion for determining an appropriate educational program for a child and placement;

(e) The evaluation is made by a multidisciplinary team or group of persons, including at least one teacher or other specialist with knowledge in the suspected disability;

(f) The child is assessed in all areas related to the suspected disability, including, where appropriate, health, vision, hearing, social and emotional status, general intelligence, academic performance, communicative status, and motor abilities. (20 U.S.C., section 1412[5][C])

Providing appropriate data

Not only are the above-mentioned procedures mandatory components of determining the most appropriate educational programs for a pupil and for complying with federal and state guidelines, but they have special significance for parent and family involvement. Although with various degrees of difficulty, program modifications may (or may not) be effected without parental permission, the desired option, of course, is to obtain parental input and support for the recommendations made. Consequently, the diagnostic team must be able to present data justifying the conclusions drawn and recommendations made. Interpretation and feedback contacts that take place between parents and school personnel often set the tone for future interactions, including collaboration; thus, it is crucial that both the evaluation process itself and the interpretation of results be the basis for future positive contacts. Finally, because parental or legal guardian permission must be obtained prior to placing, reassigning, transferring, or otherwise altering a child's program due to an exceptionality, it is essential that supporting data and attitudes assure the parents that their child is receiving the most appropriate education possible.

The foregoing does not imply that educational diagnostics and staffings must take on a game atmosphere, in which parents are willed into complying with the wishes of educators, but rather that appropriate procedures and data, including legitimate parental input, form the basis for program recommendations. Only through the adoption of such standards can schools avoid the arduous and unrewarding task of arbitrating differences through due process hearings. Although the due process alternative is a legitimate right that schools and parents may choose to exercise in select instances, rigid assessment procedures, meaningful parental and family involvement, and adequate interpretative standards can effectively increase the working relationship between educators and parents and reduce the need for more formal recourse.

Right to Due Process

Probably no single phrase in education produces such a visceral response as "due process." Both parents and educators alike seem to associate it with legal involvement, conflict, and proceedings more aligned with a courtroom than an educational setting. However, the provisions of procedural due process, as specified in the Individuals with Disabilities Education Act to govern the assessment, educational placement, transfer, and rights of children and youth with exceptionalities, essentially comprise the parent's, pupil's, or school district's right to challenge a course of action recommended because of an alleged exceptionality. The basic concepts associated with educational due process were initially articulated in *Pennsylvania Association for Retarded Children v. Commonwealth of Pennsylvania* (1972). In the decision, the court stipulated that no child with mental retardation can be assigned or reassigned to either regular or special education status, or kept from receiving a public education, without a prior recorded hearing before a special hearing officer. The court decision was also accompanied by a series of steps detailing the operational elements of due process, much of which is currently, at least in concept, a part of the due process proceedings contained in the Individuals with Disabilities Education Act. The primary due process procedures afforded parents and children under IDEA include parental access to records, independent evaluations, surrogate parents, parental notice, and right to a hearing.

Parental access to records

Parents or legal custodians have access to all records and data pertaining to the identification, assessment, and programming of their child. As noted in the assessment section, this component accentuates not only the need for a complete and thorough evaluation but also for an accurate and professional report of the findings and recommendations to parents.

Independent evaluations

Parents and legal custodians are also entitled to obtain an evaluation of their son or daughter from qualified (licensed or certified) examiners not affiliated with the district or agency recommending the action. Again, the importance of initial rapport and an adequate multidisciplinary and comprehensive evaluation cannot be overemphasized, because parents are entitled to present data from an alternate source in instances in which they question or are dissatisfied with the findings and recommendations presented them. As dissatisfaction is frequently associated with a lack of parental input or involvement, diagnostic teams should both be able to support their findings and provide parents with the opportunity for input into the analysis of the issues and intervention strategies.

Even though parents may seek their own independent evaluation and even though schools or agencies may be required to recommend appropriate individuals to conduct the evaluation, the parents may have to assume the costs of the outside testing. Only in instances in which hearing officers request additional independent data or in which schools or agencies acknowledge, or parents can demonstrate in a hearing, that the evaluation conducted was deficient or biased, or that the district or agency did not have available qualified examiners, can the parents be exempted from assuming financial responsibility. However, regardless of the financial responsibility issue, assessment data solicited from independent diagnosticians must be considered by individuals charged with making disposition recommendations.

In one example, a couple acknowledged that their son had a "learning problem," but they questioned the ability of the school district's diagnostic team to conduct an adequate evaluation. They consequently sought out community professionals to assess their son simultaneously with the evaluation being conducted by school district personnel. Because the majority of the private evaluation findings matched those obtained by the district, the parents were required to assume financial responsibility for the private testing. The one exception was the audiological exam conducted by a private practitioner. Because the school district did not assess the child's hearing, and because this was considered potentially related to his problem, the district agreed to pay for this service. In all instances the information generated by private professionals was considered by district personnel.

Appointment of surrogate parents

In instances where a child or adolescent is a ward of the state, or the parents are unavailable or unknown, the appointment of a surrogate parent must take place. Surrogate parents are commissioned to represent the child in all matters pertaining to evaluation and program planning. The criteria for the selection of a surrogate parent is that the appointee have the necessary competence to represent a child or adolescent with an exceptionality, as per state guidelines, and that no conflict of interest exists. Thus, individuals employed by or affiliated with an institution or setting in which a child or adolescent is a resident may not serve as surrogate parents. Due process hearings exist as the means for resolving conflicts over the appointment of parent surrogates.

Right to parental notice

As discussed earlier, parents, legal custodians, or surrogates must be provided written notice whenever a school or agency proposes to conduct an evaluation or make a change in the educational program for a pupil with an exceptionality. This requirement also applies in instances where parents request changes or evaluations. As previously noted, these formal notices must follow a written format and be in the parents' or guardian's native language. When the parents cannot read, or if their native language is not written, it becomes the responsibility of the school or agency to apprise them in an appropriate manner of the proposed action and their rights to due process safeguards.

Right to a hearing

Parents and legal custodians must have a formal opportunity to present complaints on any matter relating to the identification, evaluation, programming, or educational placement of their child. This process is designed to afford parents, schools, and agencies the chance for an objective and structured hearing, the outcome of which will lead ostensibly to the most appropriate educational placement possible for the child. Hearings can be held by the state, intermediate, or local educational agency, depending on the situations and locale.

School districts and agencies must apprise parents of their due process rights under the Individuals with Disabilities Education Act. These rights include the following:

- The right to a fair and impartial hearing that is open to the public. This right specifically affords the disputing parties the opportunity for an orderly hearing coordinated by a qualified and objective hearing officer who has neither a professional nor personal conflict in the outcome of the hearing. Hearing officers thus cannot be employees of the school or agency involved in the action.

- The right of the parents to have both their child and the counsel of their choice present at the hearing. Those who function as counsel can be professionals (e.g., attorney, educator, or psychologist) or another parent or advocate whom the parents or legal custodian considers appropriate to represent their interests and those of the child. Both the parents and their counsel are guaranteed access to information and data employed by the school or agency in recommending the disputed action. The parents and their counsel also have authority to present expert witnesses and testimony (e.g., educational, medical, or psychological) in support of their position and to cross-examine individuals presenting information on behalf of the agency or school. Only evidence that is disclosed at least 5 days prior to the hearing can be presented.

- The right of the parents to a verbatim recording of the hearing. This record must be made by a mechanical recording device or an official court reporter. Unless the involved parties agree to an extension, the hearing must be held and a final decision rendered by the hearing officer within 45 days after the request for hearing is made. The parents must be provided a copy of the decision report.

- The right of both parents and school districts to appeal the decision of the hearing officer. The first level of appeal is to the state education office. However, further appeals can be made through the traditional court system. Between the time of the request for a due process hearing and extending through the appeal process, or until a satisfactory compromise can be obtained, the child can remain in the setting he or she was assigned to prior to the recommended action.

Although due process procedures exist as a necessary and essential safeguard, they should not serve as a routine mode for arbitrating differences. Individuals with experience in formal due process hearings are quick to point out that this option rarely leads to mutually satisfying decisions. Accordingly, both educators and parents must develop other means for resolving differences and gaining appropriate services for children. Indeed, more and more school districts and agencies are relying on conflict resolution measures and related avenues to avoid, whenever possible, a formal due process hearing. Accordingly, only after all other options have been exhausted should the parties consider due process proceedings.

Whelan (1988) developed a procedural due process checklist for parents, school district personnel, and hearing officers in Kansas. This instrument, as shown in Figure 9.1, was specifically designed to ensure that the rights of all parties have been explained and guaranteed.

Least Restrictive Environment (LRE) Assurances

According to this provision of the Individuals with Disabilities Education Act, children and youth with disabilities must be educated to the maximum extent appropriate with normally developing and achieving students. Indeed, children and youth with disabilities may receive a placement outside the regular classroom environment only when the severity or nature of their disability demands a more restrictive setting. The specific policy of this important component of the Individuals with Disabilities Education Act reads as follows:

> to the maximum extent appropriate, children with disabilities, including children in public or private institutions or other care facilities, are educated with children who are not disabled, and that special classes, separate schooling, or other removal of children with disabilities from the regular education environment occurs only when the nature or severity of the disability is such that education in regular classes with the use of supplementary aids and services cannot be achieved satisfactorily. (20 U.S.C., section 1412[5][B])

		Parent		District	
Section	**Item**	Yes	No	Yes	No
District Written Prior Notification to Parent of Proposed Special Education Action	1. Notice is given by restricted mail or personal delivery.				
	2. Notice is in generally understandable terms, and in primary language of home.				
	3. Notice includes procedure to ensure that parent signs written statement of rights regarding the action.				
	4. Consent of written notice must:				
	a. Describe proposed action and reasons for it, the evaluation records upon which it is based, and reasons for consideration and rejection of other options.				
	b. Give parent right to consent or object in writing upon forms provided by district.				
	c. Describe all procedural due process rights.				
	d. Inform parent that failure to consent may result in district request for a due process hearing.				
	e. Inform parents of any free or low-cost legal or other relevant services in the area.				
	f. Indicate opportunity to obtain independent evaluation at district expense unless a due process hearing decides district evaluation is appropriate.				
	g. Describe parent right to access school records related to proposed action.				
					(continues)

Figure 9.1. Procedural due process checklist.

		Parent		District	
Section	**Item**	*Yes*	*No*	*Yes*	*No*
District Written Prior Notification to Parent of Proposed Special Education Action (continued)	h. State that child remains in present placement until decisions following due process hearing or until proposed action accepted by parent and distict.				
	i. Parents told of state toll-free number for information about special education rights and procedures.				
Hearing Officer's Responsibilities to Parties Prior to Hearings	1. Will verify that parent understands right to:				
	a. Independent evaluation				
	b. Access school records related to proposed placement.				
	2. Will verify that parent and district understand rights of parties in due process hearing to:				
	a. Have counsel of their choice present and to receive advice of such counsel.				
	b. Have parent attend and testify at hearing.				
	c. Have child and counsel hear or read full report of testimony from witnesses including those responsible for recommending proposed action.				
	d. Cross-examine witness.				
	e. Present witness in person or testimony by affidavit, including expert medical, psychological, or educational.				
				(*continues*)	

Figure 9.1. *Continued*

		Parent		District	
Section	*Item*	*Yes*	*No*	*Yes*	*No*
Hearing Officer's Responsibilities to Parties Prior to Hearings (continued)	f. Have child testify in own behalf, and give reasons for or against proposed action.				
	g. Notify parties 10 days prior to hearing of the right to prohibit evidence or testimony not disclosed to other party at least 5 days prior to hearing.				
	h. Have an orderly hearing.				
	i. Have fair and impartial decision based on evidence.				
	j. Have a record of hearing made.				
	3. Will determine if presence of interpreter required.				
	4. Will ensure that notice of hearing date, time, and place is given at least 5 days prior to hearing.				
	5. Will obtain from both parties:				
	a. Written summary of evidence each will present at hearing.				
	b. List of persons who represent parties, and/or appear as witnesses at hearing.				
	6. Will determine if use of subpoenas for attendance of witnesses and/or production of relevant records is required.				
	7. Will determine if parent decides to have pupil attend/testify at the hearing. (Pupil 18 or older who not adjudicated to be incapacitated has the right to attend/testify at the hearing.)				
					(continues)

Figure 9.1. *Continued*

Section	Item	Parent		District	
		Yes	No	Yes	No
Hearing Officer's Responsibilities to Parties Prior to Hearings (continued)	8. Will determine if hearing is closed/ open to public.				
	9. Will ensure that prehearing conference is held at least 5 days prior to hearing to provide each party with a hearing agenda which includes written summary of evidence, and a list of representatives/witnesses.				
Hearing Officer's Responsibilities to Parties Subsequent to Hearing	1. Will render a written decision based on evidence and send such decision by restricted mail to both parties not later than 10 days after hearing concluded.				
	2. Will send the decision, without personally identifiable information, to the Kansas State Advisory Council for Special Education.				
	3. Will arrange for each party to have a summary of hearing proceedings, including such materials or statements either party wishes to appear in the record.				
	4. Will describe appeal procedures for State Board review.				

Reprinted from *Special Education Procedural Due Process Checklist* by R. J. Whelan, © 1988.

Figure 9.1. *Continued*

Years ago the National Association for Retarded Citizens (1973) emphasized the concept of normalization and contact with peers, noting that persons with disabilities should be aided in achieving "an existence as close to the normal as possible, making available to them patterns and conditions of everyday life . . . close to the norms and patterns of society" (p. 72). The least restrictive environment component of the Individuals with Disabilities Education Act derives directly from this theme. In this regard, restrictiveness refers to (a) the physical setting of the educational facility, including its proximity to the student's home, (b) the degree to which the educational program itself is normalized (i.e., the pupil population, the curriculum and materials used in the program, the instructional methods used), and (c) the structure and rules of the program (i.e., the degree to which students are permitted the same choices and freedoms as other students in other schools).

Assigning students with disabilities to regular classrooms, whenever possible, revolves around two basic arguments. The first is that research has asserted that the separate special class model produces less than adequate academic and social results (Dunn, 1968; O'Neil, 1995; Stainback & Stainback, 1992b). The second argument relevant to the desirability of the regular classroom comes from theories of homogeneity and heterogeneity. A number of advocates (Baker, Wang, & Walberg, 1995; Brown, Nietupski, & Hamre-Nietupski, 1976a) have contended that heterogeneity in classroom populations—whereby students with differences in a number of areas learn to experience and interact with one another—is superior to the establishment of homogeneous groups. Advocates of this position emphasize that individuals with disabilities must be able to interact with a variety of people if they are to function successfully in a heterogeneous community environment later in life. Although parents have not advocated the advantages of regular class placement in such an esoteric manner as these researchers, they have voiced concerns based on many of the same principles and concepts (Avis, 1985; Wilmore, 1995).

Historically students with disabilities were functionally and socially segregated, even when physically assigned to the same buildings as their general education peers. In fact, relatively little attention was paid to the setting in which students with disabilities received their education prior to the enactment of PL 94-142. Professionals and parents were generally content to be allowed access to public schools, even if the programs offered limited access to nondisabled students. This perception of the importance of educational settings for special needs students changed as a result of the work of Brown, Nietupski, and Hamre-Nietupski (1976b). Brown and his colleagues argued that if professionals and parents wanted students to be independent and competent, they needed to be taught specific skills, not behaviors representative of those skills. Based on their notion of the "criterion of ultimate functioning," Brown et al. (1976b) advocated for teaching functional skills to individuals with disabilities in natural environments. Their position set the tone for parents and professionals to advocate for maximally normalized settings for students with disabilities, including opportunities for contact with normally developing and achieving peers.

An additional event that spurred demands for the integration of students with disabilities was related to findings that skill generalization and maintenance were best achieved in natural settings (Stokes & Baer, 1977). Not surprisingly, students with disabilities were consistently unable to generalize skills and knowledge that they acquired and practiced exclusively in segregated settings.

Work conducted subsequent to these two significant events demonstrated the positive influence of integration experiences on the behavior and skill development of students with disabilities (Gaylord-Ross & Haring, 1987; Sasso, Simpson, & Novak, 1985) as well as increasingly strong arguments that integrated settings best served the needs of children and youth with disabilities. As educators and parents sought to provide integrated school experiences for students who historically had been denied public school access, full-time general education placement for all students inevitably became a goal for some (Sailor et al., 1989; Stainback, Stainback, & Forest, 1989).

It is important to recognize that in spite of least restrictive environment policies that support the regular classroom as the desired arena for instruction, children and youth whose needs cannot be met in that setting must be afforded other placement options. Thus, the concept of the least restrictive environment has roots in the assumption that children and youth with exceptionalities should be educated along with their nonexceptional peers to the maximum extent appropriate. IDEA specifies that this educational placement decision process *begin* with a consideration of the pupil in a general education classroom. In the event the team determines that a student with a disability cannot be satisfactorily educated in a regular classroom, he or she may be placed in an alternative setting (e.g., self-contained special education classroom). However, this alternative setting must provide for contact and interactions with nonexceptional peers to the maximum extent appropriate for the student with a disability. The identification of the least restrictive environment, which is reviewed and determined at least annually, must be based on each pupil's ability and performance, as translated through the Individualized Education Plan (IEP). As parents or legal custodians are major participants in this decision, such a disposition cannot be made by school or agency personnel independent of parent input.

The least restrictive environment and the inclusion debate

Many would contend that the primary current issue in the education of children and youth with disabilities relates to the least restrictive environment, specifically *full inclusion* in regular classrooms (Kauffman & Hallahan, 1995). Indeed, inclusion has been an extremely divisive issue for both professionals and parents. Kauffman and Hallahan (1995) described the inclusion movement as "special education's largest bandwagon ever, one having gathered such great mass and momentum that it seems to many unstoppable," and a movement whose "size, velocity, and direction have become potentially fatal not only to those on board but to the entire special education community through which it is traveling" (p. ix). Others have cautioned that the full inclusion movement lacks a scientific foundation (Kauffman, 1993). Simpson and Sasso (1992) have criticized the underpinning of much of the full inclusion movement, noting that it is often based on references to "'the moral and just thing to do' rather than scientifically established benefits" (p. 3). As they continued,

> The full inclusion debate has too often been reduced to superficial arguments over who is right, who is moral and ethical, and who is a true advocate for children. Much of this simplistic posturing obscures the real issue (i.e., what is best for children) via claims of moral and ethical "high ground" and denouncements of "nonbelievers" as not knowing what is best and not caring about children and youth with disabilities. While perhaps effective in the short term, this process can lead to results that are directly opposite of those intended, including impediments to maximally effective programs for children and youth. We are of the opinion that full inclusion . . . is the right thing to do only if it benefits students with disabilities, their normally developing peers, or (ideally) if it is beneficial for both groups. That is, "the right thing to do," in our estimation, is that which provides the most benefits, not something that someone or some group deems appropriate because it fits their value system, is congruent with a fashionable trend, or appears to be a suitable, albeit unsupported alternative. (Simpson & Sasso, 1992, p. 4)

Obviously, there are parents and professionals who strongly advocate for full inclusion, believing it a logical step in the advancement of services and programs for students with disabilities (Sailor, 1991; Stainback & Stainback, 1992b; Wilmore, 1995). Advocates of inclusion argue that service provision outside general education has been associated with instructional discontinuity (Wang, Reynolds, & Walberg, 1986), reduction of curricular options for students with disabilities (Stainback & Stainback, 1984), and impediments to developing knowledge and skills that facilitate the full-time integration of pupils with disabilities into general education and adult society (Sailor et al., 1989). Purportedly, negative outcomes associated with pull-out and other segregated programs are self-concept and self-esteem problems for students with disabilities (Rogers & Saklofske, 1985), impaired social skills (Madden & Slavin, 1983), and lack of preparation for post-school life, as evidenced by exceptionally high unemployment rates among persons with disabilities (Reynolds, Wang, & Walberg, 1987; Will, 1984).

Although the controversy over inclusion is complex and multifarious, this appears at least in part to be a function of variable terminology. That is, professionals and parents often use terms related to inclusion in different ways. A related problem is that individuals who have written and lectured on the subject of integration and inclusion have sometimes significantly altered their positions on this topic without clarifying their use of terminology, thus causing further confusion. Stainback and Stainback (1984), for instance, recommended that inclusion of children and youth with disabilities in regular education classrooms be encouraged, but they cautioned that "students would still need to be grouped, in some instances into specific courses or classes according to their instructional needs" (p. 108). In 1992 these same authors advocated that "an inclusive school or classroom educates all students in the mainstream" (Stainback & Stainback, 1992a, p. 34).

At least five basic terms are essential to understanding the inclusion debate and to making appropriate least restrictive placement decisions: *least restrictive environment, regular education initiative, integration, mainstreaming,* and *inclusion.* As noted earlier, the *least restrictive environment* component of the Individuals with Disabilities Education Act requires that pupils with disabilities be educated along with students who do not have disabilities to the maximum extent appropriate. Placement decisions relating to students with disabilities must begin with a consideration of educating them in regular classrooms. If it is determined that a student with a disability cannot learn satisfactorily in a regular classroom, an alternative setting may be recommended, with the stipulation that these alternatives allow for contact with nonexceptional peers to the maximum extent appropriate. Thus, the least restrictive environment concept is based on the availability of a range of services and environmental alternatives capable of meeting individual students' needs.

A term historically related to inclusion is the *regular education initiative* (REI; Reynolds et al., 1987). REI proponents challenged the assumption that regular and special education programs should be separate, and they advocated for a single educational system capable of responding to all students' needs. Supporters of the REI movement contended that the existence of separate regular education and special education systems created barriers to responding effectively to the needs of both students with and without disabilities who were experiencing educational problems.

The term *integration,* as related to LRE and inclusion, generally refers to placement of students with disabilities in settings attended by their classmates without disabilities. Integration frequently refers to contact between students with disabilities and their nondisabled peers in other than shared classroom activities. For instance, integration may refer to common experiences between general education and special education students in a hallway or cafeteria. *Integration* and *inclusion* are not synonymous terms.

Mainstreaming refers to the selective placement of children and youth with disabilities in one or more regular education classes. An underlying assumption of mainstreaming is that students with disabilities should have the necessary basic knowledge and skills to benefit from a general education curriculum. That is, students who are mainstreamed are considered capable of making progress with their nondisabled peers in regular classroom settings when provided appropriate support, curricular and instructional adaptation and assistance, and individualization.

Inclusion refers to a commitment to educate students with disabilities in regular education classrooms to the maximum extent possible. Inclusion involves making support services available in general classrooms as opposed to pulling students out for services. Unlike mainstreaming, inclusion requires only that pupils profit from being in a regular education classroom (e.g., social benefits occur), not that they successfully compete with their nondisabled peers. Inclusion can be full or selective.

The practice of *full inclusion* stems from basic principles that are important for both parents and professionals to recognize. First, full inclusion is a "zero reject" model; that is, it is designed to accommodate, without exception, all students with disabilities in general education classrooms. Second, pupils in full-inclusion programs receive their education at the same neighborhood schools or attendance centers as other same-age students who live in their area. Third, children and youth with disabilities are placed in regular education classrooms at a rate consistent with disability prevalence statistics. In accordance with this provision, no more than one to three students with disabilities would be assigned to typical general education classrooms. Fourth, children and youth with disabilities receive their education along with same-age peers as opposed to taking classes with younger or older normally developing and achieving students. Fifth, general classroom teachers and other regular education personnel assume primary responsibility for educating pupils with disabilities, with the assistance and support of special education teachers and related services staff. Finally, regular classroom experiences are designed to develop and enhance students' peer relationships and social development, regardless of their overall functioning and ability.

Just as the name suggests, the term *selective inclusion* refers to regular class placement of some students with disabilities some of the time. That is, this moderate inclusion perspective stems from the assumption that not all children and youth with disabilities are appropriate for full-time regular class placement. Moreover, selective inclusion (a) requires availability of a continuum of service options, (b) may be unavailable at certain schools, (c) involves some students with disabilities receiving at least a portion of their instructional services from special education and related services personnel, and (d) requires that IEP teams determine the appropriateness of general education placement for individual students with disabilities.

There is no question that the problems associated with selecting the least restrictive environment for students with disabilities are due at least partially to confusion over the various terms that relate to this process. Accordingly, professionals should help parents and other professionals deal with this difficult issue through careful clarification of terminology, including analysis of the theoretical and procedural underpinnings of various options. Knowledge of such elements should assist parents and professionals in reaching informed decisions about the least restrictive environment for a particular student, including the advisability of inclusionary placement. It should also be obvious that placement of students with disabilities in inclusive settings will necessitate availability and usage of suitable support resources, including adequate teacher planning time, a pool of paraprofessionals, appropriate staff in-service training, trained support personnel, reduced class size, appropriate outside consultants, supportive attitudes and a positive school climate, plus knowledge of basic regular classroom management and structuring tools.

Given the controversial nature of inclusion, integration, and mainstreaming and the interpretation of the least restrictive setting, it is imperative that professionals work particularly closely with parents in establishing this component of a pupil's program. Included should be consideration of the following:

- In determining the least restrictive environment, the educator should remember that the parent is not an opponent but rather shares a common goal. Pursuant to that end, the focus should be on the student; that is, the least restrictive environment should be determined by each pupil's needs and the educator's and parents' interpretation of those needs rather than by the services available in the district.

- As suggested previously, one can expect parents to be active participants relative to gaining an appropriate education for their child only when the proper interpersonal conditions exist. The conferencer must be able to establish conditions of trust and rapport in order to reach consensus on significant educational decisions, including the least restrictive environment.

- Educators should not be overly anxious to transfer pupils with disabilities into general education classes when special classes or settings are producing desirable results. Evidence shows that many parents view special class placement favorably. If a more structured setting offers an appropriate environment and is supported by the parents, educators and parents should carefully evaluate the advantages of recommending a transfer to a general education setting.

- Educators should seek ways to have children and youth with disabilities participate with their regular class peers in social, extracurricular, and nonacademic school and community activities, even if those with special needs remain in segregated settings. Many parents may be reluctant to give up programs that they have struggled so hard to obtain and return their offspring to a setting that has been unrewarding. Nonetheless, attempts should be made to phase pupils with exceptionalities into normalized situations as much as possible.

- Educators must be able to offer a continuum of educational placement alternatives for students with exceptionalities. Thus, parents and educators must be able to select from among a variety of services those that seem most appropriate for a given pupil.

Making informed and appropriate decisions related to inclusion

There is no question that decisions relating to inclusion (especially full inclusion) of children and youth with disabilities in general education settings requires prudent consideration of a number of factors. It is also clear that this emotionally charged issue will be the source of a good deal of disagreement for some professionals and parents (Lieberman, 1992). Thus, individuals considering LRE and inclusion-related issues should consider the following recommendations (Simpson & Sasso, 1992).

Acknowledge parents' and professionals' positive regard for students with disabilities, regardless of their full-inclusion viewpoint. The vast majority of professionals and parents involved in raising, educating, and treating individuals with disabilities are decent, honest, and compassionate people, and thus the differences of opinion they hold regarding full inclusion should be viewed as arising from different attitudes, training, and experiences. It should also be apparent that these differences are not only natural but a potentially rich catalyst for cooperative problem solving.

Covey (1989) has noted the importance of "synergistic communication," or how differences of opinion creatively stimulate effective problem solving. He described this process as "[valuing] the mental, the emotional, the psychological differences between people. . . . realizing that all people see the world, not as it is, but as they are" (p. 277), and thus using the energy from these differences to generate creative and maximally effective solutions to problems. Relative to full inclusion, Simpson and Sasso (1992) offered the following observations regarding the focus of full inclusion discussions and debates:

> Too much energy has already been invested in the full-inclusion debate in terms of defining who is the "most right", who cares most about children, who has the most worthy values, and so on. We contend that the vast majority of individuals associated with children and youth [with disabilities] are committed to promoting the best interests of these individuals. By assuming this attitude, differences of opinion over full inclusion can be used to stimulate creative and mutually beneficial problem solving. Consequently, the debate can be redirected to focus on the utility of full inclusion, as opposed to whether one group's values are as good as those of another. (p. 11)

Recognize that it is unrealistic to expect that nondisabled children and youth and regular education teachers and staff will independently and exclusively make all necessary adjustments to accommodate students with disabilities in full-time general education settings. Expecting general education students and educators to make all the necessary accommodations related to inclusion implies that pupils with disabilities are unable to positively change their behavior and that special educators are incapable of providing effective instruction. Current strategies provide remarkable opportunities for behavioral, social, language, and cognitive change. Thus, when provided appropriate training and intervention, students with disabilities can make significant gains. Accordingly, the most appropriate program is that which most effectively serves individualized needs of students, regardless of its physical setting.

Make full-inclusion decisions for students with disabilities on a case-by-case basis. In spite of its positive aspects, full inclusion of all violates the concept of individualized education, as does any procedure that is advocated for *all* children. Thus, children and youth with disabilities should be integrated on an individual basis, based upon consideration of a variety of placement alternatives, including (but not limited to) general education classrooms.

Full inclusion should be viewed as one placement option rather than the preferred choice for every student with a disability. Though advocated by some, full-time general education placement is probably not appropriate for all students with disabilities. Moreover, full inclusion may be appropriate during one phase of a student's school program but not at other times. For example, some students with severe disabilities may require skills that are better developed and trained in a segregated setting (e.g., self-help, toileting). In such situations, skill development may progress more rapidly and effectively in a special education setting.

Balance integration and functional-skill development needs for students with disabilities when making full-inclusion decisions. Integration and functional-skill development constitute two core curricular areas for many children and youth with severe disabilities. Thus, concern for contact with nondisabled peers should not completely overshadow the need for functional skills that are necessary for disabled persons to live an independent adult life. As noted by Simpson and Sasso (1992),

> the only planned integrated post-school activity is work. Young men and women [with disabilities] who leave school without job, self-care and independent-living skills more often spend their lives in segregated settings than individuals who have acquired functional skills. To prevent such potential waste of abilities, educational experiences must be provided in settings that are most congruent with the skills and knowledge being taught. (p. 12)

Full-inclusion plans for students with disabilities should consider the needs of both disabled and nondisabled children and youth. Integration experiences rely on the involvement of normally developing and achieving peers. Though integration primarily benefits pupils with disabilities, nondisabled children and youth also gain from these interactions. Unfortunately, special education policies such as inclusion have been perceived by some regular educators, administrators, parents, and members of the general population as a factor associated with the poor performance of some general education students. Further, some parents of nondisabled students have questioned special educators' reliance on normally developing children to benefit those with disabilities. Accordingly, appropriate educational experiences for *all* children and youth must be assured. With regard to inclusion decisions, teams must consider the needs of both students with disabilities and their regular education peers.

Consider full inclusion for students with disabilities as experimental placement options pending appropriate validation studies. The jury is still out on the long-term efficacy and utility of full-inclusion programs. Accordingly, parents and professionals who consider this option should do so on the basis of its advantages, disadvantages, and proven effects with individual students rather than on the basis of its purported moral and ethical correctness.

Individualized Education Plans (IEPs)

Although each of the major components of the Individuals with Disabilities Education Act has received significant attention by parents and educators, the section that many contend has the most direct impact on students' outcomes, curricula, services, placements, and overall programs has been the requirement that an Individualized Education Plan be developed and monitored for each child or adolescent with an exceptionality. This regulation specifies that each state and local educational agency must provide an IEP for each pupil identified as having an exceptionality:

> The term "individualized education program" means a written statement for each child [with a disability] developed in any meeting by a representative of the local educational agency or an intermediate educational unit who shall be qualified to provide, or supervise the provision of, specially designed instruction to meet the unique needs of children [with a disability], the teacher, the parents or guardian of such child, and whenever appropriate, such child, which statement shall include (A) a statement of the present levels of education performance of such child, (B) a statement of annual goals, including short-term instructional objectives, (C) a statement of the specific educational services to be provided to such child, and the extent to which such child will be able to participate in regular educational programs, (D) the projected date for initiation and anticipated duration of such services, and appropriate objective criteria and evaluation procedures and schedules for determining, on at least an annual basis, whether instructional objectives are being achieved. (20 U.S.C., section 1401[20])

There are two general elements of the IEP process: meeting(s) of parents and professionals wherein joint decisions are made regarding students' educational programs, and the IEP document itself, which describes the decisions made by the parents and professionals. Thus, as stated in the *Federal Register* (57[208]), the IEP requirement serves a number of functions:

(a) The IEP meeting serves as a communication vehicle between parents and school personnel, and enables them, as equal participants, to jointly decide what the child's needs are, what services will be provided to meet those needs, and what the anticipated outcomes may be.

(b) The IEP process provides an opportunity for resolving any differences between the parents and the agency concerning the special education needs of a child. . . .

(c) The IEP sets forth in writing a commitment of resources necessary to enable a child with a disability to receive needed special education and related services.

(d) The IEP is a management tool that is used to ensure that each child with a disability is provided special education and related services appropriate to the child's special learning needs.

(e) The IEP is a compliance/monitoring document . . . used to determine whether a child with a disability is actually receiving the FAPE agreed to by the parents and school.

(f) The IEP serves as an evaluation device for use in determining . . . progress toward meeting the projected outcomes. (p. 48695)

Individualized education programs, which must be in effect prior to the commencement of special education and related services, must be reviewed or revised at least annually. Further, it is expected that special education and related services identified on a pupil's IEP will be provided immediately. Thus, while some delays may occur because of vacations or transportation arrangements, services identified on the IEP must be provided as soon as possible after the meeting. As placement, programming, related services, and other significant decisions are made at the IEP meeting, students may be temporarily placed in a program as a part of an evaluation process, prior to finalizing the IEP, to aid in identifying the most appropriate placement. If a student with a disability transfers from one school district to another, the new district may not need to develop a new IEP (if the current one is available, the parents are satisfied with it, and the plan is considered appropriate by the new district). There is no set length for IEP meetings as long as there is sufficient time for decision making, development of the IEP document, and parent participation.

The IEP format can vary between states, school districts, and agencies. However, certain basic components, as previously noted, must be included: (a) description of present levels of performance, (b) annual goals, including short-term instructional objectives, (c) specific special education and related services to be provided, including a description of general education program participation, (d) projected dates and duration of services, and (e) objective criteria, schedules, and evaluation methods for determining if short-term instructional objectives are being achieved. Beginning no later than age 16 (and frequently beginning at age 14), IEPs for youths must provide a transition plan. Although the IEP is not intended as a legally binding contract whereby districts and agencies must demonstrate that progress specified in the annual goals and objectives has been met, it does serve to solidify the cooperative involvement of parents and educators.

The development of the IEP is so structured that it is functionally impossible to comply with the established protocol and not produce a cooperative document. Thus, the development of a program prior to the official IEP conference or by a limited number of personnel constitutes a severe breach of policy. As noted in guidelines to parents from a national publication designed to apprise them of their rights under PL 94-142, "If you have reason to think that school people met 'behind the scenes' to agree on the IEP, effectively keeping you out of the act, you have grounds to complain loudly" (Parents Campaign for Handicapped Children and Youth, 1977, p. 7).

Who should participate

Individuals who should be involved in the IEP conference include a representative of the school or agency providing the services (other than the teacher) who is qualified to provide or supervise special education services; the pupil's teacher(s) who will actually implement the IEP (schools may designate which teachers will participate in the meeting); the parent(s) or legal custodians; the pupil, when appropriate; and others at the discretion of the parents or school. During the development of the initial IEP, the district or agency recommending the program modification should also have available someone who can interpret testing and diagnostic procedures to parents. When transition issues are to be considered, the school or agency should attempt to include the pupil and appropriate agencies involved in providing transition services.

Because parents are considered such an integral part of the IEP conference, provisions exist for guaranteeing their participation. Specifically, parents must receive advance notice of the conference, including the purpose, time, location, and those who will be in attendance. When the purpose of the meeting is to consider transition issues, parents must be so notified and informed of the agencies that will be sending a representative to the meeting and of the fact that the school or agency would like the student to attend the meeting. Districts and agencies must also guarantee that IEP meetings are held at times and places mutually convenient to the parents and educators. Those individuals coordinating the conference must also ensure that parents can comprehend and have input into the session (e.g., interpreters must be provided for deaf or non-English-speaking parents) or, in the event that they cannot attend, that the school uses other methods to allow their participation (e.g., conference telephone calls). Although IEP conferences can take place without parental representation, the district or agency must be able to document that parents were provided an opportunity to participate. This documentation must include accounts and results of telephone calls made or attempted, copies of letters and responses to letters sent, and reports of the results of home and employment visits. Though this information is not required for every case in which parents are not involved in an IEP conference, it must be available in situations in which parents claim that they have been excluded from the conference.

Rights and responsibilities of parents

Because the concepts, principles, and protocol involved in the Individuals with Disabilities Education Act are both numerous and complex, and because school districts often provide parents limited or incomplete information, educators frequently find it necessary to develop alternative procedures for apprising parents of their rights and responsibilities. Although published books and periodicals may be able to meet this need, they are threatening to some parents and at the very least will lack precise information about a specific program, class, or district. As a result, educator-developed parent handbooks may be more effective in disseminating the information that parents require. Selected rights of parents listed in a portion of one such parent handbook, developed by a teacher of children with disabilities for use in a rural area of central Kansas, appear below:

— You have the right to be notified before the school district changes anything to do with the identification, evaluation, or placement of your child. That is, your school must notify you of any change in your child's program.

— You have the right to have that notice in writing and in your native language (the language you use at home) or another way which is understandable to you. If reading is difficult for you, you may request any and all information be given to you in another way that you can understand.

— Notices you receive from the school pertaining to your child's special education program must describe that program and why it was considered the best possible choice. All other options must be considered, and you must be given an explanation of why they were rejected.

— You have the right to have a complete and individual evaluation of your child's educational needs. You can choose to have your child evaluated by someone of your choice in the community. However, if you make that choice you may have to pay for the evaluation.

— Your child will be evaluated by qualified school professionals. For example, a school psychologist will give intelligence tests, a speech clinician will give language and speech assessments, and so forth. Your child will be assessed in all areas related to a suspected problem. For example, if your child has a speech or language problem, he or she will be evaluated by a hearing specialist.

— Your child will be re-evaluated for continued special education progress and eligibility on a regularly scheduled basis, or more frequently if you or your child's teachers request it, to see if his/her school placement is still the most appropriate option. (Huxman, 1976, pp. 3–7)

Ensuring parental participation

Even though the efforts involved in scheduling and conducting a functional IEP conference are extensive and time-consuming, it should be obvious that such a process carries enormous benefits. It must be pointed out, though, that complying with minimum federal requirements may do little to ensure parental cooperation. As noted by Meyen (1978b), "merely setting up procedures which comply with the law and thus allow for parental participation is not sufficient. Emphasis needs to be placed on establishing relationships which capitalize on parental involvement" (p. 22). Although not an easy task, several procedures, when correctly identified and planned for, will help the educator to include the parents more effectively in the IEP process.

THE NEED FOR TRUST. Throughout this text readers have encountered the message that only under conditions of shared confidence in the integrity and honesty of professionals and parents will the true intent of the IEP conference be realized. Although this position has been advocated by many (Kroth, 1985; Kroth & Simpson, 1977; Robinson & Fine, 1994; Rutherford & Edgar, 1979; Sontag & Schacht, 1994) and thus should be an acknowledged principle, its importance must not be underestimated. Schools and parents all too often have had an adversarial relationship, making the development of trust and a collaborative interaction less than easy. However, without these basic ingredients, even the most precise adherence to mandated requirements will be meaningless.

The staff of a federally supported public school demonstration program for pupils with severe emotional disorders thought it somewhat peculiar when the mother of an adolescent being considered for placement in the program presented two rather strong demands. The first was that the initial parent-teacher interview, conducted as one component of the evaluation, be held in the home, and second, that a former teacher, residing in a community some distance away, be contacted regarding the boy's past performance. Both requests were honored. After the IEP conference, at which she actively participated, this mother revealed that she had been "testing" the staff. She indicated that although she had received a number of promises over the years from school personnel regarding the services to be provided her son, few had been honored. She confided that if the school personnel who contacted her were willing to come to her house and to contact a teacher whom she personally respected, "then they probably had Calvin's best interests in mind." This parent also reported that this demonstration convinced her that her input into the development of her son's IEP would be considered worthwhile.

THE ISSUE OF ADMINISTRATIVE AND BUREAUCRATIC RESTRAINTS. Even though teachers and other educational personnel may understand the components and protocol involved in developing an IEP, the standards adopted by school districts or agencies may be in direct conflict. District policy, though unwritten, may specify that only services readily available in the district are to be noted on the IEP, regardless of a pupil's needs. Other policies may require authors of IEPs to word components of the document in an intentionally nebulous or difficult-to-interpret fashion. The unfortunate thing about these practices is that they unceremoniously thrust educational personnel into the awkward position of demonstrating allegiance either to their employer or to the children they serve. Although some may argue to the contrary, the adoption of either position, regardless of how cleverly presented, cannot serve to accomplish the goals originally intended.

One director of special education for a large Midwestern school district, although knowledgeable of IEP guidelines, required that evaluation criteria for short-term instructional objectives be stated in nonspecific and nonmeasurable terms. For example, goals were frequently stated in terms of "demonstrating indications of improvements" rather than in more empirical and easily evaluated ways. Although the special services staff did not agree with this approach, they understood that the policy was a nonnegotiable dictate they were required to follow if they wished to keep their jobs.

THE ISSUE OF LANGUAGE. In order for parents and educators to collaboratively develop an individualized program for a pupil with an exceptionality, they must share a common language and vocabulary. Frequently educators become so accustomed to using sophisticated terms and concepts that they assume other people, including parents, share their lexicon. Parents may be somewhat reluctant to reveal their lack of understanding and, in some instances, may actually employ terms and phrases for which they have little comprehension. It is essential that the importance of a shared language not be underestimated. The selection of appropriate words and phrases, as free from jargon as possible, will ensure that parents feel more like contributing members of the IEP team.

One mother, when asked about the IEP conference she attended, coolly replied that she learned that "the CEC is aiding the SEAs and LEAs in interpreting the rules and regs of 94-142, 99-457, and 101-476 so as to ensure the proper development of IEPs, IFSPs and IIPs for MRs, LDs, EDs, and other DDs."

THE PROBLEM OF INTIMIDATION. Because the development of a pupil's IEP requires wide representation, parents and family members often end up in a planning conference with a number of other individuals, most of whom are professionals. Although this wide participation presents a number of advantages, it has the obvious disadvantage of intimidating many parents. Because the majority of parents will have had little or no prior contact with either the other IEP participants or the guidelines of these meetings, and because they may very well just be coming to grips with having a child with an exceptionality, it should come as no surprise that many have reported a great deal of apprehension and discomfort at these sessions. In addition, a number say they feel somewhat ill equipped to make a realistic contribution. Yet, because parents do represent a significant resource in the IEP conference, the team must encourage them to be a contributing component of the planning delegation. Even though this is not an easy task to accomplish, certain procedures will facilitate the process:

- No more participants than necessary should be allowed in the meeting. Although no one should be denied admission whose contribution may be of benefit, neither should the effective composition of the group be compromised by marginally involved persons. Indeed, Department of Education 1992 IEP guidelines noted that

   > the number of participants at IEP meetings should be small. Small meetings have several advantages over large ones. . . . they allow for more open, active parent involvement, are less costly, are easier to arrange and conduct, and are usually more productive. (*Federal Register*, 57[208], p. 48699)

- Nonessential and nonproductive "professionalism" should be eliminated from the session. In particular, an informal and friendly conference style can most effectively create an atmosphere of warmth for parents and a willingness to form partnerships.

- Parents should be encouraged to bring a friend or confidant to the conference, particularly someone who is familiar with the IEP process.

- Parents should have at least one professional at the conference with whom they are familiar and to whom they can relate. It is simply unrealistic to assume that parents can enter a group of professional strangers, without the benefit of at least one previously established relationship, and function as a contributing and collaborative member of an IEP team.

The mother of a recently identified child with mental retardation reported that she felt the same anxiety at entering her son's IEP conference as she did walking into her dentist's office. She described being particularly overwhelmed at "entering a roomful of strangers who knew more about Arnie than I did." Although she acknowledged that periodically someone would ask for her opinion, she reported feeling too intimidated to respond, "even though later on I wish I had since I knew some things they didn't." This mother later said, "If I had just known someone at the meeting or if I had someone to go with me, I wouldn't have felt so scared."

THE NEED FOR TRAINING. In order for parents to be meaningful and collaborative IEP conference participants, they must receive appropriate training. As suggested earlier, it is extremely unrealistic to assume that parents of children with exceptionalities can function in a productive manner with professionals when developing an IEP for their child if they lack adequate training and experience. The National Education Association (1978) has endorsed the need for this type of systematic training, noting that only with such instruction could parents be expected to fulfill their responsibilities.

Simpson and Fiedler (1989) have recommended systematically training parents to fulfill their roles and responsibilities associated with IEP involvement as well as training professionals to involve parents as collaborative partners. These investigations also suggested specific procedures for facilitating the participation and collaboration of parents in IEP conferences. As noted by McAfee and Vergason (1979), "the issue is not whether parents should be involved, nor the extent of involvement, but rather how the situation can be structured to best utilize parents in efforts to maximize the educational achievement of children" (p. 4). These efforts must include planned and sequenced parental training activities.

Individualized Family Service Plans (IFSPs)

PL 99-457 requires an Individualized Family Service Plan (IFSP) for infants and young children with exceptionalities. These plans, which resemble IEPs in many ways, are designed to identify and structure services for young children and their families. Thus, PL 99-457 explicitly recognizes the importance of parent and family involvement, and calls for a blueprint for addressing both childrens' and families' needs.

Components of IFSPs include the child's developmental functioning level and skills; the expected outcomes for the child, including procedures, criteria, and an evaluation timeline; services needed to meet the child's and family's special needs; and dates for service initiation. In addition, IFSPs require an identification of the family's strengths and needs relative to responding to their young child's special needs, the name of the parent liaison who will manage the IFSP, and a transition plan.

Involvement of Parents in Their Children's Education

The Individuals with Disabilities Education Act guarantees not only the right to a free and appropriate education for all children with exceptionalities, it also ensures the involvement of parents in decision making, educational planning, and implementation. This mandated policy of parent involvement represents a radical departure from past practices. Historically parents and families often have been blamed for their children's exceptionalities and educational problems, and isolated from professional decision making concerning their disabled children. In contrast, the Individuals with Disabilities Education Act allows and encourages parent involvement in educational matters that affect their children. Thus, through the IDEA, parents have participatory rights with regard to their children's education—rights that schools and agencies have never before had to respect. Moreover, parents currently have significant opportunities to collaborate and form partnerships with professionals.

It should be obvious that mandated parent involvement is not sufficient to establish and maintain a productive professional-family relationship. That is, trust, rapport, and similar interpersonal ingredients form the true basis for effective relationships. Yet, it is indisputable that the Individuals with Disabilities Education Act provides a legislative structure for the meaningful and collaborative involvement of parents, families, and professionals.

Summary

For decades parents were required to shoulder the task of raising and educating their children with exceptionalities alone. Presently, however, both parents and professionals are assisted in their common task of providing appropriate services to children and youth with exceptionalities by a series of laws, legislative positions, and court decrees. However, these elements serve as nothing more than tools and, as such, must be employed to facilitate the development of services and programs for children and youth with exceptionalities. This process, if it is to be successful, cannot derive exclusively from litigation contingencies but rather from a partnership in which parents and educators collaborate for the common good of children. Accordingly, procedures guaranteeing mere minimal legislative compliance will not be sufficient in and of themselves to produce desired results. Without an emphasis on the development of parent-educator relationships, the level and quality of involvement necessary to ensure the educational gains possible for every pupil will not be achieved.

Exercises

1. Prepare a handbook on the Individuals with Disabilities Education Act for parents and family members of the children in your classroom.

2. Prepare a list of procedures that you could use in training parents to serve more effectively as advocates for their children and in becoming more collaboratively involved in IEP conferences.

3. Conduct a simulated due process hearing.

4. Conduct a simulated IEP conference using the role-playing materials provided in Appendix B. Because these simulation scripts are extensions of those presented for the initial contact conference simulation exercise, you should continue with the same materials (i.e., students with mental retardation, physical disabilities, learning disabilities, behavioral disorders, or giftedness). In conducting this exercise, one individual should assume the part of the parent. Another person, taking the part of the teacher, should structure his or her responses around the educator materials. These materials, although in need of refinement and expansion, will serve to structure the content of the conference. Although individuals assuming the parent's role have not been provided script materials, they should participate in the conference by reacting to IEP suggestions made by the teacher and by using the simulation materials provided for the initial conference exercise (Appendix A). A third individual should assume the role of evaluator, using the evaluation form provided.

As a part of the session, educators should complete the IEP form that has been provided. Individuals should change roles after completing the exercise.

Chapter 10

Training Parents and Family Members to Be Treatment and Intervention Agents

T he process of helping the parents and families of children and youth with exceptionalities to effectively serve their own children requires instruction in basic behavioral change strategies and home tutoring methods. Such an approach allows parents to effect planned behavioral and academic changes in the natural environment, thereby extending the influence of professionals beyond the classroom setting. Target behaviors include those occurring exclusively in the home setting and problem behaviors occurring both in the home and school environments. Such home-school collaboration is a significant means of involving parents and family members in the management of behavior concerns as well as in academic remediation or acceleration programs.

Historical Perspective and Overview of Issues

Ample empirical documentation exists to show that the parent-child relationship affects behavior (Harlow, 1958; Kauffman, 1977; Quay & Werry, 1972). Consequently, it is not surprising that professionals have attempted to influence the social and academic behavior of children through work with parents and families. However, historically parents and family members have not received the training necessary to effectively apply therapeutic and educational strategies with their own children. Rather, a counseling model was predominantly used with parents and families; that is, attempts were made to facilitate the development and progress of children through counseling or therapy with parents. As a result, parents were not only denied access to strategies and procedures that would allow them to become collaborative members of a "therapeutic alliance" (Berkowitz & Graziano, 1972), but many became the object of therapists' crafts (i.e., were thought to be in need of treatment themselves). In some instances, this approach was supposed to uncover factors associated with developmental and school-related difficulties through an analysis of the parent-child relationship. Because for many years teachers and most school personnel were not trained to provide therapy for parents and families, few problem-solving procedures involving parents and family members were employed in school environments. Almost without exception, parents and family members were not perceived as resources who could augment school-applied procedures.

This traditional perspective has undergone significant change in recent years, and with increasing regularity parents and family members now are being trained to use problem-solving procedures with their own children in natural environments.

Use of Behavioral Intervention Strategies by Parents and Families

One of the most prominent and efficacious problem-solving alternatives available to parents and family members derives from behavioral technology. This approach, which applies experimental analysis strategies to specific human behaviors, is based on the assumption that parents and family members should have an opportunity to assume active roles in the intervention programs implemented with their children rather than being passive onlookers.

The procedures associated with behavioral interventions are designed to focus on observable and measurable behaviors. As used in the model, behavior refers to any observable and external response (Sulzer-Azaroff & Mayer, 1977), and behavioral interventions assume that children's operant responses can be controlled through systematic application of learning theory principles. Further, because the model assumes that behavioral principles can be taught to parents and family members and that "problem behaviors" represent inadequate or incorrect learning (rather than underlying pathology on the part of the parent or child), parents and family members can be taught ways of teaching their offspring to make more appropriate and developmentally mature responses. Thus, the behavioral model, in the present context, assumes that parents and family members will function in a systematically designed training role with their own children.

Behavior management techniques are designed to modify the frequency, rate, duration, or intensity of a specific behavior through the systematic application of learning theory principles. The selection of appropriate *observable* and *overt* behaviors is a basic concept in behavior modification. For example, if the parents of a child were directed to apply behavioral principles to increase their son's "actualization of potentiality," it undoubtedly would be extremely difficult not only to obtain agreement among independent observers on the frequency, rate, intensity, or duration of the behavior, but also on the effectiveness of any intervention procedure applied. However, although it is very difficult to define and measure "actualization of potential," the parents could be instructed in how to precisely determine the number of minutes their child studied at home each evening. Only with such precision can the techniques associated with behavioral interventions be utilized effectively. The emphasis on overt behaviors enables the person devising a program to eliminate not only unobservable behaviors and processes but also indirect intervention approaches. Thus, from a behavioral position one could argue that a child's lack of social interest does not necessarily indicate a "personality" problem or some other equally unobservable problem; any intervention procedure that might be implemented would focus on training the child in more appropriate and useful interpersonal skills rather than attempting to remediate a "defective personality." Thus, although a child's personality might improve as a function of an intervention procedure, the intervention would be designed to directly modify some observable and measurable behavior.

Behaviorists assume that the observable environmental events that precede and follow a response are the agents responsible for a given behavior, and that systematic manipulation of these factors will be associated with predictable changes in behavior. Therefore, the procedures associated with behavior modification are of such nature that parents and other laypersons can learn how to apply them, thereby extending the treatment process to the natural home setting. Traditional therapeutic approaches, on the other hand, focus on more unobservable variables and intervention techniques that, in addition to being difficult to evaluate, cannot easily be transmitted and applied by parents and families, who have extensive contact with the individual of concern in the natural environment.

One additional benefit to the behavioral approach is its wide applicability. Even though up to about 15% of all children and youth may be considered *exceptional*, one should not interpret this to mean the remainder do not have intervention needs or problems. Obviously, the parents of even the most well-adjusted child would acknowledge that management, structuring, and tutoring techniques are needed from time to time. Consequently, because of the complexity of child development and child rearing, parents and family members at some point will be faced with tasks for which they have little or no preparation. The techniques associated with applied behavior analysis and behavior modification are appealing and rewarding to parents and families because of their effectiveness and relative ease of use. In addition, behavioral interventions do not automatically assume abnormality and, therefore, avoid "labeling" individuals with whom the technique is used. Because behavioral principles assume that all maladaptive behaviors are governed by the same laws that govern adaptive behavior, no attempt is made to differentiate between "normality" and "abnormality." Rather, behaviors are evaluated relative to their own unique adaptiveness, and techniques are differentially developed for behaviors deemed to be maladaptive.

Parent- and Family-Applied Tutoring Programs

Evidence continues to mount showing that parents and family members can promote and augment specific academic skill development with exceptional children, thereby underscoring the importance of their involvement in children's educational programs (Duvall, 1987; Greenwood, Whorton, & Delquadri, 1984; Van Reusen, Bos, Schumaker, & Deshler, 1994). An underlying assumption for such involvement is that "active" student responses (e.g., writing, task participation, oral reading) are more functional than passive ones (e.g., listening to a lecture). As a result, providing numerous opportunities to respond in a variety of settings (i.e., home, school) becomes critical for mastery.

Instructional systems designed to increase active academic participation not only give students higher rates of academic responding via direct ecobehavioral assessment, these rates also correlate with higher academic achievement on criterion-referenced and standardized measures (Barbetta & Heron, 1991; Cronin, Slade, Bechtel, & Anderson, 1992; Greenwood, Whorton, & Delquadri, 1984; Delquadri, Greenwood, Whorton, Carta, & Hall, 1986). Parent and family member application of home tutoring programs is an effective means of increasing children's opportunities to practice and learn (Greenwood, Delquadri, & Hall, 1984).

As previously noted, individualized parent and family involvement programs tend to be most effective (Harry, Allen, & McLaughlin, 1995). Not every parent or family member of a child or adolescent with an exceptionality is interested or effective for conducting a home tutoring program, but when they do have the interest and aptitude, tutoring programs are invaluable. Thurston (1977) demonstrated that parents can be trained to carry out specific tutoring procedures that positively affect their children's reading skills. Similarly, Keele and Harrison (1977) observed that structured tutoring "is an effective avenue for providing reading readiness skills for kindergarten children and remedial work for first grade children who have not mastered certain prerequisites" (p. 18). Finally, the generalization benefits of home tutoring programs also have been noted (Baer & Guess, 1971; Christenson & Cleary, 1990; Robinson & Fine, 1994; Strain, Cooke, & Apolloni, 1976).

Regardless of the technology employed or the orientation favored, the rationale for using parents and family members as planned facilitators of academic and social change must be addressed. One justification relates to the paramount role parents play in child development. Indeed, parents and family members exert the most significant influence in a child's life, especially during the formative years. In addition to concurring with the numerous benefits in relying on parents as a valuable resource, O'Dell (1974) suggested training them to use a learning theory approach. O'Dell noted a number of advantages to this strategy: (a) behavior modification techniques can be transmitted to individuals with little or no knowledge of traditional therapeutic procedures; (b) behavior modification is an orderly and empirically based model; (c) groups of individuals can be trained in the technology of behavior modification simultaneously; (d) individuals can be trained to use the procedures in a relatively short period of time; (e) the procedures allow for maximum use of professional staff talent; (f) the model does not assume "sickness" as the basis for the problem; (g) a majority of childhood behavior problems are responsive to the approach; and (h) a behavioral approach allows for treatment in the natural environment by the individuals who routinely experience the problem. As a further argument for developing parent-implemented behavioral programs, O'Dell recommended that

> parents must become involved if effective preventive mental health programs hope to meet the demand for professional services. Also, parent training follows the growing trend toward working in the natural environment and behavior modification offers a relatively easily learned and empirically derived set of concepts for such a parent training model. (1974, p. 419)

Williams (1959) was among the first to report parents' use of a simple extinction procedure to eliminate bedtime tantruming in a 21-month-old child. The parents achieved cessation of bedtime crying in a relatively short period of time and the problem behavior did not reappear. Although not extraordinary in its methodology or results, this study demonstrated that parents could be taught to effectively utilize behavior modification procedures in a natural environment. Thus, in essence it initiated an era of parent and family participation in the training of their own children. Since Williams's study, innumerable other research reports have unequivocally demonstrated the efficacy of employing parents and family members as behavioral change agents (e.g., Arndorfer, Miltenberger, Woster, Rortvedt, & Gaffney, 1994; Bernal, Williams, Miller, & Reagor, 1972; Christophersen, Arnold, Hill, & Quilitch, 1972; Fox & Savelle, 1987).

Even though behavior and academic change principles are empirically derived and highly efficacious, their ultimate success rests on the skill of the individuals using them. Thus, even the most efficient and well-planned parent and family program must be implemented correctly in order to produce change. As a means of isolating factors that may be correlated with successful parent- and family-applied programs, several researchers have evaluated the characteristics of those involved. Using a direct teaching format rather than a lecture or reading approach, Mira (1970) failed to find a relationship between parents' intellectual abilities, education, and socioeconomic status and their ability to employ behavior modification procedures. Others (Patterson, Cobb, & Ray, 1972), however, have suggested that parents of lower socioeconomic status without formal education are difficult to instruct. Likewise, poorly functioning families, those lacking in cooperation, and individuals evidencing psychopathology have proved poorer candidates for the role of change agent than parents and families without such problems (Bernal et al., 1972; Ehly, Conoley, & Rosenthal, 1985; Patterson, 1965).

Data suggest that when appropriately trained, motivated parents and family members can be effective in the role of change agent (Simpson & Carter, 1993). Further, academic progress can be facilitated when parents, family members, and educators work in concert to achieve specific school goals (Adelman, 1994). Finally, when parents and family members are trained to manage maladaptive behavior in the environment in which the response is manifested, the greatest degree of success and generalization will be realized. As suggested by Ross (1972),

> If behavior is to be modified, the modification must take place when and where the behavior manifests itself. This is rarely the therapist's consult-

ing room, and as a consequence, behavior therapists working with children frequently find themselves working through the adults who are in a position to be present when the target behavior takes place, and who have control over the contingencies of reinforcement. (p. 919)

A word of caution: Where a problem is manifested and where the intervention is applied relate directly to problem ownership and the level of anticipated parent/family and educator involvement. That is, some parents and family members may have limited motivation to participate in solving an academic problem that occurs exclusively in the classroom. Likewise, educators may be uninterested in serving as a resource for behavior problems that take place at a baby-sitter's or at Sunday school. As a result of these factors, the primary responsibility for problems and their solutions must be determined. And as suggested by Gordon (1970) and Kroth (1985), until the ownership for a problem has been identified, proposed problem-solving strategies will prove ineffective. Thus, until the parents and educators can agree on the nature of a given problem as well as the person most responsible for its occurrence and solution, interventions cannot be expected to show progress.

Thus, because the success of any change program is a function of both the skill with which the various components are implemented and the motivation of the participants, the anticipated levels of motivation and responsibility on the part of the individuals involved must be considered carefully. In particular, the models presented in the sections that follow are most appropriate for problems that occur in home environments or settings where parents and family members are most apt to be responsible or motivated to bring about changes; therefore, these procedures should be applied only when parents and family members will assume at least partial problem ownership and intervention responsibility.

Parents and Families as Behavioral Change Agents

As noted in the procedural flow depicted in Table 10.1, a successful behavior management program cannot be developed and implemented in a single conference session. The model is time sequenced for procedural objectives and activities. In addition, the process assumes that individuals who utilize these procedures have a basic working knowledge of operant conditioning and applied behavior analysis procedures. Individuals who

Table 10.1. Parent- and Family-Applied Behavioral Intervention Training Procedures

Procedural Steps	Specific Activities
Session 1	
Identify and operationally define the most significant problem response.	List and operationally define the parents'/families' concerns about specific problem behaviors shown by the child.
	Prioritize parent/family concerns.
	Identify the child's adaptive, positive, and desirable behaviors.
	Select one problem behavior for modification, choosing a behavior for which success is probable.
Identify those environments and situations in which the target behavior most frequently occurs, and a functional analysis of the response.	Determine the individuals, situations, times, and circumstances surrounding the occurrence of the problem behavior, and identify possible variables and factors that may be affecting or controlling the behavior.
Identify contingencies that operate to support the target behavior.	Determine the responses of the parents, family members, and others in the environment following the emission of the target response.
Train parents and family members to identify, observe, and record the target behavior.	Identify and demonstrate simple observation and recording procedures to the parents/family.
	Aid the parents/family in applying these systems in order to evaluate the target behavior in the home environment.
	Train parents/family in procedures to establish reliability.
	Make adjustments in the observation and recording systems based on feedback from the parents/family.
Session 2	
Train the parents/family to chart and inspect the target behavior data.	Train parents/family to use simple visual displays to chart the target behavior.

(*continues*)

Table 10.1. *Continued*

Procedural Steps	Specific Activities
	Train parents/family to record daily observations on the chart.
	Train parents/family to inspect the baseline data for variability and trend.
Establish intervention procedures and performance goals.	Select with the parents/family appropriate consequences for modifying the target behavior. Intervention procedures should be positive (if possible), practical, economical, simple, and realistic.
	Establish appropriate outcomes.
	Train parents and family members to apply the intervention program in the home, employing the behavioral principles of consistency, constancy, and immediacy.
	Train parents/family to continue observing, recording, charting, and analyzing the target behavior after the intervention procedures have been applied.
Session 3 and Subsequent Meetings	
Show parents/family methods of analyzing and interpreting data relative to the target behavior.	Aid parents and family members in inspecting and analyzing the data with respect to desired outcomes.
Make changes in recording, charting, and intervention procedures, as needed.	Implement program modifications, as needed.
Encourage parents/family to maintain contact with the behavioral conferencer and to apply the same model with other behaviors.	Adopt a follow-up schedule for parents and family members to use in reporting the success of the home-based program.
	Encourage parents and family members to apply the general model techniques with other problems.

do not meet this basic criterion are encouraged to supplement this outline with basic behavioral information.

Session 1 Procedures

Identify and operationally define a behavior of concern. An initial step in establishing a parent/family coordinated behavior management program consists of soliciting a statement of concern from parents/family members specifically related to those behaviors they consider most in need of change. This basic step is contingent upon parent and/or family motivation and at least partial acceptance of ownership for the problem. Accordingly, the educational conferencer cannot expect parents and families to identify "problem behaviors" they do not perceive as problems in the home setting or to accept ownership of problems that occur exclusively in the classroom.

Even though applied behavior analysis principles are characterized by versatility and adaptiveness, they are most effective when observable and measurable responses can be pinpointed. Furthermore, the response selected for modification must be defined in such a fashion that it allows the individuals involved with the child to perceive the behavior in an identical manner. For example, *hyperactivity* to one parent may consist of crying, screaming, and distractability, while to another it may mean primarily failing to complete homework assignments. Consequently, it is essential to the success of any applied behavior analysis program that each participant be trained to observe the target behavior in the same way.

In addition to determining that the target behavior is observable, measurable, and defined in such a manner as to allow for reliability, the educator implementing an applied behavior analysis program must solicit other basic information from the parents/family. First, he or she must determine whether the pinpointed behavior is under the child's control. Behaviors such as "taking out the trash," "fighting," and "studying" are typically under a child's control, while parasympathethic functions such as sweating, breathing, and salivating lie beyond a child's influence. In most instances, the process of determining whether a behavior is under an individual's control, and then selecting the type of behavior analysis procedure to employ, consists of establishing whether the problem behavior follows or precedes a controlling environmental stimulus.

Respondent behavior (classical conditioning) is a response elicited by a stimulus. That is, the presentation of a particular stimulus event will provoke a response. Respondent behavior typically includes involuntary responses such as those involving the smooth muscles or glands of the body (e.g., a child sweating profusely and becoming agitated when his father calls him for dinner). Thus, a respondent behavior is typically a function of a stimulus event that occurs prior to a response. *Operant behaviors*, in contrast, are a consequence of the stimulus events that follow them. Operant responses are under voluntary control and are frequently maintained by the environmental events that follow them. The behavioral counselor must be able to discriminate between a respondent and operant behavior because the change process involves understanding the controlling environmental stimuli. Although one can employ behavioral principles with respondent-type behaviors, the most efficacious use of the principles for most parent counselors will occur with operant responses. Consequently, in the discussion that follows, primary attention will focus on using the model with operant behaviors.

Applied behavioral analysis and intervention techniques are designed for use with responses that contain movement. Therefore, the parent/family counselor employing a behavioral strategy should determine, through either interviewing or direct observation, whether or not the proposed target behavior contains movement. For example, parents can be trained to see a child wash the dinner dishes or hit a sibling. In contrast, behaviors with minimal movements are difficult to analyze. Daydreaming, for example, would typically not be as acceptable a choice of target behavior as a response containing more visible movement.

An additional consideration relative to selecting an appropriate target behavior concerns whether the response selected for modification is repeatable. Although the family of a child who engages in severe temper tantrums may wish to modify this response, if the behavior occurs only once per month it is a poor choice for a formal applied behavior analysis program.

Prior to developing a parent-applied behavioral intervention program, the conferencer should also determine whether the response selected for change has a definite starting and stopping point. For most efficient management, a target behavior should have a definitive cycle of repeatable movement. For parents and families to accurately measure a behavior, it should consist of a relatively short cycle with both a clear starting and stopping point. Completing an assigned task or throwing objects, for example, both possess such cyclical characteristics. Sleeping, on the other hand, has relatively obscure starting and stopping points. In addition, it involves a cycle far too long for most parents and family members to measure accurately.

A major task of the parent/family counselor consists of translating into operational definitions the concerns parents and family members have about their child's behavior, and thus establishing targets for modification. Typically, parents and family find it reasonably easy to list these behaviors if the task has been adequately explained and if they are motivated to effect change. The educational counselor may discover that some parents and family can identify only one behavior in need of change. When this is the case and if the response appears appropriate for modification via an applied behavioral analysis and intervention approach, the single target behavior will suffice. This limiting process makes the establishment of priorities for change an easy matter. Even when a number of "problem responses" are generated, parents and families will often have fixed in their own minds a priority problem most in need of modification.

In situations where a problem response occurs exclusively in a school environment but parents and families are involved in the management process (e.g., home reinforcement for acceptable school behavior), the conferencer is responsible for operationally defining the behavior. The procedures defined for aiding parents/families in identifying a behavior are followed.

The importance of asking parents/families to focus on their child's positive or adaptive behaviors cannot be overemphasized. This tactic can provide a perspective to the family regarding their child's overall behavior pattern. For example, it is not unusual for a single behavioral excess or deficit to generalize in the minds of the parents to the extent that they perceive the youngster as demonstrating virtually no positive qualities. Statements such as "He always causes problems at home—he just can't seem to do anything right" are common. However, the process of pinpointing a behavioral excess or deficit for modification coupled with an analysis of a child's strengths places the complaint in proper perspective. Identifying a child's strengths may construct the one positively oriented component of an otherwise "problem oriented" model, thus making it an extremely significant program feature and one that should not be underestimated.

In addition to careful consideration of the motivation and interests of parents and family members in selecting a target behavior for modification, care must be taken in selecting a response with which success is a possibility. Especially in programs designed for children with exceptionalities, one should not initially select behaviors that have totally resisted other treatments. Although professionals must be responsive to the goals of parents and families in applying the technology, they must also be aware that when success is forthcoming, it tends to bolster the implementer's confidence and make it possible to successfully intervene with other more difficult problems. Thus, even though the parents of a 10-year-old non-verbal child with autism might want their son to talk, this immediate outcome would probably be a poor choice for an initial target behavior. After the counselor has established his or her personal validity and the validity of the proposed procedures, and after the parents have determined their own ability for successful intervention, more difficult problem responses can be considered.

Identify environments and situations where the target behavior occurs, and conduct a functional analysis of factors that may affect or control the target behavior. In addition to identifying an appropriate target behavior for change, the behavioral conferencer must seek information about the environments and circumstances surrounding the occurrence of the response. Although frequently overlooked, it is crucial to gain an understanding of the relationship of the environment to the response, including whether the response is generalized across settings or is environmentally specific. As noted by Bersoff and Grieger (1971), "obtaining knowledge about environments and situations in which the behavior appears is a necessity" (p. 487).

The behavioral conferencer must also determine which individuals are most frequently in contact with the child when the problem response appears. In just a few instances will the response pattern be independent of the individuals involved, hence the importance of understanding this factor. As observed by Bandura (1969), "under naturalistic conditions behavior is generally regulated by the characteristics of persons toward whom responses are directed, the social setting, temporal factors, and a host of verbal and symbolic cues that signify predictable response consequences" (p. 25).

Environmental and situational factors also aid in determining the appropriateness of a behavior management strategy. That is, in the course of obtaining information about the environments and situations surrounding the problem, the conferencer may conclude that a given behavioral strategy is not appropriate and that other solutions should be considered. For example, a student's mother requested an appointment with his classroom teacher to discuss "problems" she was having at home in controlling his behavior. Discussing the circumstances surrounding the situations revealed that the problem ("antisocial behavior") occurred only when the child was at the sitter's during a 2-hour period in the late afternoon. Further discussion revealed that the sitter frequently abandoned the child during the time he should have been under her care, and that the "antisocial" act consisted of "wandering around" an adjacent neighborhood. On the basis of this information, the teacher suggested engaging another baby-sitter instead of developing a behavior modification program.

Behavioral engineers are increasingly recognizing the importance of conducting a functional analysis of problem behaviors (Cooper, Wacker, Sasso, Reimers, & Donn, 1990), and the significance of this preintervention component of the behavioral model must not be minimized. As suggested by Arndorfer et al. (1994),

> Without a functional assessment of the variables controlling problem behaviors, researchers may be more likely to rely on aversive and restrictive procedures and less likely to teach functionally equivalent behaviors or implement other educative or proactive interventions. (p. 65)

Identify factors that may be operating to support the target behavior. According to the tenets of operant conditioning, both adaptive and maladaptive behaviors are controlled by environmental conditions (Bandura, 1969). Consequently, one must assume that a problem behavior occurring in or around the home environment is a function of existing stimulus conditions or related factors there. Thus, a preintervention functional analysis should include gaining an understanding of those variables associated with the maintenance of the problem response, or understanding the results of a child engaging in a particular undesired response. For example, a youth with a severe disability may engage in a particular aberrant response because he lacks a way of communicating his needs.

Although an easy strategy for interpreting and understanding the effects of behavior is not forthcoming, an attempt should be made to identify significant variables correlated with the occurrence of a target response. Specifically, the major factors of concern include (a) the discriminative stimulus or environmental circumstance that alerts the subject to the fact that conditions are correct for a particular response, (b) the operant response itself, (c) the reinforcing or consequent stimulus, and (d) the results or effects of a response (i.e., what the child is getting or trying to get out of the effort). In this paradigm, and in the successful construction of a parent-applied behavioral intervention program, operant responses are a function of their consequences or communicative intent. Therefore, understanding and modifying variables that control behaviors, and implementing proactive programs based on these findings that assist students in meeting their needs, are essential.

As behavioral interventions may involve manipulation of conse-quences and antecedent conditions, the goal here is to solicit information from parents and family members about what happens prior to and imme-diately after the occurrence of the target behavior. The following types of questions are useful in this respect: "What happens right before he tantrums?" "What happens right after the tantrum starts and ends?" "How do others in the family respond to the tantruming?" and "What does she get from her tantrum?" Bersoff and Grieger (1971) also suggested that con-ferencers focus on the interactions that take place between the parents and child, the parents' perception of these interactions, the punishment tactics employed by the parents, and the manner in which expectations, praise, and punishment are presented to the child by his or her parents.

Train parents to identify, observe, and record the target behavior. In keep-ing with standard behavior management procedures, parents/families should be instructed to employ simple measurement and evaluation proce-dures (Simpson & Poplin, 1981). Even though some parents and family members may appear threatened and overwhelmed by this seemingly diffi-cult task, the conferencer should be able to quell such anxiety. To this end, he or she can inform parents and others of the importance of accurate behavioral measurements, pointing out that this feature is an integral and basic element of successfully employing the system (Phillips, 1978). One can typically convince parents and family members being counseled in the use of behavior management to participate in the measurement process by stressing that only through measurement can a thorough analysis of the behavioral excess or deficit and its antecedent and consequent events be gained. Besides, without such exact observation and recording activities, the team cannot determine whether the contingencies being manipulated are having the desired results.

The second prerequisite for achieving measurement compliance relates to ensuring that participating parents/family members are knowledgeable about the measurement process to be used. Thus, carefully considered expla-nations, programming, and modeling must accompany each set of proce-dures. Only when parents and family members have received proper instruction can competence be assumed. Because the remaining compo-nents of the model hinge on successful measurement, it is essential that appropriate attention be given to this aspect of the overall methodology.

Almost without exception parents and others should be advised to use observational recording techniques. Hall (1970) identified five varieties of observational recordings, all of which can be employed by parents: con-tinuous, event, duration, interval, and time sample recordings.

Continuous measurements (anecdotal records) involve recording the various responses manifested by a child over a given period of time. Although this procedure allows the parents/family an opportunity to record a variety of behaviors, it lacks reliability and requires great investment of resources that may not be available to families. Besides, this recording technique would rarely be the most useful alternative for parents and families being counseled in the use of behavior management methodology.

Event-recording techniques, on the other hand, are typically very functional for parent and family use. These procedures consist of making a cumulative account of specific behavioral events. For example, parents can use an event-recording system to note the number of times a child follows commands or the frequency of one child kicking another. In addition to being relatively easy for parents and family members to understand, event-recording systems are highly adaptable to a variety of target behaviors.

Duration recording, another observational system appropriate for parent and family use, involves calculating the amount of time a child engages in a particular behavior. This alternative is most preferable when the length of time a given behavior occurs is considered the most significant response descriptor. For example, the amount of time children engage in tantruming is often a far more accurate descriptor of their behavior than the frequency with which the behavior occurs.

Interval-recording systems involve dividing a predetermined observation period into equal time segments. Parents and families who use this procedure should be advised to record whether the target response occurs during each interval. Although this recording technique requires the undivided attention of the observer, it offers the advantages of allowing the person to observe more than a single target behavior.

Time sampling, although similar to interval recording, offers the advantage of not requiring continuous observations. Parents and/or family members are trained to determine whether or not the child being observed is engaging in the target behavior at the end of a specific time interval. For example, a child's study behavior might be observed by his parents for one hour, with recordings made at the end of each 5-minute period. Every 5 minutes the parent or family member would observe whether or not the child was studying. This procedure is efficient as it generates a significant amount of data while allowing the parents to carry on other activities.

Regardless of which measurement alternative the behavioral counselor selects, it is essential that parents and families have collaborative input into its selection and a thorough working knowledge of its use. Thus, rather than advising parents and family members to "record the number of times John refuses to comply with a request you make," one must provide more precise instruction, including a statement of the specific time period during the day when the measurement will occur, and the specific procedure (tally sheet, golf counter, kitchen timer, stopwatch, etc.) for measuring and recording. Further, parents should be instrumental in determining which measurement approach would be easiest for them to integrate into their lifestyle. This collaborative process should result in clear and concise agreed-upon procedures, including a written product for the parents or others to use as a reference.

During this initial conference, the behavioral engineer should also provide the parents/families with a format for recording the target behavior. Because graphing and charting procedures should be pursued during the second conference, this format can, and should, be as simple as possible. (A sample format appears in Figure 10.1.) The baseline observation should be structured such that it can be completed within 5 to 7 days. Fewer observation days will provide a less than adequate picture of the response, whereas longer baselines may endanger parents' willingness to participate in the program.

Although reliability procedures offer an excellent addition to the behavioral system, this component is not as imperative. That is, if obtaining reliability data appears to present a problem, it may be eliminated. Even though a major advantage of the reliability process is allowing for the active participation of more than one family member, it should not become a deterrent to overall program participation.

Finally, during the baseline period, parents and family should be able to consult freely with the behavioral engineer. At a minimum, the conferencer should make at least one phone contact. In addition, parents and family members must feel free to contact the educator if problems or questions arise.

Each of the steps involved in developing a successful parent/family-applied behavior management program is critical; however, the importance of a successful first session is paramount. Specifically, the majority of "failures" can be traced to procedural problems in the initial behavioral planning session. If the behavioral engineer can successfully establish his or her own validity and the validity of the program, select an appropriate target behavior for management, accurately analyze the environments, situations, and variables surrounding the response, and obtain measurement data from the parents/family, the overall success of the program is greatly enhanced. Again, one essential ingredient in the process consists of convincing the parents/family to follow through with each component of the program.

Child's Name _____

Observer's Name _____

_____

Target Behavior _____

Operational Definition of Behavior _____

_____

_____

Time of Observation _____

Date	Frequency or Duration	Comments
_____	_____	_____
_____	_____	_____
_____	_____	_____
_____	_____	_____

Figure 10.1. Sample recording form.

Session 2 Procedures

Train parents and family members to chart and analyze the behavioral data.
One of the initial tasks in the second session of the behavioral intervention training sequence will be to demonstrate graphing and charting procedures. Prior to meeting with the parents/family, the educator should construct a demonstration graph similar to the one shown in Figure 10.2. As illustrated, all components should be labeled and completed except the actual data points.

By using a form similar to the one shown, the behavioral engineer can demonstrate how data points are inserted and connected. The same train-

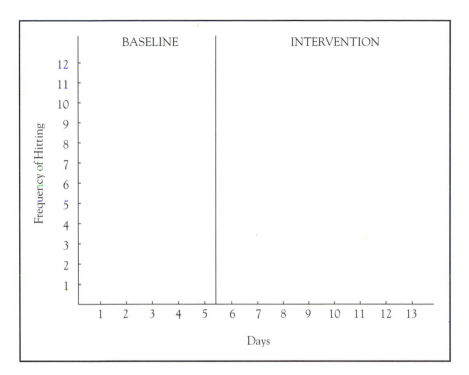

Figure 10.2. Demonstration graph form.

ing format can be used to train the charting procedures for the remainder of the program. The use of modeling and tangible products makes charting and graphing relatively simple to teach.

During the same training session the behavioral engineer should acquaint parents and family members with the information that is ultimately derived from the baseline data and how these data will be compared with subsequent measures. Finally, the behavioral engineer should apprise the parents and family of concepts related to baseline trend and variability. The extent to which this information is conveyed is, in large measure, a function of the interest and abilities of parents and family members.

Establish and implement intervention procedures and performance goals. Parents and families involved in applied behavior analysis programs with their own children are confronted with target behaviors that can be classified as either behavioral excesses or deficits. That is, parents and family members may consider their offspring lacking in a particular response, such as completing homework assignments or engaging in desirable social interactions with neighborhood children, or they may consider him or her excessive on some dimension of behavior. For example, parents may think that their child cries or quarrels too often or manifests an unnecessary level of some other behavior. Because of the nature of the model and the manner in which problem responses are operationally defined, behavioral principles are designed to either *increase* or *decrease* the occurrence of a *specific* behavior under *specific* conditions. This goal is accomplished via systematic manipulation of antecedent variables and consequences.

Operationally, an *operant reinforcer* is an environmental event that strengthens the behavior it follows (Skinner, 1953). A *punisher,* on the other hand, weakens the behavior it follows (Millenson, 1967). Hence, parents and family members must recognize that if an environmental event fails to change a behavior, it does not operationally qualify as a meaningful consequence, regardless of whether they or the parent counselor perceive it impressive. In addition, the only valid method of judging whether a stimulus event is effective consists of observing its influence on the behavior it follows. For that reason one should remind parents and families to continue the measurement procedures throughout the program as a means of determining the influence of a given consequence.

The selection of an effective consequence or antecedent condition is not an easy task. However, through functional assessment of the target behavior, including observing children and asking them about their preferences, potentially motivating reinforcers may be designed. Often parents and family members can accurately identify a number of potentially useful consequences. In other cases (Edlund, 1969; Homme, 1969), a reinforcement menu, or a listing of possible reinforcers from which a child can choose, is an excellent way to make available a variety of positive consequences.

Even though punishers and negative consequences may have some appeal, parents and family members should be encouraged to utilize positive strategies whenever possible. A number of researchers have demonstrated that parents and family members can be effective in modifying the behavior of their own children through reliance on positive reinforcement programs. Risley and Wolf (1966), for example, used shaping and reinforcement procedures to train an institutionalized child with severe emotional disturbance to engage in adaptive behaviors. After successful results had been achieved in a laboratory setting, the child was returned to the home environment, where the mother was instructed in applying the same behavioral techniques. This transfer of the intervention procedure to the home resulted in a significant increase in adaptive behavior. Hawkins, Peterson, Schweid, and Bijou (1966) trained mothers in procedures for interacting with their own children in the natural environment, resulting in improved interactions between the parents and children and generally improved child behavior.

Others (Haring & Phillips, 1962; Polsgrove, 1991; Reith & Hall, 1974) have engineered home reinforcement programs to increase desirable school behavior. Edlund (1969) reported that parents were able to promote desirable school behaviors by reinforcing their children for completing assignments and engaging in acceptable social behavior. Kroth, Whelan, and Stables (1970) also reported that they were able to accelerate academic and social progress in school by training parents to apply behavior change techniques in the home.

Parents and families have also successfully used token reinforcement programs with their own children. Specifically, they have been trained to reward desired behaviors with tokens that can be exchanged at a later time for a reinforcer. O'Leary, O'Leary, and Becker (1967) trained the parents of a 6-year-old aggressive child to effectively employ a token economy system. Initially the parents provided verbal praise and food reinforcement when their son and his brother were involved in cooperative play activities; later tokens exchangeable for reinforcers were successfully phased into the program. Within a relatively short time, the parents could independently employ all the procedures originally developed by the behavioral engineer. They reported that as a result of this program their son's behavior became more cooperative and his social skills began to improve.

Selection of an appropriate behavior consequence should hinge not only on an evaluation of the child but also on the needs and characteristics of the parents and family. That is, the intervention selected should be compatible with the parents' and family's demeanor, skills, and resources, based on collaborative parent/family input. In particular, consequences that are realistic, feasible, economical, and practical tend to be more effective. For instance, a couple had become extremely concerned about their 9-year-old son's nocturnal enuresis. The child, according to his parents, wet the bed at least five or six nights a week. During an informal conference the parents asked the boy's learning disabilities teacher for assistance, and she recommended they purchase a "P-P-Vigilante," a monitoring device designed to awaken youngsters when they begin to urinate. Unfortunately the device, which cost $589.00, was far beyond the financial means of the family.

As suggested in this example, a number of family-related factors must be considered when selecting an appropriate consequence, even though the child remains the most significant factor. As noted throughout this text, decisions should be made collaboratively whenever appropriate.

The agreed-upon experimental procedures should be communicated to parents/families in both oral and written form (Simpson & Regan, 1986). That is, rather than simply explaining to parents and families what to do, the educator should provide them with a plan sheet that details the procedures to follow. If parents or family members later forget or do not clearly understand particular segments of the spoken explanation, they will have access to a written procedural plan. An example of such a procedural plan sheet appears in Figure 10.3.

The first column, "Description of Program," is reserved for a general statement of the objectives of the project, including who will be responsible for carrying out the procedures, what times (hours) of the day the program will be in effect, where the program will be implemented (home, neighborhood, store, etc.), and the procedures that will be involved. The "Description of Target Behavior" column provides an operational definition of the target behavior. This description should be stated in such a fashion that the parents and family can easily comprehend it. In addition, the strategy to be used in measuring the target behavior should be briefly described here.

In the third column, "Procedures Prior to Observation of Target Behavior," one should describe any pertinent responses and structuring procedures, particularly those based on a functional analysis of the behavior. For example, if a parent-applied behavior management program is designed to decrease tantruming at bedtime, parents should receive specific instructions on how to structure conditions related to the target behavior. For instance, the parents should tell their child to prepare for bed at a certain time each evening. To be consistent with the intervention program, these instructions should be delivered in a systematic fashion. Likewise, if a program were established to increase compliance behavior, the conferencer should instruct parents in when and how to deliver commands. Although professionals are encouraged to be collaborative in their approach, they must also recognize that the technical aspects of most behavioral intervention programs will require direct instruction.

The fourth column, "Procedures Following Observation of Target Behavior," allows for a description, in specific and sequential fashion, of the consequences or procedures to apply when the target behavior occurs. This information must be communicated to parents/family in an easy-to-follow manner. Because the plan sheet is intended for the benefit of parents and family members, appropriate language should be used throughout.

The importance of preparing a written plan sheet for use by parents and family members cannot be overemphasized. This procedure provides a

Child's Name _Chuck Downs_

Parent's Name _Ms. Lois Topps_

Date Started _September, 1995_

Description of Program	Description of Target Behavior	Procedures Prior to Observation of Target Behavior	Procedures Following Observation of Target Behavior
The program is designed to reduce Chuck's tantruming. The program will be implemented at home on a daily basis at bedtime (8:30 p.m.). Chuck's mother and father will carry out all procedures.	Tantruming consists of severe crying, screaming, hand and leg flailing, and other out-of-control behavior, including jerky extensions of the body. Target behaviors will be observed daily at bedtime, at home, from 8:30 p.m. until 7:00 a.m. the following morning.	At 8:00 p.m. daily, Chuck will be told that he has to start getting ready for bed. Specifically, his mother will assist him in washing, brushing his teeth, and changing his clothes. She will also inform him that she will read to him until 8:30 p.m. after he has gotten into bed. At 8:30 p.m. the mother will inform Chuck that it is time for him to go to sleep, and then she will leave the room, closing his door as she departs.	Chuck's mother, along with other members of his family, will refrain from entering his bedroom (except for emergencies) after 8:30 p.m. Thus, regardless of Chuck's behavior, he will not be allowed to receive visitors, leave his room, or otherwise interact with family between 8:30 p.m. and 7:00 a.m. the following morning. The subsequent evenings during which Chuck does not tantrum, he will be provided special reinforcement by his mother and other family members (e.g., "I liked the way you quietly went to bed last night").

Figure 10.3. Procedural plan sheet.

basic way to reduce parents' and family members' uncertainty while increasing their faith and ability to collaborate in following the program, thus increasing the overall probability of success. Modeling, demonstration, and monitoring techniques should also be utilized to aid participants in implementing agreed-upon procedures. Hence, as a means of augmenting the verbal and written program instructions and avoiding misunderstandings, actual demonstration or modeling should be used.

The importance of this step was illustrated in the implementation of a parent-applied behavior management program with a 6-year-old boy with mental retardation. An intervention program had been designed to reduce the child's negativism. In particular, both parents had experienced difficulty in getting the child to obey their requests or commands, and hence they described him as "headstrong" and "set in his ways." Although expressive language was not his primary mode of communication, the youngster frequently did use phrases such as "no-no," "I won't," and "I can't."

In this case *negative behavior* was operationally defined as a refusal, either verbal or nonverbal, to obey a parental request or command. An event-recording procedure was employed to measure oppositional behavior daily between the hours of 2:00 to 4:00 p.m. and 6:30 to 8:30 p.m. Both observation and experimental procedures were carried out in the child's home. Baseline data indicated that the boy displayed an average of 21.85 specific instances of negative behavior per day (median 23). This measure was found to be fairly stable, although slightly ascending, during the 7 days of baseline.

Following baseline procedures, learning theory principles and procedures that had proved effective with other children in decreasing oppositional episodes were discussed with the parents. A two-point program of experimental procedures was agreed upon, with the goal of diminishing oppositional behavior: the parents agreed to eliminate attention for oppositional behavior, while introducing attention and social praise for cooperative behavior, and they agreed to place the child on a chair in a corner for 3 minutes immediately following each instance of oppositional behavior.

During the initial phases of the experimental procedures, the professional who collaborated with the parents in designing the program received several anxious phone calls from the mother. With each contact the mother appeared more upset and less sure of her ability to carry out the prescribed program. Supportive efforts proved only marginally successful. The child was described as "uncontrollable" when attempts were made to implement the time-out procedures. In addition, he was said to "kick the wall and me [mother]," "chew on his chair," and "scream" when placed in the corner. The mother also stated that only by physically holding her son could the procedure be implemented.

The child and his mother returned to the behavioral engineer's office for further instruction. Because specific instructions obviously were needed, a tele-coaching system was devised whereby the mother could follow verbal instructions via a radio and earplug that the child could not hear. The behavioral engineer stood on one side of a one-way mirror and made suggestions to the mother regarding what to say and do—when to reinforce, when to ignore, and when to implement time-out procedures. Comments included "Tell him that was very good," "Ignore that," and "Take him to the time-out chair now." After a single instruction period the mother commented that she felt much more knowledgeable of the intervention procedures.

Following this training session the number of negative episodes decreased significantly. Specifically, the mean number of oppositional incidents was reduced to 3 (median = 2). According to parental comments, the child became "much easier to live with." They also reported that he had begun to use expressive language more, arguing against requests rather than totally refusing. Although still negative, they considered this tactic more sophisticated than a mere "no."

Even though these procedures were time-consuming, the benefits were obvious. Although many parents and family members do not require such explicit training, most can benefit from behavioral demonstrations and modeling procedures. In all instances, the conferencer must ensure that parents and families are familiar with the procedures to be followed.

The conferencer must also play an active role in helping parents and families establish acceptable program goals and outcomes. Without this safeguard, the conferencer has a tenuous ethical basis for training parents and families to apply experimental procedures with their child. For example, the conferencer must not allow parents and families to indiscriminately determine that they will eliminate a behavior that is developmentally normal. Although it is important to make parents and families collaborative partners in developing their child's management program, such involvement must be carefully monitored by a professional.

Session 3 and Subsequent Meetings

Follow-up meetings are primarily designed (a) to assess the influence of program procedures, (b) to establish and modify performance goals, and (c) to make program changes. Although parents and families must have access to the behavioral engineer at other than established follow-up meeting times, most modifications will be made at these sessions.

The conferencer must be cautious when suggesting or supporting program changes. That is, consequences and antecedent modifications must be given ample opportunity for success. Though amendments should be made in instances where intervention programs lack efficacy, it is important that the process not involve capricious changes.

Finally, subsequent sessions must be structured so as to provide reinforcement for parent and family efforts. Because parents will be instrumental in determining the success of any program and their behavior will be a function of consequent stimuli (Skinner, 1953), positive feedback must be offered. This often neglected element is frequently the basis for successful program results.

Parents and Families as Academic Tutors

In this discussion and procedural outline of parent and family tutoring procedures, the term *academic* refers to more than traditional academics (e.g., reading, math, spelling). Within this section the term will refer to a variety of school-related activities, including prereadiness, readiness, independent living, self-help, prevocational, and so on. As with the application of behavioral intervention procedures, the proposed model here assumes that individuals utilizing it possess a working knowledge of applied behavior methods. Not every parent or family member of a child or adolescent with an exceptionality will make an acceptable tutor. Due to interest, time, motivation, temperament, skills, or other factors, some families and family members will not— or should not—serve as tutors. Thus, professionals must not aggressively pursue tutoring as an option for all families. Instead, based on a collaborative partnership format, one should prudently consider this option for those parents and family members who demonstrate appropriate interest, skills, and resources. As with other aspects of parent and family participation and partnerships, tutoring should be based on parent/family choice, not professionals' coercion. The procedures for family tutoring appear in Table 10.2.

Session 1 Procedures

Identify and operationally define an academic subject for tutoring. As with parent/family behavioral intervention programs, identifying an appropriate

Table 10.2. Parent- and Family-Applied Tutoring Procedures

Procedural Steps	Specific Activities
Session 1	
Identify and operationally define appropriate academic areas for parent and family tutoring.	List and define professionals' and parents'/family members' academic skill concerns.
	Prioritize teacher, parent, and family concerns.
	Identify student's academic strengths.
	Select and define one subject/area for tutoring
Identify appropriate tutoring materials.	Select tutoring materials for parent and family use.
Train parents and family members to use tutoring materials and methods.	Train parents/family members to use instructional materials.
	Train parents/family members to use instructional procedures.
Train parents/family members to observe and record academic response(s) of the student being tutored.	Identify and demonstrate simple observation and recording procedures for parents/family members.
	Aid parents and family members in applying an observation system to evaluate the target response in the home setting.
Session 2	
Amend tutoring methods and materials, as needed.	Make adjustments in tutoring materials and methods based on data and feedback from parents and family members.
	Make adjustments in the observation and recording systems based on feedback from the parents/family.
Train parents and family members to chart and inspect the target academic data.	Train parents and family members to use simple visual displays to record and chart academic data.
Establish suitable performance goals and outcomes.	Establish appropriate performance goals, expectations, and outcomes.
Session 3 and Subsequent Meetings	
Show parents/family members methods of analyzing, interpreting, and sharing data with educators.	Instruct parents and family members in methods of inspecting and analyzing data relative to previously established goals and outcomes, and in sharing tutoring data, results, and issues with educators.
Make changes in materials, procedures, recording, and charting, as needed.	

subject for remediation, practice, or acceleration forms the initial step in establishing a parent/family tutoring program. This basic step is a collaborative effort, and thus it hinges on parent/family interest, concern, skill, temperament, and at least partial problem ownership. When these factors are not evident, or when other evidence suggests that parents or family members would not make satisfactory tutors (e.g., poor academic skills, temperament problems, limited child rapport), training should be deferred to others, including private tutors.

Though collaborative in nature, decisions relating to tutoring programs and materials should reflect a strong professional influence. Accordingly, educators should solicit parent/family academic concerns, assist them in ranking their concerns, and then ultimately guide them in the selection of tutoring subjects and areas. Thus, after considering parent and family input, the educator assists parents in selecting an appropriate tutoring area and then writes an operational definition of a behavior for tutoring intervention (see the preceding section's discussion of how to write target behavior definitions). Tutoring targets must be congruent with a child's needs, abilities, parent/family skills and resources, and the overall school program. Drill-and-practice activities (e.g., color identification, math facts, word identification, etc.) are particularly appropriate and responsive for many parent and family tutoring programs.

Identify appropriate tutoring materials. As suggested, tutoring materials should be selected primarily by a professional. Thus, as part of this process, educators must consider a pupil's strengths and weaknesses, including IEP goals and objectives, as well as parent/family strengths and resources. As noted, for many parents preference should be given to drill-and-practice activities. Educators should provide parent and family tutors with *all* materials required for successful implementation of a given program; that is, rather than advising parents or family members to construct math fact cards, for example, these materials should be made available, and updated, as needed. Almost without exception, educators should select parent and family tutoring activities from subjects with which the child and his or her teacher(s) are familiar. Thus, subjects and activities that reinforce and enhance basic classroom skill development should be chosen over novel curricular areas and activities.

Train parents and family members to use tutoring materials and methods. As with behavioral intervention programs, parents and family members should receive specific tutoring instructions. Instructions should include the following oral and written information:

1. A specific time should be designated for tutoring. Tutors should start and stop on schedule, as agreed upon with the teacher. Although the duration of tutoring sessions will vary with a child's age, exceptionality, and so forth, most sessions should be limited to approximately 30 minutes daily, 5 days per week.

2. As much as possible, tutors should conduct all tutoring sessions in the same place at a table or desk. In addition, the site should be quiet (e.g., free from TV or stereo noises).

3. Tutors should strive for consistency. When different family members act as tutors, they should attempt to maintain the same conditions and setting, including an appropriate atmosphere.

4. Tutors must recognize the importance of following directions agreed upon in program development, especially those specified by the teacher. Deviations from this protocol, such as introducing new materials, procedures, or activities, should be avoided.

New tutoring materials and methods are best introduced via demonstration. That is, procedures and materials should be both explained and demonstrated to parents and family members. This activity should include opportunities for parents/family members to apply tutoring procedures under simulation conditions (i.e., with the teacher role-playing the part of the child demonstrating typical behaviors).

Specific tutoring procedures will vary according to materials, children to be trained, the target, and a host of other factors. Yet, several common methods should be followed. First, tutors should be trained to present materials, instructions, or tasks only when the child is quietly attending to the tutor or the task. Second, tutors should be advised of cues appropriate for prompting the desired responses. In the case of word recognition, for example, tutors must know *when* (e.g., after a specified duration, after an incorrect response) and *how* (e.g., sounding out the first syllable) to prompt a child who is encountering difficulty. This process may also involve training in such techniques as modeling, fading, shaping, and chaining. Finally, tutors should be trained to respond to children's responses, including dispensing appropriate reinforcers and other consequences for a given behavior. In particular, parents and family members should be advised to provide reinforcement for correct responses *immediately following* the desired response and in a consistent and clear manner. (Positive consequences appropriate for use by parent and family member tutors are discussed in an earlier section of this chapter.)

Train tutors to observe and record children's responses. As with parent- and family-administered behavioral intervention programs, tutors should be trained to observe, record, and monitor children's progress. Without such data, neither parents nor educators will have a basis for interpreting pupils' gains and the effectiveness of tutoring programs. Event recording, discussed earlier in this chapter, typically affords the most appropriate and effective means of parent and family data collection. For monitoring purposes, data are often recorded as frequencies or percentages. Thus, tutors may record the number or percentage of correctly identified math facts or the number and percentage of correctly identified word cards.

Session 2 Procedures

Amend tutoring methods and materials. Based on parent and family member feedback as well as observational daily data, educators must make the necessary adjustments in the original tutoring program. If, for example, a child fails to make the expected progress, the educator, in collaboration with the parents, must determine modifications necessary for success. To be effective, teachers should be familiar with the curricula being tutored and thereby with anticipated response patterns. That is, teachers should have classroom baseline data for the children being tutored in order to determine whether or not they are progressing in accordance with the rate shown in the classroom

Train parents and family members to chart and inspect tutoring data. In a manner similar to charting and inspecting behavioral data, tutors should maintain daily progress profiles on the children they work with. Typically, parents and family members who conduct tutoring sessions do not conduct baseline assessments; however, they must chart children's progress over training sessions. These data form the basis for subsequent curriculum modifications and adjustments, and thereby play a significant role in any home tutoring program.

Establish performance goals and outcomes. In accordance with a collaborative model, educators and parents involved in home tutoring programs should jointly recommend performance goals and outcomes. However, because this is often a professional task based on a variety of factors, educators typically should take a leadership role in this regard. It is important to identify goals consistent with IEP objectives, classroom instructional goals and outcomes, and students' needs and abilities. For example, if an IEP objective requires that the child be able to identify 25 specific words, home tutoring in this area should be geared toward accomplishing this goal. Such coordination facilitates not only appropriate parent and family tutoring expectations, but also development of a partnership between home and school.

Session 3 and Subsequent Meetings

The third session as well as subsequent meetings between family tutors and educators will focus mainly on student progress and/or tutoring problems. Educators should maintain regular contact with parent and family tutors, making adjustments and introducing new methods and materials as required. Many of these contacts may be informal, as opposed to face-to-face meetings.

Summary

As noted throughout this chapter, behavioral and educational principles often can be effectively applied in natural environments by the parents and families of children and youth with exceptionalities. The success of the proposed model depends both on the effective use of a collaborative strategy and the conferencer's ability to translate technical tenets into functional procedures. Accordingly, the conferencer must recognize parent- and family-implemented behavioral intervention and tutoring as tools that can only be effectively applied through a partnership process in combination with effective conferencing skills. Without attending, listening, rapport, and other fundamental conferencing elements, it is unlikely that these approaches will be effective.

─────────────── # Exercises ───────────────

1. Conduct a behavioral intervention simulation conference using the materials in Appendix C. Descriptions are provided for the cases previously presented for the initial interview and IEP role-play exercise (students with mental retardation, physical disability, emotional disturbance, etc.). Use those materials most aligned with your career goals or experiences or those you have used in the previous role-playing exercise.

In conducting the simulation exercise, one individual should assume the part of the parent, using the materials labeled "Parent Role." The conference should be parent initiated; that is, assume that the parent in the exercise contacted the educator to obtain aid for a home-based problem.

No materials are designated for the person playing the role of the conferencer. However, background information on each case can be obtained from the descriptions provided for the earlier simulation conference. The third individual, who plays the role of evaluator, is to use the evaluation forms provided in Appendix C.

The behavioral conference should be separated into two separate sessions. The first should cover those elements identified in Table 10.1 as "Procedural Steps" in Session 1. At the completion of this session, individuals playing the part of the parent should generate baseline data on the identified target behavior. This information should be written on a form similar to the one in Figure 10.1 (sample recording form).

Following the first segment, individuals assuming educator roles should prepare a graph similar to the one shown in Figure 10.2 to demonstrate how baseline data are transferred to a chart. Those in educator roles should also develop a list of consequences or intervention procedures to discuss with parents and a procedural plan sheet as shown in Figure 10.3. (The plan sheet is not to be completed until Session 2.)

The second phase of the simulation conference should adhere to the "Procedural Steps" in Session 2. As noted previously, this session will make use of the data generated by parents following the first conference, the graph for translating the parent-generated data, the possible consequences generated by the educator, and the educator-developed plan sheet. Because the text provides only basic information regarding appropriate reinforcers, extinction methods, punishers, and antecedent programs, individuals unfamiliar with fundamental behavioral intervention methods are advised to review a text specifically devoted to this topic. For instance, the role-play materials for individuals interested in working with students who have learning disabilities focuses on a parent's concern over a child who lacks social interaction skills. Individuals who are unfamiliar with interventions in this area (e.g., direct instruction, peer-mediated programs, adult antecedent prompting) are advised to review a text focusing on this topic prior to conducting the role-play exercise.

Individuals should change roles after completing both phases of the conference.

2. Conduct a tutoring simulation conference for a child and family described in Appendix A and B. Use those materials most aligned with your area or those you have used in previous role-playing exercises. In conducting the simulation exercise, one person should assume the role of par-

ent, another that of teacher. The conference should be parent initiated; that is, assume that the parent in the exercise contacted the educator regarding establishing a home tutoring program.

No materials have been developed either for the individual playing the role of the conferencer or for the person who plays the part of the parent. Thus, specific parent and teacher academic concerns and tutoring materials must be developed by participants, based on descriptions provided in Appendix A and B. Individuals are also advised to rely on the IEP they developed as a part of conducting the IEP role-play session.

The conference should be divided into two separate meetings: the first should comprise those elements identified in Table 10.2 as "Procedural Steps" in Session 1 and the second should follow the "Procedural Steps" in Session 2. This session will require a week's tutoring-progress data so that charting may be demonstrated to tutors. Thus, persons playing parent roles must manufacture percentage or frequency data for educators to use in demonstrating charting procedures.

Individuals should change roles after completing Session 1 and Session 2 procedural steps.

Chapter 11

Progress Report
Conferences

Individual parent-educator conferences that focus on students' school progress are among the most common and significant of all parent-professional interactions. These sessions allow for the clarification of information exchanged via non-face-to-face means (e.g., notes and grade cards) and for the direct dissemination of information relevant to a pupil's education. In addition, progress report conferences allow for an evaluation of individualized education program (IEP) goals and objectives and serve as a mechanism for maintaining contact among parents, family members, and professionals.

Although there may be disagreement regarding the most appropriate timing for the progress report conference, research maintains that these sessions should be held on a regular basis (Harry, Allen, & McLaughlin, 1995; Kroth, 1985). Kelly (1974) suggested that these meetings should at least coincide with report card or grade reporting schedules and that they not be held exclusively at times of crisis. Such conferences also should be scheduled to meet the individual needs of parents and pupils. Just as students with exceptionalities receive individualized schedules that correspond to their unique needs, so must their parents have individually scheduled feedback conferences (Adelman, 1994; Espinosa & Shearer, 1986).

Even though the professional's preparation for and skill in the progress report conference will be significant, the most crucial factor related to a favorable conference outcome will be the success of previous parent-educator contacts (McNaughton, 1994; Schulz, 1978). In particular, it is typically unrealistic to expect a completely satisfactory progress reporting session if prior positive contacts have not occurred. In such instances parents most likely will lack the rapport, trust, and/or prior information required for effective participation and collaboration. Consequently, professionals must recognize that parent-educator interactions are cumulative and in particular that, regardless of one's skill in conducting the conference, success will depend on prior positive contact.

Discussing Student Progress with Parents and Family

A variety of factors will dictate the specific agenda for each progress report conference, including the nature and extent of a pupil's exceptionality and the needs of parents and families. However, several common areas should be examined as a part of each session. These areas include a cursory review of factors associated with the diagnosis and intervention procedures along with academic growth and performance, social/behavioral factors, and educationally related physical variables.

Parents should receive prior written or spoken notice of both the nature and purpose of the conference and the areas that will be reviewed. In addition, this prior notice should inform parents and family members that they will be allowed to discuss any concerns they have related to their child's program. Thus, the conferencer should be able to structure the session without giving the impression that all aspects have been predetermined; otherwise, parents and family members may either assume that they have no input into the direction of the conference or may attempt to discuss matters that would be more appropriately dealt with in other types of conferences.

Especially with parents and family members who may be relatively unfamiliar with special education and their child's specific educational or treatment program, the educator should provide an overview of the events that led to the pupil's diagnosis and program, and the current status of the program. Although the degree of attention given this phase of the conference will depend largely on participants' familiarity with this information, each conference should include this material. The cursory review of presenting issues should be followed by a brief recap of diagnostic findings, the pupil's IEP, the educational and intervention program being used, and a summary evaluative statement. The intent of this overview is to refresh the parents regarding the somewhat complicated process that led to the diagnosis and programming/placement of their child and then bring them up to date on the nature and efficacy of the resulting intervention program. In addition, parents and family members should have an opportunity to raise issues or ask questions about any of these factors.

Providing Feedback on Academic Progress

Independent of an exceptionality, parents are concerned with the academic progress of their child. Hence, even in instances where a program modification was implemented for other than learning issues, parents still want information on their child's academic performance. *Academic*, in this context, refers not only to traditional school-related subjects and skills but also to self-help, prevocational, vocational, and similar areas.

The format for discussing academic information with parents and family members resembles that used in a general progress report overview, with content relating specifically to academic and academically related performance. Accordingly, parents and family members should first hear a brief review of the academic issues existing prior to the program modification and the diagnostic findings relative to this exceptionality. This process is designed to establish a historical basis for the intervention program and to aid the parents and family members in more adequately understanding the nature of the exceptionality. The extent to which the group discusses this content area is based on the parents' needs and interest, the characteristics of the academic exceptionality, and the general familiarity of the parents and family with this information. Consequently, a conferencer may invest relatively little time in this topic with parents and family members who have had recent opportunities to discuss the diagnosis and its implications prior to the conference. Thus, it is essential to gauge the needs of parents and family members in this area accurately, taking care to provide sufficient information to answer their questions and form a basis for other components of the interpretation process without excessively reviewing materials with which they are familiar.

One aspect of this interpretation and review is to be prepared to discuss with parents and family members the tests and procedures employed in the diagnostic process. Because these procedures may consist at least in part of formal, standardized tests administered by other professionals, the classroom teacher, if he or she is to conduct the interpretation, should be familiar with the measures and the manner in which they were used in the evaluation process.

The ability to review test data and interpret diagnostic findings to parents and family members (especially standardized assessment measure data) will necessitate having a thorough knowledge of the instruments being discussed. As standardized procedures are designed to compare a child's performance with normative data, it is imperative to the accurate interpretation of the data at hand that the professional be thoroughly familiar with these procedures, including a knowledge of the standardization samples and the reliability, validity, and adaptability of the procedure for children and youth with exceptionalities. Only with this information should the conferencer attempt to interpret test data to parents and family members. Individuals lacking this background should request assistance from those with specific expertise in this area.

Conferencers who lack formal training in administering/interpreting standardized tests and other such measures should also recognize that informal assessment results, trial teaching findings, and other criterion-referenced assessment data are not only more easily disseminated by teachers but may also be far more meaningful to parents and family members (Fuchs & Deno, 1994; Hammill, 1987). Above all the conferencer should remember that the intent of reviewing assessment procedures is to recapitulate for the parents, in language they can understand, the nature of the issues existing at the time of referral for special service and the nature of the evaluation findings relative to these issues. Wallace and Larsen (1978) noted several advantages to informal procedures, which also serve as strengths during the process of disseminating information to parents and family members. These strengths include the similarity of the assessment items to the skills that are under development in the classroom, the involvement of the classroom teacher in the assessment procedure, the relative ease of administering and interpreting informal techniques, and the wide range of skills that can be evaluated. The reliance on informal measures, including a review of the "Present Levels of Educational Performance" section of the IEP, should also aid the conferencer in minimizing the use of esoteric diagnostic findings and in facilitating the dissemination of functional information. As suggested by Deno (1971), the commitment of the educator "should be to make the assessment as worthwhile as we can in terms of its contribution to improved learning on the part of the child" (p. 3). Certainly this same commitment must also guide the educator in his or her interpretation of assessment information to parents and family members.

After discussing the nature of a student's academic exceptionality with the parents, the conferencer should shift to an analysis of the academic intervention, academic acceleration, or curriculum modification program and its effect on the student. In particular, this process will involve a discussion of the academic remediation or acceleration model, curriculum, and programming procedures in use and the measured efficacy of these treatments. Although the progress reporting conference is not exclusively designed to serve as an IEP evaluation session, one can facilitate an interpretation of academic progress by following the format established on the IEP. That is, each annual goal should be presented to the parents and family members for review and discussion, followed by a statement of the various short-term academic objectives that were developed to accomplish the annual goal and the means of accomplishing each objective. Finally, the conferencer should discuss with the parents and family members the effectiveness of the curriculum or academic remediation program in achieving the desired goals. This model for disseminating information appears in Figure 11.1.

Though obviously in certain situations academic progress reports may unfold independent of a student's IEP, in many instances student progress can be disseminated effectively through adherence to the IEP model. This process has the major advantage of utilizing an instrument in which parents and family members should have had prior input. In addition, this strategy allows for interpretation of progress made on a previously agreed-upon approach. In particular, this can serve as a demonstration that the conferencer is truly following a joint parent-educator collaborative plan. Though this message is frequently given to parents and family members, the present strategy represents one means for actually demonstrating the authenticity of the message.

Providing Feedback on Social Progress

In addition to requiring information on their child's academic performance, parents are also interested in their child's social functioning. The format for providing this information resembles that used for disseminating academic progress. That is, the interpretation should involve a discussion of the child's school social history and any particular behavioral or social issues associated with the referral for program modification. A discussion then should follow the assessment findings relative to these issues, the intervention procedures employed to manage these concerns, and an evaluation of these procedures. Just as with academic functioning, this dissemination process can be facilitated, at least in part, through an interpretation of IEP annual social goals and short-term objectives.

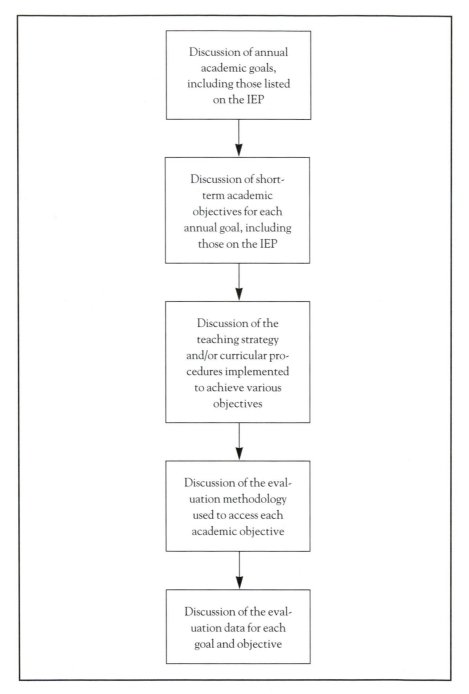

Figure 11.1. Model for disseminating academic progress information to parents.

The conferencer should also be able to comment on social or behavioral problems that have developed since the time of referral or placement. Patterns of conduct disturbance, shyness, immaturity, or social withdrawal, particularly when representative of a marked change in behavior, should become items for discussion. Although educators should discuss these social patterns with parents when first observed rather than hold them as agenda items for a scheduled progress conference, they frequently can be dealt with at such sessions. Particular social/behavioral patterns that the conferencer will want to note include the items listed below:

1. Rejection by peers
2. Shyness
3. Preoccupation
4. Excessive daydreaming
5. Social withdrawal
6. Excessive anxiety
7. Depression
8. Inability or unwillingness to sustain effort and complete tasks
9. Confusion
10. Rigid patterns of behavior
11. Extreme sensitivity
12. Patterns of regression
13. Truant or chronic tardiness
14. Impulsiveness
15. Physical aggression and violent tendencies
16. Defiance
17. Responses suggesting that rules and regulations apply only to others
18. Disruptiveness
19. Difficulty in responding to authority figures
20. Hostility

Although this list is in no way complete, it does suggest those general patterns of behavior to which educators should be sensitive and on which appropriate attention should focus in parent-educator conferences. In discussing this information the educational conferencer should not attempt to place the responsibility for a school social problem with parents. It is appropriate, of course, to apprise parents of a classroom social behavior and to solicit their thoughts on its nature and cause, but it is essential that the conferencer also provide a possible solution or intervention strategy. Although the conferencer may justifiably suggest ways in which the parents can be involved in the progress reporting, it is grossly inappropriate to identify a school-based social problem without a possible solution or to attempt to make the parents independently responsible for arriving at a solution to the problem.

It is also important when social/behavioral excesses, deficits, or other issues are identified in the progress reporting conference to present them in an empirical fashion. That is, rather than relating to parents and family members that a child is "defiant," "withdrawn," "hyperactive," or "inattentive," without an adequate explanation of the nature and extent of the problem, the conferencer should offer a more scientifically based analysis of the situation. This may take, for example, the form of a line or bar graph that illustrates the nature and significance of a particular social behavior. The important element is that parents and family members be able to understand the nature of the problem and be convinced that the professionals have thoroughly analyzed the situation. In addition, the data presented must demonstrate that the child's behavior represents a change and/or that the pattern falls outside the classroom norm. This probably can be achieved best by offering a comparison of the child's behavior with that of his or her peers. Finally, this process can serve as the basis for entering into a discussion of the present intervention strategy and later as a means of evaluating the procedure. An example in which this empirically based interpretation process was employed follows.

A 9-year-old fourth-grader presented a concern to his teacher because of his chronic failure to hand in written assignments. She noted that this child was a disruptive element in the classroom but that he "had good potential." In preparation for a progress reporting conference, the teacher began keeping a record of the daily English, spelling, social studies, and writing papers the boy completed and handed in within the appropriate class periods on the given day assigned. The measure did not include homework assignments nor did it impose quality criteria for the material submitted.

The teacher found that the child's mean rate of assignment completion was 31.2%, while that of the other class members was 88%. She noted, however, that differences occurred in his rate of assignment completion as a function of becoming aware that he was being observed. In particular, his mean rate of performance prior to awareness of being observed was 21%; this rate increased to 55.6% after he determined that his behavior was under scrutiny.

During a regularly scheduled conference this teacher shared this information with the parents, along with a proposed strategy for managing the problem. She explained to the parents that the child would be exposed to a three-point reinforcement program to increase his number of completed assignments. The program would involve (a) social reinforcement immediately following his submission of papers, (b) a self-charting program, and (c) the privilege of being the "teacher's errand boy" on days when at least 90% of his assignments were completed. At a follow-up conference, the teacher shared the results of this program with the parents in the format shown in Figure 11.2.

Videotapes and other forms of technology can also be used to communicate students' progress to parents and families. Alberto, Mechling, Taber, and Thompson (1995) reported that 48% of the parents they surveyed preferred videotapes as a progress reporting option. Indeed, educators can

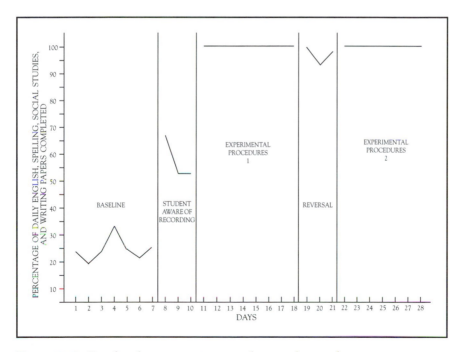

Figure 11.2. Results of program to increase the completion of written assignments.

use videotapes to communicate students' progress at face-to-face progress report meetings, and Alberto et al. (1995) noted that many parents "indicated that it is much easier for them to take a tape home than to schedule meetings and arrange childcare" (p. 18). Though videotapes can be used to communicate students' academic progress, visual products of social and behavioral problems and issues have obvious advantages.

Providing Feedback on Physical Progress

Parents and family members of children and youth for whom a physical exceptionality is the basis for a program modification or curriculum adaptation will be interested, of course, in receiving feedback in this domain. In such cases, a format similar to that employed in the academic and social/behavioral areas will serve. That is, the educational impact of the physical exceptionality and the diagnostic findings relative to the disability should be discussed with parents, followed by a discussion of the intervention and curriculum strategies being employed to deal with the problem and the efficacy of these strategies.

Although the majority of children and youth with exceptionalities will receive services for other than physical problems, it is nonetheless important for the education conferencer not to dismiss this category of information as unrelated. Indeed, even in situations where a child's exceptionality is of a cognitive or social nature, the conferencer should consider the physical domain in preparing for the parent feedback conference. To encourage sensitivity to possible sensory problems, the educator may reflect on items from the Keystone Visual Screening Tests (Keystone View, 1971), examples of which follow:

Appearance of the eyes

- Eyes crossed—turning in or out at any time
- Reddened eyes
- Watering eyes
- Encrusted eyelids
- Frequent tearing

Using the eyes

- Headaches

- Nausea or dizziness
- Burning or itching of eyes

Behavior indicative of possible vision difficulty

- Body rigidity while looking at distant objects
- Thrusting head forward or backward while looking at distant objects

The educator should be equally sensitive to indications of possible hearing impairment. Signs such as language delay, atypical speech patterns, inattentiveness, erratic school performance, apparent inability to follow oral directions, confusion, and cupping of hands behind ears or favoring one ear in conversations present potentially significant information and should be both discussed with the parents and professionally evaluated.

In preparation for the progress dissemination conference, the educator should also be aware of other physically related symptoms, signs, and patterns that may require further investigation. Indications of substance abuse or dependence, illnesses, frequent school absence or tardiness, signs of extreme fatigue, poor gross and/or fine motor coordination, enuresis and encopresis—all may be potentially significant and thus become necessary items for discussion with parents. Although the educator may simply request information from parents and family members regarding these patterns, he or she should be ready to suggest a method for acquiring further data or an intervention strategy for dealing with the problem. Although ownership of problems (Kroth, 1985; Simpson & Carter, 1993) must be clarified, professionals nonetheless must avoid presenting educationally significant problems and concerns without also offering intervention alternatives.

Staging the Progress Report Conference

In addition to having a set dissemination format for providing parents and family members with information, the educational conferencer should have an appropriate style, guidelines, and methods for structuring and transmitting data. These skills should allow both for the effective transmission of information and for the successful disposition of problems and issues that may arise in the course of a session.

Satisfying the Information Needs of Parents and Family Through Collaborative Discussion

According to Langton and Stout (1954), progress reporting conferences are designed to allow parents and educators an opportunity to discuss a child's school behavior and academic performance. Although these conferences should facilitate sharing, the progress report conference has been typified by a one-way flow of information (Redl & Wattenberg, 1959). Consequently, the conferencer must ensure that the session represents a collaborative discussion process. That is, though some individuals may consider parents solely the receivers of educational data, a progress conference can only be successful when it involves educators and parents discussing and sharing information, attitudes, concerns, and positions (Nahmias, 1995; Schulz, 1987; Sicley, 1993). As noted by Chinn, Winn, and Walters (1978), effective communication requires interaction. Furthermore, they noted that "through a 'two-way' process we are able to learn from one another, share our ideas, provide feedback and enhance the probability that quality communication will take place" (p. 60). It is essential then that the educational conferencer not lose sight of this basic fact and that, regardless of time constraints and the amount of information to be dispensed, he or she *discuss* information with parents and family members rather than lecture. In particular, this will involve (a) being sensitive to the emotions and feelings of parents and family members and to the goal of achieving a satisfactory understanding, (b) being attentive to questions presented by the parents, and (c) making them collaborators in the progress report rather than exclusively receivers.

Notifying Parents and Family of the Progress Report Conference

Lack of parental attendance is a major challenge confronting educational conferencers. Because face-to-face progress conferences obviously cannot proceed without parents and family members present, educators must identify procedures for securing their attendance at the meetings.

First, one must recognize that parents and family members will be motivated to attend parent-educator conferences only after having been exposed to prior reinforcing experiences with school professionals. Therefore, successfully conducted initial conferences, IEP planning sessions, problem-solving meetings, and other collaborative contacts will all serve to promote the attendance and participation of parents and family members in progress report conferences. As part of American Education Week, one school district in Idaho organized a "Substitute Student Day." This involved having parents attend school for one day in place of their sons and daughters. This or similar programs should serve to sensitize parents to their child's educational program and should facilitate the development of rapport upon which attendance and participation in parent-educator conferences can be based.

Clements and Simpson (1974) reported that parents were most responsive to handwritten notices of scheduled parent-educator conferences sent through the mail. These researchers also found that parental attendance at conferences increased when transportation and a baby-sitting service were provided. Other considerations can also help promote the attendance of parents:

- Provide sufficient notice of the scheduled conference for parents and families to plan accordingly. This may involve announcing the schedule for progress conferences early in the school year and then following up at a later time with a letter regarding the specific date of each conference. These announcements should specify meeting time and place, time allotted, topics to be discussed, and specific expectations. Parents should also have input into scheduling the time of the conference.

- Employ whatever means necessary to ensure that parents and family members know how to reach the conference site. Maps, guides, or well-planned directions should be provided if appropriate.

- Identify community resources that can facilitate the participation of parents and family members in conferences. Agencies providing transportation and baby-sitting, for example, are particularly important.

- Be willing to conduct the session in the parents' home, if necessary.

Allotting the Correct Amount of Time for the Conference

Ideally, the conferencer should be able to individualize the time requirements of each session to best meet the needs of parents, families, and pupils. However, administrative personnel frequently schedule progress conferences, including time allotments, for entire buildings or districts; consequently, one may not have a major role in determining the time available for each conference. At a minimum, no less than 30 minutes should be scheduled. In addition, it is often advisable to set a time limit for the session. This frequently will serve to keep both parents and professionals "on task" as well as to facilitate growth and reduce irrelevant discussions. Parents and family members should be advised, of course, that changes may occur as needed and as schedules permit, and that additional time can be provided at a later date if required. Indeed, the limited time available for most progress conferences may require that follow-up sessions be scheduled to deal with special problems or other agenda items that the parent or conferencer may wish to discuss.

Preconference Planning

The success of the parent-educator progress report conference will correlate highly with preconference planning efforts (Barsch, 1969; Ehly, Conoley, & Rosenthal, 1985; Robinson & Fine, 1995). These planning efforts should involve attention to the following:

- The child's records, including the IEP and previous parent-educator conference notes, should be reviewed carefully.

- An outline of those items to be discussed should be prepared.

- The conferencer should review standardized test data and informal assessment information that may need reinterpretation to the parents and family members.

- A careful selection of papers and work samples should be made in preparation for the conference. These portfolio samples should be representative and illustrative of particular concepts and should be dated and sequentially arranged for comparative purposes.

- Parents should be provided a portfolio folder of their child's work to take with them after the conference. This work sample should be representative of their child's performance and consistent with feedback provided by the conferencer. Evaluative comments should appear on the papers to aid parents and family members in understanding the concepts being illustrated.

- Educators should plan for an acceptable environment for the session, including a professional and confidential setting. In addition, the conferencer should make arrangements for adult-sized furniture for all participants and pads and pencils for note taking.

- Parents and family members should be prepared to participate in the conference. (This important component is addressed in depth later in this chapter.)

- The educator should prepare each student for the conference, which basically consists of apprising him or her of the purpose and nature of the session and the materials to be reviewed. The pupil also should be offered an opportunity for input into the agenda. Finally, one should consider the possibility of the pupil's participation in the session. In instances in which such involvement is appropriate, the student should receive training (e.g., information, discussion opportunities, and role playing) for participating in the conference.

These preliminary efforts can aid in reducing the anxiety of both the pupil and the parents.

Conducting the Conference

According to a number of practitioners and theorists, the parent-professional relationship is basic to effective communication (Cronin, Slade, Bechtel, & Anderson, 1992; Ginott, 1957; Gordon, 1970; Harry et al., 1995; Nahmias, 1995; Turnbull & Turnbull, 1986). Consequently, as an integral component of the conferencing process, the educator should be able to establish and maintain rapport and a collaborative relationship with parents and families. One can initiate this relationship by means of a warm greeting, and a positive lead, and a willingness to listen and work together.

The conferencer should attempt to create as informal and relaxed an atmosphere as possible. It is important, in addition to communicating aspects of a child's progress, that the conferencer also listen to parents and family members. As noted previously, providing parents and families exposure to a good listener is frequently the most effective relationship builder.

Being clear and specific

Other preliminary procedures include reviewing the purpose of the conference with parents and family members and clarifying the role of the conferencer or other individuals involved in the session. That is, the sophisticated nature of educational service delivery systems and their related personnel may require some explanation for parents and families. Thus, for example, it is important for parents to recognize the role of a resource or consulting teacher, or the function of an inclusion specialist, as well as the manner in which these individuals form part of the service delivery team and impact on students and their families. It is also helpful for the conferencer to remind parents and family members of any time limitations for the session and that the agenda items not covered in the time allotted or not related specifically to the progress conference can be dealt with at a later time. Finally, in initiating the meeting, the conferencer should encourage parents and family members to participate in the session by asking questions or commenting on the educator's observations or related matters, and by collaborating on decisions and interventions.

The conferencer should address areas of growth and progress prior to focusing on problem issues (an appropriate strategy throughout the conference). That is, in the overview process and in reviewing the academic, social, and physical areas, one should address areas of success and growth before attending to less positive components. Further, for these positive comments to have maximum impact, they must be specific. The conferencer must specifically detail and document the nature of the gains shown for this information to be most meaningful. Typically, one can accomplish this by showing parents and family members portfolio samples of work and curriculum completed by the student. As suggested previously, these materials should be given to parents to take home following the conference.

Following the review of growth components, parents and family members should be apprised of weak areas or those in which additional improvement is needed. The educator should transmit this information, just as with growth feedback, in clear and empirical terms. Especially with regard to social problems, the conferencer must be able to explain and document the nature of a problem clearly. Thus, for example, one could share a graph or show a videotape of the times a child is out of his or her seat without permission as opposed to telling parents that their child is "hyperactive" or "noncompliant." In addition, it is mandatory that the educator provide possible solutions to any weaknesses that are identified. This process should also include allowing parents and family members an opportunity to discuss the nature of the problem and to collaborate on solutions. This will take the form of discussing what the educator suggests doing to remediate the problem (e.g., "Jerry will work 20 minutes extra per day with the class aide on his math flash cards") as well as what parents and families can do (if they so desire) to aid in solving the problem (e.g., using a note-home system that will allow parents to praise a child daily for good social behavior). The educator should also build in a time and mechanism for providing parents and family members feedback on the effectiveness of the agreed-upon intervention strategy.

Maintaining a professional attitude

Although the conferencer will want to establish a warm, accepting, and collaborative atmosphere where parents and family members can feel free in expressing their concerns, it is important to maintain professional ethics and decorum. In particular, parents and family members should have an opportunity to share concerns about their child and the individuals who work with him or her without creating a forum for criticizing other educators, agencies, or school policy. The conferencer must thus be able to offer parents and families an airing of matters related to their child's education without promoting griping and gossip about issues only tangential to the true issues under scrutiny. In instances where parents and family members focus on complaining about other teachers or educational personnel, one may need to direct the discussion to more appropriate areas, perhaps simply by reminding everyone of the limited amount of time available for discussing the student and suggesting they should attempt to focus on that task.

Although prompting participants to attend to the conferencing task may be required in some situations, it is also important to note that parents and families must have an opportunity to be heard, even if the subject of their discussion is not specifically related to their child's school progress. Consequently, the conferencer must not be too quick to direct the attention of parents and family members away from a topic they consider worthy of discussion—such a strategy would run counter to collaboration. Thus, only in instances where an unproductive focus dominates the session or when the intensity of the content raises ethical issues should the session be redirected. Given the nature and the frequency of this situation, the conferencer can listen to the concerns of parents and family members without agreeing, can refer parents and family members to the individual most able to effect some type of appropriate change (e.g., principal, school board members, hospital superintendent), and can employ subtle redirection techniques (reinforcing, attending to content more directly related to the session) as alternatives to direct confrontations about the appropriateness of content.

Concluding the conference

The conference should wrap up with a summary of the discussions that occurred. Included should be a brief review of the high points of the student's progress and a restatement of those activities that will be implemented to deal with identified weaknesses and problems. In particular, the summary should include individual responsibilities for the various programs to be followed, methodology for evaluating success, and the manner and dates for exchanging this information.

Just as the conference was initiated on a positive note, so should it be concluded. In particular, the conferencer should reinforce parents and family members for their participation, extend an invitation for them to stay in touch when they experience a problem or require further information (this may involve scheduling a follow-up conference on the spot to discuss agenda items not covered or items not specifically related to the progress conference), and encourage parents and family members to maintain their interest, participation, and collaborative spirit.

After the Conference

Even though the conclusion of a parent-educator conference will most likely be celebrated with feelings of relief and possibly also optimism and accomplishment, it is important to remember that responsibilities do not end when parents and family members leave the session. Rather, the conferencer should attend to the following tasks: (a) record the results of the session, (b) provide feedback to other appropriate school or agency professionals, (c) perform activities agreed upon in the conference and promptly provide feedback to parents regarding the results of these efforts, (d) review the progress report conference with the student, and (e) evaluate the conference.

Record results

Making an accurate and meaningful record of the progress report conference is a basic professional duty, integral not only to that particular conference but also to future interactions. Because it is not at all unusual to exchange significant and elaborate information and to devise cooperative intervention programs during parent-professional conferences, the proceedings must be captured in written form. In these written reports the reader should find an integrated summary of discussions that ensued, including academic, emotional/social, and physical information exchanged. The conferencer should take care to present this information in a fashion reflective of the discussions and parent/family reactions that occurred as opposed to providing only a summary of the student's progress. Although the report should contain a summary of progress, it should also capture the interactions that passed between the parent/family and professional participants.

The summary report should also make reference to recommendations that emerged and the manner in which these recommendations will be collaboratively implemented. Included should be items for later discussion at the annual IEP review meeting. Finally, the report should identify the individual responsible for carrying out each agreed-upon recommendation, activity, and evaluation procedure.

Conferencers should record the discussions that take place in progress report conferences in as accurate a fashion as possible. Because professionals must be able to validate the accuracy of their reports and inferences, it is essential that extreme care guide the preparation of parent conference reports. As observed by Kroth and Simpson (1977), "some school records may contain potentially libelous material, and not only can parents challenge the accuracy of information contained in their child's records, but they also have legal recourse in situations where the recorded information provides an unsupported or damaging picture of the student" (p. 118). Conference reports must provide clear and functional summary information that is free of damaging data and inferences.

Provide direct feedback to other professionals

In addition to preparing a written report of the conference, the educator may wish to disseminate information to some individuals directly. This should occur especially when the information may directly result in curriculum, attitude, or procedural modification, and when questions persist regarding the degree to which information will be seen if available only in written form.

For example, a junior high–level learning disabilities resource room teacher learned from one of her student's parents during a progress report conference that their son had recently started taking antihistamines for hay fever. She had noted that the child seemed extremely lethargic and distractible for the past several weeks during the 2 hours he was in her resource program. Although this teacher was not aware that similar problems were occurring in the student's general education classes, she made individual visits to his other teachers following the conference to apprise them of his medical condition.

Even in the best of programs, reports may go unseen by those individuals who most need the information. As a result, highly significant data should be disseminated face-to-face to ensure that in fact it is shared.

Perform agreed-upon duties

Although rapport and trust can take hold through the use of basic interpersonal skills, parents' ultimate satisfaction and belief in an educator and a program will come only with the performance of agreed-upon tasks and the communication of results. In the final analysis, delivery on promises is the fundamental determinant of rapport and collaborative success.

Review results of the conference with the student

In instances where a pupil is not a part of his or her own progress report conference, the teacher and/or parents should provide feedback. This process should consist of an overview of the items discussed, the progress results noted, and the various recommendations made. As much as appropriate, the pupil should be exposed to the same collaborative format and information as the parents. Thus, he or she should also have an opportunity to raise questions, to be part of any problem-solving efforts, and to have input into the various recommendations. Among the most significant components in this process is the need to stress that the purpose of the conference is to apprise parents and family members of the student's progress (an effort that will be of direct benefit to him or her) and that progress report conferences are routinely scheduled for all parents and family members.

Evaluate the conference

The evaluation of efforts is needed in all areas of education, including parent and family involvement. School and agency personnel, along with almost every other professional, should be able to demonstrate the efficacy of their efforts. Although assessment efforts may appear to be a cumbersome burden that requires unnecessarily extensive resources and is associated with few positive gains, evaluative strategies serve to provide feedback necessary for change. Especially with regard to self-evaluation, the conferencer should streamline any assessment system such that it yields information directly associated with desired goals and objectives. This need for evaluative feedback is further highlighted by noting that personal satisfaction with a conference may not always indicate true success. Thus, a teacher who talks incessantly during a conference may conclude that the session went well, but in spite of this personal feeling of satisfaction she may have given others few opportunities to voice an opinion or collaborate and may have actually failed to provide certain basic information. Consequently, the conferencer should, as a regular practice, conduct an evaluation of the session. As noted by Carkhuff and Berenson (1976), "at every point where the helpers intervened in the lives of their helpees, the efforts could be 'for better or for worse'" (p. 16).

One suggested procedure for obtaining this feedback appears in Figure 11.3. This instrument can serve as a self-evaluation measure or as a means of allowing one's colleagues (or the parents!) to provide feedback. The questions can also become a preconference checklist for remembering the specific components to address.

Responding to Questions from Parents and Family Members

Parents and family members of children with exceptionalities will have questions regarding their child and the future long after an initial diagnosis has been made and special educational provisions delivered. Consequently, the conferencer should expect that questions will arise in the course of the progress report conference that may or may not relate directly to the agenda. It is important, of course, to make the discussions collaborative and to keep them related to the task at hand, but it is also mandatory to address the issues and questions that parents and family members raise. As a result, the professional must be able to contain the session within certain parameters without being so rigid as to extinguish items not associated with the preconference agenda. Making this discrimination while at the same time providing appropriate feedback to parents, all within a somewhat unrealistic period of time, is in no way an easy task.

One of the most important points to remember is that parents and family members may raise a "question" for which they are not seeking a response but which will provide them an opportunity to redirect the session. Thus, for example, a parent who asks "Why is our child retarded?" may simply wish to offer his or her perceptions. On one occasion when this very question was raised, the conferencer noted that it was a difficult question with many possibilities and asked the parent for her thoughts. The mother stated that she believed it was related to her heavy cigarette smoking during pregnancy. She revealed that her in-laws had chided her for smoking while pregnant and specifically warned her that such behavior could produce mental retardation, poor health, or small stature in children. Although the mother had been told previously that her smoking had not caused her son's disability, and thus did not need another professional to repeat the message, she did feel a strong urge to talk about the situation. As this example shows, the conferencer should attempt to determine when parents and family members desire information and when they just

Pupil's Name: _____ Date: _____

Conferencer: _____

Person Completing Evaluation: _____

	Yes	No	Needs Improvement
I. Preconference Evaluation			
1. Was the conferencer familiar with the pupil's and family's background and related information, including the IEP?	☐	☐	☐
2. Was an agenda developed and followed?	☐	☐	☐
3. Was a review of previous test data and informal assessments conducted such that a reinterpretation of results could be conducted if necessary?	☐	☐	☐
4. Was a portfolio of the pupil's representative work prepared for the parents?	☐	☐	☐
5. Was an adequate environment prepared for the conference?	☐	☐	☐
6. Was the pupil prepared for the conference?	☐	☐	☐
7. Were the parents prepared to participate and collaborate in the conference?	☐	☐	☐
8. Was sufficient time allotted for the session?	☐	☐	☐
9. Were the parents appropriately notified of the conference?	☐	☐	☐
II. General Conferencing Evaluation			
1. Were the parents appropriately informed of the purpose of the conference?	☐	☐	☐
2. Was the session conducted in a systematic and sequential manner?	☐	☐	☐
3. Was the conferencer able to keep the interview flowing and on course?	☐	☐	☐

(*continues*)

Figure 11.3. Progress report conference evaluation procedure.

	Yes	No	Needs Improvement
4. Did the conferencer provide the parent with an opportunity to ask questions?	☐	☐	☐
5. Was the conferencer able to attend to the parent rather than to notes?	☐	☐	☐
6. Was the conferencer able to include the parents as collaborative participants?	☐	☐	☐
7. Did the conferencer appropriately rephrase when necessary?	☐	☐	☐
8. Did the conferencer summarize the session?	☐	☐	☐

III. Evaluation of Specific Conference Content

	Yes	No	Needs Improvement
1. Was the conferencer able to provide a general progress report to the parents?	☐	☐	☐
2. Was the conferencer able to provide an adequate report of academic progress?	☐	☐	☐
3. Was the conferencer able to interpret previously administered tests/evaluation procedures?	☐	☐	☐
4. Was the conferencer able to clearly explain the pupil's academic program (remediation strategy) to the parents?	☐	☐	☐
5. Was the conferencer able to interpret the pupil's success as a function of the academic program (remediation or acceleration strategy)?	☐	☐	☐
6. Was the conferencer able to interpret to the parents the future outcomes, pro-gressions, and expectations for the pupil?	☐	☐	☐
7. Was the conferencer able to provide an adequate report of social/emotional progress?	☐	☐	☐
8. Was the conferencer able to provide the parents with a remediation plan if a social/emotional problem was targeted?	☐	☐	☐

(continues)

Figure 11.3. *Continued*

	Yes	No	Needs Improvement
9. Was the conferencer able to provide an adequate report of physical progress?	☐	☐	☐
10. Was the conferencer able to solicit and respond to questions raised by the parents?	☐	☐	☐
11. Was the conferencer able to identify information that would later be used to amend the pupil's IEP?	☐	☐	☐

IV. Additional comments:

_____

_____

Figure 11.3. *Continued*

need someone to listen. As noted by Benjamin (1969), "Not every question calls for an answer, but every question demands respectful listening and usually a personal reaction on our part" (p. 74).

Frequently conferencers observe that they are asked to respond to "difficult" or "sensitive" questions only after having had several prior meetings with parents and families. That is, only after rapport, trust, and a collaborative relationship have been satisfactorily established will parents and family members feel sufficiently comfortable in sharing this type of information. Thus, the conferencer should regard these difficult questions, many of which have no answers, as a sign of rapport and a request for the professional to listen and collaborate.

Atwell and Clabby (1971) identified a list of common questions (with suggested responses) that parents of children with mental retardation are likely to ask. Among those most frequently posed are questions referring to cause, why the condition affected their child or family, whether or not their other children will have a similar disability, and the impact of the child's condition on their children and family. As noted previously, the situation demands that the professional be sensitive to the nature of the question and to whether it is a request for information or an opportunity to talk.

Preparing Parents and Family Members to Participate

With ever-increasing frequency parents and families are being asked and expected to participate actively and productively with professionals in developing and maintaining appropriate educational services for their children (Fine, 1990). As a result of the work of parent groups, advocates, legislators, and other forces, parents have been accorded the rights and privileges commensurate with a colleague relationship. More than ever before we seem to be adopting Hobbs's (1975b) position that professionals must learn to be consultants to parents. Some researchers, such as McAfee and Vergason (1979), have focused on more immediate and practical issues. In particular, they suggest that "the issue is not whether parents should be involved, nor the extent of involvement, but rather how the situation can be structured to best utilize parents in efforts to maximize the educational achievement of children" (p. 4).

With respect to progress report conference participation, this approach suggests the need to prepare parents and family members to engage in planning and participate in the various activities associated with their child's educational program. This should include information on being a legitimate collaborative component of the parent-educator progress report conference. As noted by Simpson and Poplin (1981), "In order for the educational program of a child to be truly a joint effort between home and school, parents must be supplied the knowledge to be effective treatment surrogates and to effect change within given school situations" (p. 24).

Accordingly, greater emphasis has focused on making parents and family members more acceptable conference participants and collaborators. In pursuit of this goal, educators should equip them with questions to think about prior to the session, including the skills parents are most interested in the student developing, the strengths and weaknesses of the student, and other related issues.

Without doubt, parents and family members can be trained to engage in conference activities that will facilitate their participation. Listed below are suggestions to offer parents and family members to aid them in becoming more functional conference participants.[1]

---

[1] As this list may appear somewhat self-serving for professionals, the information will be most effective when disseminated by someone other than the teacher—a parent advocate or support group, a school administrator, and so forth.

- Arrange your schedule so that you can arrive on time. If you are not familiar with the school or neighborhood, ask for directions or secure a map of the area.

- Arrange for a sitter for your other children. It is disruptive to a conference to have children distract the educator and parent/family members.

- Determine how much time has been allotted for the session and stay within that time frame. If you are not able to complete your business within that period, you can make another appointment.

- Discuss the upcoming conference with family members and the pupil. Ask for input from these individuals, especially if they will not attend the meeting with you. If you feel comfortable with the idea, discuss with the educator the possibility of including your child in the conference. A number of educators recommend including students in their own conferences. This strategy may demonstrate to the pupil that the responsibility for an education is a personal one. It also eliminates the problems associated with disseminating secondhand information to the pupil.

- Do not gossip about other teachers, students, or families. However, be candid in relating information that may be beneficial to professionals.

- Review any notes and school documents (including the child's IEP) that you have prior to the conference.

- Bring a written list of questions and items that you want to discuss with the teacher. Do not rely on your memory. Included should be information related to academic, social/emotional, and physical areas. Specific questions such as "Is he reading at grade level?" "What is his reading level compared with children his age who are in the regular classroom?" "Do you have disciplinary problems with Sue?" and "How do you discipline Hector?" can all be useful in eliciting specific feedback.

- Do not come to the conference looking for a fight or an apology from the teacher for your child's school-related problems. Rather, arrive ready to work and collaborate for the child's benefit. However, if you feel the professional is in error or does not understand the entire situation, share information that you have. Whatever the situation, you should constantly be looking for ways to resolve conflicts and to solve problems associated with your child's educational program.

- Make a list of information you believe should be shared with the student's teacher and other professionals. Include the child's particular likes, dislikes, and attitudes, as well as specific information that may aid the teacher in better understanding the student's particular situation.

- Consider taking notes during the conference. After the conference attempt to summarize the important points and happenings that took place.

- Praise the teacher and educational system for things they do well.

- If the conferencer uses a term or concept that you are unfamiliar with, ask for an explanation.

- Accept responsibility for problems that are yours. Likewise, follow through with any plans or activities that you agree to.

- Do not expect the conferencer to solve your personal problems or those of your family. The person conducting the progress report conference will most likely be a teacher. Although educators may be able to make referrals, they are not therapists.

This list, of course, is far from comprehensive. Messineo and Sleeman (1977), for example, developed a protocol form for aiding parents in gathering information and structuring their participation in conferences. Above all, the educator must remember that the maximum growth of a child will be facilitated by parents, family members, and educators collaboratively working together. However, for parents and family members to be most productive in conferences, they must receive appropriate training. As suggested by a number of authorities, parents who are educated in school-related matters will be more satisfied with the system, because they will have been involved in the establishment of its design (Drucker, 1976; Friend & Cook, 1992; Harry et al., 1995).

Summary

Progress report conferences remain among the most common of all parent-educator interactions and, consequently, are among the most significant. These meetings afford the opportunity for parents, family members, and teachers to exchange information and develop and expand a collaborative relationship. In addition, these meetings provide an opportunity for significant information to be exchanged for the benefit of children and youth. However, in spite of the potential significance of these meetings, one must remember that the success of the parent/family and professional progress report conference will closely align with the establishment of rap-port, trust, and a cooperative relationship, and with the participation training parents and family members have received. Thus, the educator cannot realistically expect the progress report conference to be effective in the absence of prior positive associations. However, when parents, fam-ily members, and educators who have well-established collaborative rela-tionships make use of the progress report conference as one means of sharing information, the results can be highly facilitative of the goals and desired outcomes of everyone involved.

Exercises

1. Conduct a progress report simulation conference using the materi-als in Appendix D. Descriptions are provided for the cases previously pre-sented for other role-play exercises (i.e., students with mental retardation, physical disability, behavior disorders, and so forth). Consequently, you should use those materials most aligned with your area of interest or those that you have used in previous role-playing exercises.

In conducting the simulation exercise, one individual should assume the part of the educator. Those persons should employ both the materials labeled "Teacher Role" and the IEP previously developed for their respec-tive pupil in structuring their responses.

Although individuals assuming the parent's role are not provided script materials, they should participate in the conference by reacting to the information provided by the teachers and by reviewing the initial interview simulation materials outlining the parent's role. A third individ-ual should play the role of evaluator, using the evaluation form included at the end of the appendix.

Individuals should change roles after completing the exercise.

2. Conduct a progress report conference with parents. Following the session, ask the parents, a colleague, or both to evaluate your performance using the instrument shown in Figure 11.3. Compare the ratings you gave yourself with those assigned by the others. Based on the feedback, develop a list of procedures that will enable you to function more effectively in your conference.

Chapter 12

Unplanned
Conferences

It is becoming increasingly apparent that in order for parent-educator conferences to be successful, educators must become trained and prepared for a variety of encounters and situations (Berger, 1995; Fewell, 1986; Hobbs, 1975; Simpson, 1988; Simpson & Simpson, 1994). In particular, the profile of good conferencers must reflect the following traits:

- Aware of the various factors impacting and influencing families of children with exceptionalities

- Competent in establishing and maintaining collaborative relationships

- Knowledgeable of basic communication skills

- Competent in sharing information with parents and families

- Skillful in apprising parents of legislation relating to children with disabilities, including methods for helping them serve as advocates for their own children and as more effective consumers of educational services

- Effective in training parents and family members to function as change agents within the natural environment

- Competent in solving problems and resolving conflicts with parents and families

- Skillful in conducting a variety of individual and group conferences

- Adroit in helping parents and families more effectively accommodate and integrate their children with exceptionalities into family units

In addition to acquiring skill and competence in these areas, educators must be prepared to contend and interact with parents and family members at times other than during scheduled sessions. As any educator will attest, numerous situations can arise in which parents expect to see or talk with their child's teacher or other educational personnel during non-scheduled times and without first having called for an appointment. In fact, because many schools require that teachers be in their classrooms before and after school to talk with parents who want to "drop in," many parents and families likely will assume that conferences can and should occur at their discretion (including in the checkout line of the neighborhood supermarket or over the telephone). Finally, as a number of conferencers have discovered, it is during unscheduled meetings that parents seem most apt to manifest very intense emotions and sentiments, including anger, sorrow, guilt, and despair.

Thus, educators must be equipped with suitable attitudes and skills to deal with parents and family members on these and similar occasions. Although unscheduled conferences have received far less attention from researchers and writers than more traditional parent-educator meetings, this omission in no way indicates a lack of importance for these interactions.

Developing Attitudes and Strategies for Unplanned Conferences

Although educators might understandably prefer scheduled and structured meetings, they must nonetheless acknowledge that at least some of their contacts with parents and family members will be unplanned. Conferencers must not only accept the inevitability of these contacts but also develop appropriate attitudes and strategies for enhancing their success.

Educators must be able to understand themselves and their behavior as related to unscheduled parent and family meetings. That is, they must be able to access their beliefs and honest feelings about parents and family members calling on them unexpectedly, telephoning them at home to talk about students with special needs, and attempting to conduct conferences in noneducational settings. When professionals become cognizant of their own anxieties, fears, and resentments at being unprepared to deal with certain issues, values, and educational philosophies regarding unplanned interactions with parents and families, they will usually be more adept at handling these situations. Moreover, this self-understanding can assist them in structuring situations to jointly meet needs.

Educators must accept all types of parent and family involvement as a basic component of program success. Two premises basic to the effective collaborative involvement of parents, families, and educators are that (a) parents and families must be perceived as integral and legitimate components of any educational or treatment program for children, and that (b) a variety of options for serving the needs of parents and families must be made available, including unscheduled interaction opportunities. Unless educators willingly accept this position, little can be anticipated from the implementation of parent/family programs. Both families and educators must be able to perceive the other party as having a justifiable role in facilitating a child's growth and development and as worthy of cooperative and collaborative involvement for a child's benefit. In particular, both planned and unplanned conferencing opportunities must be extended to parents and family members as a means of facilitating both the development of children and the enhancement of parent-professional communication.

Educators must have confidence that planned change can occur with and through collaborative parent and family involvement programs. Educational conferencers must believe in their capacity to positively influence the behavior of parents and families and the capacity of parents and family members to facilitate the growth and development of their children. Thus, conferencers must accept the premise that children with exceptionalities and their families can positively change when exposed to appropriate conditions and contingencies and that educators can engineer and effect such changes. However, in order for parents and family members to achieve desired change, they must receive a variety of interaction and communication opportunities with educational personnel, including both planned and unplanned meetings. The acceptance both of families' ability to change and conferencers' ability to facilitate this process through both planned and unplanned interactions is basic to the successful implementation of many parent and family programs.

Educators need to be assertive in unplanned conferences. As noted, some meetings with parents and family members of children with exceptionalities will be unplanned but also necessary and productive. However, educators must also recognize that circumstances surrounding these conferences are characterized by variant levels of acceptability. For example, one teacher became concerned because a pupil's mother who had never attended a planned conference routinely called her at home after 10:00 p.m. to discuss her child's school progress. That these and similar situations regularly occur can be attested to by anyone who has ever worked in an educational setting; therefore, educators must be able to exercise appropriate assertiveness in structuring unscheduled conferences. Though the educational conferencer must be tolerant and accepting of unplanned meetings, as well as aware of their potential value, he or she must also be appropriately expressive relative to the circumstances surrounding these sessions.

Assertiveness can serve both to reduce an educator's vulnerability during unplanned parent meetings and to direct interactions into more productive areas. That the process can aid conferencers in expressing their rights without infringing on the interests of others (Alberti & Emmons, 1974; Ivey, Ivey, & Simek-Downing, 1987; Lambie & Daniels-Mohring, 1993) and in evincing positions in a positive and productive manner makes assertiveness an obviously desirable trait for conferencers to possess. Though educators must be appropriately accommodating of parent and family member requests for unplanned meetings, they must also recognize the need to offer structure and guidance regarding these requests. In particular, educators must know when to say "no," how to express emotions and perceptions truthfully, and when to continue, reschedule, and terminate meetings with parents and family members. Failure to act assertively in conferencing will facilitate neither the parent-professional relationship nor a child's school progress; in fact it likely will restrict the development of collaborative relationships.

Educators need to provide structure and guidelines for unplanned conferences. Informing parents and family members of guidelines, protocol, and rules of conduct for unscheduled conferences offers one essential means of enhancing the productivity of these meetings and avoiding misunderstandings. Although such information may be shared during a conversation, it should also be disseminated in written form. Some educators describe such ground rules during initial conferences and then follow up with a written reference (and an additional explanation) at "open house" meetings. The information should include an explanation of when an unscheduled conference is appropriate, the hours available for such meetings, situations that may be inappropriate for a "drop-in" session, and conditions and times during which an educator will accept calls from parents and family members at school and at home.

It is essential that administration staff aid in establishing and implementing such guidelines so as to ensure district or school endorsement and some consistency across programs. Information regarding unplanned conferences also should be considered for dissemination through other modes, such as meetings of the parent-teacher association, local newspapers, parent-coordinated service organizations, and educational television.

Parents and family members in all likelihood will need and appreciate information regarding their participation in unscheduled meetings. Therefore, just as parents must learn to be functional participants in IEP conferences and other school-related sessions, so must they become aware of the variables and procedures associated with unscheduled meetings. Such structure is necessary to make unplanned conferences an appropriate and maximally beneficial form of parent-educator communication.

Educators need to have effective communication skills. As suggested earlier, parents or family members who arrive at unscheduled times for conferences with educational personnel will frequently have a particular concern or need. In conjunction with these absorbing and acute needs one often will see atypical manifestations of emotion. That is, parents who appear without first scheduling an appointment are likely to be concerned about a specific incident at home or school, overwrought with a particular feeling, or in some other way agitated and disquieted. Thus, conferencers can expect to encounter a greater proportion of angry, guilty, and otherwise discomposed parents and family members at unscheduled conferences.

Educators must be prepared, therefore, to apply appropriate communication skills. Although good communication is an integral component of any parent-educator conference, special attention to the characteristics associated with maximizing interactions should be considered at unplanned encounters. In particular, conferencers should strive (a) to attend to parents' and family members' messages, both manifest and affective content as well as nonverbal behavior; (b) to recognize and value parents' and family members' perceptions and concerns (even if one does not agree with them), accepting rather than interpreting what is being shared; and (c) to address the conflict directly. Consideration of these and similar communication facilitators may enable conferencers to convert potentially unhealthy situations into collaborative problem-solving sessions.

Educators need to prepare for unscheduled conferences. Though by their very nature unplanned meetings between families and educators exclude comprehensive planning, conferencers can anticipate and prepare for many unscheduled encounters. For instance, educators should consider maintaining well-organized and up-to-date files on each pupil; having lists of names, addresses, and telephone numbers of school and community agencies available for families; having written guidelines available for parents to use in structuring their child's home-study schedule; and being familiar with the use of conflict resolution strategies. Even though educators may be unfamiliar with the specific types of unplanned meetings they will have with parents and families, they can anticipate and make general arrangements for most of the sessions they will encounter.

Specific Types of Unplanned Meetings

Although a variety of unscheduled encounters with parents and family members can be expected, educational conferencers are most apt to contend with several recurring types of meetings: telephone conferences, meetings in noneducational settings, and encounters with angry parents, emotionally overwrought individuals, garrulous parents, family members who are seeking counseling or therapy for their own problems, and parents who insist on observing their child or talking with an educator during class time.

Telephone Conferences

Just as no businessperson could hope to be successful without making appropriate use of the telephone, fax machine, computer, and so forth, neither can educators. Telephone communication affords the professional an easy and personalized means of interacting with parents and family members. Furthermore, it reduces the problems of misinterpretation and message delay so often experienced when notes are sent home. Yet, in spite of the numerous advantages, telephone interactions present a variety of concerns. First, the telephone should always be considered a "less than equal" alternative to face-to-face meetings. Not only do telephone conversations deny the educator full access to an individual and his or her nonverbal responses and demeanor, they can also limit a conferencer's capacity to provide clear and meaningful feedback. That is, the conferencer will not be able to rely on or produce visual displays, examples of academic work, or other permanent products. Accordingly, telephone interactions are totally dependent on the ability of parents, family members, and conferencers to send and receive messages effectively, a capacity that cannot always be counted on (Rabbitt, 1978; Turnbull & Turnbull, 1986). The telephone is often a weak mode of communication in attempting to resolve conflicts, reach joint solutions to problems, or respond to emotions. Although conferencers may be required to respond to the initial needs of parents and families on the telephone, one is well advised to follow such initial interactions with face-to-face meetings during problematic situations.

Educators would also be well advised to structure their telephone interactions with parents and family members early in a relationship. This structure can be offered at initial conferences or "open house" meetings in the form of suggestions as to when parents should call, matters that are appropriate for telephone communication, and under what conditions parents and family members should telephone educators at home. In a similar manner, conferencers should obtain permission from parents to call them at home or work as well as inquire about convenient times for their conversations. The telephone can be a particularly effective tool when used by conferencers to reinforce children, family members, and parents, to maintain open lines of communication, and to provide ongoing feedback. Parents can also facilitate communication with educators by relying on the telephone primarily as an information exchange device. However, correct use of telephones by parents and family members can be anticipated only with appropriate structuring.

A teacher of adolescents with learning disabilities provided a specific time when parents could call her at school to discuss matters of concern. She arranged with the secretary in her school to take messages and to remind parents who called at other times that she would receive nonemergency telephone calls only at specific times (previously negotiated with the parents). This same teacher routinely requested that parents telephone to alert her of changes occurring in their home or with their child's behavior, to clarify notes sent home, or to discuss other matters of their choice.

Meetings in Noneducational Settings

One teacher of children with learning disabilities confided that she had transferred her church membership to another community so that she would not have to contend with the parents of her students on Sundays. Other educators have noted that they are apprehensive about meeting their students' parents and families in public or nonschool settings because of similar experiences. Although this represents a significant issue for some professionals, a solution can be offered. That is, educators who are uncomfortable talking with parents in out-of-school settings must insist on conducting their conferences only at particular times and places. When approached by parents and family members outside the classroom, these educators must politely, yet assertively, instruct parents and family members about the appropriate manner for setting up a conference. Just as physicians and dentists are reluctant to discuss professional matters with their patients at ball games and restaurants, so must educators be equally resistant.

Some professionals might assume that the protocol associated with this matter is so universally understood that it does not require further attention. Nevertheless, parents and family members should be informed early on of educators' preferences regarding unplanned meetings; only then can a mutually understood expectation exist.

One special education teacher who was new to a small rural community found that she was constantly being approached by parents wishing to discuss their children in a variety of settings outside of school. As one means of contending with this situation, she began carrying cards printed with her name and school telephone number. When approached by parents hopeful of conducting an on-the-spot conference, the teacher would give them a card along with instructions for setting up an appointment. As part of these instructions she also indicated that without the necessary time or materials she could not serve their informational needs adequately.

Meetings with Angry Parents and Family Members

For many educators there is no situation quite as intimidating as the prospect of an angry parent or family member arriving without prior notice. Yet, as unfortunate as these situations may be, they do occasionally occur. Even good relationships between families and professionals can sometimes involve conflict. Hence, even in situations where conferencers have invested time and effort establishing rapport and a spirit of collaboration with parents and families, serious disagreements and misunderstandings may develop. Furthermore, the frustrations experienced by parents and families of children with exceptionalities may result in periodic displays of anger toward a child's teacher or other educational personnel independent of these individuals' behaviors.

Recognition of these basic factors may enable the conferencer to maintain a suitable frame of reference and a willingness to involve parents and families in joint problem solving. In fact, a major problem associated with these conflict situations is their potential impact on future relationships. Failure to contend with parent and family anger effectively can result in reduced cooperation and willingness to collaborate, exacerbated suspicion, and eventual destruction of good communication. On the other hand, conferencers who contend with anger effectively and convert these situations into opportunities for joint problem solving can enhance feelings of trust and value in parents, families, and educators cooperatively searching for solutions to problems.

Rule number one is that conferencers' communication skills will determine their success in unplanned meetings with angry parents and family members. In particular, an effective conferencer must be able to listen accurately and creatively without becoming defensive, recognize and appropriately respond to emotions, maintain a willingness to collaboratively solve problems rather than to patronize or retaliate against aggressive individuals, communicate to parents and family members that it is acceptable for them to have different values and opinions than educators, maintain an adult-to-adult relationship rather than a superior-subordinate attitude, and be willing to offer explanations and information without being sanctimonious.

In addition, conferencers may wish to consider the following when interacting with angry parents and family members:

- Allow parents and family members to talk about their concerns without interruption. Rather than attempting to respond as issues are raised, the conferencer should allow persons to exhaust or fully explain their problems.

- Attempt to record the concerns voiced by parents and family members; however, first consideration should be given to maintaining an acceptable listening environment.

- Be aware that some of the issues raised by angry parents and family members may not actually be significant concerns to them. In their anger parents and family members may comment on issues that are obviously not relevant, and thus educators must be able to help irate persons focus their concerns.

- Be aware of your own body language and the nonverbal responses of parents and family members during these exchanges. Concentrate on keeping your voice low, relaxing, and avoiding defensive or intimidating gestures.

- Avoid attempts at discounting problems or parents' feelings regarding issues (e.g., "Now let's not overreact," "You couldn't possibly feel that way").

- Avoid arguing with parents and family members.

- Respond to feelings without putting parents and family members on the defensive (e.g., "You are very angry," "I see a great deal of hostility in you today") and without using clichés (e.g., "I feel that you are say-ing to me . . . ," "Now just calm down, honey").

- Avoid strong emotional reactions and insensitive responses, includ-ing sarcasm, disbelief, pain, anger, and disapprobation.

- Request clarification from parents and family members on points you do not understand but avoid constantly interrupting, asking two ques-tions at once, or using leading questions.

- Attempt to keep angry persons on task without eliminating the opportunity for them to voice additional concerns.

- Avoid attempts to engage parents and family members in collabora-tive problem solving before they have had an opportunity to express fully their concerns and to vent their anger.

- Be sensitive and sympathetic to parent and family problems without assuming responsibility or ownership.

- As much as possible, avoid responding to wrongful and generalized allegations (e.g., "If you were a decent teacher this wouldn't have happened") or threats (e.g., "You can expect to hear from my lawyer," "I plan to call the superintendent of schools").

- When confronted by parents and family members with a confirmed history of being physically abusive toward professionals, ask that a colleague sit in on the session.

- Recognize that most anger is motivation that can be translated into collaborative problem-solving efforts.

The teacher of a group of intermediate-grade children with severe dis-abilities was surprised one day after school by an irate parent. This individ-ual, whom the teacher had known for several years, accused her and her colleagues of several wrongdoings, including a lack of concern over the well-being and future of their pupils. By simply allowing the parent to talk about her concerns and by not responding defensively, the educator was able to determine that her family had recently been under a severe emo-tional stress and this situation had been aggravated by a note from the teacher outlining a new "inclusion" program. After the parent had an opportunity to vent her feelings and concerns, a discussion of the new pro-gram ensued. In addition, the educator was able to suggest several alterna-tives for alleviating the stress factors in the home.

Meetings with Parents and Families
Who Are Emotionally Overwrought

As described previously, one can expect parents and families of children and youth with exceptionalities to have a number of strong emotional reactions to their children's conditions (Roberts, 1986; Paul & Simeonsson, 1993; Roos, 1978; Simpson & Carter, 1993). Included may be shock (Hardman, Drew, & Egan, 1984; Ross, 1964), grief (Solnit & Stark, 1961), guilt (Ziskin, 1978), and frustration (Akerley, 1978; Fewell, 1986). Accordingly, educators can anticipate periodically interacting with emotionally upset parents and family members.

Although the process of effectively responding to overwrought parents and families consists of a number of components, the conferencer should keep two basic points in mind. The first relates to the need to confirm and legitimize emotions and to indicate that it is acceptable for parents and family members to have certain feelings. Furthermore, educators should be willing and able to communicate that they are comfortable and capable of helping parents and families contend with such feelings. Thus, more than anything else, conferencers must assure parents and families that their behavior is both acceptable and understandable.

Second, responding to the emotional reactions of parents and family members must take precedence over other agenda items. For example, parents who become emotionally upset in the course of an unscheduled conference ostensibly initiated to deal with other matters should be dealt with as if their emotional response were the single most salient issue rather than a concern that must be eliminated so that attention can refocus on the initial topic. Frequently when parents arrive at unscheduled times for meetings with educators and subsequently manifest strong emotions, their major concern is associated with their own feelings rather than with the stated issue.

Conferencers should consider the following points during interactions with emotionally upset parents and family members:

- Listen. Avoid attempts at talking parents and family members out of their feelings or aiding them in denying their responses.

- Become aware of your own reactions when confronted with emotionally overwrought persons. Such self-examination will help educators recognize how they manifest their anxieties, including avoidance of eye contact, shifts in body posture, and body movements.

- Recognize that emotionally overwrought persons are in a highly vulnerable position. Therefore, conferencers must be able to verbally support parents and family members (e.g., "It's OK for you to cry"), physically offer assurance (e.g., touch an arm, offer tissues), and psychologically communicate a sense of understanding. At all costs, conferencers should avoid being critical (e.g., "Come on, pull yourself together") or intolerant of emotional responses (e.g., "My job as teacher only allows me to talk with you about your daughter's performance in school, not that other stuff").

- Avoid offering quick solutions; frequently the best strategy for dealing with emotionally upset parents and family members is to allow them to talk without interruption.

- Avoid patronizing remarks and clichés when interacting with emotionally upset parents and family members.

- Do not discount or refute the descriptions of feelings or events offered by emotionally upset parents and family members; rather, let the emphasis rest on understanding these perceptions.

During one unscheduled conference initiated by a parent seemingly to discuss her daughter's school progress, it quickly became obvious that the mother's major concern was not her child's academic development. This parent had been traumatized by a severe accident that had befallen her daughter, and, while she had begun to recognize her child's need for special school services, she continued to experience a number of strong feelings associated with the accident and its effects. As a result, the educator redirected the focus of the conference toward the mother's feelings and emotional concerns. This session was later followed by a scheduled progress report meeting.

Meetings with Garrulous Parents and Family

Parents and family members who chronically show up for unscheduled conferences without any more serious purpose than an interest in chatting can be exasperating. Conferencers may hold open portions of each day or week for unplanned meetings, but with the plan of using such opportunities to discuss relevant items. When a loquacious parent or family member fails to make appropriate use of this time resource, conferencers must firmly and positively structure the situation. Failure to do so can result in a waste of professional time, interference with persons actually requiring legitimate attention, and a deterioration in parent-educator relationships.

Educators confronted with garrulous persons may wish to consider the following ideas:

- Apprise parents and family members early in the school year that, although unscheduled meetings can be held, these sessions should occur on an aperiodic basis and they are not designed for casual visitations.

- Confront parents and family members who consistently arrive for unplanned conferences without a purpose or agenda. Such a straightforward strategy is typically more profitable than devising more circuitous measures for ending or avoiding these meetings.

- Consider setting a time limit for all unplanned conferences. Although conferencers must be willing to make adjustments according to the needs of individuals, this strategy can serve to reduce time spent in nonpertinent areas.

After having tried a number of more subtle approaches, one teacher finally confronted a parent of one of her pupils who routinely showed up in her classroom after school without an appointment. When confronted, the parent explained that she enjoyed seeing the teacher and hearing about her child's progress, albeit in an indirect fashion. After being made aware of her behavior and the restrictions it placed on the teacher and other parents, the mother became more appropriate and collaborative in her conferencing behavior.

Meeting with Parents and Families Who Are Seeking Counseling for Themselves

Occasionally conferencers find that parents and family members who frequently call on them to discuss their children are actually seeking counseling for themselves. This may be the case when parents arrive without prior notice and the focus of each session revolves around the family and the difficulties experienced by that individual. In such instances, it is extremely important that educators distinguish individuals who simply want to chat from those needing psychological counseling. In situations where parents and family members require psychological counseling, the conferencer should refer them to other professionals better qualified to serve their needs. Hence, conferencers must be cautious not to dismiss a parent who chronically "drops by" as someone who simply wants to pass the time of day when the individual may indeed be seeking professional services.

Although educational conferencers must be cognizant of their role and recognize their professional limitations, they also must be aware of their obligations. That is, educational conferencers must not simply terminate a relationship with a parent or family member because that individual needs in-depth counseling. Rather, educators must rely on their relationship with a parent or family member along with their clinical skills to reach a point where they can be assured that the person will not be threatened by referral to another person or agency. Failure to act in this manner may result in persons both rejecting referrals for counseling and discontinuing relationships with educators that may be needed for their children's continued growth and development.

As a strategy for dealing with a father who was obviously seeking help for himself, an educator initially concentrated on building a trusting relationship. Subsequently, she suggested that this parent consider counseling from the individual associated with the school system who was better trained to provide psychological services to parents. The offer of this suggestion after a collaborative relationship had been developed helped the father give it serious consideration.

Meetings with Parents During Class Time

Occasionally educators may be confronted by parents who either wish to observe their children without having made prior arrangements or wish to engage in a teacher conference during class time. Obviously, these situations can be both troublesome for educators and disruptive to pupils.

One mechanism for clarifying procedures for parents wishing to observe their children in class or to meet with educators is to inform them of the protocol surrounding these activities. This information should be given parents at the same time their children are placed in a program and followed by periodic updates dictated by changes and individual needs. These guidelines may be provided verbally, but they should also be disseminated to parents and family members in written form for later reference.

Educators may determine that allowing a parent to observe a class without prior arrangements does not constitute a problem. However, in such instances some educators may request that the parent wait in an office area until the teacher or another educator can determine if they have a particular concern and what they are specifically interested in observing. This procedure also gives the educator a chance to remind the parent of guidelines and rules for classroom observation. Taking the time to attend to these considerations can often convert a potentially distressing situation into a good collaborative learning experience. Conversely, in instances where parents have not made prior arrangements to observe a class and when doing so would not be in the best interests of a program, the educator must courteously, yet firmly, insist that the parent arrange to visit on another occasion.

Educators confronted with parents and family members desiring an immediate meeting must be able to determine whether the circumstances warrant an on-the-spot conference. School psychologists, counselors, and some itinerant and consulting personnel may be able to see persons under these conditions with only minor difficulties; however, classroom teachers face a much more difficult situation.

One particular policy that can eliminate problems in this area is to require that all visitors to a school or agency check in at the central office. Indeed, if this policy is followed, classroom teachers will not be required to contend with a parent and a class simultaneously. Rather, an administrator, counselor, or another person can make judgments regarding the needs of a parent or family member and decide whether a teacher's presence is required in a conference. Finally, when warranted, these same individuals can make arrangements for a teacher's class to be covered by someone else or for the meeting to take place during a free period.

After receiving a note from his child's teacher describing a behavior problem, one father of a boy with an emotional/behavioral disorder arrived at school the following day just as classes were starting with the intent of meeting with his son's teacher. This individual was allowed to confer with the school counselor until the teacher's planning period. At that time, the counselor, parent, and teacher were able to meet regarding the incident. This session led to more adequate evaluation systems and a more regularly scheduled series of conferences.

Undoubtedly, parents and family members who arrive at their child's school during class hours demanding to hold a conference will not be particularly welcome. Nonetheless, educators must not be so rigid and insensitive as to deny parents access to professional services. Rather, efforts should be made to negotiate a time when pertinent parties can be brought together. In addition, when a parent or family member wishes to see an individual who is not available at the moment, arrangements should be made to have the person meet with someone else whenever possible. Frequently when parent's or family members' concerns are so pressing that they arrive at a school without prior notice, they should receive immediate attention. Failure to do so can lead to unfavorable outcomes.

Summary

Even though educators may prefer to hold conferences with parents and family members at scheduled times, unplanned meetings will occur. Consequently, educators can and must be prepared for these encounters in order to work successfully with parents and families.

—————————————— **Exercises** ——————————————

1. Conduct unplanned role-play conferences with another individual. Your sessions should be structured around the following:

- a parent-initiated telephone conference

- attempts by a parent or family member to conduct a conference in a noneducational setting

- a meeting with an angry parent or family member

- a meeting with an emotionally upset parent or family member

- a meeting with a garrulous parent or family member

- a meeting with a parent or family member seeking personal professional help

- a meeting with a parent who insists on observing a child or conferring with a teacher during class time

In conducting the exercise, one individual should assume the part of a parent or family member, another the part of the educator, and a third the role of an observer and discussant. Following each session the observer should discuss with the participants those procedures that were employed to deal with the situation and the strategies that might have been more appropriate.

Each group of three should assume each role in the exercise.

Chapter 13

Group Conferences

In spite of indications that it may be highly beneficial to hold individual conferences with every parent and family member (Duncan & Fitzgerald, 1969; Kroth & Simpson, 1977; Voltz, 1994), group sessions prove more desirable in certain situations. In particular, group conferences can serve as follow-ups to individual parent-educator meetings and as a means of allowing for dynamic interactions between a number of parents and family members, including those with similar types of children.

One of the most obvious advantages of group conferencing or training is a reduction in time and effort requirements: It is much more efficient to have conferences and train parents in groups than individually (Gordon, 1980; McDowell, 1976; Miller & Hudson, 1994; Rose, 1969). Hence, just as public schools are limited in their capacity to provide individual instruction to children, so, too, are many educators restricted in their individual conferencing resources. In addition, research has offered some indications that group models offer the most efficacious means of accomplishing certain goals (Dembo, Sweitzer, & Lauritzen, 1985; Kelly, 1974; McWhirter, McWhirter, McWhirter, & McWhirter, 1993; Weissbourd & Kagan, 1989). For instance, by having conferencers transact general business in group settings and disseminate basic information of interest to all parents, they may be able to accrue the necessary time to conduct individual sessions with parents who require more specific or specialized attention. As suggested by Wyckoff (1980), "The time savings noted with the group delivery over the individual delivery has been attributed to the opportunity the grouped parents had to exchange ideas and learn how others solved problems with their own children" (p. 295).

In addition, and perhaps most importantly, group interactions can be both enlightening and stimulating for the participants. In some instances

299

parents and family members may discover other families with issues similar to their own, or in others they may gain the confidence necessary to apply new techniques with their children. In still other situations, group sessions may provide parents and family members a forum for discussing their perceptions and feelings about their children with a truly empathic group. As observed by Rutherford and Edgar (1979), "group training provides support for parents who feel socially isolated from parents of normal children. In some cases, the friendships formed during these training sessions have been maintained long after the training sessions have terminated" (p. 161). When provided an opportunity to interact in the right kind of group setting, parents and families of children with exceptionalities frequently respond by becoming more actively and productively involved with their children and the educators who serve them.

Although the structure, characteristics, and goals of each parent/family group meeting are dictated by the needs and distinctive features of the participants and by the objectives and training of the person conducting the session, most will focus on one of the following five areas: (a) group information exchange programs, (b) training sessions to aid parents and families in their role as educational consumers and child advocates, (c) family-applied intervention and tutor training programs, (d) group counseling, support, and education programs, and (e) service programs for parents and family members.

Group Information Exchange Programs

Although parents and family members should have an opportunity to exchange information with educators on a one-to-one basis when their child first enters a program and thereafter as required, many of their basic information needs can be satisfied effectively through group meetings. Thus, even though group sessions must not supplant individual conferences, they can serve as a vehicle for disseminating common information, discussing shared issues, and allowing for communication between parents and family members with collective concerns. In particular, sessions focusing on the nature, characteristics, etiology, and prognosis of an exceptionality, a description of the general educational program being utilized, and the manner in which pupils are evaluated are highly compatible with a group format. As suggested by Kelly (1974), "To be successful, the teacher-planner must take care to select a theme which is most relevant to her children's parents. All other aspects of planning revolve around the theme selected" (p. 33).

Information Regarding an Exceptionality

One of the most common needs expressed by parents of children with exceptionalities is for information on the nature, characteristics, etiology, and future implications of their offspring's condition (Chinn, Winn, & Walters, 1978; Simpson, 1988; Simpson & Zionts, 1992). The search for this kind of information represents both an immediate reaction to an exceptionality as well as an ongoing concern of parents and families. Accordingly, educators should be aware that information relating to an exceptionality presents a commonly requested agenda item. In this regard parents and family members may benefit as much (if not more) from being allowed to discuss their own perceptions and to share their own information regarding an exceptionality as from facts disseminated by a professional.

The importance of addressing the characteristics, etiology, and prognosis of an exceptionality should not be underestimated. First, the complexity of these issues may make their comprehension by parents and families extremely difficult. Certainly if professionals have as much difficulty understanding the various exceptionalities as they appear to, parents and family members can be expected to share the same plight. In addition, even when families have a cognitive understanding of a condition and its related factors, they can still be expected to demonstrate emotional needs that require attention. Group interactions and the support that can come from families meeting together frequently serve to satisfy this need. Though group sessions focusing on this type of information must not take the place of individualized and in-depth interpretation, planning, and evaluation conferences, they can help clarify and facilitate understanding and acceptance by parents and families.

One teacher of children with learning disabilities held a parent group session each year on factors associated with her pupils' exceptionality. As a part of her discussion she focused on a commonly used definition of learning disabilities, including an interpretation of its components (e.g., involvement of one or more of the basic psychological processes, minimal brain dysfunction). Furthermore, she made available a list of common terms associated with "learning disabilities" (e.g., attention deficit disorder, poor self-concept, vocal encoding) and discussed these items with parents and family members. Finally, she employed her list of terms as a vehicle for stimulating discussions with the participants. This veteran educator revealed that when she gave parents lists of terms she not only was supplying them with a future reference, she was also generating questions and stimulating lively discussions that might not otherwise have come forth.

Other means of structuring informative group sessions on characteristics and related issues include videotapes, filmstrips, guest speakers on a particular topic, and adults with disabilities commenting on their personal experiences. However, regardless of the format used, time should always be allotted for discussions. As suggested earlier, family interaction opportunities typically are the most salient part of any group meeting.

Educational Program Description

Conferencers can also expect families of children with exceptionalities to be interested in the educational and related services programs and procedures designed for their children. When taken up in group sessions, topics on these issues should support (not replace) information provided in individual conferences and present items for general discussion. Areas of discussion and information exchange will occur on topics similar to those pursued during initial parent conferences, including classroom/school schedules, policies, and orientation, academic and social intervention and enrichment programs, ancillary services and personnel available to students, and parent and family programs. Because parents (and family members) should have had an opportunity to pursue these matters individually at the time of the initial conference, group sessions should be designed to reacquaint families with the original information plus any changes that may have taken place and then to allow for discussions among the participants.

A number of educators address general information relating to educational programming at annual "open house" meetings. Of course parents should be invited to make individual appointments at a later time to discuss specific matters as needed.

One teacher of students with learning disabilities gave parents a written description of her educational program at the time she provided an oral overview. She reported that this strategy served both to provide parents and family members with a resource for later referral and to stimulate discussion. The meeting took place in the special education resource room and was structured to accommodate questions, demonstrations, and comments, all of which aided in facilitating a discussion. The teacher discussed the classroom schedule with the parents and, because each of the students was in an inclusive classroom for a significant part of each day, she spent a considerable amount of time discussing the general education support and communication system she used. Finally, the teacher also provided a thorough description of the reinforcement and behavior management system she used in her class, and the manner in which this system was coordinated with the students' general education teachers. Again, this topic was structured so as to facilitate discussion.

Evaluation Procedures

Group meetings can offer an appropriate vehicle for discussing the manner in which a student will be evaluated and the mode in which this information will be communicated to parents and family members. In many instances, children with exceptionalities enter special education programs with a long history of school failure, making the topic of evaluation particularly interesting. Moreover, as the majority of children and youth with exceptionalities receive at least a portion of their education in regular classrooms, it is important to discuss the manner in which educators will coordinate evaluations across various settings and classrooms. Just as with other topical areas within this domain, information should serve as a follow-up to discussions during individual conferences and be presented in a fashion facilitative of group interaction. Accordingly, in order to facilitate discussions, the conferencer should carefully plan ways of assuring parent and family participation. Without such prior planning, the major benefits of group conferences may go untapped.

Group-Oriented Consumer and Advocacy Training Programs

Instruction on procedures for helping parents and families become better consumers of educational services and advocates for their children is particularly well suited for group training. Though this training can be provided individually and through printed materials that parents and families can use independently, optimal training success seems associated with group processes (Miller & Hudson, 1994). This is particularly true when group sessions allow for discussions along with simulation, role-playing, and modeling opportunities. Specifically, training sessions are needed that familiarize parents and families with their rights and responsibilities relative to their child with an exceptionality and with methods for more effective participation in educational conferences.

The role of parents as chief advocates for their children with exceptionalities requires that they determine whether their offspring are receiving appropriate services and that the schools serving their children are in compliance with local, state, and federal policies and guidelines (Fiedler, 1991). Without information and training on these topics, parents and family members will probably be less than completely effective representatives for their children. Hence, a primary training activity for educators must involve familiarizing parents with the guidelines and procedures associated with various special education mandates and policies, including the Individuals with Disabilities Education Act, Americans with Disabilities Act, Section 504 of the Rehabilitation Act of 1973, and so forth.

An example of one unit of a training document used to transmit information about the Individuals with Disabilities Education Act in group conferences is shown below. The training format was structured around a booklet, which families were allowed to keep. In addition, the conferencers planned discussions to ensure familiarity with the various concepts presented. Participants were instructed that according to the Individuals with Disabilities Education Act, parents had the following rights:

- The right to have your child educated with students who do not have disabilities to the maximum extent appropriate. When at all possible, your child has the right to remain in a regular classroom situation to receive his or her education. However, regular classroom placement at all times may not be appropriate for some students. If your child requires a more restrictive settings, such as special education classroom, as deemed by you along with other members of the IEP team, then such provisions will be made available to meet your child's needs.

- The right to have your child attend the school he or she would attend if they did not have an exceptionality, unless the IEP requires some other arrangements. If the school your child would normally attend does not have the appropriate instructional services your child needs, your school district may provide those services elsewhere (perhaps in another school within the district), and shall also be responsible for your child's transportation between home and his instructional site.

- The right of your child to participate with normally developing and achieving children as much as possible, including in nonacademic and extracurricular services and activities such as meals, recess, counseling, clubs, athletics, and special groups. Your child has the right to participate in any of the above activities with other children unless such activities are deemed inappropriate jointly by you and the IEP team. (Simpson, 1992, pp. 3–4)

In addition, parents and family members should also be given instruction in how to participate in the various types of conferences they will be asked to attend, including initial, interpretation, individualized education program (IEP), and progress report sessions. Without appropriate training, parents and family members cannot be effective conference participants and best represent the interests of their child. Training in this area often can be provided most effectively in group situations, in which discussions, role models, simulation activities, and encouragement can become an integral part of the learning experience.

Turnbull (1981) suggested that educators provide parents a list of questions they should consider prior to attending a conference. The list recommended included skills parents would like their children to learn, areas of behavior and socialization that they would like to see dealt with at school, parental perceptions of their children, and their attitudes regarding their child interacting with children who do not have exceptionalities. Turnbull noted that with such training one can expect parents to become more productive conference participants.

Simpson and Fiedler (1989, pp. 167–169) offered suggestions for maximally involving parents in their children's IEP meetings. These considerations, shown in Table 13.1, are grouped by levels of preferred parental involvement: prior to the IEP conference, at the actual conference, and after the IEP conference has been completed.

With proper training and motivation, parents and families of children and youth with exceptionalities can function with skill and authority as consumers of educational services and advocates for their children. In many instances, the training associated with developing this proficiency can be delivered effectively via a group format.

Group Behavior Management and Tutorial Training Programs

Another area for which the group format can prove highly appropriate is in training parents and family members to serve as behavioral change agents and tutors for their own children in nonschool settings. As described by a number of authorities, parents can learn to be both managers of social behavior and academic tutors, thereby extending the service options available to exceptional children beyond the classroom environment (Adelman, 1994; Berkowitz & Graziano, 1972; Greenwood, Whorton, & Delquadri, 1984; O'Dell, 1974; Sasso, Hughes, Critchlew, Falcon, & Delquadri, 1980; Simpson & Fiedler, 1989).

Table 13.1. Considerations for Parent IEP Involvement, by Level of Involvement and Phase of Participation

Pre IEP conference[a]	During IEP conference	Post IEP conference
	Attendance and Approval	
Plan for meeting: (1) determine the site of the conference, (2) plan to arrive on time, (3) identify a baby-sitter to avoid having to bring young children to the meeting, (4) determine how much time has been allotted for the conference, (5) attempt to identify who will attend the meeting.	Maintain a positive attitude during the conference.	Be willing to attend future meetings and to offer support and approval.
Consider bringing a friend or relative to the meeting if you are uncomfortable attending alone.	Maintain a businesslike demeanor: (1) dress in a businesslike manner, (2) bring writing materials, (3) avoid isolation via the seating arrangement, (4) listen carefully, (5) introduce yourself and request that others at the meeting do the same, including specifying their role.	
Develop a positive attitude regarding the meeting as opposed to assuming an adversarial position.	Be willing to accept responsibility for problems which are outside school. Similarly, do not expect school personnel to solve your personal or family problems. However, you may seek referrals from school personnel for such services.	
Familiarize yourself with legal and legislative special education mandates. In particular, review handbooks and pamphlets relating to PL 94-142.		
	Sharing Information	
Maintain and organize developmental, school, and clinical records on your children and review these records (including previous IEPs).	Bring writing materials, background information, and other information which you may wish to share at the conference.	Obtain and file a copy of the IEP and any other information needed for future reference.
		(continues)

[a] Activities at each level of involvement are cumulative (e.g., activities at the second level include those of the first level).

Table 13.1. *Continued*

Pre IEP conference	During IEP conference	Post IEP conference
Develop a list of information and other data you wish to share at IEP conferences. Write this information down because you may not remember it at conference time.		Provide conference information to family members, including the child about whom the meeting was held (if appropriate).
Identify with family members' (including the child about whom the conference will be held) prioritized goals for the child.	*Suggesting Goals* Assertively maintain a participatory status during the conference. Ask for clarification about items and concepts which you fail to understand and which are not explained; solicit input and feedback from individuals who might not otherwise share information; make suggestions you consider important; request a copy of the completed IEP; and request additional meeting time if the allotted schedule is insufficient for completing the IEP. Present to IEP participants parent and family goals for the child.	*Prepare notes about the meeting. These notes should reflect happenings during the conference and should be filed with the student's IEP.* Contact the appropriate personnel if clarification or additional information is required. Reinforce educators for their work, for example, through letters and phone calls.
Consider enrolling in assertiveness training and problem-solving workshops.	*Negotiating Goals* Positively and assertively work with educators. Present and advocate priority goals. However, avoid arguing over minor details or attempting to dominate the meeting.	

(continues)

Table 13.1. *Continued*

Pre IEP conference	During IEP conference	Post IEP conference
	Monitoring Implementation	
Consider enrolling in workshops on child and program assessment and evaluation.	Establish the manner in which goals and objectives will be monitored and how this information will be communicated to educators.	Maintain an ongoing record of IEP progress and skill development.
	Engaging in Joint Programming	
Familiarize yourself with teaching strategies and behavior management techniques.	Establish the manner in which goals and objectives will be jointly monitored and how this information will be communicated.	
	Engaging in Independent Programming	
Develop proficiency in independently carrying out teaching strategies and behavior management procedures.	Establish the conditions under which goals and objectives will be independently pursued by parents and the manner in which this information will be communicated.	

Note. From *The Second Handbook on Parent Education* (pp. 167–169), by R. Simpson and C. Fiedler, 1989, New York: Academic Press. Copyright 1989 by Academic Press. Reprinted with permission.

An example of an instructional program designed to train groups of parents of children with exceptionalities in the use of behavior management procedures is presented below. This program, developed by Simpson and Combs (1978) to instruct parents of children and youth with autism, is based on a three-part slide/tape presentation (Simpson & Swenson, 1978). Part I provided an overview of behavioral techniques, including procedures for identifying a target behavior. Part II focused on training parents to employ behavioral measurement procedures, and Part III dealt with graphing behavioral records and applying intervention techniques. The program was designed to operate for a minimum of 4 consecutive weeks, with the fourth meeting serving as follow-up. Reproduced below are selected sections from the training manual (Simpson & Combs, 1978) that was written to provide structure to educators and other users of the training model.

Guidelines for Program Use and Selection of Participants

Careful planning has gone into the development of the workshop procedures described in the following sections. The validity of the program will depend on the appropriate implementation of the procedures described in this manual. For that reason, it is mandatory that workshop leaders follow the suggested guidelines. This training program is designed for use by workshop leaders with professional training and experience in both parent counseling and behavior modification. Specifically, the program is designed for individuals holding at least a master's degree in counseling, child development, special education, psychology, or a related field. In addition, the level of professional expertise of manual users should enable them to screen prospective participants. Specifically, it should be recognized that a group format is not equally appropriate for all parents and that some individuals may be in need of more intensive or individualized intervention.

Planning and Organizing the Workshop

The behavior management workshop is not only adaptable to a variety of parents and children, but also to a number of situations. For instance, the series can be used with a group of parents who will continue to meet after completion of the behavior management program, as an initial means of organizing a group, or as a program for parents who will meet only for the management workshop. Regardless of the design, it is imperative that parents participating in the workshop attend all sessions. Equally important, parents and guardians participating in the program must agree to complete all exercises and assignments, including some home-based activities. Since the workshop content is sequentially arranged, parents who do not attend one or more sessions will probably experience difficulty in successfully completing the program and in correctly applying the concepts.

As an aid in securing parental cooperation, it is recommended that participants be notified in advance of the importance of attending all sessions and that they sign an agreement form acknowledging their willingness to complete the program. Use of a contract has been found to be a functional procedure for increasing the probability of attendance, although the parents should be made aware that the contract is legally nonbinding and that they are not required to sign it to take part in the sessions.

An example of a workshop invitation [Figure 13.1] and a sample participation contract [Figure 13.2] are provided for illustrative purposes. It is suggested that the invitations be sent to parents and family members through the mail and that the contracts be presented verbally as a means of increasing the probability of success. Basic information about the child should also be elicited in planning the workshop [Figure 13.3 and Figure 13.4].

The Workshop Environment

Experienced counselors and group facilitators generally agree that physical and environmental factors can either facilitate or detract from the desired goals of a workshop. However, the exact design of the workshop environment is difficult to specify because of resource limitations and individual preferences. More importantly, workshops are frequently conducted in situations that allow for only limited environmental manipulation. Nonetheless, it is essential to secure a setting that is characterized by both professionalism and comfort. Professionalism, as shown in the physical environment, implies an atmosphere that is commensurate with the goals of the workshop. Although difficult to precisely specify, the furniture and facilities should be appropriate for a nonsocial meeting among adults and yet be comfortable. Since it is essential that the environment not interfere with the workshop procedures, session coordinators should provide participants with adequate furniture, lighting, and other physical features.

Since the series format calls for both full-group and small-group participation, appropriate space arrangements must be made. These arrangements include a room large enough to accommodate all participants and adequate for an audio-visual presentation and either several small rooms for small group work or one room large enough to allow several small groups to meet simultaneously. Finally, workshop leaders should have available audio-visual equipment, an overhead projector, screen, movable chairs, and work tables.

Dear Mr. and Mrs. (Jones):

You are cordially invited to attend a Parent Workshop on behavior management techniques. The workshop will meet on Thursday evenings for 4 consecutive weeks beginning September 14. The sessions will be coordinated by (Dr. Sally Smith) and will meet in room (31) at (Central Junior High School).

The purpose of the workshop series is to share information about procedures for more effectively allowing parents and family members to manage the behavior of their children. Parents and family members will be encouraged to participate in the program and to apply the techniques with their own children. Since the four-part workshop series is sequentially arranged, it is imperative that participants attend all sessions.

If you would like additional information about the workshop, please call the district administrative offices (849-1403, extension 41). If you do plan to participate, please complete the attached forms (Figures 13.3 and 13.4) and return to the district office in the enclosed stamped envelope. This information will be used in applying the workshop principles to your child.

Sincerely,

(Peter Foxx)
(Director of Pupil Services)

Figure 13.1. Sample letter of invitation. (p. 15)

I wish to participate in the workshop on behavioral management techniques sponsored by the school district. I have been informed of the nature of the workshop series and I understand the importance of attending each of the four sessions. In addition, I agree to participate in all activities related to the workshop.

_____
Parent or Guardian Signature

_____
Date

Figure 13.2. Sample participation contract. (p. 15)

Name of Child _____

Name of Person Completing Form _____

Relationship to Child _____

Date _____

I. List the things which your child does that you like, that other people
    like, and that he or she does well or relatively well.
    1.
    2.
    3.

II. List the things that your child does too often, too much, or at the
    wrong times that get him or her into trouble. List everything you can
    think of.
    1.
    2.
    3.

III. List the things that your child fails to do, refuses to do, does not do
    properly, does not do often enough, or does not do as you would like.
    1.
    2.
    3.

IV. Considering the above, list the three things that you consider to be
    the most important and in need of change or strengthening. List these
    in order of importance.
    1.
    2.
    3.

Figure 13.3. Child information form. (p. 16)

Child's Name _____

Name of Person Completing Form _____

Relationship to Child _____

Date _____

Please complete this form according to your knowledge and observation of your child. You may wish to directly ask your child many of these questions since it is important that the answers truly represent the child's likes and dislikes.

1. What sorts of things does your child like to do?

2. If given a choice, how does your child spend his (or her) time?

3. What privileges does your child have?

4. What does he (or she) frequently ask you for?

5. If school-aged, what does he (or she) like to do after coming home from school?

6. What games does your child like to play?

7. What are your child's favorite things to eat?

8. How does your child spend time on the weekends?

9. Who does your child like to visit? (friends, grandparents, other relatives, other adults)

10. Where does your child like to go? (swimming pool, library, grocery, certain stores, shopping, the park)

11. What are your child's favorite television programs?

12. What are your child's favorite indoor activities?

13. What are your child's favorite outdoor activities?

14. What does your child like to do most with mother?

15. What does your child like to do most with father?

16. What does your child like to do most with brothers and sisters? (list each sibling)

17. List three things your child least likes to do.

18. List three things your child would most like to have.

Figure 13.4. Reinforcement inventory. (p. 17)

Conducting the Workshop

Although not totally designed for large groups, aspects of the workshop series can be used with as many as 100 persons. Thus, introductory information, audio-visual presentations, and certain other activities can be presented to relatively large groups; however, a large part of the workshop is designed for small groups of 10 to 12 persons. Each group of 10 to 12 parents and family members should have its own leader. These leaders should have the same training and background as previously described for session leaders and should remain with the same participants during the four-session workshop series. It is also recommended that groups be developed to accommodate parents, guardians and family members of children of similar ages. Although families may have children with wide age ranges, they will frequently be motivated to apply the techniques with one child in particular. Thus, as much as possible, parents and family members should be grouped according to the age of the child with whom they are most concerned. In addition, especially with regard to children and youth with exceptionalities, attempts should be made to homogeneously group parents and family members according to the characteristics of the child or adolescent. Since some parents may find it difficult to participate in the workshop activities if their offspring is significantly different from those described by other participants, prior grouping arrangements may need to be made. (pp. 7–9)

As a further example of the use of this program, the guidelines associated with the initial components of the four-part series (developing and maintaining adaptive behavior) are presented. Readers should note that these guidelines are also appropriate for use in other types of parent and family programs.

Participant Orientation to Workshop

Purpose. To welcome parents and family members and to describe the objectives for the workshops, the agenda for the evening, and to give information regarding future meeting times.

Materials Needed:
—name tags and pencils,
—participation agreement forms.

Procedure. The participants should be greeted as they arrive for the meeting. Each parent should be asked to find or fill out a name tag. You may also wish to offer coffee or tea as this can contribute to a more genial and informal atmosphere. In addition, if coffee is readily available, interruption of the session for a special break can be avoided.

At the first session, wait about ten minutes after the scheduled starting time to start. This extra time should allow all participants ample time to locate the meeting site. It should be noted that future sessions will start on schedule.

The leader's introduction, which is designed to orient the participants to the workshop and to give essential information, should last no more than five to ten minutes. The introductory comments should include:

—a welcome to participants and reinforcement for their participation
—the general purpose of the workshop
—the date and times of future meetings
—the importance of attendance and participation
—an overview of the workshop series
—an introduction to the agenda for the evening.

An example of the type of introduction appropriate for this orientation session is provided in Figure 13.5. It is suggested that this material be used as a guide and not as information to be read to the participants.

Presentation of Information

Purpose. To prepare parents and family members for the evening's session and to provide instructions and activities to facilitate the establishment of a cognitive framework to enhance learning.

Materials Needed:
—pencils
—videotape or slides and tape
—videotape player or slide projector and tape player
—screen
—posttest questionnaire—A
—overview reference sheet

Procedure. Before the videotape or slide-tape presentation is shown it may be helpful to give each participant a sheet specifying the name of the workshop and workshop leader(s); a brief statement of the overall purpose of the workshop; topics to be covered in each workshop; meeting dates, times, and places; and relevant telephone numbers. This information should be accompanied by a brief comment on the nature of the information. Participants should also be provided an opportunity to ask questions or make comments prior to and following the slide-tape presentation.

In order to provide feedback regarding the effectiveness of the videotape/slide-tape presentation and to aid in identifying particular problems or misconceptions, a posttest questionnaire is administered to participants following each presentation. It is helpful to prepare participants

Welcome to our workshop on Managing Child Behavior. Each of you is here to learn techniques for managing and working with your children. In addition, each of you here is demonstrating by your presence that you are aware that your child can benefit from parent-school cooperation and that you are a concerned parent or guardian.

This is the first of four workshop sessions designed to help parents of typical and exceptional children. The purpose of the workshop series is to help each of you learn and apply behavior management techniques. The skills can be used to deal with actual problems encountered in raising typical as well as handicapped children, since behavior management techniques have been shown to be effective with both groups of individuals. We will meet here each (Thursday) night from (7:00 p.m.) to (9:30 p.m.). We will be sure to end on time, and after tonight, we will also be starting on time. It is crucial that you attend the next two sessions if you hope to develop a behavior management program for your child. The fourth and final session is also important because at that meeting we will attempt to "put together" previously discussed information.

It is necessary that you participate fully in the workshop by completing "homework" assignments and attempting the exercises given during each session. Parents who attend all sessions and complete all assignment have the greatest chance for successful improvement of their child's behavior.

I would like to talk more specifically about the objectives of the workshops and to give you an overview of the next three sessions, as well as a preview of what we will be doing this evening. But, first, I would be interested in any questions or comments any of you may have.

Our goal for this evening's session is to help each of you identify a specific behavior problem that you would like to work on with your child. You have been asked to complete a child information form [Figure 13.3] that we will be using in tonight's work.

During our next session, you will be shown how to observe and record systematically the behavior you wish to change. During the third session you will learn how to design a program to produce actual behavioral changes. During the final session, we will meet to discuss your progress and any specific problems or questions that you may have regarding your own child's program and procedures for setting up future programs.

By the end of this four-part series, many of you should be seeing or beginning to see improvement in your child's behavior. Research has shown that a majority of the parents who systematically follow a behavior management approach are eventually successful in changing the behaviors they identify. However, we must emphasize that attending all sessions, participating in practice exercises, and completing homework assignments are crucial to success.

Tonight and during each of the next two sessions you will be shown a slide-tape presentation that is the basis of the information for these workshops. However, before showing the slide and providing you with additional information, let me answer any questions that you might have up to this point.

Figure 13.5. Sample workshop welcome. (p. 20)

for the questionnaire by explaining that its purpose is to help determine how well the audio-visual presentation was able to convey the information. Participants should be informed that the sheets will be collected but that no one needs to sign the test. (pp. 12–14)

Additional Guidelines for Working with Parents and Family

The foregoing program example focuses only on the first of four group sessions and is only one of several such available group training alternatives in the behavior management area (Hall, 1976; Kerr & Nelson, 1983; Wagonseller, Burnett, Salzburg, & Burnett, 1977; Zionts & Simpson, 1988). However, it does demonstrate the specificity and structure required for successful use with parents and family members. When such precision is a part of a program, the overall effectiveness in most instances will be significantly increased.

The structured training procedures employed with parents and family members to enable them to modify social behavior can also be implemented to augment children's academic programs (Greenwood et al., 1984; Hoover, 1993; Karnes & Lee, 1978). However, to be effective such programs should stem from previously established home-school cooperation. Kelly (1974) observed that

more than any other form of involvement, active parental facilitation of specific subject matter learning must reflect a marked degree of parent-teacher cooperation. Without this type of working relationship, most specific subject matter involvements, from simple parental encouragement to tutoring, can never be fully realized. (p. 120)

In addition, these family-oriented tutorial programs should be coordinated by a child's teacher and only after parents and family members have received sufficient instruction and structure.

Finally, group tutorial training programs for parents and family members should be based on the following guidelines:

- Only parents and family members who are motivated and appear appropriate to tutor their own children should be involved. This type of training and level of participation is not for every family member.

- Parents and family members should receive structured training before conducting tutoring sessions with their own children. These training programs should make use of lectures, discussions, role model demonstrations, and simulation exercises.

- Parents and family members should be provided with ongoing training to match their child's changing needs and skills. Karnes and Zehrbach (1972) suggested that trainers consider using single-topic and small-group training sessions so that parents and family members with the same specific training needs can be dealt with at the same time.

- Carefully monitored evaluation and feedback systems should be incorporated into every program.

- Educators should design their training and feedback systems in such a manner as to provide regular and systematic reinforcement for parents and family members.

Abundant evidence supports the contention that many parents and family members can serve as tutors with their own children and that a group training format may offer the most efficient and efficacious means of developing tutorial competency (Adamson, 1970; Adelman, 1994; Hoover, 1993; Reusen, Bos, Schumaker, & Deshler, 1994; Stokes & Baer, 1978). However, positive results from such programs can be expected only in conjunction with carefully structured and monitored training programs and ongoing evaluation systems.

Group Counseling, Support, and Family Education Programs

As suggested previously, educational conferencers must be able to determine when the needs of parents and families require traditional counseling methods. In this context, conferencers must be aware of their own strengths and weaknesses and be willing to refer parents and families to appropriate professionals (e.g., mental health workers) as needed. Moreover, conferencers should recognize that many parents and family members will benefit from support groups even if they don't require formal counseling and therapy (Miller & Hudson, 1994; Phillips, 1985).

In part, the process of determining which parents and family members are most appropriate for group educational conferences as opposed to psychological counseling depends on the distinction made between conferencing, counseling, and psychotherapy. Unfortunately, the literature's attempts to make such distinctions have been unclear. Perry (1976), for example, observed that attempts at comparing counseling and psychotherapy have been clouded

> by an interest either in making one exclusive of the other, or in making the two entirely indistinguishable. Even less biased comparisons have not been illuminating, for they have referred to peripheral matters of institutional settings, function, or training, seldom to process. (p. 5)

Nonetheless, relatively good agreement exists that psychotherapists are more inclined to be involved where intrapsychic and interpsychic conflict are the most salient issues and where obvious psychopathology exists. Counselors, on the other hand, tend to work with individuals who evidence specific adjustment problems, especially with regard to role or position. For example, adjusting to the role of parent of a child with an exceptionality would in many instances fall within a counselor's domain. In instances where minimal levels of conflict exist and in which significant pathology is absent, an individual may be more appropriate for counseling as opposed to psychotherapy.

The task of differentiating conferencing from counseling can also prove difficult. However, in spite of the confusion and the significant overlap between the two roles, educational conferencers are more inclined to focus on exchanging information with parents and families and training them to function more productively relative to their child's educational program, while counselors tend toward involvement with family adjustment problems and related conflicts.

With regard to conducting group sessions, educational conferencers must acknowledge that, in most instances, they are not counselors or psychotherapists and that parents and family members requiring such services are most appropriately dealt with by other professionals. In such situations the primary role of the educational conferencer should become one of referral agent, collaborator, and supporter.

Although educators may be restricted in their capacity to conduct group therapy and counseling sessions, they can play a significant role as group facilitators and trainers in parent and family education programs. In particular, parents can learn strategies for facilitating communication and reducing conflict in their homes and with their children and families through involvement with educational conferencers. A brief description of several programs and models for parents that have been successfully disseminated and implemented through group meetings follows.

One very popular program that has had enormous impact on parents is Parent Effectiveness Training (PET; Gordon, 1970). According to Gordon (1980), PET was devised as a strategy for facilitating communication and enhancing relationships between parents and their children. The model was developed as an educational approach best suited for group situations. After completing a training program, educational conferencers can instruct parents in the use of the system.

The PET model is designed to educate parents in the use of interpersonal skills associated with more effective communication. Specifically, Gordon (1980) described his model as being associated with

> reciprocal relationships; relationships in which there is social equity; relationships in which there is mutual need satisfaction; collaborative relationships; humanistic relationships; relationships in which there is mutual respect for the rights of each; and therapeutic relationships (p. 108)

The model (Gordon, 1970) is based on a variety of interpersonal skills, including active listening, "I messages," problem ownership, and "no lose" methods of conflict resolution. These and related skills are established and enhanced through the use of discussions, role model demonstrations, and role playing. Through the training program, parents are shown the value of listening and expressing their own feelings and of encouraging their children to do likewise.

The PET model has proven effective for enhancing parents' relationships with their children (Gordon, 1978). Moreover, as the model has been used and variously updated, it continues to have significant influence under a variety of names and through a variety of procedures years after its initial introduction. This model and its many variations have been successfully disseminated by educational conferencers within a group environment.

The Systematic Training for Effective Parenting (STEP) program (Dinkmeyer & McKay, 1976) also provides an educational model appropriate for group dissemination to parents by educational conferencers. Based on Adlerian concepts (Adler, 1977; Dreikurs & Solz, 1964), the kit contains a leadership manual, group discussion guidelines, cards and questions, and cassette tapes for parents to use in developing and practicing specific communication skills. The program is designed to teach parents a theoretical explanation of behavior as well as procedures for more effectively communicating with and influencing the behavior of their children.

During STEP training sessions, attention focuses on descriptive family conflict situations. Parents are encouraged to discuss strategies for handling the various situations based on STEP-related information and discussions. The program also makes use of the "parent 'c' group" concept (Dinkmeyer & Carlson, 1973), a procedure designed to aid parents in acquiring information and evaluating their beliefs and attitudes. The strategy was titled "c group" because the components include collaboration, consultation, clarification, confrontation, concern and caring, confidentiality, commitment, and change. According to Dinkmeyer and Dinkmeyer (1976), "The 'c' group goes beyond the study of principles and involves the sharing not only of procedures and ideas but helps members become more aware of how their beliefs, feelings and attitudes affect their relationship with their children" (p. 5).

Although the STEP program is a multifaceted approach, it can be implemented by educational conferencers with the necessary training, time, and motivation. The model works particularly well for ongoing parent and family groups. Other interpretations of the Dreikurs model, similar to the STEP program, are available as well, including Popkin's (1983) video-based Active Parenting program.

A family systems philosophical model is also commonly used in counseling, therapy, and support programs for parents and families of children with exceptionalities. A fundamental premise of family counseling is that individuals can be understood best within the context of their entire family, and further, that families are interconnected units organized in such a fashion that a change in one component of a system results in changes in other systems. For example, understanding a parents' exaggerated investment of time and resources in a child with a disability may help participants comprehend the negative attitudes of other children in the family. Thus, family counseling programs frequently focus on clarifying and supporting boundaries and roles of family members, and enhancing lines of communication. Although most educational conferencers will not be trained to conduct family counseling sessions, knowledge of the fundamental principles of this approach can enable educators to play a meaningful collaborative role in the process.

The role of the educator as a source of group counseling and therapeutic aid is limited. Thus, as mentioned previously, educators must be aware of their therapeutic limitations and be willing to refer parents and families with more intensive needs to trained mental health personnel. Yet, adequately trained, educational conferencers can structure meetings for parents to share information and experiences with other parents and families as well as use structured programs and organize parent and family support groups. Accordingly, educators must be considered a valuable source of assistance to parents interested in enhancing their ability to communicate with their children and families, as well as collaborators with parents and other professionals who are involved in meeting families' support and counseling needs.

Group Service Programs

Some parents and families of children and youth with exceptionalities may be interested in community action programs. Particularly suited are individuals who have had their own basic needs satisfied and would like to serve a broader range of individuals with exceptionalities. Community action roles include volunteers, advisory board members, and "parent-to-parent" group workers, for example.

Though educators must be cognizant of the importance of these activities and the significance of family-coordinated service ventures, they must also realize that the primary characteristic of these programs is that they are structured and governed by parents and families themselves. Hence, the educator must be cautious in assuming a leadership role in this area. A more appropriate strategy might be to arrange for an initial group session with interested parents and families in order to present information and alternatives regarding service programs. At such a session parents and family members should be encouraged to arrange for leadership from among their own ranks and to structure their own activities. Although the educator can and must serve as a collaborator and resource to these groups, the activities themselves should be undertaken by parents and families.

Although educators will be required to implement certain service program suggestions (e.g., train parents wishing to volunteer as aides in a classroom), they must remember that the positive benefits of groups can and will accrue independently of their presence.

Summary

Even though parents and family members of children and youth with exceptionalities must have opportunities to interact with educational personnel on an individual basis, the value of group interactions cannot be overestimated. Not only can these alternatives save time and energy, but they also allow parents and family members to benefit from each other's experiences and perceptions. When used judiciously, the group conference can perform as one of the most valuable and effective tools in the conferencer's repertoire.

Exercises

1. Prepare a group conference agenda for exchanging information with parents and families in your class or program. Compare similarities and differences between your agenda and those of others. In addition, compare differences in your agenda and that which you would use in an individual information exchange session.

2. Develop handbooks on the Individuals with Disabilities Education Act (IDEA) and parent-educator conference participation appropriate for dissemination and discussion at group meetings. Compare your booklets with those of others who may be involved with different ages and types of children.

3. Conduct a tutorial training or behavior management training program for a group of parents and family members in your class or program. Share your experiences and curricula with others who have conducted similar sessions.

4. Observe a Parent Effectiveness Training (PET), Systematic Training for Effective Parenting (STEP), or similar session. Discuss with the group leader and participants their particular likes and dislikes regarding the program.

Chapter 14

Resolving Conflicts

In many respects the ideal parent-educator relationship is considered one that embodies harmony, unity, understanding, and a collaborative attitude. Further, in the minds of at least some this relationship should be free from conflict. The basis for this position, albeit inaccurate, is understandable. That is, much attention has focused on the need to establish and maintain rapport and trust and to be sensitive to values, both personal and those of families with whom we relate. The resulting erroneous concept has been the need to establish and maintain a working relationship without conflict and disagreements. In this context, conflict refers to differences in goals and opinions, which actually should be encouraged in order to facilitate collaborative problem solving and interpersonal growth.

Although one cannot deny the need for an acceptable working relationship and atmosphere, it is important not to confuse this with an association in which conflicts are totally absent. Interactions among individuals with diverse goals, backgrounds, and motivations will periodically involve differences and conflict. Accordingly, it is necessary that this normal and healthy product of human interaction not be perceived incorrectly. To totally preclude conflicts, collaborators would need to either avoid situations that could potentially breed differences of opinion or fail to recognize their own feelings and needs. In instances where differences of opinion and conflict are totally absent, so, too, is effective communication. Jourard (1966) believed that "interpersonal relationships, besides being a rich source of satisfaction for the participants, also provide a rich source of problems for each participant. The solution of these problems results either in growth of personality toward health or away from health" (p. 345). Similarly, Covey (1989) observed that valuing and accommodating differences facilitates creative problem solving.

These opinions in no way support the need or desirability of severe interpersonal conflicts in parent-educator relationships, but they do suggest that differences of opinion among adults will periodically arise and can serve as facilitators in the development of new and creative solutions to problems. Thus, normal disagreements among parents, family members, and professionals should be viewed as indications of open communication, interpersonal maturity, a willingness to collaborate, and the basis for meeting the individualized needs of children and adolescents with exceptionalities most effectively. Consistent with this perception, the educator should not actively seek strategies for avoiding healthy conflicts but rather ways for arbitrating differences and selecting mutually satisfying and collaborative solutions to problems.

Factors Associated with the Development of Unhealthy Conflict

In the course of developing and implementing educational and training programs for children and youth with exceptionalities, opportunities for a multitude of decisions will arise. Each of these decisions will reflect the values, training, experiences, and goals of the individuals involved in the process, and thus each will potentially be the source of differences and conflicts. In situations characterized by free and open communication, the expression of different opinions and the resulting resolutions can enhance the interpersonal relationship between family members and professionals and subsequently the appropriateness of the services provided children (Covey, 1989; Fisher, 1994).

There are, however, other conditions associated with the development of conflict that are not products of open communication and are more difficult to resolve. These situations cannot be considered healthy and do not reflect differences of opinion based on free and open communication. Rather, these conflicts develop as a reaction to situations that lack effective avenues of communication. Solutions to these problems usually do not come through the use of standard conflict resolution models but rather through the development of acceptable family-professional relationships and communication strategies. Ways in which unhealthy conflict situations can develop are discussed below.

Conflict, expressed as anger, hostility, or fear, may become the sole form of self-expression. The capacity to express differences of opinion and position exists as a necessary and vital means of maintaining an open and effective collaborative relationship. No opportunity to express differences deprives parents and family members of a primary avenue of appropriate communication and often results in strong emotion, such as anger or sorrow, employed to gain attention or to release a buildup of minor frustrations that could have been dealt with through effective communication.

There may be insufficient opportunity for parents, family members, and professionals to exchange information. In the absence of an adequate information exchange system, both families and educators are more likely to misunderstand and to blame the other for the development of problems. When parents and family members are not a part of the decision-making process and when information does not flow between parents and professionals (such that the basis for decisions and changes is not clearly understood), one can anticipate conflicts.

Professionals may fail to offer viable models and direction for problem-solving collaboration and conflict resolution. Although differences of opinion may be a normal by-product of a healthy adult-to-adult relationship, the professional must set the tone and provide directions and a model for managing problems and conflict. In particular, the conferencer must be able to clearly communicate that it is appropriate for parents and family members to have opinions different from those of the professional and that strategies exist for reconciling differences such that the needs of children will still be met most effectively. This message must be supported by actual demonstrations of problem-solving and conflict resolution behavior.

Professionals and parents/family members may lack a shared language and knowledge of established protocol. Conferencers can expect anger, despair, or withdrawal when parents and family members are exposed to language and procedures that they fail to comprehend (Harry, Allen, & McLaughlin, 1995; Schulz, 1987). Long (1976) and Dembinski and Mauser (1977b) advised that educators use only language appropriate for each parent's social, cultural, and ethnic background. Hardin and Littlejohn (1995) elaborated on the elements of collaborative programs, including the need for parents to be familiar with the procedures utilized in exceptional education programs. These authorities have each recognized the necessity of making parents an active part of the communication process as well as the potential for unhealthy interpersonal discord in the absence of common language and shared information.

There may be an absence of trust and acceptance of value differences. The creation of an effective environment in which communication can occur necessitates a basic measure of trust and an acceptance of one's own values and those of others (Chinn & McCormick, 1986; Mundschenk & Foley, 1995). Without this basic ingredient of effective communication, parents, family members, and professionals will lack the basis for both collaboration and healthy conflict resolution. Wagonseller (1979) observed that "many confrontations between parents and children could be avoided through the use of good communication skills which assist in settling problems before they turn into major wars" (p. 21).

Parents and family members may lack appropriate methods for influencing their child's educational system. In order for parents and professionals to communicate and arbitrate their differences in an effective and functional manner, they must have acceptable modes of influencing the child's educational program (Carkhuff, 1985; Ramos, 1995). Without this option, families have no alternative but to withdraw from interactions with the school, bitterly accept the situation, or create conflicts.

Conflicts resulting from one of these or related deficiencies or policies can be effectively resolved only by addressing the underlying issues. Though crisis intervention and short-term solutions are possible, ultimate and lasting success will come from the development of mutually satisfying responses to underlying problems.

The Communication Process: An Analysis

In the final analysis, the capacity to resolve conflicts effectively or to create conditions in which productive conflict resolution strategies can be applied is a function of the quality of the communication process. The essential components of this process, according to Barnlund (1973), are the sender, who encodes a message; the message itself; and the receiver, who must correctly decode the message. In order for effective communication to occur, all components must be coordinated and functional.

The encoder (sender) must be able to transmit information in such a fashion that another individual will be motivated to attend and respond. The success of this endeavor, according to Berlo (1960), will relate directly to the sender's communication skills, attitudes, socioeconomic status, and technical knowledge. In addition, the encoder's nonverbal messages will also play a significant part of the communication process. Gestures, posture, facial expression, body language, and voice tone are only a few of the ways in which nonverbal communication occurs (Stuart, 1986). As suggested by a number of authorities (Fast, 1971; Robinson &

Fine, 1995), communication is a multifaceted affair and frequently occurs independent of verbal content.

The communication process also depends on the accurate decoding of the sender's messages. This capacity relates directly to the receiver's attitudes, communication skills, background, experiences, and ability and willingness to collaborate. In addition, the accurate reception of messages relates to the receiver's ability to solicit feedback regarding assumptions made and the exactness of information decoded (Rogers, 1951). In particular, this involves asking for clarification or examples to verify one's understanding of a message. One need only ponder the many nuances of language and the multitude of ways in which the same stimuli can be interpreted to gain an appreciation of the importance of this process (Fine, 1991; Rubin, 1994). Benjamin (1969) devoted an entire chapter to questioning, noting that "the question is a useful tool when used delicately and sparingly" (p. 86).

A related skill is the ability to provide feedback to senders. Although it is important to avoid making moral or value judgments, the receiver must be able to generate appropriate feedback. Without this mechanism the sender has no way of determining whether the message has been accurately received.

Finally, receivers, especially educators, must be sensitive to emotional and verbal cues. That is, in addition to the manifest content of the sender's message, receivers must also be able to focus and respond to affect. Numerous researchers and practitioners (Deutsch, 1994; Hammond, Hepworth, & Smith, 1977; Lambie & Daniels-Mohring, 1993; Rogers, 1951; Zionts & Simpson, 1988) have concluded that the emotional content of a message may be the most salient feature and thus the listening and responding process must consider this feature.

Communication: The Key to Conflict Resolution

Though talking and exchanging information are typical, everyday functions, the process of really communicating and collaborating with another individual is different and often more difficult. True communication and collaboration, whether between parents and professionals, friends, or lovers, requires mutual acceptance, attentiveness, trust, and an atmosphere of "good feelings." In these situations the participants assert an interest in and an understanding of another person as well as the information this individual attempts to impart.

Even though this propitious level of communication is ideal, it also lies within the bounds of many parent-educator conferences. One would be naive, of course, to expect this level of involvement in the absence of prior parental contact and rapport or with every parent; however, without at least a basic atmosphere of effective communication, a fruitful interpersonal relationship will remain unattainable. Interestingly, although both parents and educators have revealed the need and desire to communicate (Dembinski & Mauser, 1977b; Friend & Cook, 1992; Green, 1988; Sicley, 1993), a high level of dissatisfaction persists regarding communication and collaboration opportunities. Without question, effective resolution of conflicts will be possible only in a suitable interpersonal atmosphere. In addition, such an atmosphere will aid in preventing irreconcilable disunion and conflict between parents and professionals.

Variables Associated with Conflict Resolution

A variety of factors will impact on any interpersonal conflict and the approach selected for resolving the dissonance, including the nature of the conflict and its importance to the individuals involved in the discord, the time and resources required to gain resolution, the willingness of the participants to compromise and allow for concession, and the relationship and rapport that existed prior to the conflict. These factors influence not only the conflict resolution strategy chosen but also the potential for resolution. In situations involving cooperation, conflict resolution is likely; likewise, it is unrealistic to expect that any strategy will be effective when one or both parties are unwilling to collaborate and make adjustments. An illustration of this potential for resolution appears in Figure 14.1.

The Nature of the Conflict and Its Perceived Importance

The nature of the conflict and its perceived importance to parents, family members, and professionals presents a major variable influencing any reconciliation. A situation perceived as significant will more frequently be associated with a position of obduracy and steadfastness than one considered less consequential. When parents, family members, and educator all regard an

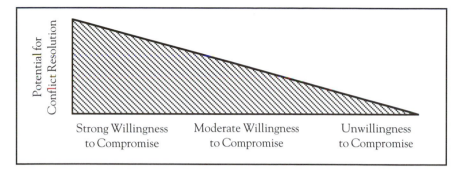

Figure 14.1. Potential for resolution of conflict.

issue as highly important, the conflict resolution process becomes even more intricate and difficult.

One set of parents, for example, had toiled several years to establish an association for children with exceptionalities in their community, and they considered their efforts directly responsible for the services their 12-year-old with a learning disability was receiving. When the recommendation was made to fully include their son, these parents openly and firmly resisted, noting that the boy had been unsuccessfully "mainstreamed" for several years prior to the development of what they considered an appropriate educational program. The child's teacher felt equally strongly that this pupil would benefit from an inclusion program, observing that he had made significant progress and was capable of functioning in a regular class setting. The strength with which the parents and teacher assumed their respective positions made the negotiation of a mutually satisfying outcome much more difficult than if such strong stands had not been taken.

Time and Resources Required for Resolution

Although resolution is possible in a majority of conflict situations, the success of the process will be associated with the amount of effort and the number of resources required to reach a solution. Because most educators (particularly classroom teachers) and families have time and resource limitations, the resolution of conflicts becomes possible only when the process operates within the means of the participants.

One classroom teacher involved in a curriculum conflict with the parents of an adolescent with retardation was unable to invest the time necessary to resolve the issue satisfactorily. Although the teacher felt that progress was being made, the amount of time required to work with the parents became inordinate. The teacher ultimately referred the parents to a district administrator. Although not as well versed in knowledge of curriculum as the teacher, the administrator had more time to spend with the parents in negotiating a resolution.

Willingness of the Participants to "Lose"

Unfortunately, the conflict resolution process can sometimes take on an atmosphere in which the involved individuals perceive the inability to prevail as a failure. Especially when polarization occurs, or when extreme positions are adopted and strong affect is present, the resolution process— regardless of how strongly based on reason—can take on a "win-lose" flavor. It is mandatory that the conferencer dissolve this atmosphere if successful conflict resolution is to occur.

Prior Relationship and Rapport

Perhaps the single most significant factor in resolving conflict between parents and educators is the nature of their preconflict relationship. Not surprisingly, when parents and educators have a sound collaborative perspective based on mutual respect and effective communication, the resolution process will be much easier to achieve. Covey (1989) refers to this relationship as "an emotional bank account" (p. 18), a metaphor for the trust that has been developed between two individuals. In this regard, he notes that trust in a relationship develops in accordance with factors such as honesty, courtesy, kindness, and keeping commitments. Similarly, when individuals make "withdrawals" from their emotional bank accounts, because of failing to listen, betraying trust, overreacting, and so forth, they erode the amount of trust in a relationship, and thus may be vulnerable to "overdrawing" their account. Without question a sound relationship based on mutual respect and trust bodes well for parents and educators working out their differences effectively.

Approaches to Conflict Resolution

Just as with any problem-solving strategy, a variety of ways emerge in which conflicts can be expressed and dissipated. Some are by nature more effective and appropriate than others, plus different conflict situations will create a need for different resolution approaches.

Avoidance

According to Lewin (1935), individuals in conflict situations can either avoid the issues involved (and with it the disunion) or deal with them directly. Avoiding conflicts is an obvious option but by far the least acceptable. Not only is it difficult to avoid conflicts, but doing so can severely limit the growth potential of any collaborative relationship. As suggested by a number of researchers and practitioners, open, effective communication occurs only when participants feel confident in expressing their thoughts and feelings (Dinnebeil & Rules, 1994; Turnbull & Turnbull, 1986).

Accommodation

Although conciliatory and accommodating attitude is a necessary component of the effective conflict negotiation process, it is counterproductive as the sole means of resolving issues. Individuals may avoid conflicts and stressing their relationships simply by always accepting another individual's position. This strategy, however, has at least two major limitations. First, it is virtually impossible to be accommodating in all situations, particularly with individuals who are quite demanding or who request conditions that are inappropriate or unachievable. Second, this approach will almost always cause frustration and anger, thus serving to strain rather than support a collaborative relationship. Although an accommodating attitude is a basic requisite for effective conflict resolution, it offers neither an end in itself nor an adequate strategy for resolving conflicts.

Collaborative Problem Solving

An alternative to avoidance and accommodation is collaborative problem solving. This strategy has the distinct advantage of providing a means for meeting parents', families', and educators' needs while serving the best interests of the child. These circumstances, according to a number of authorities, lead to "win-win" situations (Covey, 1989; Warschaw, 1980).

Successful problem solving depends on a variety of factors, including an awareness that conflict resolution requires effective use of negotiation skills. Although some may consider *negotiation* alien to education, in fact educational conflict resolution resembles negotiations in business and politics. In particular, negotiation success is associated with three major factors: (a) availability of factual information surrounding an issue, (b) power of the mediator, and (c) institutional support.

Availability of pertinent facts

Availability of factual information surrounding the issue is a sine qua non of conflict resolution. Educators cannot resolve conflicts by means of facts alone, nor can they enter into meaningful problem solving without background information and facts. Accordingly, those attempting to resolve conflicts with parents and families must have accurate information, such as student files, professional records, knowledge of pertinent protocol and policies, reports from other professionals, and so forth.

A teacher of a child with mild mental retardation discovered the importance of accurate information when attempting to resolve a conflict that involved withholding lunch from the student as a consequence of failure to complete assignments. The teacher was unaware that the student was diabetic and hence needed to follow a rigid eating schedule. Availability of such information could have prevented the conflict.

Power of the mediator

The mediator's power presents another critical element in the negotiation process. "Power" here refers to one's capacity and willingness to take action and create change. The importance of such power in conflict resolution should be apparent, in that individuals who lack the desire or capacity to make change when appropriate or who fail to take suitable action cannot engage in conflict resolution. If parents or family members determine (or consider) that professionals are unable to take necessary action, their capacity to engage in problem solving becomes severely limited.

One element of power involves acknowledging one's capacity to create change. Educators often consider themselves relatively powerless, commenting that administrators, legislators, and other agencies hold the power and that they themselves have little decision-making authority. Yet, educators have tremendous potential to implement change and, in so doing, engage in problem solving and conflict resolution with parents and families. One of the first orders of business for educators wishing to enter into conflict resolution, therefore, is to acknowledge their capacity to produce change. Although not all conflict resolution and problem solving involves making changes, the potential for creating such conditions must exist.

Another power element involves the willingness to take risks. Thus, educators must be willing to admit when they or their program is in error, when their program or policy must be maintained in spite of pressure to the contrary, and when popular decisions are not the most appropriate. Further, risk taking requires conceptualizing problems in a creative manner and selecting novel solutions and strategies. Obviously, the backing of administrators and colleagues is a major consideration in one's willingness to take risks.

A third element of power within the context of conflict resolution involves the ability and willingness to follow through on decisions and agreements. Nothing undermines families' confidence in professionals more than failure to carry out what was agreed upon. Educators must not only follow through on commitments and agreements but also ensure that others in the system (e.g., administrators, colleagues) do so as well. Productive conflict resolution may ultimately depend on professionals' skill in identifying and using appropriate power.

Institutional support

Institutional support, as related to conflict resolution, involves obtaining support from administrators and others. This process entails making administrators and others aware of pertinent situations and, when necessary, including them in decision making. Thus, one teacher who anticipated a parental conflict over a decision to exclude an adolescent with a mild disability from a school bus for 3 days because of unacceptable behavior shared relevant facts and perceptions with his building principal and the director of special education. These individuals' attention to the matter resulted in support for the bus-exclusion decision during the resulting conflict with the youth's parents.

Effective communication skills

Effective problem solving also requires effective communication and interaction techniques, including an awareness of the needs and emotions of the parent/family and professional involved in the conflict. Above all else, successful problem solving relies on good communication skills.

As previously noted, a basic feature of effective communication is the use of active listening skills (Rogers, 1961); that is, attention to both the manifest and emotional content of messages. Related to this listening process is the ability to respond empathically. This feedback mechanism presents a primary means by which educators can communicate interest and understanding, including acceptance of parents' feelings. This acceptance will in no way detract from the ability of the conferencer to negotiate; it will, in fact, produce the opposite effect. Although educators may not agree with parents and family members on particular issues, they must be able to understand the latter's position before attempting to resolve a conflict. Conferencers who can listen effectively provide a supportive environment for parents and family members where they can be heard without fear of blame. This atmosphere increases the parents' feelings of safety and their willingness to engage in collaborative problem solving, which can occur only when threatening conditions are removed.

The listening and responding process is also designed to provide feedback. This clarification and perception-checking mechanism serves to assure the person talking that the message is being received accurately and that the receiver is truly interested and listening. Listening does not require the conferencer to agree with the position taken by a parent or family members; rather, it simply means communicating interest and understanding. The listener may also find it beneficial to acknowledge particular components of a person's message. By attending and acknowledging the validity of portions of the person's position, and looking for areas of mutual agreement, the conferencer maintains an atmosphere conducive to problem solving while establishing a basis for inquiring, questioning, and negotiating on areas of disagreement. Such a procedure is far superior to attempts at arguing without this rapport-building mechanism.

Constructive openness

Mutual problem solving also requires an atmosphere of constructive openness. Although one might assume that withholding feelings and opinions may reduce the chance of hurting, angering, or alienating parents and family members, it seldom accomplishes that goal. In instances where the conferencer is not open, the parent/family member is denied access to the feedback needed to build and maintain a relationship and to engage in collaborative problem solving. Constructive openness, as opposed to undifferentiated candor, is limited to responses that are facilitative of the relationship and problem-solving process. That is, confrontation and openness that are ends in themselves and that lack the potential to improve the relationship or solve the conflict should be avoided.

Constructive openness does make use of confrontation. Although confrontation may generate an image of anxiety and open dissension, and thus be perceived as a detractor to the conflict resolution process, it can form an essential part of the negotiation process. In order to be effective, however, confrontation must be accompanied by other problem-solving tools and communication facilitators; it is a counterproductive process when employed independently of other basic communication and negotiating procedures. Conferencers should note that the intensity of any confrontation should be only as strong as the parent-educator relationship and thus avoid strong and frequent confrontation in new and weakly formed collaborations.

Constructive confrontation allows for the opportunity to authentically identify one's feelings and frustrations. That is, it can serve as one primary avenue for expressing anger, emotion, or concern without producing additional conflict or stress. In particular, "I" messages (e.g., "I am concerned," "I am upset by . . . ") have been identified as useful for this purpose (Gordon, 1970; Hammond et al., 1977). These responses tend to be safer and more appropriate than "you" statements (e.g., "You are not doing what we agreed on," "You don't seem to be as concerned as you should be").

Constructive confrontation also tends to be most functional when employed in descriptive form. That is, the conferencer should report what is seen (e.g., "I have observed that James has not had his daily report card signed for 2 weeks"), what is felt (e.g., "I am concerned," "I am uncomfortable"), and what is desired or expected (e.g., "I would like to see us arrive at a mutually agreed-upon plan"). Above all, the confrontation process must focus on the situation or behavior of concern rather than become an attack on the parents or family. Personal attacks simply do not facilitate the goal of improving communication or interpersonal openness.

Constructive confrontation is not an easy tool to use, but it offers a way of voicing concern while creating an atmosphere of openness and effective communication. It must thus be maintained as one possible strategy in the conferencer's repertoire.

A Model Conflict Resolution Process

Educators called upon to resolve conflicts with parents and family members should adopt a strategy based on collaborative problem solving, active listening, mutual respect, shared decision making, and active negotiation. Moreover, the model used should be designed to produce "win-win" outcomes, as opposed to creating one winner and one loser. Such a strategy is described below.

Step 1: Set the Conditions for Collaborative Conflict Resolution

A significant part of setting the conditions for collaborative conflict resolution relates to active listening. That is, the parties involved in the conflict should each demonstrate a willingness to understand the position of the other without challenging, interrupting, or otherwise interfering with an individual's ability to communicate. Because professionals will likely have little control over parents' willingness to listen reciprocally, they should take a leadership position in this regard by indicating the advisability of this process (e.g., "I would like to recommend that each of us listen to the other person so that we can understand one another and see where we agree and disagree") and by setting a good example for active listening (including attempts at understanding the emotions that accompany a message). Though these steps will guarantee neither an understanding of the differing perceptions and positions involved in a dispute nor an effective problem-solving atmosphere, they will obviously go a long way toward achieving these goals.

A second element associated with this process involves professionals' attempts to separate their perceptions and feelings toward the individual(s) with whom they are disagreeing from the substantive issues of the conflict. In all too many cases individuals become so entangled with the personal variables in a conflict that they lose sight of the end goals. As a case in point, the parents of a young child were asking the school district to make substantial curricular and procedural classroom changes to accommodate their child. Their approach, however, was extremely adversarial, threatening, and demanding, and eventually the district personnel involved in the conflict began losing sight of the substantive issues associated with the case (i.e., the merits of what the parents were asking). That is, rather than focusing on the requests and concerns, the district representatives instead primarily reacted to the parents' attacks, criticisms, and threatening demeanor. Such a reaction is, of course, understandable and natural, but educators must remind themselves that whether or not they like or dislike a parent should remain separate from their attempts to resolve substantive issues. Because neither professionals nor parents will be immune to personal attacks and criticism, and because such variables will likely generate emotions that may interfere with problem-solving, techniques such as cognitive self-prompting (e.g., reminding oneself to concentrate on the issues), constructive confrontation, and delaying problem-solving attempts until both parties are more in control of their emotions may be advisable.

Fisher and Brown (1989) have advised that individuals involved in conflict resolution be "unconditionally constructive" (p. 24). Such an approach, in spite of its difficulty, sets a tone that facilitates reconciliation of differences, encourages reciprocal responses on the part of parents (thereby furthering a productive collaborative climate), and helps both parents and educators concentrate on salient points of agreement and difference. As observed by Fisher and Brown (1989), "The Golden Rule is a useful rule of thumb in helping me understand how my behavior is likely to affect you and how you might want me to behave" (pp. 31–32).

Setting the conditions for collaborative conflict resolution also involves identifying the problem, its owners, and the individuals associated with the conflict. Gordon (1970, 1980) emphasized this point in dealing with conflicts. Kroth (1985) also noted the importance of determining the owner of a problem, and Fine (1979) observed the need to determine ownership of feelings. Gordon (1980) has suggested that the individual experiencing discomfort regarding a particular situation is the person with the problem, and that only those individuals directly involved in a particular problem should participate in its solution.

Gordon (1970, 1980) has recommended the conflict resolution process begin with an "I" statement; that is, a statement of concern about a particular problem or situation made to another individual believed to have joint ownership in the issue. Gordon (1970) noted the necessity of addressing specific issues as opposed to dealing in generalities. This initiating response should be followed by active listening, whereby the individual commencing the process attempts to understand the other individual's position and perception. This component of the process requires that a relationship appropriate for conflict resolution exists, that the parents be able to engage in verbal interactions, and that sufficient time be allotted for the process. Finally, the process requires that both parties be willing to work toward a solution to the problem.

Step 2: Identify and Evaluate Possible Solutions for Resolving the Conflict

Based on the aforementioned effective communication principles, and subsequent to an agreement by the parents and professionals to try to solve the problem, parents and professionals should attempt to jointly and collabora-tively generate possible solutions to the identified problem. Gordon (1970, 1980) recommended that all persons affiliated with the issue participate in the process, that individuals involved in the process be encouraged to be creative in their problem solving, and that each suggestion be given serious consideration. Only after individuals have had ample opportunity to gener-ate possible solutions should evaluations of alternatives proceed. Again, this process should be structured such that both the parents/family and conferencer have equal opportunities to evaluate alternatives.

Step 3: Identify and Implement a Mutually Agreed-Upon Problem-Solving Strategy

Participants should recognize at this point in the problem-solving process that substantial resolution progress has been made. That is, important interpersonal and communication factors ostensibly have been addressed, and conditions for conflict resolution have been set in motion. Moreover, the individuals involved have had opportunities to recommend possible solutions to the problem as well as to evaluate each solution suggested. Accordingly, the next step is for participants to collaboratively select and implement the problem-solving strategy with the most apparent utility. As was noted earlier, the success of this component of the resolution process will depend on the participants' willingness to contribute their efforts to the program, to collaborate and compromise, and to seek "win-win" solu-tions. In selecting a solution to a conflict, Brown and Fisher (1989) have advised that participants not make a relationship contingent upon an agreement (i.e., neither parents nor professionals should demand adoption of a particular recommendation as a contingency for maintaining a rela-tionship), and that neither parents nor professionals make problem-solving concessions in order to "buy" a good relationship.

Step 4: Evaluate the Mutually Agreed-Upon Problem-Solving Strategy and Make Modifications as Needed

This final, equally important stage of conflict resolution consists of evalu-ating the solution and the participants' satisfaction with the selection. In instances where success or consensus is not within reach, the conflict reso-lution process may be reinitiated or other problem-solving steps may be taken.

Use of the recommended collaborative conflict resolution process is illustrated in the case of a dispute involving the parents of a student with a learning disability. In this example, the parents were notified by their son's former learning disability teacher that the child, who had been mainstreamed for several months, was having "problems" in his regular class setting. The child's general education teacher questioned his appropriateness for a regular classroom, but his parents were strongly committed to their son being in an inclusive setting. The special education teacher, who was serving as a consultant to teachers of children in inclusion programs in the district, requested a conference to discuss the problem. At this meeting, attended by the parents, the regular class teacher, and the special educator, the parents were informed that although their son's academic performance was satisfactory, he had recently developed a number of behavioral excesses. The parents were shown behavioral charts that indicated excessive vocalizations and noncompliance. Both teachers revealed concern over the behavior and suggested that a strategy for managing the problem be selected. The educators acknowledged that the problem was in their domain and thus was their responsibility (and that they were willing to take total charge of the problem); however, they indicated a desire to include the parents in the solution. This approach was taken in part because on several occasions in the past the parents had complained that school personnel had not included them in their planning efforts nor kept them informed.

The parents, when informed of the problem, responded that they had not experienced an increase in behavioral problems at home. However, they did accept partial ownership of the problem and voiced a willingness to be involved in the intervention process. The parents and educators subsequently discussed alternatives for managing the problem. Options included additional individualized classroom attention, psychotherapy, periodic visitations to the school counselor, medication, various punishment contingencies, and a cooperative home-school communication program. Once presented, the advantages and disadvantages of each alternative were discussed.

These discussions resulted in the selection of a home-school communication program as the best option. In particular, this program consisted of the teacher issuing 10 behavioral evaluations to the child over the course of each day. Each evaluation, reported as "satisfactory" or "needs improvement," was recorded on an index card and given to the child immediately after it was made. The child was required to bring home at least seven satisfactory cards per day in order to receive a reward of his choosing. Following the initial conference between the parents and teachers, the program was discussed with the child and subsequently implemented. The educators and parents remained in close contact throughout the course of the program in order to judge its effectiveness and make necessary adjustments.

Analyzing Your Conflict Resolution Style

If educators were to honestly analyze their style in interacting and resolving conflicts with parents and family members, they would probably discover they have some characteristics that are far more facilitative than others. Therefore, it important that conferencers be aware of how conflicts arise, the ways in which their manner contributes to conflicts, and the options that are available for resolution.

Figure 14.2, "Analyzing Your Style," provides educators a simple method for examining the manner in which they interact with parents and family members. Respondents should be honest, of course, in completing the form. After personally responding to the survey, it is helpful to ask a colleague or parent to complete it as observers of one's style. Analyzing and discussing with others how that style impacts on relationships and conflict resolution approaches with parents and family members can help educators get a better picture of themselves in these interactions. Although this survey does not purport to make quantitative comparisons or predictions, it does offer a revealing means of looking at problem-solving styles.

Problem-solving and conflict resolution skills must be a reliable part of each conferencer's repertoire. In addition, it is important to realize that an individual's style, personality, attitude, and demeanor will impact on the resolution process. Even more significant than the conflict resolution model or the problem-solving approach ultimately selected are the participants' interpersonal characteristics. Thus, educational conferencers must not only work to develop their listening, negotiation, and other communication skills but must also find ways of becoming aware of their own interpersonal style. Without such awareness, the most salient component of problem solving will remain an enigma.

Summary

Planning for children and youth with exceptionalities and coordinating the viewpoints and goals of the parents and professional educators involved will periodically result in conflicts. Although at times formidable, the process of

Are you . . .	Always	Frequently	Sometimes	Never
1. Able to stay informed about the parents with whom you relate and their family situation?	☐	☐	☐	☐
2. Irritated by parents who offer alternatives for managing the classroom behavior of their children?	☐	☐	☐	☐
3. Willing to let parents tutor their own children at home?	☐	☐	☐	☐
4. Honest with parents?	☐	☐	☐	☐
5. Able to confront parents?	☐	☐	☐	☐
6. Prone to arguments with parents?	☐	☐	☐	☐
7. Aware of how your emotions are communicated through your body language?	☐	☐	☐	☐
8. Willing to "take risks" with parents?	☐	☐	☐	☐
9. Prone to active listening with parents?	☐	☐	☐	☐
10. Annoyed by parents who suggest curriculum ideas?	☐	☐	☐	☐
11. Threatened by parents who initiate a conference?	☐	☐	☐	☐
12. Threatened by parents who request access to school records and data?	☐	☐	☐	☐
13. Willing to engage in joint problem solving with parents?	☐	☐	☐	☐
14. Uneasy about admitting to parents that you don't have all the answers?	☐	☐	☐	☐
15. Threatened by aggressive parents?	☐	☐	☐	☐
16. Uncomfortable with parents who display emotional behavior?	☐	☐	☐	☐
17. Prone to make assumptions about the parents with whom you interact?	☐	☐	☐	☐
18. Creative in problem-solving strategies?	☐	☐	☐	☐
19. Reluctant to make changes in the ways you deal with parents?	☐	☐	☐	☐
20. Troubled by what you wish you had said but did not say in conferences with parents?	☐	☐	☐	☐

Figure 14.2. Analyzing Your Style (*Note*. Although reference is made to "parents," items also refer to family members.)

negotiating mutually satisfying alternatives can provide a powerful growth experience for both parents and educators and can lead to creative planning for pupils. When parents and educators are open and willing to engage in problem-solving and conflict resolution processes, most issues can be dealt with satisfactorily. Although conflict may appear to be an area to avoid, its pervasive and salient nature in the parent-educator relationship mandates appropriate strategies for its eventual occurrence and resolution.

Exercises

1. Complete Figure 14.2, "Analyzing Your Style." Discuss characteristics of parents and professionals that can facilitate and detract from a desirable conflict-resolution atmosphere.

2. Conduct a conflict resolution simulation conference using the materials in Appendix E. Descriptions are provided for the cases previously presented for other role-play exercises (i.e., student with mental retardation, physical disability, behavior disorder, etc.). Consequently, you should use those materials most aligned with your area or those that you have used in previous role-playing.

In conducting the simulation exercise, one individual should assume the part of the parent, using those materials labeled "Parent Role." Another person, taking the part of the teacher, should structure his or her responses around the teacher materials. A third individual should take the role of the evaluator, using the evaluation form provided.

Participants should assume that the conference is parent initiated; that is, that the parent in the exercise contacted the educator regarding the described issue. Individuals should change roles after completing the exercise.

Appendix A

Initial Interview Role-Playing Materials

These materials are to be used in conjunction with the exercises at the end of chapter 8 and chapter 10. See the exercises at the end of chapter 8 for specific directions.

INITIAL INTERVIEW ROLE-PLAYING MATERIALS: YOUTH WITH A BEHAVIOR DISORDER

Billie—Age 13

Teacher Role

The 13-year-old student described below has been placed in your learning center class for students with behavior disorders for 2 hours daily. As this youngster is new to your program, the information you have about him is from the reports of others.

Report of Regular Class Teacher

Billie was referred for special education evaluation and placement because of behavior problems in his regular classes. His regular class teachers report that he has a number of behavioral excesses and academic problems. His general education teachers have each independently described Billie as aggressive; specifically, the teachers have noted that he is constantly fighting with other students. Billie was also described by his teachers as socially immature. For example, Billie "verbally provokes" the other students and has consistently attempted to manipulate the teachers. His teachers describe him as a very insecure and frightened boy. They also noted he will work best for teachers who assure him that he is capable of good work. He was also described as needing physically, socially, and academically firm teachers. According to each of his teachers he was in the lowest group and generally worked at about one to three grade levels below his peers. Billie's teachers reportedly are firm believers in inclusionary programs for students with special needs, but they consider his social and behavioral problems so severe as to require special education intervention.

School Psychologist's Report

Individualized intelligence testing results indicated that Billie is functioning at the low-average range of intelligence. Previous test results and teacher observations confirmed this intellectual estimate.

Direct classroom observation indicated that Billie attended to task approximately 25% less than his peers. In addition, he daydreamed and was out of his seat without permission significantly more than the others in his class.

Standardized academic assessment measures indicated a reading recognition level of 5.5. His reading comprehension level was 3.5. Arithmetic performance was 4.0.

Parent Role

Parents' Perception of Problem

Mr. and Mrs. Carder moved to this district from out of state approximately 6 months ago. They stated that Billie has always been a problem child.

However, his behavior has worsened within the last 2 years. Mr. and Mrs. Carder are most concerned with Billie's destructive behavior. They related three incidents in recent weeks when he vandalized neighbors' homes and tortured neighborhood animals. The mother also recalled a recent episode when a baby-sitter found Billie trying to shoot his sister with a bow and arrow. Billie told his mother they were "just playing." A neighbor asked Billie to go home recently, and he retaliated by throwing a rock through her front window. Billie, according to his parents, picks on his younger sister, especially when mad at other people. His parents report that he does not interact with the neighborhood children and prefers to stay indoors and watch TV or go to his room.

Development

The parents report that early development appeared normal. In particular, his development was similar to that of the other children in the family. He was completely toilet trained by 3½ years and has had no problems with bed-wetting. He began talking at 17 months and was talking in short sentences by 2½ years.

Family Structure

Billie lives with his natural parents, a 31-year-old laborer father and a 29-year-old unemployed mother. They have been married 13 years. Siblings include a 12-year-old brother and two younger sisters, 7 and 8. The maternal grandparents care for Billie and the other children when the parents are gone.

Interaction

According to Mrs. Carder, Billie disturbs the entire household. She related a story of Billie chasing his younger sister with a bow and arrow. When he was confronted, he said that he was "just playing." Following the incident he was taken to the family physician, who told the parents Billie would probably outgrow his problems. The doctor did suggest that the parents curtail Billie's TV watching, especially shows displaying graphic violence.

Mrs. Carder said they bought another TV so Billie could watch his own programs in his room without disturbing other family members.

Billie threatens his mother. He recently fought her when she tried to spank him. The mother, however, is able to physically manage Billie's behavior. The parents feel his problem is one of behavior and not a learning difficulty. They speak of him as a "smart boy" who learns quickly. The mother notes that Billie causes problems between her and her husband. For example, he annoys his mother, increasing his disturbing behavior when the father is due home. The mother, nervous and distraught, nags at him. The father tells her she is yelling too much, and Billie smiles as he hears the parents "bicker." He tells his dad his mother has been mean all day to him. Billie also makes his mother feel guilty for her treatment of him.

Bill has low self-esteem and often makes remarks that no one in the family likes him, everybody hates him. He has poor relationships with both his siblings and peers. The parents feel he is selfish and rough in play. He was on the soccer team at his last school, but was removed due to inappropriate behavior.

Discipline

The father indicates he is authoritarian with his son although the mother is able to control him. The father whips him and sends him to bed. If the mother threatens to whip Billie, he threatens to tell his dad.

Significant Medical History

Early childhood illnesses included both measles and mumps at age 5. Billie has no known allergies, but according to his mother, he does have "asthmatic fever." This is characterized by difficulty in breathing following running or hard playing and occurs in the spring. Billie is a small boy for his age, with his weight and height falling in the lower 30th percentile compared to boys his age. Other than the above, Billie is a healthy boy who is rarely ill.

Sleeping Patterns

Mrs. Carder reports that Billie seems to need little sleep. He constantly gets out of bed at night and "gets into things." He does complain of occasional nightmares. He sleeps in the basement in a room of his own by his own preference. His mother also stated she feels he "lies" about what he does at night when he gets up.

Family Constellation

The 31-year-old father, who completed 10 grades, is employed as a laborer. The natural mother is a full-time housewife and mother. She dropped out of school after completing the ninth grade.

INITIAL INTERVIEW ROLE-PLAYING MATERIALS: GIFTED CHILD

Howard—Age 8

Teacher Role

The 8-year-old child described below has been placed in your Enhanced Learning Center (1 hour daily) for gifted students and in the district's Challenge Program for underachieving gifted students. You have had minimal contact with the child and you have not talked to the parents, but since you attended the staffing on the child you have the following information.

Report of Regular Class Teacher

Howard's regular classroom teacher described him as follows:

1. Doesn't turn work in on time.

2. Daydreams.

3. Becomes involved in something that interests him and then pays little attention to class activities.

4. Is a perfectionist.

5. Is very verbal and tends to dominate class discussions.

6. Reading: Tests indicate he is two grade levels above his peers but he rarely completes his skill sheets on time.

7. Math: Howard has been working on computation skills as required by the district. His standardized test math scores indicate he is 2½ grade levels ahead of the average second-grader. He used to show me some new shortcuts he had discovered for dividing but hasn't shared them recently. He has not consistently mastered his addition and subtraction facts.

8. Handwriting is barely legible.

Miss Precocious described Howard's interpersonal relationships with his classmates as good. At times his classmates seem to be in awe of his responses during discussions. Some students call him "Brain" or "Smartsy." He says he is bored, but there is a lot of work he could be doing and doesn't. Many times when he should be doing his skill sheets in reading or math his teacher finds him engrossed in a library book.

School Psychologist's Report

This 8-year-old is currently functioning in the very superior range of mental ability. In spite of this child's level of ability, he evidenced some anxiety during parts of the test. His overall intellectual functioning was in the 99th percentile rank on a standardized intellectual measure. The Performance section was 3 points higher than the Verbal section, which is not a significant difference. The scaled scores ranged from a high of 19 (Block Design) to a low of 11 (Coding). Most of the scaled scores clustered close to 2 standard deviations above the mean. Howard was cooperative and friendly. He has excellent verbal expressive skills.

School Social Worker's Report

Howard is the younger of two children; he has an older sister in junior high school. The parents reported that his developmental milestones were slightly accelerated. He has had a history of ear infections and has a 10% hearing loss in both ears when his ears become inflamed. The parents also report that he has mild allergy problems.

The parents report that Howard attended preschool at age 3 and remained in this program for 1 year. He has also attended summer programs at private schools since age 5. His hobbies include soccer, working riddles, and reading, which he does 1 hour per day.

Parent Role

Your history and attitude are described as follows:

Parent's Perceptions

Howard's parents are pleased with their child's abilities, although concerned over his reluctance to complete work requested by the classroom teacher. He expresses a feeling of boredom, and his regular teacher has indicated that Howard is not motivated or achieving. The parents feel that this conflict at school has frustrated him. His self-concept and relationship with his peers are now also concerns for the parents. Howard appears sullen and withdrawn much of the time. He insists that the worksheets in the classroom are "baby" work, and he frequently refuses to do them. He gets interested in a book or game and "forgets" to turn in many of the other required assignments.

Development

Howard's birth was full-term. The delivery was natural without the aid of any medication. He walked at 12 months, talked quite well at 15 to 18 months. He was always active and restless. He had few childhood diseases, but because of a hearing loss caused by fluid buildup in the inner ear, he had ear surgery with tubes inserted at 14 months. He has a slight hearing loss any time the ears are infected, but this clears with medication. He has some allergies, but these are not considered severe.

Because the neighborhood where the Huges have lived all of Howard's life has allowed so much social interaction, a preschool was dropped after 1 year. He attended this program between the ages of 3 and 4. In addition to attending summer programs at private schools since age 5, Howard has attended art classes for children conducted at an art gallery. He was also enrolled in a music awareness class. The family has also been involved in many outings, trips, and trips to the library. Mrs. Huge is a former teacher and seems to enjoy her time with Howard.

Howard read before entering kindergarten, which presented problems for both him and the teacher. At a conference called because of Howard's disruptive behavior in the classroom, the parents asked the teacher if she was aware that Howard was reading. The teacher was not aware, and because the school policy was that kindergarten students could not check out books at the school library, the teacher was helpful in securing books for the classroom, and Howard was allowed to read after his work was finished.

Howard had a satisfying first-grade experience. One of the things the teacher did was set up a contract arrangement for math. She allowed spelling words to be chosen from the dictionary, and she introduced him to books that were more on his reading level. He also learned to enjoy biographies. Finally, the teacher challenged him and allowed him to progress at his own pace.

The second grade has not been a continuation of the success felt in first grade. Howard has received low marks in areas in which he knew success last year. The parents are aware that their son's second-grade inclusion-oriented classroom has several children with disabilities, but do not know of any other gifted children in the class.

Howard did begin piano lessons at the beginning of last summer. He has continued these lessons, and the teacher is pleased with his interest and progress. Howard and his father have talked about his joining a baseball team for the coming summer. Howard has expressed an interest, and if the situation is not too competitive, he probably will enroll in the program.

Family Dynamics

Howard's family includes his father, age 36; mother, age 36; and an older sister in junior high, age 12. Mr. and Mrs. Huge have been married 14 years. They feel they have a good marriage with positive feelings of commitment for each other. Both Mr. and Mrs. Huge seem like intelligent, concerned parents. Mrs. Huge is very spontaneous, sensitive, and expressive. Mr. Huge appears to be somewhat of an introvert, very analytical, and not too expressive. Mr. Huge is an accountant, while Mrs. Huge is a housewife.

Mrs. Huge does give a great deal of attention to Howard. His father's attentiveness toward him seems to be to a lesser degree. There does appear to be some inconsistency in the way the parents relate to Howard. Mr. Huge's responses tend to be very analytical, while Mrs. Huge tends to be more spontaneous and perhaps emotional in her interpersonal reactions with her son.

INITIAL INTERVIEW ROLE-PLAYING MATERIALS: CHILD WITH A LEARNING DISABILITY

Sally—Age 9

Teacher Role

The 9-year-old female described below has been referred for placement in your resource strategy room for 2 hours daily. You have had minimal contact with the child and you have not talked to the parents, but because you attended the staffing on the child, you have the following information.

Report of Regular Class Teacher

The regular class teacher identified Sally's major problems as severe academic deficits and "social immaturity." In particular, the third-grade teacher reports that the child is able to identify all of the letters and some of the sounds of the alphabet, but has difficulty blending the sounds into words. She is reported to have a four-word sight vocabulary. In the area of mathematics, Sally is able to do simple addition and subtraction if allowed to manipulate objects. She does seem to understand most basic mathematical concepts (e.g., carrying, borrowing) in class discussion, but tends to "forget" how to do the math process from day to day, especially during independent practice.

The teacher is also concerned as to Sally's ability to comprehend. Specifically, she does not know if Sally is simply not listening or unable to comprehend. Sally frequently responds to teacher queries with phrases such as "I don't know" or "I can't remember." Sally is also described as a sensitive student who is aware that she is not making the same rate of progress as the others. The teacher described Sally's interpersonal skills as immature. She is withdrawn, desiring to be by herself much of the time. The other students in the class are accepting of her and attempt to help.

Report of Social Worker's Home Visit

The mother described Sally's problems as directly related to her academic deficits. She and her husband believe that Sally's academic expectations are relatively high and that she becomes frustrated when she is unable to function on the same level as her class peers. The mother noted that her daughter typically manifests her frustration by becoming sullen and withdrawn. According to the mother, this is the same pattern that her husband employs to demonstrate his anger and frustration. She further noted that this pattern is typical of how Sally interacts with her peers.

To a lesser extent the parents are concerned about Sally's lack of self-confidence. They feel, however, that academic success will improve her self-concepts and her peer relationships. The parents reported that their daughter does not have a behavior problem.

School Psychologist's Report

According to intellectual measures Sally is functioning in the average range of mental ability with some indication of bright normal potential. She was motivated to perform and was goal oriented the entire session. As previously reported, Sally did show significant academic deficits. Educational instruments indicate she is functioning on a readiness level. Deficit areas included sight word recognition and ability to blend sounds into words. No perceptual problems were noted in Sally's performance. It was also noted that Sally tended to be somewhat shy and withdrawn during the testing session.

Parent Role

Your history and attitude are described as follows:

Sally's Problem

The parents' major concern is Sally's poor academic achievement. Specifically, they are concerned over her difficulties in doing her schoolwork, especially learning to read, and the frustration accompanying this failure experience. The parents further stated that because Sally expects so much from herself, she becomes frustrated when she is unable to do what she sees the other children doing. They feel that it is at these times when other problems, such as social withdrawal and sullen behavior, occur. Mrs. Slith believes that Sally is very close to her father and relies on him as a role model. She is concerned over Sally's lack of self-confidence and her poor self-image. Finally, the parents are somewhat concerned over her social withdrawal. They believe, however, that this is a result of her academic problems. Mrs. Slith and her husband are in agreement that Sally does not have a behavior problem. She stated that the discipline they use, restriction of privileges and talking to her, accomplishes the desired results.

Sally's Social History

Sally was the product of a full-term pregnancy and normal delivery. The parents reported that Sally's early growth and development were normal, except that she did not talk until the 20th month. Sally has been relatively healthy and has not had major illnesses or injuries. When she was 4, Sally was enrolled at a preschool in their neighborhood. She was withdrawn shortly after beginning, however, because the parents felt that it placed Sally under severe pressure. They were also dissatisfied with the amount of social interaction that occurred among the students. They had hoped to increase the amount of interaction that Sally had with other children; the school, however, allowed for few contacts of this type. Rather, it emphasized academic preparation.

Sally attended kindergarten and first and second grades at a neighborhood public school. She was reported to be a well-behaved and quiet child. She did, however, experience academic problems in each of her early school experiences. These failure experiences have been difficult for both Sally and her parents to accept.

As noted previously, Sally is a shy, withdrawn child. She tends to model her father, a shy and retiring individual who avoids social interactions. Both parents described Sally as having a "keen respect for books and toys she enjoys." They also feel she wants to read very badly, and that she is sensitive and very conscious of others' feelings in all areas of interpersonal interaction.

Family Dynamics

Sally's family includes her father, age 36; mother, age 31; and one younger brother, age 6. Mr. and Mrs. Slith have been married 12 years. They feel they have a good marriage, although there are areas of conflict. In particular, the mother is quite extroverted and active in community activities, while Mr. Slith is introverted and socially retiring. Both individuals take their parenting responsibilities seriously and strive to do what is right for their children. Mr. Slith works as a repairman for an appliance company and Mrs. Slith is a secretary for an insurance company.

INITIAL INTERVIEW ROLE-PLAYING MATERIAL: CHILD WITH A PHYSICAL DISABILITY

Eddie—Age 6

Teacher Role

The 6-year-old described below is placed full time in a first-grade general education classroom. However, because he has been identified as having an educationally significant disability, you will be providing itinerant support services. You have never seen the child nor talked with the parents, but you have the following information.

Previous Medical Records

Eddie was born with meningomyelocele, which was repaired when he was 6 months of age. He was the product of a full-term pregnancy and uncomplicated delivery. However, he was reported to have tremors and possible seizures during the first weeks of life. This condition, along with the meningomyelocele, resulted in hospitalization for the first 4 weeks of life.

At the age of 1 Eddie began having frequent grand mal seizures. These were successfully controlled with antiseizure medication (Dilantin). At present, he has a grand mal seizure about once every 5 or 6 months. These seizures are extremely upsetting to both the child and his parents.

School Psychologist's Report

Intellectual assessment procedures indicated Eddie functioning in the bright normal range of mental abilities. He did particularly well on tasks requiring a verbal response. The examiner noted, in fact, that Eddie was quite adept in structuring the tasks on the tests administered and at verbally manipulating the situation (e.g., "I bet you can't do that one"; "If I get this one right will you give me some gum?" etc.).

Eddie did experience some difficulty with some of the perceptually oriented tasks. However, this was considered to be a function of his lack of interest and inexperience with these tasks.

The examiner was particularly impressed by this child's verbal skills and his manipulative strategy. Although the psychologist considered Eddie's verbal prowess to be a strength, she also noted that his desire to manipulate people could be a problem.

Academic assessment procedures revealed several readiness skills. Eddie was able to follow four-step commands, match shapes, identify colors, identify basic body parts, string beads, and rote count to 50. He demonstrated a significant weakness in fine motor activities, including writing, cutting with scissors, and duplicating geometric shapes with blocks. His first-grade teacher considers him to fall within the lower 25th percentile of academic skills when compared to his classmates.

Parent Role

The child's history and parent attitudes are as follows:

Parent's Perception of Problem

Eddie was born with meningomyelocele, which was repaired when he was 6 months of age. He was the product of a full-term pregnancy and uncomplicated delivery. However, he was reported to have tremors and possible seizures during the first weeks of life. This condition, along with the physical handicap, resulted in his hospitalization for the first 4 weeks of life.

At age 1 he began having frequent (daily) grand mal seizures. These consisted of tremors and unconsciousness. These seizures were successfully controlled with the antiseizure medication Dilantin. At present he has a grand mal seizure about once every 5 or 6 months. These seizures are extremely upsetting to both the child and his parents. Although the parents know how to respond when Eddie has a seizure, they confess that they are overcome with a combination of guilt, anger, and embarrassment when they occur. The parents have few first-grade academic goals for their son, although they do consider him to be bright and motivated.

Development

Except for Eddie's physical impairment, the parents described him as normal. They note, for example, that most major developmental milestones were achieved within normal limits. He was talking at 11 months, for example, and has been walking with the aid of crutches since he was 3.

The parents report that they tended to shelter their son for the first few years of his life. He was, in particular, expected to do little for himself, with the mother responding to his every need. The parents also resisted placing him in a preschool for children with disabilities, preferring to keep him at home. During these years at home he was rarely taken outside the house. The parents reported that this was because of the problem in transporting him and the anger they felt when "people stared at him."

The parents were quite impressed over their son's verbal aptitude. Although irritated by his manipulative behavior, they believe this skill will allow him to live a relatively normal and independent life. Their expectations are relatively high for Eddie; they anticipate he will be able to attend college and pursue a profession. The parents, especially Mrs. Haskell, are extremely resentful of anyone who suggests otherwise.

The Family

The 28-year-old parents are happily married. Mr. Haskell travels in his selling job and is rarely home except on weekends. Mrs. Haskell, consequently, is the primary parenting figure for her two sons. She is not unhappy with her full-time homemaking job but does hope to pursue a career someday. She is a high school graduate and worked as a secretary up until she became pregnant with Eddie. Her other son, Todd, is a "normal" 4-year-old.

INITIAL INTERVIEW ROLE-PLAYING MATERIALS: CHILD WITH MENTAL RETARDATION

Barbie—Age 8

Teacher Role

The 8-year-old girl described below has been placed in your noncategorical special education resource room 2 hours daily. You also provide itinerant consultation and support services to the general education teacher. You have had minimal contact with the child, and you have not talked to the parents, but you have the following information.

Report of Regular Class Teacher

Barbie is assigned to a first-grade classroom where she is repeating that grade. She is assigned to the same teacher she had last year. The first-grade school placement was Barbie's initial experience, having been held out of kindergarten because she was "immature."

Barbie is functioning significantly below the academic and social level of her peers. She has few reading readiness skills (unable to identify the letters of the alphabet or identify colors) or math abilities (unable to rote count to 5). In addition, she has poor social skills; she stays to herself and initiates few interactions. The other children in her class are kind to her, although they tend to treat her like a much younger child. Barbie seems to enjoy this treatment.

Finally, Barbie has poor speech articulation. This deficit, combined with her shy demeanor and soft voice, makes understanding her difficult. Both the teacher and her peers are becoming more adept at understanding her, however.

Though Barbie does not have a behavior problem, she is extremely active and appears to have difficulty maintaining attention to any task for even a short time. This "attention" deficit pattern has been effectively controlled by verbal cues from the teacher, individual attention, and individualized academic programs. However, the teacher noted that this control was not immediately gained. Rather, Barbie was in the classroom several weeks before responding appropriately to the teacher.

School Psychologist's Report

The single most significant observation made during the testing session was Barbie's noncompliance and hyperactivity. She required constant attention and vacillated between ignoring and manipulating the behavior of the examiner. She was able to follow directions to a minimal degree and was successful on several items for which the difficulty was commensurate with her chronological age. Although she could be persuaded at times to attend to the task at hand, she was difficult to maintain at any one task for more than a few minutes.

Barbie gives evidence of adequate receptive language, but her expressive skills are far less developed; at least part of this behavior is believed to be a function of her negativism. She does spontaneously employ language on occasion, but for the most part her verbalizations consist of repeating what has been said to her and of answering direct examiner questions. She also gave evidence of having a severe articulation problem.

Intellectual instruments were attempted, but this child's lack of cooperation and oppositional behaviors made strict adherence to testing procedures impossible. Specific strengths were noted in her ability to take disjointed elements and unite them into meaningful wholes.

Barbie also demonstrated a deficit in perceptual motor functioning. She was specifically weak at tasks requiring fine muscle coordination and visual-motor integration. However, as her visual-motor skills are consistent with her tested mental age, the exact nature of her perceptual-motor difficulties are unknown.

Indicators of socialization skills suggest this child's social maturity to be below her chronological age. Specific deficits appear to be concentrated in the area of communication; this finding correlates with previous observations.

Parent Role

The child's history and parent attitudes are as follows:

Parent's Perception of Problem

The parents are most concerned about Barbie's "hyperactivity" and non-compliant behavior. The mother and father are also concerned about Barbie's speech problems.

Both the mother and father report that Barbie has been oppositional for as long as they can remember. She has not responded to the various disciplinary techniques that have been used and typically will do what she wants. The parents also noted that she will occasionally do just the opposite of what she is asked to do or will act as if she does not hear commands. When the mother or father attempts to interfere with this behavior, Barbie will throw a tantrum.

Development

Mrs. Diddle's pregnancy was significant in that she was extremely ill much of the first trimester. It was also noted by the mother that "I was so heavy I could hardly walk with her." Barbie was a full-term infant who weighed about 8½ pounds at the time of birth. Barbie was discharged with her mother in good health at the age of 4 days.

The developmental landmarks are obscure due to the mother's poor memory for detail. Allegedly Barbie crawled at 16 months, walked at 19 months, was toilet trained at 2, and began talking at age 3. This child, according to the mother's report, has been speaking in sentences for only about 3 years.

At approximately 3 months of age Barbie had a number of "seizures," which were characterized by "rolling her eyes, jumping, and getting limber." Barbie reportedly has periodic petit mal seizures today.

School History

Barbie is presently repeating the first grade, having skipped kindergarten. The decision to not place Barbie in kindergarten was made by the parents because of their daughter's "immaturity."

Barbie is with the same first-grade teacher she had last year. During the first year in this class the parents were told that she was academically and socially unable to function in the first grade. Although she was described as not having a behavior problem, the teacher described Barbie as "very slow" and "probably in need of special education." The teacher further revealed to the parents that their daughter did not have a normal relationship with the other children. Rather, the teacher noted that the other kids respond to Barbie like they do their younger sisters.

The teacher sought to have Barbie evaluated for special education, but the parents wanted to see if their daughter could "mature over the summer and catch up with the other kids." Consequently, it was decided that Barbie would repeat the first grade.

Expectations of the Parents

Mr. and Mrs. Diddle are frustrated and overwhelmed by their daughter's poor performance in school. They believe that if she is developmentally delayed she should receive special education services, yet they are not sure that that is what she needs. In addition, they are perplexed over the differences in Barbie's behavior at home and school. Although the classroom teacher reports that Barbie does not have a behavior problem, the parents are experiencing a variety of problem behaviors at home.

INITIAL CONFERENCE EVALUATION

Date_____

Name of Child_____

Name of Person Playing Parent Role_____

Name of Person Playing Conferencer Role _____

Observer(s) _____

Circle the response that most closely describes the performance of the individual you are evaluating for each of the items below. Following evaluation, you should provide verbal feedback to the individual playing the conferencer role for each of the items.

I. General Conferencing Evaluation

A. Ability of the conferencer to inform parents of the purpose of the conference

1	2	3	4	5
Poor	Below Average	Average	Above Average	Excellent

B. Ability of the conferencer to conduct the session in a systematic and sequential manner

1	2	3	4	5
Poor	Below Average	Average	Above Average	Excellent

C. Ability of the conferencer to keep the session flowing and on course

1	2	3	4	5
Poor	Below Average	Average	Above Average	Excellent

D. Ability of the conferencer to solicit and respond to parent questions

1	2	3	4	5
Poor	Below Average	Average	Above Average	Excellent

E. Ability of the conferencer to attend to the parents

1	2	3	4	5
Poor	Below Average	Average	Above Average	Excellent

F. Ability of the conferencer to rephrase questions

1	2	3	4	5
Poor	Below Average	Average	Above Average	Excellent

G. Ability of the conferencer to summarize the conference

1	2	3	4	5
Poor	Below Average	Average	Above Average	Excellent

II. Evaluation of Information Requested

A. Chief issues

1. Ability of the conferencer to solicit the parents' perception of the issues

1	2	3	4	5
Poor	Below Average	Average	Above Average	Excellent

2. Ability of the conferencer to resolve discrepancies in the parents' and professionals' perception of the issues

1	2	3	4	5
Poor	Below Average	Average	Above Average	Excellent

B. Ability of the conferencer to secure developmental history information from the parents

1	2	3	4	5
Poor	Below Average	Average	Above Average	Excellent

C. Ability of the conferencer to secure information about the child's likes and dislikes from the parents

1	2	3	4	5
Poor	Below Average	Average	Above Average	Excellent

D. Ability of the conferencer to secure information about the child's school history from the parents

1	2	3	4	5
Poor	Below Average	Average	Above Average	Excellent

E. Ability of the conferencer to secure information about the parents' expectations for their child

1	2	3	4	5
Poor	Below Average	Average	Above Average	Excellent

F. Ability of the conferencer to secure sociological information about the child and family from the parents

1	2	3	4	5
Poor	Below Average	Average	Above Average	Excellent

III. Evaluation of Information Disseminated

A. Ability of the conferencer to disseminate assessment and diagnostic information to the parents

1	2	3	4	5
Poor	Below Average	Average	Above Average	Excellent

B. Ability of the conferencer to disseminate information to parents about the educational program to be used with their child

1	2	3	4	5
Poor	Below Average	Average	Above Average	Excellent

C. Ability of the conferencer to disseminate information to parents on procedures for evaluating the progress of pupils and the manner in which this information will be communicated

1	2	3	4	5
Poor	Below Average	Average	Above Average	Excellent

D. Ability of the conferencer to disseminate information to parents regarding community and school problem-solving alternatives and resources available

1	2	3	4	5
Poor	Below Average	Average	Above Average	Excellent

IV. Summary Information

_____

_____

_____

_____

_____

_____

_____

_____

_____

Appendix B

Individualized Education Program (IEP) Role-Playing Materials

These materials are to be used in conjunction with the exercises at the end of chapter 9. They are intended for persons playing the professional role; there are no materials designated for the person playing the role of the parent. However, background information on each case can be obtained from the case description provided in Appendix A.

IEP ROLE-PLAYING MATERIALS: YOUTH WITH A BEHAVIOR DISORDER*

Billie—Age 13

---

*Additional information on this child is available in the initial conference simulation materials.

Summary of Present Levels of Performance

	Strengths	Weaknesses
Reading:	Sight word vocabulary, which permits independent and group classroom participation.	Reading comprehension is significantly lower than recognition.
Math:	Currently working at the fourth-grade level and is able to do most of the activities.	Extremely low frustration tolerance for new concepts.
Handwriting:	Making more frequent attempts at cursive writing.	Does not know all the letters in the cursive form and is easily frustrated over assignments.
Language:	Ability to express himself is good, and he is very willing to converse with adults.	His greatest degree of trouble is with capitalization, punctuation, and contractions.
Behavioral/ Social:	Anxious to please teachers; works well for teachers who demand good work.	Difficulty in getting along with peers, and frequently threatens them. Some incidents of stealing from other students.

Possible Annual Goals**

Reading:	Improved reading comprehension.
Math:	Improved accuracy on work at grade level; increased frustration tolerance and fewer incidents of going "blank" on previously acquired math skills.

**The Possible Annual Goals should form the foundation for short-term objectives.

Handwriting:	Recognition of all letters in cursive form and legible cursive writing.
Language:	Correct use of capitalization, punctuation, and contractions.
Behavioral/ Social:	Decreased incidence of threatening others, arguing, stealing, fighting, and manipulative behaviors.

Regularly Planned Activities with Nondisabled Children

Billie is mainstreamed in general education classes for all except two class periods daily.

Recommendations for Specific Special Education Services

Itinerant support services to be provided by the learning center teacher.
Monthly parent meetings with the teacher and school psychologist.
Reevaluation by the school psychologist at the end of the academic year.

Other Information

Medical concerns

None

Stimulus control information

Billie responds well to a very structured program that includes scheduling; a behavior modification, token reinforcement program; and shaping. He works best for teachers who assure him that they know he is capable of good work, and teachers who demand good work.

Precautions

Billie has at times become very aggressive and physically fought with peers. A highly structured program appears to be the best measure for the prevention of such incidents.

IEP ROLE-PLAYING MATERIALS: GIFTED CHILD*

Howard—Age 8

Summary of Present Levels of Performance

	Strengths	Weaknesses
Reading:	Tests indicate he is two grade levels above his peers.	Does not complete skill sheets and is slow to do his assignments.
Math:	Key Math scores indicate that he is 2½ grade levels ahead of the average second-grader. Able to do complex division problems.	Has not mastered his addition and subtraction facts; is often sloppy and careless.
Handwriting:	Knows all the letters in the cursive form.	Handwriting is barely legible.
Language:	He is very verbal and his ability to express himself is very good.	
Behavioral/ Social:	Displays no acting-out behavior.	Has recently decreased his amount of contact with other children. He also displays a weakness in motor skills.

Possible Annual Goals**

Reading:	Improved comprehension of reading materials; increased incidence of completing assignments.

---

*Additional information on this child is available in the initial conference simulation materials.

**The Possible Annual Goals should form the foundation for short-term objectives.

Math: Increased accuracy on work at grade level; decrease in careless and sloppy work.

Handwriting: Legible cursive writing with appropriate spacing between letters and words.

Language: Increase in appropriate use of capitalization and punctuation.

Behavioral/   Increased incidence of interactions with peers, com-
Social: pleting tasks, and following through on contractual agreements.

Regularly Planned Activities with Nondisabled Children

Howard will be in a regular classroom. He will attend the Enhanced Learning Center resource room for gifted students 1 hour each day. In addition, he will attend the district's Challenge Program for underachieving gifted students 30 minutes per week.

Reevaluation by the school psychologist at the end of the academic year.

Other Information

Medical concerns

A few years ago Howard had a minor hearing loss caused by fluid buildup in the inner ear. He still has a slight hearing loss, especially when the ears become infected. This condition clears with medication. In addition, Howard has some allergies, but these are not considered severe by his physician. He is not currently receiving any medication.

Stimulus control information

Howard responds well to a very structured program that includes scheduling, shaping, and a social reinforcement program. He works best for a teacher who demands good work.

Precautions

None

IEP ROLE-PLAYING MATERIALS: CHILD WITH A LEARNING DISABILITY*

Sally—Age 9

Summary of Present Levels of Performance

	Strengths	Weaknesses
Reading:	Prereading skills, such as identification and discrimination of letters, and some of the sounds of the alphabet.	Sight vocabulary is limited; cannot consistently identify all of the sounds of the alphabet; comprehension difficulties.
Math:	She is able to grasp basic math concepts; when allowed to manipulate objects she can do basic math operations such as adding or subtracting.	Unable to understand abstract mathematical concepts; tends to "forget" how to do math procedures during independent practice.
Handwriting:	Letter formation is very good.	Difficulties in spacing between letters.
Language:	Adequate expressive language.	Frequently does not listen, or may occasionally have comprehension difficulties.
Behavioral/ Social:	Increase in social interactions with peers in the classroom.	Even though there has been some improvement, she has a very obvious deficit in peer interactions, especially outside of the classroom.

Possible Annual Goals**

Reading:	Improved sight and word vocabulary; improved accuracy in reproducing individual sounds.

---

*Additional information on this child is available in the initial conference simulation materials.

**The Possible Annual Goals should form the foundation for short-term objectives.

Math: Improved performance on daily mathematics papers.

Handwriting: Legible reproduction of a printed model with appropriate spacing between letters and words.

Language: Increased capacity for listening and/or verbal comprehension.

Behavioral/ Increase in peer interactions.
Social:

Regularly Planned Activities with Nondisabled Children

Sally will be assigned to a regular classroom except for the 2 hours daily she will be in a resource strategy room.

Recommendations for Specific Special Education Services

Itinerant consultation and support services to be provided by the resource strategy teacher.

Reevaluation by the school psychologist at the end of the academic year.

Other Information

Medical concerns

None

Stimulus control information

Sally responds very well to a high degree of structure, which includes a shaping process, scheduling for predictable activities, and a behavior modification based on social reinforcement.

Precautions

None

IEP ROLE-PLAYING MATERIALS: CHILD WITH A PHYSICAL DISABILITY*

Eddie—Age 6

Summary of Present Levels of Performance

	Strengths	Weaknesses
Reading:	Possesses several reading readiness skills, including the ability to match shapes and colors.	Lacks ability to identify letters of the alphabet and their associated sounds; lacks sight word vocabulary.
Math:	Ability to rote count to 50.	Lacks consistent one-to-one correspondence skills; inability to consistently do simple addition and subtraction.
Self-Help Skills:	Capable of independent self-help skills.	Lacks motivation in carrying out independent self-help skills.
Handwriting:	Improvement in frustration tolerance and attempts at pencil manipulation and writing.	Fine motor skills are poor. He has difficulty with coloring within the boundaries and cutting with scissors.
Language:	Able to relate personal experiences logically and sequentially; follows 4-item commands.	His speech is characterized by misarticulation and his auditory discrimination may be slightly delayed.
Behavioral/ Social:	Displays considerable personality strength; he is outgoing and friendly; interacts appropriately with peers.	Frequently displays manipulative and tantruming behavior; constantly demands attention.

*Additional information on this child is available in the initial conference materials.

Possible Annual Goals**

Reading: Acquisition of reading skills necessary for first-grade success.

Math: Development of simple addition and subtraction skills.

Self-Help Skills: Improvement in independent self-help skills.

Handwriting: Increased incidence of attempts at writing; legible repro-
                   duction of all printed letters; decrease in incidence of
                   carelessness.

Language: Improvement in articulation; improvement in auditory
                   discrimination.

Behavioral/   Decreased incidence of manipulative behavior and tan-
Social: trums; increase in independent work and compliance.

Regularly Planned Activities with Nondisabled Children

Eddie will be in a regular first-grade classroom full-time daily.

Recommendations for Specific Special Education Services

Itinerant collaborative and consultative support service by an itinerant
special eduction teacher.
  Speech therapy 1½ hours weekly.
  Physical therapy 30 minutes daily.
  Reevaluation by the school psychologist at the end of the academic year.

Other Information

Medical concerns

Eddie has a seizure disorder, which results in grand mal seizures about once
every 5 months. He is presently taking Dilantin to control his seizures.

Stimulus control information

Eddie responds best to a teacher who assures him that he is capable of good
work, demands good work, and does not respond to his attempts to manipulate.

**The Possible Annual Goals should form the foundation for short-term objectives.

IEP ROLE-PLAYING MATERIALS: CHILD WITH MENTAL RETARDATION*

Barbie—Age 8

Summary of Present Levels of Performance

	Strengths	Weaknesses
Reading:	Occasionally able to recognize her name, and she scored above average on the Word Meaning subtest of a standardized reading readiness scale.	On a standardized reading readiness test she performed in the low normal category (13th percentile), and she has very few reading readiness skills. She also had low scores on the Copying and Matching subtests of the reading readiness scale.
Math:	Currently able to count to 3.	Outside of counting to 3, she appears to have few mathematical skills, including one-to-one correspondence.
Perceptual/ Motor:	Barbie is able to hold a primary-size pencil.	Weak at tasks requiring fine muscle coordination and visual motor integration. She has a very awkward manner of holding her pencil.
Speech/ Language:	Relatively good receptive language skills.	Makes a few spontaneous verbalizations. Subtest scores on a preschool language scale ranged from $3\frac{1}{2}$ to 5 years. She has articulation problems.
Behavioral/ Social:	Gets along well with her peers at school and has shown some improvement in adjusting to the classroom situation.	She tends to be a participant rather than an observer; she has on occasion become extremely negative toward the teacher and refused to carry through with structured demands. She is also thought to have an attention deficit.

---

*Additional information on this child is available in the initial conference simulation materials.

Possible Annual Goals**

Reading: Ability to recognize the letters of the alphabet and their corresponding sounds; increased accuracy in reproducing initial sounds; development of basic sight word vocabulary.

Math: Increased accuracy in rote counting; development of basic math readiness skills; development of basic addition and subtraction skills.

Handwriting: Improved performance in legibly reproducing printed letters.

Language: Increase in spontaneous verbalizations; development of expressive language skills comparable to a kindergarten to first-grade child.

Behavioral/   Increase in peer interactions; decrease in negativism;
Social: decrease in noncompliance; decrease in tantruming.

Regularly Planned Activities with Nondisabled Children

Except for the 2 hours Barbie is in a special education resource room, she will be in a regular first-grade classroom.

Recommendations for Specific Special Education Services

Full-time paraprofessional support.

Itinerant collaborative and consultative services by the resource room teacher.

Reevaluation by the school psychologist at the end of the academic year.

Monthly parent meetings in behavior management programming for dealing with Barbie's tantrums and related behavior problems.

Other Information

Medical concerns

Barbie periodically has petit mal seizures.

Stimulus Control information

Barbie responds well to a highly structured approach as a means of remediating her social and educational difficulties.

**The Possible Annual Goals should form the foundation for short-term objectives.

IEP CONFERENCE EVALUATION

Date_____

Name of Child_____

Name of Person Playing Parent Role_____

Name of Person Playing Conferencer Role _____

Observer(s) _____

Circle the response that most closely describes the performance of the individual you are evaluating for each of the items below. Following evaluation, you should provide verbal feedback to the individual playing the conferencer role for each of the items.

I. General Conferencing Evaluation

A. Ability of the conferencer to inform parents of the purpose of the conference

1	2	3	4	5
Poor	Below Average	Average	Above Average	Excellent

B. Ability of the conferencer to conduct the session in a systematic and sequential manner

1	2	3	4	5
Poor	Below Average	Average	Above Average	Excellent

C. Ability of the conferencer to keep the session flowing and on course

1	2	3	4	5
Poor	Below Average	Average	Above Average	Excellent

D. Ability of the conferencer to solicit and respond to parent questions

1	2	3	4	5
Poor	Below Average	Average	Above Average	Excellent

E. Ability of the conferencer to attend to the parents

1	2	3	4	5
Poor	Below Average	Average	Above Average	Excellent

F. Ability of the conferencer to rephrase questions

1	2	3	4	5
Poor	Below Average	Average	Above Average	Excellent

G. Ability of the conferencer to summarize the conference

1	2	3	4	5
Poor	Below Average	Average	Above Average	Excellent

II. IEP Content

A. Ability of the conferencer to review the pupil's level of functioning, including academic, physical, social, prevocational/vocational, emotional, psychomotor, self-help, etc.

1	2	3	4	5
Poor	Below Average	Average	Above Average	Excellent

Was legitimate input obtained (or opportunity for input provided) from the parent in this area?

1	2	3	4	5
Poor	Below Average	Average	Above Average	Excellent

B. Ability of the conferencer to develop annual goals for the child

1	2	3	4	5
Poor	Below Average	Average	Above Average	Excellent

Was legitimate input obtained (or opportunity for input provided) from the parent in this area?

1	2	3	4	5
Poor	Below Average	Average	Above Average	Excellent

C. Ability of the conferencer to develop short-term objectives (steps between present functioning and annual goals) for the child

1	2	3	4	5
Poor	Below Average	Average	Above Average	Excellent

Was legitimate input obtained (or opportunity for input provided) from the parent in this area?

1	2	3	4	5
Poor	Below Average	Average	Above Average	Excellent

D. Ability of the conferencer to develop evaluation procedures (criteria for determining whether the objectives are being achieved) for the pupil

1	2	3	4	5
Poor	Below Average	Average	Above Average	Excellent

Was legitimate input obtained (or opportunity for input provided) from the parent in this area?

1	2	3	4	5
Poor	Below Average	Average	Above Average	Excellent

E. Ability of the conferencer to identify educational services need (without regard to the availability) for the pupil

1	2	3	4	5
Poor	Below Average	Average	Above Average	Excellent

  1. Was legitimate input obtained (or opportunity for input provided) from the parent in this area?

1	2	3	4	5
Poor	Below Average	Average	Above Average	Excellent

  2. Ability of the conferencer to identify special instructional media, materials, or services needed for the pupil

1	2	3	4	5
Poor	Below Average	Average	Above Average	Excellent

  3. Ability of the conferencer to specify when services for the pupil will begin and the specific length of time and extent provided

1	2	3	4	5
Poor	Below Average	Average	Above Average	Excellent

F. Ability of the conferencer to describe the extent to which the pupil will participate in regular education programs

1	2	3	4	5
Poor	Below Average	Average	Above Average	Excellent

Was legitimate input obtained (or opportunity for input provided) from parent in this area?

1	2	3	4	5
Poor	Below Average	Average	Above Average	Excellent

G. Ability of the conferencer to justify the type of educational placement/program to be provided the pupil

1	2	3	4	5
Poor	Below Average	Average	Above Average	Excellent

Was legitimate input obtained (or opportunity for input provided) from parent in this area?

1	2	3	4	5
Poor	Below Average	Average	Above Average	Excellent

III. Summary Information

_____

_____

_____

_____

_____

_____

_____

_____

_____

_____

_____

_____

_____

_____

_____

_____

_____

_____

INDIVIDUALIZED EDUCATION PLAN

Student's Name: _____   Date: _____

School: _____

Summary of Present Levels of Performance

_____

_____

_____

Annual Goals

1. _____   4. _____

2. _____   5. _____

3. _____   6. _____

Short-Term Objectives	Special Education and Related Services	Person Responsible	Beginning and Ending Dates	Review Date

Regularly planned activities with general education children (%) _____

_____

Committee recommendations for specific procedures/strategies, materials, information about learning style, etc. _____

_____

_____

Committee members present

_____

_____

_____

_____

Appendix C

Behavior Management Role-Playing Materials

These materials are to be used in conjunction with the exercises at the end of chapter 10. There are no materials designated for the person playing the role of the conferencer; however, background information on each case can be obtained from the case description provided in Appendix A.

BEHAVIOR MANAGEMENT ROLE-PLAYING MATERIALS: YOUTH WITH A BEHAVIOR DISORDER

Billie—Age 13

Parent Role

Billie has recently been a concern to his parents because of his "pouting" behavior. When displeased, Billie will show his displeasure by making facial grimaces, stomping around the house, and sulking. Although he has always had this behavior in his repertoire, he is currently displaying it to an inordinate degree. He has few friends in the neighborhood and, according to the parents, seems to be spending a great deal of his time pouting.

This behavior is quite pervasive, and Billie displays it whenever he is at home, regardless of who is there. Because his mother and siblings are most frequently at home at the same time, they experience it most.

The parents have tried scolding, isolation, ignoring, and reasoning in attempting to deal with the problem but have had little success in decreasing its rate. Billie's brother and sisters make fun of him for his "baby" behavior, and his father threatens "to beat hell out of him."

Everyone in the family is upset over the situation and all are looking at the mother to solve the problem. Mother is upset and is purportedly considering leaving the family. She has told Billie this in hopes of "straightening him up." The father's attitude is that Billie is seeking punishment when he pouts, and the father is not going to disappoint the youth by ignoring it.

BEHAVIOR MANAGEMENT ROLE-PLAYING MATERIALS: GIFTED CHILD*

Howard—Age 8

Parent Role

Howard's parents have recently become quite upset over their son's solitary play behavior. Extremely little of his day is spent in any interaction with other kids in the neighborhood. He typically plays alone in a quiet area of the house and interacts only with his parents. The parents are becoming increasingly upset by his isolated play and feel that he should be spending at least some of his leisure time engaging in social behavior.

The parents have begun nagging their son in hopes of persuading him to adopt more socially appropriate play behavior. The mother especially spends a great deal of time and energy after school and on weekends trying to entice him to play with the neighborhood children. She has even threatened to withhold his allowance until he makes some friends and begins to play with the neighborhood kids.

---

*Individuals using this role-playing script are advised to use intervention programs that combine consequences with antecedent manipulation, including direct skill instruction, adult prompting, and/or peer mediated procedures.

Mother and father disagree somewhat in their perceptions of the future. Mr. Huge feels that Howard will outgrow his isolation and begin making friends. However, he does not feel that he will ever be an extrovert. Mrs. Huge, on the other hand, has read in several women's magazines about the problems that can arise if a child is withdrawn and poorly equipped socially. She is frightened that he may later develop a "mental problem." She thinks that perhaps by displaying to him how much his behavior upsets her, the situation will improve.

BEHAVIOR MANAGEMENT ROLE-PLAYING MATERIALS: CHILD WITH A LEARNING DISABILITY*

Sally—Age 9

Parent Role

Mr. and Mrs. Slith are concerned about their daughter's withdrawn behavior. Sally has always been considered to be "socially immature" and "withdrawn." However, this pattern of shyness and reclusiveness has recently become more acute. In addition, several of the Sliths' relatives have told them that shyness in children can lead to severe problems in later life. Mrs. Slith has begun prompting Sally to spend more time playing with neighborhood children. When this has not worked, she has resorted to punishment (withholding dessert) and nagging, and has recently threatened to send Sally to a psychiatrist if she doesn't start spending more time with children her own age. The mother spends a considerable amount of time and effort on weekends and after school trying to get Sally to be more social. Although this is a pervasive behavior, Mrs. Slith is by far the most concerned.

Mr. and Mrs. Slith vary in their overall perception of the problem and its future implications. Mr. Slith is somewhat concerned, yet he truly believes that Sally is "just shy" and will outgrow her reclusiveness in time.

---

*Individuals using this role-playing script are advised to use intervention programs that combine consequences with antecedent manipulation, including direct skill instruction, adult prompting, and/or peer mediated procedures.

Mother is not nearly as optimistic. She feels that Sally will develop other more severe emotional problems if she does not develop a more extroverted personality. The mother also believes that by displaying to Sally how much her behavior upsets her, the condition will be improved.

BEHAVIOR MANAGEMENT ROLE-PLAYING MATERIALS: CHILD WITH A PHYSICAL DISABILITY

Eddie—Age 6

Parent Role

Just recently (last few weeks), Eddie has begun to display rather severe tantrum behavior to control the actions of his parents. As his father is gone during the week, this action is directed at his mother.

Eddie now demands that the mother remain with him during his afternoon nap and after he is put to bed at night. If the mother leaves the bedroom after putting him to bed, he screams and cries until she returns to the room. As a result, the mother has been unable to leave the bedroom until after Eddie goes to sleep. If the mother tries to read while in the bedroom, Eddie will cry until the reading material is put down. The mother feels that Eddie enjoys his control over her and that he fights off going to sleep as long as possible. For the past 2 weeks she has been spending from 30 minutes to 2 hours each bedtime just waiting until Eddie goes to sleep.

The mother has received medical assurance that there is no physical reason for the problem. Her physician has indicated that Eddie will probably outgrow the problem.

Mother feels obligated to stay with Eddie when he begins crying in the bedroom. She feels that if he did not have a disability, she would probably be able to deal with the situation. As it now stands, though, she feels guilty about punishing the youngster and even more guilty about ignoring him when he is crying. She thus returns to the child's room, but states that she is bitter about his obvious manipulation of her. Mother feels somewhat lost without an effective disciplinary method.

Although the mother does not currently know how to handle the behavior, she feels that he will spontaneously overcome the problem with time. Maturity, she feels, will be the answer to this youngster's problem. In addition, she feels that displaying to Eddie how much of an inconvenience he is to the family will instill a feeling of responsibility that will decrease the problem behavior.

BEHAVIOR MANAGEMENT ROLE-PLAYING MATERIALS: CHILD WITH MENTAL RETARDATION

Barbie—Age 8

Parent Role

The parents have noted that Barbie has always been an immature personality whose primary concern has been to manipulate her environment. For example, Barbie may state that she will not participate in a task and, if implored to participate, will attempt to physically leave the situation or resort to actively negative behavior.

Recently this negativism has become an even more acute problem. Specifically, both parents have experienced marked difficulties in getting Barbie to obey parental requests or commands. Barbie was described as "headstrong" and "set in her ways." Although expressive language is not this child's primary mode of communication, she does use phrases such as "no-no," "I won't," and "I can't" at a high rate of frequency.

Although this behavior has been rather consistent across environments, the parents notice it more at home. In addition, the behavior appears to occur more frequently in the mother's presence. This may be related to the fact that the mother spends a great deal more time with the child than the father.

Neither the mother nor father knows how to deal with the behavior. They suggest that they have "tried everything." They have talked to her, spanked her, taken her dinner away, and put her in her room by herself. Because they have not employed any procedures consistently, though, it is difficult to say what works best.

Presently the parents are tremendously upset about what to do. The father has even talked about institutionalization because of his inability to handle the problem. The mother feels inadequate to handle the problem and considers herself a "bad mother." Presently the parents don't know what to do, but have the attitude that if they try hard enough, they can find an answer to the problem. This attitude of perseverance means experimenting with a number of procedures, hoping to stumble across something that will work.

BEHAVIORAL CONFERENCE I EVALUATION

Date_____

Name of Child_____

Name of Person Playing Parent Role_____

Name of Person Playing Conferencer Role _____

Observer(s) _____

Circle the response that most closely describes the performance of the individual you are evaluating for each of the items below. Following evaluation, you should provide verbal feedback to the individual playing the conferencer role for each of the items.

I. General Conferencing Evaluation

A. Ability of the conferencer to inform parents of the purpose of the conference

1	2	3	4	5
Poor	Below Average	Average	Above Average	Excellent

B. Ability of the conferencer to conduct the session in a systematic, sequential manner

1	2	3	4	5
Poor	Below Average	Average	Above Average	Excellent

C. Ability of the conferencer to keep the session flowing and on course

1	2	3	4	5
Poor	Below Average	Average	Above Average	Excellent

D. Ability of the conferencer to solicit and respond to parent questions

1	2	3	4	5
Poor	Below Average	Average	Above Average	Excellent

E. Ability of the conferencer to attend to the parents

1	2	3	4	5
Poor	Below Average	Average	Above Average	Excellent

F. Ability of the conferencer to rephrase questions

1	2	3	4	5
Poor	Below Average	Average	Above Average	Excellent

G. Ability of the conferencer to summarize the conference

1	2	3	4	5
Poor	Below Average	Average	Above Average	Excellent

II. First Session Procedural Steps

A. Target Behavior

1. Ability of the conferencer to secure an adequate definition of the target behavior

1	2	3	4	5
Poor	Below Average	Average	Above Average	Excellent

2. Ability of the conferencer to explain how the parents were to evaluate (count) the target behavior

1	2	3	4	5
Poor	Below Average	Average	Above Average	Excellent

B. Evaluation of Stimulus Situations

1. Ability of the conferencer in obtaining adequate information on where the problem behavior occurred

1	2	3	4	5
Poor	Below Average	Average	Above Average	Excellent

2. Ability of the conferencer in obtaining adequate information about whom the child is with when the behavior of concern occurs

1	2	3	4	5
Poor	Below Average	Average	Above Average	Excellent

C. Evaluation of Contingencies

Ability of the conferencer in uncovering the major factors that might have been perpetuating the problem behavior

1	2	3	4	5
Poor	Below Average	Average	Above Average	Excellent

III. Additional Comments

_____

_____

_____

_____

_____

_____

_____

_____

_____

_____

_____

_____

_____

_____

_____

_____

_____

_____

_____

_____

_____

_____

_____

_____

BEHAVIORAL CONFERENCE II EVALUATION

Date _____

Name of Child _____

Name of Person Playing Parent Role _____

Name of Person Playing Conferencer Role _____

Observer(s) _____

Circle the response that most closely describes the performance of the individual you are evaluating for each of the items below. Following evaluation, you should provide verbal feedback to the individual playing the conferencer role for each of the items.

I. General Conferencing Evaluation

    A. Ability of the conferencer to inform parents of the purpose of the conference

1	2	3	4	5
Poor	Below Average	Average	Above Average	Excellent

    B. Ability of the conferencer to conduct the session in a systematic and sequential manner

1	2	3	4	5
Poor	Below Average	Average	Above Average	Excellent

    C. Ability of the conferencer to keep the session flowing and on course

1	2	3	4	5
Poor	Below Average	Average	Above Average	Excellent

    D. Ability of the conferencer to solicit and respond to parent questions

1	2	3	4	5
Poor	Below Average	Average	Above Average	Excellent

    E. Ability of the conferencer to attend to the parents

1	2	3	4	5
Poor	Below Average	Average	Above Average	Excellent

F. Ability of the conferencer to rephrase questions

1	2	3	4	5
Poor	Below Average	Average	Above Average	Excellent

G. Ability of the conferencer to summarize the conference

1	2	3	4	5
Poor	Below Average	Average	Above Average	Excellent

II. Conference Content

A. Charting and Inspecting Target Data

Ability of the conferencer to train parents to chart baseline data

1	2	3	4	5
Poor	Below Average	Average	Above Average	Excellent

B. Intervention Procedures

1. Ability of the conferencer to devise and present appropriate consequences and other interventions to modify the target behavior

1	2	3	4	5
Poor	Below Average	Average	Above Average	Excellent

2. Ability of the conferencer to establish desired interim rates for the target behavior

1	2	3	4	5
Poor	Below Average	Average	Above Average	Excellent

III. Additional Comments

_____

_____

_____

_____

_____

_____

Appendix D

Progress Report Conference Role-Playing Materials

These materials are to be used in conjunction with the exercises at the end of chapter 11.

PROGRESS REPORT ROLE-PLAYING MATERIALS: YOUTH WITH A BEHAVIOR DISORDER

Billie—Age 13

Teacher Role

In preparation for a progress report conference, you have available the records and information listed below.

Background Information and Diagnostic Data

Billie was originally referred for assessment because of both behavioral and academic problems. In particular, his regular class teachers described him as aggressive with other students, manipulative, "socially immature," and functioning academically below his peers. Individual intelligence testing revealed this child to be functioning at the low-average range of abilities. This finding was consistent with previous assessment results. Observations conducted in the regular classroom by a diagnostician revealed that Billie attended to task about 25% less than his peers, that he daydreamed, and that he was out of his seat without permission significantly more than the other children. Finally, educational testing revealed a reading recognition level of 5.5, a reading comprehension level of 3.5, and arithmetic performance at a 4.0 grade level.

Although his regular class teachers noted that Billie was anxious to please them and responded to a structured routine, they considered his social and behavioral problems so severe as to require special education intervention and support.

At Billie's IEP conference the following annual goals were discussed and adopted*:

Reading:	Improved performance in reading comprehension.
Math:	Improved performance in math, increased frustration tolerance for math problems; fewer incidents of going "blank" on previously acquired math skills.
Handwriting:	Recognition of all letters in cursive form and legible cursive writing.
Language:	Correct use of capitalization, punctuation, and contractions.
Behavioral/ Social:	Decreased incidence of threatening others, arguing, stealing, fighting, and manipulative behavior.

At the time of the progress report conference, Billie was working at approximately the fifth- to sixth-grade level. However, his academic level varied considerably, usually in direct relation to his social behavior. Listed below is a summary of his academic levels and skills.

Reading

Although Billie's reading comprehension has improved (4.5 grade equivalent level), it continues to be a problem. He becomes easily frustrated when he is asked comprehension questions that require looking back through what he has read for specific answers. Billie has been using a workbook that requires locating specific answers from the text to answer

---

*Individuals are encouraged to use the IEP developed in an earlier simulation exercise.

workbook questions. He has also been using teacher-made reading lab materials.

Writing

Billie has had extreme difficulty with cursive writing, and his handwriting is still almost illegible. He has actively resisted attempts at cursive writing and has tantrumed routinely when confronted with this task. However, he is able to recognize all cursive letters.

Language arts

Although he has shown significant improvement in this area since the writing of the IEP, Billie continues to experience problems. Specific deficit areas include capitalization, punctuation, and contractions.

Math

Billie is currently working in Modern School Mathematics 6. He seems able to do most of the activities, although on some days his frustration tolerance is so low that he seems to go "blank" on all previous math skills and will tantrum when faced with even the simplest math assignment. This has been a chronic problem since the time of the last progress report conference and one that the classroom teacher has not been able to find a key to, even though she has employed a number of different strategies. He is currently showing a 65% to 70% fifth-grade accuracy level.

Social studies

Billie has been working in a book entitled *A Journey to Many Lands* and the accompanying workbook. Just as in other academic areas, he seems able to comprehend the materials but actively resists answering comprehension questions. This particular academic area has been the source of a number of tantrums.

Emotional-Social Behavior

At the time of the progress report conference with the parents, Billie was still emitting a great number of inappropriate behaviors. He was crying and tantruming almost daily over academic work well within his capabilities. He also regularly stole articles from the learning center classroom and from other classrooms in the building, was chronically belligerent, and threatened other children. Finally, he was involved in a great many verbal arguments with both students and adults. Two recent examples of Billie's emotional-social behavior reveal the current situation:

Situation 1

Billie started out the day in his general education social studies class in a rather poor frame of mind. He was extremely antagonistic toward the other students in the classroom and was called down several times for breaking and knocking over the classroom projects of others in the room. He was sent to his seat for engaging in this behavior.

During independent seatwork, Billie was extremely ill-tempered and had his hand raised constantly, wanting the teacher to give him answers so that he would not have to actively search for them. With a great deal of "hurdle help," Billie finished his assignment, but as soon as he started another assignment, he became extremely agitated and upset. He said that he could not understand what was meant by some very simple instructions. He refused to attempt to respond to these questions and claimed that he could not comprehend the directions. He began crying and had to be removed to the hallway until he could gain control of himself. While in the hallway, he cried for nearly half an hour.

Situation 2

One day Billie was doing fairly well in language arts class until about midway through the class. At that time he was involved in an assignment that required that he find words in the index of his book and copy the page numbers where the topics could be found. Billie was extremely uncooperative and refused to even listen to the teacher's explanation of how the task should be approached. Instead, he would raise his hand for each word and say that he was unable to find it. When the teacher insisted on aiding Billie rather than finding the answer for him, he began crying, cursing, and kicking. At this time he was required to go to the learning center to settle down. This strategy appeared to be successful, as Billie was able to calm himself down after only a few minutes. However, when he was allowed to return to language arts class, he again became very upset.

His learning center teacher also found the following data and records regarding one particular social problem that has been experienced: During one period between the present and the last parent conference, Billie had been fighting in the hallway and had become somewhat of an isolate in the class. No one in the class during that time would have much to do with him, and he was constantly sulking. Billie appeared to be bringing most of this behavior about himself. He was constantly enticing the other kids into fights by verbally abusing them and hitting and kicking them when the teacher was not looking. Billie provoked these problems and then innocently stepped back with an appearance of puzzlement when the other youngsters responded.

The teacher took some data on this behavior during one period of time when the problem was of most concern.

Times fighting in the hallway

Monday	2 times
Tuesday	1 time
Wednesday	0 times
Thursday	3 times
Friday	1 time

Times Billie has provoked a fight in the learning center class

Monday	7 times
Tuesday	14 times
Wednesday	19 times
Thursday	13 times
Friday	12 times

Although the situation has improved, Billie still has problems in this area.

Physical Information

Billie's teachers have noted no physical problems that they feel need to be discussed with the parent. Billie seems to be in good health and has had no patterns of absence, illness, or tardiness.

Classroom Structure

Billie's classroom teachers have each attempted a structured approach to try to remediate emotional and educational difficulties. Initially, this consisted of evaluating Billie's patterns of strength and weakness in the learning center so that an appropriate program could be developed. This enabled the learning center teacher to recommend curricula and materials for Billie's other classes. The highly structured program in the learning center also accentuated programming Billie for specific academic materials. The programming consisted of a shaping process whereby defined behaviors were sequentially arranged into incremental units. The goal of this programming process was to increase Billie's productive behaviors and to break the repetitive elements of his maladaptive social and academic behaviors. The structure employed by the learning center teacher also emphasized scheduling Billie for specific predictable activities. This was adopted to aid in reducing Billie's uncertainty and to help him predict the consequences of his own behavior and thus to aid in the alleviation of his failure patterns. A final component of the structured strategy was behavior modification. Specifically, positive consequences occurred when Billie's responses approximated what were considered appropriate behaviors. These strategies have also been used to varying degrees in Billie's other classes.

It has been the learning center teacher's impression that since the time Billie was placed in special education, he has had severe problems in all of his classes.

Although Billie's behavior, academic work, and general emotional state seemed to deteriorate during the first few months he was in the learning center, he has just recently started to make some progress. The learning center teacher has associated this with a heightened degree of structure in all of his classes. Specifically, he has been reinforced for doing each assignment in an appropriate way (i.e., no crying, throwing books, kicking, or tantruming). Based on this recent change of behavior, the teacher recommends that Billie be maintained in the learning center and that his general education teachers continue to use a highly structured approach.

PROGRESS REPORT ROLE-PLAYING MATERIALS: GIFTED CHILD

Howard—Age 8

Teacher Role

In preparation for a progress report conference, you have available the records and information listed below.

Background Information and Diagnostic Data

Howard was originally referred for assessment because his regular class teacher thought he was bored. She routinely observed that he evaded completing daily tasks so that he could pursue a task of his own choosing. In addition, she was concerned about the following: daydreaming in class, verbal domination of peers and class discussions, lack of knowledge of math facts, and poor handwriting.

The regular classroom teacher described Howard's relationship with his classmates as good. However, she observed that his classmates seemed to be in awe of his verbal abilities and analytical mind.

Individual intelligence testing revealed this child to be functioning in the very superior range of abilities and at the 99th percentile. The examiner was particularly impressed by Howard's ability to verbally express himself.

At his IEP conference, the following annual goals were discussed and adopted:*

Reading:	Improved performance in completing reading assignments.
Math:	Improved accuracy and decrease in carelessly completed work.
Handwriting:	Improved cursive writing.
Behavioral/ Social:	Increased interactions with peers and improved willingness to follow through on contractual agreements.

At the time of the progress report conference, Howard was progressing well in both his regular class and the Enhanced Learning Center. He has also responded positively to the district program for underachieving gifted children. Howard had recently been administered an additional series of standardized assessment measures, which yielded the following results:

Howard was found to be functioning in the superior range of general intelligence and fell 2 full years above expectations in academic performance. On a pictorial test of intelligence that required a pointing response, he demonstrated relative strength on receptive vocabulary of single words in isolation, on visual form discrimination, on general information, and on an analogies task. He also showed relative prowess for his age on size and number concepts and on a visual-memory task.

A series of visual-perceptual tasks yielded scores well within normal limits. Visual-motor tasks were performed well within normal limits, and Howard earned an above-average score on a task requiring him to draw geometric designs from memory.

---

*Individuals are encouraged to use the IEP developed in an earlier simulation exercise.

Four tasks designed to measure auditory attention span and auditory memory revealed that he performed 1 year above his age group on memory for single words, and 2 years above his age group on memory for related syllables and for a sequence of directions requiring gross motor responses. He was able to score above average on a pencil-and-paper task requiring a series of steps.

Classroom Structure

Howard's classroom teachers have adopted a highly individualized program to meet his educational needs. Initially this consisted of evaluating his patterns of strength and weakness so that an individualized Enhanced Learning Center program could be developed. This enabled the teacher to select, along with Howard, appropriate curricula and materials commensurate with his strengths and weaknesses. The program also accentuated programming him for appropriate academic materials in his regular classroom. The programming consisted of a shaping process whereby defined behaviors were sequentially arranged into incremental units. The goal of this programming process was to increase his handwriting skills and to emphasize completing assigned tasks. The structure employed by the teachers also emphasized scheduling Howard for specific predictable activities. This was adopted to aid in reducing uncertainty for him. A final component of the structure strategy that was being used by the teachers was behavior modification. Specifically, positive consequences occurred when he had stayed on task and completed assigned material.

In addition, the teacher in the Enhanced Learning Center program has implemented the following in both the center and his regular classroom:

1. A reading program that takes into account this child's skills in word recognition, comprehension, and intellectual capacity.

2. A program whereby Howard is required to complete any task he begins. Although he should be given curriculum choices, he is not permitted to begin a new project without completing previous assignments. Contracts are used for this purpose.

Emotional-Social Information

The Enhanced Learning Center teacher found the following data and records regarding one particular social problem that was experienced:

Howard's teachers have recently been concerned about his lack of contact with other children. The teachers report that this child consistently stands quietly about the yard while the other children run, play games, and climb on the playground apparatus. Although the teachers have attempted to encourage him, through suggestions or invitations, to engage in activities with the other children, he consistently declines. The teachers are also concerned over his apparent lack of strength and motor skills. The Enhanced Learning Center teacher took some data on the daily time Howard had spent in social interaction with children during a 30-minute morning recess period:

Day 1	2 minutes
Day 2	1 minute
Day 3	4 minutes
Day 4	0 minutes
Day 5	1 minute

Anecdotal note

It was raining, so the afternoon recess was spent in the gym. The children had a choice of two activities during this time: (1) jump rope and (2) kickball. Howard was asked to turn the rope with the teacher while the other children took turns jumping. He was then encouraged to try jumping the rope and he shook his head "no." When the rope was turned, he just stood where he was and did not attempt to jump. He then walked over to the door and quietly watched the children who were playing kickball. He was encouraged to participate but declined. When the recess was over, he was asked to help carry the rope back to the classroom and he did.

Although the Enhanced Learning Center teacher has not initiated a program to increase social interactions, she plans to begin a reinforcement program in the near future to modify this behavior.

Physical Information

The teacher has noted no physical problems that she feels need to be discussed with the parents. Howard seems to be in good health and has had no patterns of absence, illness, or tardiness.

Other Information

Howard continued to be involved in the following:

1. Itinerant support services provided by the Enhanced Learning Center teacher are considered to be very beneficial by Howard's regular class teacher.

2. Twice weekly Howard participates as a tutor in a peer-tutoring math program for regular students and students with disabilities.

PROGRESS REPORT ROLE-PLAYING MATERIALS: CHILD WITH A LEARNING DISABILITY

Sally—Age 9

Teacher Role

In preparation for a progress report conference, you have available the records and information listed below.

Background Information and Diagnostic Data

Sally was referred for evaluation by school district diagnostic personnel because of severe academic weaknesses and "social immaturity." Her regular classroom teacher observed that she was particularly deficient in reading and math. She was also concerned about Sally's tendency to withdraw socially and her apparent inability to comprehend verbal directions.

Individual intelligence testing revealed this child was functioning in the average range of abilities. Testing also indicated that Sally was academically at a readiness level and that she had almost no sight word vocabulary and experienced difficulty in blending sounds into words. Further evaluations revealed an absence of perceptual problems.

At her IEP conference the following annual goals were discussed and adopted:*

Reading: Establishment of basic sight word vocabulary and improved accuracy in reproducing individual sounds.

---

*Individuals are encouraged to use the IEP developed in an earlier simulation exercise.

Math:	Improved performance on daily math assignments and an improved understanding of addition and subtraction concepts.
Handwriting:	Improved handwriting.
Language:	Improved listening skills and improved verbal comprehension.
Behavioral/Social:	Increased interactions with peers.

At the time of the progress report meeting with her parents, Sally was making progress both in the resource strategy program and in her regular classroom. Sally had been given a series of formal and informal tests to help determine her academic progress. Included in the measures given were visual-motor and visual discrimination tests, a general test of intelligence, a learning aptitude scale, a standardized reading survey, and an informal spelling inventory. These procedures yielded the following findings:

Intelligence testing revealed that Sally was functioning in the average range of general intelligence. On a pictorial test of intelligence that required a pointing response, Sally scored above her chronological age on receptive vocabulary of single words in isolation, on visual form discrimination, on general information, and on an analogies task. She scored below average for her age group on size and number concepts and on a visual-memory task.

A series of visual-perceptual tasks yielded scores well within normal limits with the exception of visual-sequential memory for letters, which was slightly below the average range.

Visual-motor tasks were performed well within normal limits, although Sally earned an above-average score on a task requiring her to draw geometric designs from memory.

Four tasks designed to measure auditory attention span revealed that she performed below her age group. However, she was able to score above average on a pencil-and-paper task requiring a series of steps.

Academic assessment revealed Sally to be about 2 years below grade level. In particular, visual prereading skills, such as identification and discrimination of letters, were established, but she is still unable to reliably produce sounds corresponding to the letters, nor can she blend sounds when individual phonemes were provided for her. Her sight vocabulary has grown to 24 preprimer and primer words.

Emotional-Social Information

The resource strategy room teacher and the regular class teacher both continue to be concerned about Sally's contact with other children. They report that Sally is an isolate and rarely initiates contact or participates in games or other activities with her peers. Rather, she tends to stand by herself and watch her classmates. The teachers routinely attempt to encourage and coax Sally to interact with others, but with little success. Data taken on the number of minutes Sally engaged in cooperative or parallel play with her peers during a 15-minute morning recess confirmed this observation. These data revealed the following:

Day 1	1 minute
Day 2	0 minutes
Day 3	0 minutes
Day 4	2.5 minutes
Day 5	0 minutes

Physical Information

Neither the regular class teacher nor the resource room teacher has noted any physical problems that require discussion with Sally's parents. She seems to be in good health and has had no patterns of absence, illness, or tardiness.

Classroom Structure

Sally's resource room teacher has employed a highly structured educational approach. After having thoroughly evaluated her strengths and weaknesses, the teacher selected curriculum and materials that were commensurate with Sally's strengths and weaknesses. The highly structured program also accentuated programming for her specific academic materials. The programming consisted of a shaping process whereby defined behaviors were sequentially arranged into incremental units. The goal of this programming process was to increase Sally's productive behaviors and to break the repetitious elements of her maladaptive social and academic behaviors. The structure employed by the teacher also emphasized scheduling Sally for specific predictable activities. This was adopted to aid in reducing Sally's uncertainty and to aid in the alleviation of her failure patterns. A final component of the structured strategy was behavior modification. Specifically, positive consequences occurred when Sally's responses approximated what were considered appropriate behaviors.

Sally's regular classroom teacher has also used specific programs for dealing with this child's academic problems. Specifically, a reading program with a strong visual emphasis concentrating exclusively on regular sound patterns has been chosen. The series she is currently working in is a program using visual stimuli and closure activities to teach visual sequencing.

Sally has also been exposed to one-to-one instruction in both the resource room and regular classroom. The program is designed to improve her sight word vocabulary. A whole-word method has been chosen for this program. In addition, Sally has only recently been started in a phonics program.

The special education resource strategy room teacher has been pleased with Sally's response to these programs. In particular, she has assessed the following gains:

Reading:	A sight word vocabulary of 24 words has been established. In addition, Sally demonstrated 65% accuracy in reproducing individual sounds.
Math:	75% correct on daily mathematics, which includes some abstract understanding of addition and subtraction.
Handwriting:	Legible reproduction of a printed model with appropriate spacing between letters and words has been achieved.
Language:	Improvement of expressive language skills to a level comparable with a 2.5 grade norm; 69% accuracy in gross-motor responses to three-step directions.
Behavioral/ Social:	10% increase in peer interactions, although this pattern is variable.

Other Information

It has been the special education teacher's impression that since the time that Sally was placed in her resource room, the child has made significant progress. The teacher has associated this with a heightened degree of structure and the use of reinforcement system, in both the resource room and regular classroom. Specifically, Sally has been socially reinforced for doing each assignment in an appropriate way. Based on her progress, the teacher recommends that she continue her present programs and percentage of time in the resource strategy room.

The regular education teacher and resource strategy teacher are both very pleased with the collaborative consultation relationship they have formed.

PROGRESS REPORT ROLE-PLAYING MATERIALS: CHILD WITH A PHYSICAL DISABILITY

Eddie—Age 6

Teacher Role

In preparation for a progress report conference, you have available the records and information listed below.

Background Information and Diagnostic Data

Eddie was born with meningomyelocele, which was repaired when he was 6 months of age. This birth defect has resulted in an inability to walk without the aid of crutches. Except for occasional grand mal seizures, Eddie has no other apparent physical problems.

As a part of a comprehensive evaluation, Eddie was administered a series of psychological and educational tests. These measures indicated that he was functioning intellectually in the bright normal range of abilities, with particular prowess in verbal areas. Academic measures revealed an ability to follow four-step commands, match shapes, identify colors, identify body parts, string beads, and rote count to 50. Weaknesses were identified in a variety of fine motor areas, including writing, cutting with scissors, and duplicating geometric shapes with blocks.

At his IEP conference the following annual goals were discussed and adopted:*

Reading:	Acquisition of beginning first-grade reading skills.
Math:	Development of simple addition and subtraction skills.
Self-Help:	Improvement in independent self-help skills.
Handwriting:	Legible reproduction of printed words; decrease in carelessness in handwriting.
Language:	Improvement in articulation and auditory discrimination.

*Individuals are encouraged to use the IEP developed in an earlier simulation exercise.

| Behavioral/ | Decrease in manipulative behavior and tantrums and an |
| Social: | increase in compliance and independent work activities. |

At the time of the progress report conference, Eddie was generally working at a readiness to early first-grade level. The following is a summary of his academic levels and skills:

Reading

Eddie recently completed the McGraw-Hill series *Time for Phonics* (Book R) and has begun work on Book A. He has also worked in the *Little Green Story Book* of the Ginn preprimer series. At the beginning of the year, Eddie's frequency of correct responses for matching shapes and colors was approximately 4 per minute. The incorrect responses were 5 per minute. Presently, Eddie's frequency of correct responses has increased to approximately 17 per minute and incorrect responses have been eliminated.

Eddie displays few functional word attack skills in reading, and comprehension questions must be very specific and immediate for him to respond correctly. He is not able to do his reading workbook without a great deal of guidance.

Eddie is involved in a group phonics program using "phonovisual." This program at present is at the level of identifying initial sounds. He is very successful, but little carryover has been seen as far as attempting to "sound out" words in his reading.

Math

Eddie has been working in the SRA *Greater Cleveland Math Book I*. He is presently working on "plus ones." However, neither the general education teacher nor itinerant consultation teacher are certain that he has grasped this concept because of his erratic performance.

Self-help

Eddie has shown about a 70% incidence of independent self-help skills without the aid of external reinforcement.

Handwriting

Eddie's attempts to write, when given such assignments, have increased to approximately 90%, and he is currently able to legibly reproduce letters about 50% of the time.

Language

Eddie's incidence of correct articulations has improved to 65%, and he has shown a 25% improvement in auditory discrimination.

Emotional-Social Behavior

Eddie remains a somewhat manipulative child, particularly with adults. He is also highly prone to resist following teacher directions. However, he is relatively cooperative and increasingly plays appropriately with children his own age.

During the period between the present and the past parent conference, Eddie has become extremely demanding in the classroom. He has been demanding an inordinate amount of attention, and if the teacher is unable to stand next to him, he will not work. In addition to not working, he has occasionally initiated tantrum behavior if things do not go his way. When the teacher explains to Eddie that there are other children who need her help, he starts crying.

The following data have been collected on tantrum behavior:

Day 1	3 minutes
Day 2	11 minutes
Day 3	7 minutes
Day 4	27 minutes
Day 5	4 minutes
Day 6	11 minutes
Day 7	14 minutes
Day 8	11 minutes
Day 9	13 minutes
Day 10	16 minutes

Two recent examples of Eddie's emotional-social behavior reveal the current situation:

Situation 1

Eddie's assignment was to "read" silently in his *Little Green Story Book*. Prior to this he was working one-to-one in his math book on "plus ones." As the teacher was leaving his desk area to attend to another child, Eddie immediately pushed his book off his desk and started into a tantrum routine. Although the tantrum lasted only a few minutes, it was characteristic of situations where one-to-one sessions were terminated and he was asked to work independently. Subsequently, Eddie acts as if he cannot do the assigned task unless he has the teacher's attention.

Situation 2

The following situation occurs rather frequently when Eddie and the other children in the class are engaged in a free-time activity (usually after lunch). When it is time to put the blocks, trucks, and other toys into the toy box, Eddie becomes very "stubborn" and continues playing. Even when the other children begin putting things into the toy box, Eddie screams and takes them out again and does not let the other children put them away.

Although the teacher has not initiated a program to decrease Eddie's tantrums, she plans to begin a token reinforcement program in the near future to modify this behavior.

Physical Information

Neither the itinerant special education consulting teacher nor regular class teacher have noted any physical problems, over and above those previously reported, requiring discussion with the parents.

Classroom Structure

As a means of responding to Eddie's needs, the regular room teacher has used a highly structured routine. In particular, she has selected curricula and materials commensurate with Eddie's strengths and weaknesses. The highly structured program also accentuated programming Eddie for certain academic materials. Initially, the programming consisted of a shaping process whereby defined behaviors were sequentially arranged into incremental units. The goal of this programming process was to increase Eddie's productive behaviors and to break the repetitive elements of his maladaptive social and academic behaviors. The structure employed by the teacher also emphasized scheduling him for specific predictable activities. This was adopted to aid in reducing Eddie's uncertainty and to aid in the alleviation of his failure patterns. A final component of the structured strategy was behavior modification. Specifically, positive consequences occurred when Eddie's responses approximated what were considered appropriate behaviors. The itinerant teacher has helped the regular class teacher implement this structure.

PROGRESS REPORT ROLE-PLAYING MATERIALS: CHILD WITH MENTAL RETARDATION

Barbie—Age 8

Teacher Role

In preparation for a progress report conference, you have available the records and information listed below.

Background Information and Diagnostic Data

Barbie was referred for assessment because of both academic and social problems. Her regular first-grade teacher reported that even after repeating the first grade, the child was still unable to identify the letters of the alphabet, identify colors, or rote count past 3. In addition, her teacher was concerned because Barbie had poor articulation, initiated few contacts with other children, and had "attention deficit."

Psychoeducational testing revealed a child who was noncompliant and hyperactive. Although no specific intelligence test score was obtained, the school psychologist concluded that Barbie was performing at a level associated with mental retardation. The examiner also reported that the child demonstrated articulation problems, mild perceptual problems, and weaknesses in social maturity.

Though the regular classroom teacher said that she enjoyed working with Barbie, she believed this child needed more intensive and specialized attention. Accordingly, Barbie was placed in a noncategorical special education resource room 2 hours daily.

At the IEP conference the following annual goals were discussed and adopted:*

---

*Individuals are encouraged to use the IEP developed in an earlier simulation exercise.

Reading: Ability to identify the letters of the alphabet and their corre-
            sponding sounds; increased accuracy in reproducing initial
            sounds; development of a basic sight word vocabulary.
Math: Improved performance in counting, and development of
            basic addition and subtraction skills.
Handwriting: Improved performance in legibly reproducing printed letters.
Language: Improved performance in expressive language, including
            spontaneous verbalizations.
Behavioral/ Increased interaction with peers and decreased incidence of
Social: negativism, noncompliance, and tantruming.

Since the IEP conference, the resource room teacher has acquired additional diagnostic and assessment data. She specifically administered Barbie the *Metropolitan Readiness Test*, the *Peabody Picture Vocabulary Test*, and the *Preschool Language Survey*. These instruments yielded the following results:

On the *Metropolitan Readiness Test*, Barbie's performance was very inconsistent. Many times she would make a written response (marking a picture) before the directions or instructions were given. It was noted that she had a very awkward manner of holding her pencil. Barbie tended to grip her pencil in her fist, close to the eraser. Barbie made no spontaneous verbalizations. However, she would answer questions when they were directed toward her in a firm manner.

On the auditory comprehension portion of the *Preschool Language Survey*, Barbie obtained an age equivalent of 5-1. The verbal ability scale of this instrument yielded an age equivalence of 4-6 years.

The *Peabody Picture Vocabulary Test* yielded an expressive language quotient of 71. However, Barbie was willing to participate in this activity only when provided reinforcement for each item she attempted to answer.

The *Metropolitan Readiness Test* revealed that Barbie would probably experience difficulty in succeeding in a regular first-grade classroom. She received particularly low rankings in the areas of copying and matching.

Emotional-Social Behavior

Recently, Barbie has become extremely negative at school. She refuses to carry through with many structured demands made on her and frequently will act as if she does not hear when told by the teacher to do something. Although she has not displayed any violent or acting-out behavior, she is extremely "stubborn."

The teacher has kept a count on the number of times that Barbie has refused to do something (when told to do so by the teacher) during a 5-day period:

Monday	11 times
Tuesday	17 times
Wednesday	14 times
Thursday	19 times
Friday	26 times

The teacher has previously used a time-out procedure to deal with this problem and plans to reimplement the program soon.

The teacher also recorded the following anecdotal incidents:

Situation 1

Barbie was assigned to work independently in a workbook. She became extremely negative toward the teacher and said she "didn't want to" and closed the book. Her posture became rigid, she avoided eye contact with the teacher, and she remained seated at her desk, refusing to acknowledge the teacher's request to attempt the assignment. She remained in this state during recess time and refused to perform any assignments for the remainder of the day.

Situation 2

Barbie was involved in solitary play in the free-time area. This was her reward for completing an assignment. When the timer went off signaling the end of her free-time activity, Barbie ignored the cue and continued to play with the toys. When the teacher requested that she put the toys away and return to her seat, Barbie acted as though she did not hear. She had to be physically removed from the free-time area.

Physical Information

No physical information, other than that contained in the original records, was felt to be significant by the teacher.

Classroom Structure

A highly structured strategy has been recommended by the resource teacher and adopted by the regular class teacher in an effort to best serve this child's needs. In particular, both teachers have selected curricula and instructional procedures commensurate with Barbie's abilities. This strategy has also involved using a shaping process whereby defined behaviors are sequentially arranged into incremental units. The goal of this programming process has been to increase Barbie's productive behaviors and to break the repetitious elements of her maladaptive social and academic behaviors. The structure employed by the teachers has also emphasized scheduling Barbie for specific predictable activities. This was adopted to aid in reducing uncertainty for Barbie and to help her predict the consequences of her own behavior and thus to aid in the alleviation of her failure patterns. A final component of the structured strategy has been behavior modification. Specifically, positive consequences occur when Barbie's responses approximate what are considered to be appropriate behaviors.

This program has been largely responsible for the following gains:

Reading:	100% accuracy in recognizing the letters of the alphabet; 70% accuracy in reproducing initial sounds; and recognition of 4 Dolch sight words.
Math:	80% accuracy in rote counting to 20; 70% accuracy in counting up to 20 objects; 58% accuracy in work on the kindergarten to first-grade level.
Handwriting:	Legible reproduction of 3 printed letters.
Language:	Barbie has demonstrated a 20% increase in spontaneous verbalizations.

It is both the special education and regular education teacher's impression that Barbie has made significant progress. They associate this with a heightened degree of structure and the use of a reinforcement system. It is the teacher's recommendation that Barbie be maintained in the present program, and that the strategy of increasing the amount of structure be maintained.

PROGRESS REPORT EVALUATION

Date_____

Name of Child_____

Name of Person Playing Parent Role_____

Name of Person Playing Conferencer Role _____

Observer(s) _____

Circle the response that most closely describes the performance of the individual you are evaluating for each of the items below. Following evaluation, you should provide verbal feedback to the individual playing the conferencer role for each of the items.

I. General Conferencing Evaluation

   A. Ability of the conferencer to inform parents of the purpose of the conference

1	2	3	4	5
Poor	Below Average	Average	Above Average	Excellent

   B. Ability of the conferencer to conduct the session in a systematic and sequential manner

1	2	3	4	5
Poor	Below Average	Average	Above Average	Excellent

   C. Ability of the conferencer to keep the session flowing and on course

1	2	3	4	5
Poor	Below Average	Average	Above Average	Excellent

   D. Ability of the conferencer to solicit and respond to parent questions

1	2	3	4	5
Poor	Below Average	Average	Above Average	Excellent

   E. Ability of the conferencer to attend to the parents

1	2	3	4	5
Poor	Below Average	Average	Above Average	Excellent

   F. Ability of the conferencer to rephrase questions

1	2	3	4	5
Poor	Below Average	Average	Above Average	Excellent

G. Ability of the conferencer to summarize the conference

1	2	3	4	5
Poor	Below Average	Average	Above Average	Excellent

II. Progress Report Conference Content

A. Overview Content

1. Ability of the conferencer to provide a general overview of the issues associated with the initial referral for evaluation

1	2	3	4	5
Poor	Below Average	Average	Above Average	Excellent

2. Ability of the conferencer to provide a general review of diagnostic procedures used in the evaluation

1	2	3	4	5
Poor	Below Average	Average	Above Average	Excellent

3. Ability of the conferencer to provide a general overview of the educational and intervention program being used, including a brief overview of the IEP

1	2	3	4	5
Poor	Below Average	Average	Above Average	Excellent

4. Ability of the conferencer to provide a general evaluation statement regarding the child's progress in the program

1	2	3	4	5
Poor	Below Average	Average	Above Average	Excellent

5. Ability of the conferencer to respond to parent questions and solicit their input within the overview area

1	2	3	4	5
Poor	Below Average	Average	Above Average	Excellent

B. Academic Content

1. Ability of the conferencer to provide an analysis of the academic issues associated with the referral for evaluation

1	2	3	4	5
Poor	Below Average	Average	Above Average	Excellent

2. Ability of the conferencer to provide information associated with the assessment of academic strengths and weaknesses

1	2	3	4	5
Poor	Below Average	Average	Above Average	Excellent

3. Ability of the conferencer to provide a description and analysis of academic intervention programs, including the manner in which each IEP short-term objective is to be realized

1	2	3	4	5
Poor	Below Average	Average	Above Average	Excellent

4. Ability of the conferencer to provide an evaluative statement regarding the child's academic progress, including the future expectations for the pupil

1	2	3	4	5
Poor	Below Average	Average	Above Average	Excellent

5. Ability of the conferencer to respond to parent questions and to solicit their input within the academic area

1	2	3	4	5
Poor	Below Average	Average	Above Average	Excellent

C. Emotional/Social Content

1. Ability of the conferencer to provide an analysis of the emotional/social concerns associated with the initial referral for evaluation

1	2	3	4	5
Poor	Below Average	Average	Above Average	Excellent

2. Ability of the conferencer to provide information associated with the assessment of social/emotional concerns

1	2	3	4	5
Poor	Below Average	Average	Above Average	Excellent

3. Ability of the conferencer to provide a description and analysis of social/emotional intervention programs, including the manner in which each IEP short-term objective is to be realized

1	2	3	4	5
Poor	Below Average	Average	Above Average	Excellent

4. Ability of the conferencer to provide an evaluative statement regarding the child's emotional/social progress, including future expectations for the pupil

1	2	3	4	5
Poor	Below Average	Average	Above Average	Excellent

5. Ability of the conferencer to respond to parent questions and to solicit their input within the emotional/social area

1	2	3	4	5
Poor	Below Average	Average	Above Average	Excellent

D. Physical Content

1. Ability of the conferencer to provide an analysis of the physical concerns associated with the initial referral for evaluation

1	2	3	4	5
Poor	Below Average	Average	Above Average	Excellent

2. Ability of the conferencer to provide information associated with the assessment of physical concerns

1	2	3	4	5
Poor	Below Average	Average	Above Average	Excellent

3. Ability of the conferencer to provide a description and analysis of physical intervention programs, including the manner in which each IEP short-term objective is to be realized

1	2	3	4	5
Poor	Below Average	Average	Above Average	Excellent

4. Ability of the conferencer to provide an evaluative statement regarding the child's physical progress, including future expectations for the pupil

1	2	3	4	5
Poor	Below Average	Average	Above Average	Excellent

5. Ability of the conferencer to respond to parent questions and to solicit their input within the physical area

1	2	3	4	5
Poor	Below Average	Average	Above Average	Excellent

III. Summary Information

_____

_____

_____

_____

_____

_____

_____

_____

Appendix E

Conflict Resolution Conference Role-Playing Materials

These materials are to be used in conjunction with the exercises at the end of chapter 14.

CONFLICT RESOLUTION ROLE-PLAYING MATERIALS: YOUTH WITH A BEHAVIOR DISORDER

Billie—Age 13

Teacher Role

As a means of motivating Billie to accurately complete his assignments, his learning center teacher has implemented a program whereby he is allowed to go to free-time break only after having completed a prescribed amount of work. Although the program has resulted in some success, it has also created several problems. Specifically, after having been denied a break Billie will sulk, attempt to create disturbances with other students, and swear at the teacher. Nonetheless, the teacher believes the program should be continued because it seems to be helping Billie complete his work accurately. Data supportive of the intervention approach are shown below:

Percent of assignments completed prior to free-time break	Percent of assignments completed with at least 85% accuracy prior to free-time break
(prior to program intervention-baseline)	(prior to program intervention-baseline)
Day 1 77%	5%
Day 2 44%	15%
Day 3 61%	0%
Day 4 57%	0%
Day 5 66%	15%
(after program intervention)	(after program intervention)
Day 1 79%	20%
Day 2 77%	26%
Day 3 80%	39%
Day 4 100%	44%
Day 5 78%	21%
Day 6 90%	70%

Parent Role

Approximately 3 weeks ago, Billie's learning center teacher called to inform the parents that she would be implementing a program requiring that her students accurately complete their assignments before being allowed to go to free-time break. The teacher indicated that she was hopeful that this program would encourage Billie to be more diligent in completing his assignments.

Shortly after the program was initiated, the parents began to notice a significant increase in Billie's pouting and antisocial behavior. When confronted with this behavior, which typically takes the form of making facial grimaces, stomping around the house, and sulking, he reports that he is angry because he was denied free time at school. Though Billie's pouting has always been a problem that the family has had to contend with, it has now become a more significant issue than ever before.

The parents are also somewhat concerned that denying Billie a break may further exacerbate his problems of interacting with his peers. They have concluded that if he is denied a break, he never will learn to play and work with other students.

Although the parents are interested in seeing Billie hand in his assignments, they are troubled by the program designed to facilitate this response. They have concluded that this particular intervention strategy should be abandoned.

CONFLICT RESOLUTION ROLE-PLAYING MATERIALS: GIFTED CHILD

Howard—Age 8

Teacher Role

The special education teacher is pleased with Howard's performance in her Enhanced Learning Center room. She feels that he has benefited from the experience and that he should be maintained in the program. However, she strongly believes that he should maintain his primary association with the regular classroom and be in a position of having to relate to his regular class peers. She specifically believes that Howard should be in her gifted resource room no more than 1 hour daily.

Parent Role

Howard's parents were initially somewhat apprehensive about his placement in a gifted program, but they are currently delighted with the results. Not only has he made significant progress in several areas, but he is showing an interest in a variety of topics. They associate this newfound interest with his placement in the Enhanced Learning Center program. They are, in fact, so pleased with the gifted program that they would like to see Howard placed there full-time or at least 75% to 80% of each week. They have concluded that if the current program has been successful, increased placement will lead to even greater success. They have also concluded that Howard's problems in relating to his peers are associated with his gifted status. They are beginning to believe that Howard can only relate to children "on his own level."

The parents believe that their son's exceptionality demands appropriate attention. Accordingly, they are willing to "fight" for increased time for Howard in the gifted program.

CONFLICT RESOLUTION ROLE-PLAYING MATERIALS: CHILD WITH A LEARNING DISABILITY

Sally—Age 9

Teacher Role

Although the resource strategy room teacher has been concerned about Sally's "social immaturity," particularly her tendencies to withdraw from peers, she has aimed most of her efforts at remediating Sally's academic problems. It has been the teacher's philosophy that although Sally has some problems in interacting with other children, her greatest disability lies in her academic deficits. Consequently, the teacher has firmly adopted the position that, while in her resource room, primary attention will focus on scheduling Sally for academic remediation programs. In addition, she believes that these remediation programs will be successful only if implemented in an individualized and structured fashion.

Parent Role

Mr. and Mrs. Slith had been hopeful that Sally's learning disabilities resource strategy room experience would result in changes in her social responses as well as academic behavior. However, it is their opinion that although some attention is being focused on persuading Sally to interact more with other children, primary attention is being given to academic pursuits. The parents are not opposed to this emphasis, but they would like to see the adoption of programs whereby social interaction can also occur. In particular, they would like to see Sally and her resource room classmates placed in a more traditional seating arrangement, exposed to more group instruction and less individual programming, and with a less structured and rigid setting. Although the Sliths are somewhat hesitant to tell their child's teacher how to teach, they are convinced that Sally will develop socially only if given a different type of educational experience. Candidly, they believe that Sally could make the same academic gains that she is making if provided more opportunities for social interactions.

CONFLICT RESOLUTION ROLE-PLAYING MATERIALS: CHILD WITH A PHYSICAL DISABILITY

Eddie—Age 6

Teacher Role

Eddie's itinerant special education teacher has been generally pleased with his progress in the regular first-grade program. Specifically, feedback to his parents has revealed that Eddie has made good gains in academic areas and marginal progress along emotional-social lines. This information has been shared with Eddie's parents by both the general education teacher and itinerant special education teacher via weekly notes, phone conversations, and regularly scheduled conferences. In addition, as per school district regulations, the teachers have completed a "special education report card" on Eddie during each 9-week period. They have specifically evaluated Eddie's progress through the use of descriptive statements and ratings rather than traditional grades. The school district allows teachers to evaluate students with identified disabilities (even if in full-time general education placement) by whatever means they desire, including the use of letter grades; however, Eddie's teachers believe that they can provide a more accurate and fair report card assessment by using descriptive statements.

Parent Role

Eddie's parents are pleased with his general education placement and special education itinerant services. They are also happy with his teachers, and feel that they are able to effectively communicate with them. However, they are dissatisfied with the manner in which the teachers have chosen to evaluate Eddie on his report card. Rather than using descriptive progress-related comments on Eddie's grade report, they would like them to use a traditional grading system (i.e., A, B, C, D, F). It is their belief that they have ample opportunity to receive descriptive reports and that their son should be exposed to a more "normal" grading system.

CONFLICT RESOLUTION ROLE-PLAYING MATERIALS: CHILD WITH MENTAL RETARDATION

Barbie—Age 8

Teacher Role

In an effort to decrease Barbie's negativism and noncompliance, the special education resource room teacher and general education teacher instituted a time-out procedure. After obtaining administrative and parental permission, they implemented a program whereby Barbie is required to quietly spend 2 minutes in an isolated area each time she demonstrates noncompliant or negative behavior. The teachers are pleased with the program and feel it is yielding desirable results. Data supportive of this position are shown below.

Frequency of negativistic and noncompliant behaviors

(prior to program intervention—baseline)		(after program intervention)	
Day 1	14	Day 1	12
Day 2	20	Day 2	9
Day 3	17	Day 3	6
Day 4	16	Day 4	2
Day 5	7	Day 5	1
Day 6	14	Day 6	3
Day 7	16	Day 7	1

Parent Role

Although the parents gave their permission for the teachers to place Barbie in an isolation area at school for 2 minutes each time she is negative or noncompliant, they are now having second thoughts. They have heard that this procedure, time-out, can cause "psychological and mental damage" in children. Because they are concerned that the procedure may be injurious to their daughter's mental health and because they are aware that she has been able to make good progress without the procedure, they are convinced that they must demand the program be terminated.

CONFLICT RESOLUTION EVALUATION

Date _____

Name of Child _____

Name of Person Playing Parent Role _____

Name of Person Playing Conferencer Role _____

Observer(s) _____

Circle the response that most closely describes the performance of the individual you are evaluating for each of the items below. Following evaluation, you should provide verbal feedback to the individual playing the conferencer role for each of the items.

I. General Conferencing Evaluation

  A. Ability of the conferencer to inform or reach consensus with the parents as to the purpose of the conference

1	2	3	4	5
Poor	Below Average	Average	Above Average	Excellent

  B. Ability of the conferencer to conduct the session in a systematic and sequential manner

1	2	3	4	5
Poor	Below Average	Average	Above Average	Excellent

  C. Ability of the conferencer to keep the session flowing and on course

1	2	3	4	5
Poor	Below Average	Average	Above Average	Excellent

  D. Ability of the conferencer to solicit and respond to parent questions

1	2	3	4	5
Poor	Below Average	Average	Above Average	Excellent

  E. Ability of the conferencer to attend to the parents

1	2	3	4	5
Poor	Below Average	Average	Above Average	Excellent

  F. Ability of the conferencer to rephrase questions and concerns

1	2	3	4	5
Poor	Below Average	Average	Above Average	Excellent

G. Ability of the conferencer to summarize the conference

1	2	3	4	5
Poor	Below Average	Average	Above Average	Excellent

II. Evaluation of Communication Skills

A. Ability of the conferencer to establish rapport

1	2	3	4	5
Poor	Below Average	Average	Above Average	Excellent

B. Ability of the conferencer to engage in active listening

1	2	3	4	5
Poor	Below Average	Average	Above Average	Excellent

C. Ability of the conferencer to respond to manifest content

1	2	3	4	5
Poor	Below Average	Average	Above Average	Excellent

D. Ability of the conferencer to respond to affect (emotion)

1	2	3	4	5
Poor	Below Average	Average	Above Average	Excellent

E. Ability of the conferencer to display empathy

1	2	3	4	5
Poor	Below Average	Average	Above Average	Excellent

F. Ability of the conferencer to provide feedback (i.e., make appropriate use of clarification and perception checking)

1	2	3	4	5
Poor	Below Average	Average	Above Average	Excellent

G. Ability of the conferencer to identify areas of mutual agreement

1	2	3	4	5
Poor	Below Average	Average	Above Average	Excellent

H. Ability of the conferencer to be constructively open

1	2	3	4	5
Poor	Below Average	Average	Above Average	Excellent

I. Ability of the conferencer to use "I messages"

1	2	3	4	5
Poor	Below Average	Average	Above Average	Excellent

III. Application of Conflict Resolution Model

   A. Ability of the conferencer to set the conditions for collaborative conflict resolution

      1. Ability of the conferencer to actively listen

1	2	3	4	5
Poor	Below Average	Average	Above Average	Excellent

      2. Ability of the conferencer to separate personal perceptions from substantive issues related to the conflict

1	2	3	4	5
Poor	Below Average	Average	Above Average	Excellent

      3. Ability of the conferencer to be constructive

1	2	3	4	5
Poor	Below Average	Average	Above Average	Excellent

      4. Ability of the conferencer to determine the problem, its owners, and the individuals associated with the conflict

1	2	3	4	5
Poor	Below Average	Average	Above Average	Excellent

   B. Ability of the conferencer to generate and aid the parents in identifying and evaluating possible solutions to the identified problem

1	2	3	4	5
Poor	Below Average	Average	Above Average	Excellent

   C. Ability of the conferencer to identify and implement a mutually agreed-upon problem-solving strategy

1	2	3	4	5
Poor	Below Average	Average	Above Average	Excellent

   D. Ability of the conferencer to evaluate the mutually agreed-upon problem-solving strategy and make modifications as needed

1	2	3	4	5
Poor	Below Average	Average	Above Average	Excellent

IV. Summary Information

_____

_____

_____

_____

_____

_____

_____

_____

_____

_____

_____

_____

_____

_____

_____

_____

_____

_____

_____

_____

_____

_____

References

Adamson, G. A. (1970). *Educational modulation center: Final report*, E.S.E.A., P.L. 89–10, Title III, Unified School District 233, Olathe, KS.

Adelman, H. S. (1994). Intervening to enhance home involvement in schooling. *Intervention in School and Clinic, 29*(5), 276–287.

Adler, K. A. (1977). *Proceedings of the symposium: The individual psychology of Alfred Adler*. Eugene, OR: University of Oregon Press.

Akerley, M. S. (1978). False gods and angry prophets. In A. P. Turnbull & H. R. Turnbull (Eds.), *Parents speak out: Views from the other side of the two-way mirror* (pp. 38–48). Columbus, OH: Merrill.

Alberti, R. E., & Emmons, M. L. (1974). *Your perfect right: A guide to assertive behavior*. San Luis Obispo, CA: Impact.

Alberto, P. A., Mechling, L., Taber, T. A., & Thompson, J. (1995). Using videotape to communicate with parents of students with severe disabilities. *Teaching Exceptional Children, 27*(3), 18–21.

Alexander, R. N., Kroth, R. L., Simpson, R. L., & Poppelreiter, T. (1982). The parent role in special education. In R. L. McDowell, G. W. Adamson, & F. H. Wood (Eds.), *Teaching emotionally disturbed children* (pp. 300–317). Boston: Little, Brown.

Allen, R. M., & Cortazzo, A. D. (1970). *Psycho-social and educational aspects and problems of mental retardation*. Springfield, IL: Thomas.

Alley, G., & Deshler, D. (1979). *Teaching the learning disabled adolescent: Strategies and methods*. Denver: Love.

Anderson, G. R., & Anderson, S. K. (1983). The exceptional Native American. In D. R. Omark & J. G. Erickson (Eds.), *The bilingual exceptional child* (pp. 163–180). San Diego: College-Hill.

Arndorfer, R. E., Miltenberger, R. G., Woster, S. H., Rortvedt, A. K., & Gaffney, T. (1994). Home-based descriptive and experimental analysis of problem behaviors in children. *Topics in Early Childhood Special Education, 14*(1), 64–87.

Atwell, A. A., & Clabby, D. A. (1971). *The retarded child: Answers to questions parents ask*. Los Angeles: Western Psychological Services.

Avis, D. W. (1985). Deinstitutionalization jet lag. In H. R. Turnbull & A. P. Turnbull (Eds.), *Parents speak out: Then and now* (pp. 193–199). Columbus, OH: Merrill.

Axinn, J. M., & Hirsch, A. (1993). Welfare and the "reform" of women. *Families in Society, 74*(9), 563–572.

Baca, L., & Cervantes, H. T. (1989). *The bilingual special education interface* (2nd ed.). Columbus, OH: Merrill.

Baer, D., & Guess, D. (1971). Receptive training of adjectival inflections in mental retardates. *Journal of Applied Behavior Analysis, 4*, 129–139.

Bailey, D. B. (1987). Collaborative goal-setting with families: Resolving differences in values and priorities for service. *Topics in Early Childhood Special Education, 7*(2), 59–71.

Bailey, D. B. (1988). Assessing family stress and needs. In D. B. Bailey & R. J. Simeonsson (Eds.), *Family assessment in early intervention* (pp. 95–118). Columbus, OH: Merrill.

Bailey, D., Buysee, Y., Edmondson, R., & Smith, T. (1992). Creating family-centered services in early intervention: Perceptions of professionals in four states. *Exceptional Children, 58*, 298–309.

Bailey, D. B., & Simeonsson, R. J. (1988). Assessing needs of families of handicapped infants. *Journal of Special Education, 22*, 117–127.

Baker, B. L., Brightman, A. S., Heifetz, L. J., & Murphy, D. M. (1973). *The READ project series*. Cambridge, MA: Behavioral Education Projects.

Baker, E. T., Wang, M. C., & Walberg, H. J. (1995). The effects of inclusion on learning. *Educational Leadership, 52*(4), 33–35.

Bandura, A. (1969). *Principles of behavior modification*. New York: Holt, Rinehart & Winston.

Bane, M. J. (1976). Marital disruption and the lives of children. *Journal of Social Issues, 32*, 103–117.

Banks, J. A. (1994). Transforming the mainstream curriculum: Educating for diversity. *Educational Leadership, 51*(8), 4–8.

Barbetta, P. M., & Heron, T. E. (1991). Project SHINE: Summer home instruction and evaluation. *Intervention in School and Clinic, 26*(5), 276–281.

Barnard, J. B., Christophersen, E. R., & Wolf, M. M. (1977). Teaching children appropriate shopping behavior through parent training in the supermarket setting. *Journal of Applied Behavior Analysis, 10*, 49–60.

Barnes, E., Eyman, B., & Engolz, M. B. (1974). *Teach and reach: An alternative guide to resources for the classroom*. Syracuse, NY: Human Policy Press.

Barnlund, D. C. (1973). Introduction: Interpersonal communication. In R. W. Pace, B. D. Peterson, & R. R. Radcliff (Eds.), *In communicating interpersonally* (pp. 1–22). Columbus, OH: Merrill.

Barrera, M., Kitching, C., Cunningham, D., Doucet, D., & Rosenbaum, P. (1991). A 3-year early intervention follow-up study with low birthweight infants and their parents. *Topics in Early Childhood Special Education, 10*(4), 14–28.

Barsch, R. L. (1969). *The parent-teacher partnership*. Arlington, VA: Council for Exceptional Children.

Barsh, R. A. (1968). *The parent of the handicapped child*. Springfield, IL: Thomas.

Bath, H. I., Richey, C., & Haapala, D. A. (1992). Child age and outcome correlates in intensive family preservation services. *Children and Youth Services Review, 14*, 389–406.

Baum, M. H. (1962). Some dynamic factors affecting family adjustment to the handicapped child. *Exceptional Children, 28*, 387–392.

Bayles, E. E., & Hood, B. L. (1966). *Growth of American educational thought and practice*. New York: Harper & Row.

Beckman, P. J. (1983). Influence of selected child characteristics on stress in families of handicapped infants. *American Journal of Mental Deficiency, 88*, 150–156.

Belle, D. (1990). Poverty and women's mental health. *American Psychologist, 45*, 385–389.

Benjamin, A. (1969). *The helping interview*. Boston: Houghton Mifflin.

Bennett, W. (1987). The role of the family in the nurture and protection of the young. *American Psychologist, 42*(3), 246–250.

Benson, H., & Turnbull, A. (1985). Approaching families from an individualized perspective. In R. H. Horner, L. M. Voeltz, & H. D. Fredericks (Eds.), *Education of learners with severe handicaps: Exemplary service strategies* (pp. 127–160). Baltimore: Brookes.

Benz, M., & Halpern, A. (1987). Transition services for secondary students with mild disabilities: A statewide perspective. *Exceptional Children, 53*(6), 507–524.

Berger, E. H. (1995). *Parents as partners in education*. Englewood Cliffs, NJ: Merrill.

Berkowitz, B. P., & Graziano, A. M. (1972). Training parents as behavior therapists: A review. *Behavior Research and Therapy, 10*, 297–317.

Berlo, D. K. (1960). *The process of communication*. New York: Holt, Rinehart & Winston.

Berman, E. H. (1984). State hegemony and the schooling process. *Journal of Education, 166*(3), 239–253.

Bernal, M. E., Williams, D. E., Miller, W. H., & Reagor, P. A. (1972). The use of videotape feedback and operant learning principles in training parents in management of deviant children. In R. D. Rubin, H. Festerheim, J. D. Henderson, & L. P. Ullman (Eds.), *Advances in behavior therapy* (pp. 116–142). New York: Academic Press.

Bersoff, D. N., & Grieger, R. M. (1971). An interview model for the psycho-situational assessment of children's behavior. *American Journal of Orthopsychiatry, 41*(3), 483–493.

Biller, H. B. (1970). Father absence and the personality development of the male child. *Developmental Psychology, 2*, 181–201.

Black, A., & Pedro-Carroll, J. (1993). Role of parent-child relationships in mediating the effects of marital disruption. *Journal of the American Academy of Child and Adolescent Psychiatry, 32*(5), 1019–1027.

Blodgett, A. E. (1971). *Mentally retarded children: What parents and others should know*. Minneapolis: University of Minnesota Press.

Bloom, B. S. (1964). *Stability and change in human characteristics*. New York: Wiley.

Board of Education of Hendrick Hudson School District v. Rowley, 458 U.S.C. 176 (1982).

Brammer, L. (1985). *The helping relationship*. Englewood Cliffs, NJ: Prentice-Hall.

Brandwein, R. A., Brown, C. A., & Fox, E. (1974). Mothers and their families. *Journal of Marriage and the Family, 36*(30), 498–515.

Brantlinger, E. A., & Guskin, S. L. (1985). Implications of social and cultural differences for special education with specific recommendations. *Focus on Exceptional Children, 18*(1), 1–12.

Breslau, N., Staruch, K. S., & Mortimer, E. A. (1982). Psychological distress in mothers of disabled children. *American Journal of Disabled Children, 136*, 682–686.

Breslau, N., Weitzman, M., & Messenger, K. (1981). Psychologic functioning of siblings of disabled children. *Pediatrics, 67*, 344–353.

Bricker, D., & Sheehan, R. (1981). Effectiveness of an early intervention program as indexed by measures of child change. *Journal of the Division for Early Childhood, 4*, 11–27.

Brinker, R. P. (1992). Family involvement in early intervention: Accepting the unchangeable, changing the changeable, and knowing the difference. *Topics in Early Childhood Special Education, 12*(3), 307–332.

Bronfenbrenner, U. (1967). The split-level American family. *Saturday Review, 50*(40), 60–66.

Bronfenbrenner, U. (1974). *A report on longitudinal evaluations of preschool programs: Is early intervention effective?* (Vol. 2). Washington, DC: Department of Health, Education and Wefare, Office of Human Development.

Bronfenbrenner, U. (1979). *The ecology of human development: Experiments by nature and design*. Cambridge, MA: Harvard University Press.

Brosnan, F. L. (1983). Overrepresentation of low socioeconomic minority students in special education programs in California. *Learning Disability Quarterly, 6*, 517–525.

Brown, B. B. (1992). Designing staff/curriculum development content for cultural diversity: The staff developer's role. *Journal of Staff Development, 13*(2), 16–21.

Brown, L., Nietupski, J., & Hamre-Nietupski, S. (1976a). Criterion of ultimate functioning. In M. A. Thomas (Ed.), *Hey, don't forget about me* (pp. 16–30). Reston, VA: Council for Exceptional Children.

Brown, L., Nietupski, J., & Hamre-Nietupski, S. (1976b). The criterion of ultimate functioning and public school services for severely handicapped students. In L. Brown, N. Certo, K. Belmore, & T. Crowner (Eds.), *Madison alternative for zero exclusion: Papers and programs related to public school services for secondary age severely handicapped students* (pp. 113–139). Madison, WI: Madison Public Schools.

Bryen, D. M. (1974). Special education and the linguistically different child. *Exceptional Children, 40*, 589–599.

Buck, P. (1950). *The child who never grew.* New York: Day.

Bull, B., & Johnson, P. (1991). *Research on the school-to-community transition of behaviorally disordered adolescents: An annotated bibliography.* Manmouth, OR: Western Oregon State College, Teaching Research Division.

Bullis, M., Bull, B., Johnson, P., & Johnson, B. (1994). Identifying and assessing community-based social behavior of adolescents and young adults with EBD. *Journal of Emotional and Behavioral Disorders, 2*(3), 173–188.

Buscaglia, L. (1975). *The disabled and their parents: A counseling challenge.* Thorofare, NJ: Slack.

Caldwell, B. M., & Yahraes, H. (1975). The effects of early experience on a child's development. In J. Segal (Ed.), *The mental health of the child* (pp. 16–38). Washington, DC: Department of Health, Education and Welfare.

Calvert, S. C., & McMahon, R. J. (1987). The treatment acceptability of a behavioral parent training program and its components. *Behavior Therapy, 2*, 165–179.

Canfield, J., & Wells, H. (1976). *100 ways to enhance self-concept in the classroom: A handbook for teachers and parents.* Englewood Cliffs, NJ: Prentice-Hall.

Cansler, D. P., & Martin, G. H. (1974). *Working with families: A manual for developmental centers.* Chapel Hill, NC: Council for Exceptional Children.

Carey, J. C., Boscardin, M. L., & Fontes, L. (1994). Improving the multicultural effectiveness of your school. In P. Pedersen & J. C. Carey (Eds.), *Multicultural counseling in schools: A practical handbook* (pp. 239–249). Boston: Allyn & Bacon.

Carkhuff, R. R. (1985). *Productive parenting skills.* Amherst, MA: Human Resource Development.

Carkhuff, R. R., & Berenson, B. G. (1967). *Beyond counseling and therapy.* New York: Holt, Rinehart & Winston.

Carkhuff, R. R., & Berenson, B. G. (1976). *Teaching as treatment: An introduction to counseling and psychotherapy.* Amherst, MA: Human Resources Development.

Carnegie, D. (1936). *How to win friends and influence people.* New York: Simon & Schuster.

Carter, E., & McGoldrich, M. (1980). The family life cycle and family therapy: An overview. In E. Carter & M. McGoldrich (Eds.), *The family life cycle: A framework of family therapy* (pp. 3–19). New York: Gardner.

Cashion, B. (1982). Female-headed families: Effects on chidren and clinical implications. *Journal of Marital and Family Therapy, 8*, 77–85.

Chapman, A. H. (1965). *Management of emotional problems of children and adolescents.* Philadelphia: Lippincott.

Charleston, S. (1987). Victims of an American holocaust. *Sojourners, 16*(10), pp. 32–33.

Cherlin, A. J. (1992). *Marriage, divorce, remarriage.* Cambridge, MA: Harvard University Press.

Chestang, L. W. (1981). The policies and politics of health and human services: A Black perspective. In A. Johnson (Ed.), *The Black experience: Considerations for health and human services* (pp. 15–25). Davis, CA: International Dialogue Press.

Children's Defense Fund. (1985). *Black and White children in America: Key facts.* Washington, DC: Author.

Children's Defense Fund. (1991). *The state of America's children 1991.* Washington, DC: Author.

Chinn, P., & Hughes, S. (1987). Representation of minority students in special classes. *Remedial and Special Education, 4*, 41–46.

Chinn, P., Winn, J., & Walters, R. H. (1978). *Two-way talking with parents of special children: A process of positive communication.* St. Louis: Mosby.

Chinn, P. C., & McCormick, L. (1986). Cultural diversity and exceptionality. In N. G. Haring & L. McCormick (Eds.), *Exceptional children and youth* (4th ed., pp. 95–117). Columbus, OH: Merrill.

Christenson, S. L., & Cleary, M. (1990). Consultation and the parent-education partnership: A perspective. *Journal of Education and Psychological Consultation, 1*, 219–241.

Christophersen, E. R., Arnold, C. M., Hill, D. W., & Quilitch, H. R. (1972). The home point system: Token reinforcement procedures for application by parents of children with behavior problems. *Journal of Applied Behavior Analysis, 5*, 485–497.

Clark, G., & Kolstoe, O. (1995). *Career development and transition education for adolescents with disabilities.* Boston: Allyn & Bacon.

Clements, J. E., & Alexander, R. N. (1975). Parent training: Bringing it all back home. *Focus on Exceptional Children, 7*(5), 1–12.

Clements, J. E., & Simpson, R. L. (1974). Establishing parental support. *Pointer, 19*(1), 70–71.

Cobb, H. C., & Reeve, R. E. (1991). Counseling approaches with parents and families. In M. J. Fine (Ed.), *Collaboration with parents of exceptional children* (pp. 129–143). Brandon, VT: Clinical Psychology Publishing.

Cohen, D. J., Granger, R. H., Provence, S. A., & Solnit, A. J. (1975). Mental health services. In N. Hobbs (Ed.), *Issues in the classification of children* (pp. 88–122). San Francisco: Jossey-Bass.

Coleman, J. S. (1968). The concept of equal educational opportunity. *Harvard Educational Review, 38*, 7–22.

Coleman, J. S., Campbell, E. Q., Hobson, C. J., McPartland, J., Mood, A. M., Weinfeld, F. D., & York, R. L. (1966). *Equality of educational opportunity.* Washington, DC: Department of Health, Education and Welfare, U.S. Office of Education.

Coles, R., & Piers, M. (1969). *Wages of neglect: New solutions for children of the poor.* Chicago: Quadragh.

Coletta, A. J. (1976). *Parent involvement: A resource guide for teachers.* Wayne, NJ: William Patterson College Services.

Coletta, A. J. (1977). *Working together: A guide to parent involvement.* Atlanta: Humanities Limited.

Coletta, N. (1983). Stressful lives: The situation of divorced mothers and their children. *Journal of Divorce, 6,* 19–31.

Collarusso, R. P., & Kana, T. G. (1993). Implementing services for infants and toddlers with developmental delays. In E. L. Meyen, G. A. Vergason, & R. J. Whelan (Eds.), *Challenges facing special education* (pp. 27–43). Denver: Love.

Collier, C. (1986). A comparison of acculturation and education characteristics of referred and nonreferred culturally and linguistically different children. In O. Miramontes, G. Schafer, & J. Starks (Eds.), *4th annual symposium: Bilingual special education research* (pp. 79–81). Boulder, CO: Bueno Center for Multicultural Education.

Combs, A. N., Avila, D. L., & Purky, W. W. (1971). *Helping relationships: Basic concepts for the helping professions.* Boston: Allyn & Bacon.

Conant, M. M. (1971). Teachers and parents: Changing roles and goals. *Childhood Education, 48,* 114–118.

Cooper, L. J., Wacker, D. P., Sasso, G. M., Reimers, T. M., & Donn, L. K. (1990). Using parents as therapists to evaluate appropriate behavior of their children: Application to a tertiary diagnostic clinic. *Journal of Applied Behavior Analysis, 23,* 285–296.

Copeland, A. P., & White, K. M. (1991). *Studying families.* Newbury Park, CA: Sage.

Corbett, T. (1993). *Child poverty and welfare reform: Progress or paralysis?* Madison, WI: Institute for Research on Poverty.

Correa, V., & Weismantel, J. (1991). Multicultural issues related to families with an exceptional child. In M. J. Fine (Ed.), *Collaboration with parents of exceptional children* (pp. 83–102). Brandon, VT: Clinical Psychology Publishing.

Covey, S. R. (1989). *The 7 habits of highly effective people.* New York: Simon & Schuster.

Crnic, K., Friedrich, W., & Greenberg, M. (1983). Adaptation of families with mentally retarded children: A model of stress, coping, and family ecology. *American Journal of Mental Deficiency, 88,* 125–138.

Crnic, K., & Leconte, J. (1986). Understanding sibling needs and influences. In R. Fewell & P. Vadasy (Eds.), *Families of handicapped children: Needs and supports across the life span* (pp. 75–98). Austin, TX: PRO-ED.

Cronin, M., Slade, D. L., Bechtel, C., & Anderson, P. (1992). Home-school partnerships: A cooperative approach to intervention. *Intervention in School and Clinic, 27,* 286–292.

Curwin, R. L., & Fuhrmann, B. S. (1975). *Discovering your teaching self: Humanistic approaches to effective teaching.* Englewood Cliffs, NJ: Prentice-Hall.

Davis, D. H., & Davis, D. M. (1981). Managing parent teacher conferences. *Today's Education, 70*(2), 40–44.

Davis, K. (1977). *Human behavior at work: Organizational behavior.* New York: McGraw-Hill.

Dawson, D. A. (1991). Family structure and children's health and well-being: Data from the 1988 National Health Interview Survey on Child Health. *Journal of Marriage and the Family, 53,* 573–584.

Dawson, P., Robinson, J., Butterfield, P., Doorninck, W., Gaensbauer, T., & Harmon, R. (1991). Supporting new parents through home visits: Effects on mother-infant interactions. *Topics in Early Childhood Special Education, 10*(4), 29–44.

Day, C., & Roberts, M. C. (1991). Activities of the child and adolescent service system program for improving mental health services for children and families. *Journal of Clinical Child Psychology, 20,* 340–350.

Delquadri, J., Greenwood, C., Whorton, D., Carta, J., & Hall, R. (1986). Classwide peer tutoring. *Exceptional Children, 52*(6), 535–542.

Dembinski, R., & Mauser, A. (1978). Parents of the gifted: Perceptions of psychologists and teachers. *Journal of the Education of the Gifted, 1*(2), 5–14.

Dembinski, R. J., & Mauser, A. J. (1977a). Considering the parents of LD children: What they want from professionals. *Journal of Learning Disabilities, 10,* 578–584.

Dembinski, R. J., & Mauser, A. J. (1977b). What parents of the learning disabled really want from professionals. *Journal of Learning Disabilities, 10,* 578–584.

Dembo, M., Sweitzer, M., & Lauritzen, P. (1985). An evaluation of parent education: Behavioral, PET, and Adlerian programs. *Review of Educational Research, 55*(2), 255–200.

Deno, E. (1971). Some reflections on the use and interpretation of tests for teachers. *Focus on Exceptional Children, 2*(8), 1–14.

Deutsch, M. (1994). Constructive conflict resolution: Principles, training and research. *Journal of Social Issues, 50*(1), 13–32.

Dewey, J. (1938). *Experience and education.* New York: Collier.

Diana v. California State Board of Education, NOC-70-73-37, U.S. Dist. (N.D. Ca. 1970).

DiLeonardi, J. (1993). Families in poverty and chronic neglect of children. *Families in Society, 74*(9), 557–562.

Dinkmeyer, D., & Carlson, J. (1973). *Consulting: Facilitating human potential and change processes.* Columbus, OH: Merrill.

Dinkmeyer, D., & Dinkmeyer, D. (1976). Systematic parent education in the schools. *Focus on Guidance, 8*(10), 1–12,

Dinkmeyer, D., & McKay, G. (1976). *STEP: Systematic training in effective parenting.* Circle Pines, MN: American Guidance Service.

Dinnebeil, L. A., & Rules, S. (1994). Congruence between parents' and professionals' judgments about the development of young children with disabilities: A review of the literature. *Topics in Early Childhood Special Education, 14*(1), 1–25.

Dixon, A. P. (1992). Parents: Full partners in the decision-making process. *NASSP Bulletin, 76,* 15–18.

Doll, B., & Bolger, M. (1991). The family with a young developmentally disabled child. In M. Fine (Ed.), *Collaboration with parents of exceptional children.* (pp. 183–199). Brandon, VT: Clinical Psychology Publishing.

Dore, M. M. (1993). Families preservation and poor families: When "homebuilding" is not enough. *Families in Society, 74*(9), 545–556.

Dreikurs, R., & Solz, V. (1964). *Children: The challenge.* New York: Hawthorn.

Drucker, P. F. (1976). Managing the educated. In R. A. Sutermeister (Ed.), *People and productivity* (pp. 55–82). New York: McGraw-Hill.

Duberman, L. (1975). *The reconstituted family.* Chicago: Nelson-Hall.

Duncan, L. W., & Fitzgerald, P. W. (1969). Increasing the parent-child communication through counselor-parent conferences. *Personnel and Guidance Journal, 48,* 514–517.

Dunn, L. M. (1968). Special education for the mildly retarded—Is much of it justifiable? *Exceptional Children, 35,* 5–22.

Dunst, C. J., Leet, H. E., & Trivette, C. M. (1988). Family resources, personal well-being, and early intervention. *Journal of Special Education, 22*(1), 108–116.

Dunst, C. J. & Paget, K. D. (1991). Parent-professional partnerships and family empowerment. In M. J. Fine (Ed.), *Colloboration with parents of exceptional children* (pp. 25–44). Brandon, VT: Clinical Psychology Publishing.

Duran, R. P. (1989). Assessment and instruction of at-risk Hispanic students. *Exceptional Children, 56*(2), 154–158.

Duvall, S. (1987). *The effects of parent tutoring on reading behavior for their children.* Unpublished manuscript, Juniper Gardens Children's Project, University of Kansas, Lawrence.

Dyson, L., Edgar, E., & Crnic, K. (1989). Psychological predictors of adjustment by siblings of developmentally delayed children. *American Journal of Mental Retardation, 94*(3), 292–302.

Edelman, M. W. (1987). *Families in peril.* Cambridge, MA: Harvard University Press.

Edgar, E., & Polloway, E. A. (1994). Education for adolescents with disabilities: Curriculum and placement issues. *Journal of Special Education, 27*(4), 438–452.

Edlund, C. V. (1969). Rewards at home to promote desirable school behavior. *Teaching Exceptional Children, 1,* 121–127.

Ehly, S., Conoley, J., & Rosenthal, D. (1985). *Working with parents of exceptional children.* St. Louis: Times Mirror/Mosby.

Einstein, E. (1982). *The stepfamily: Living, loving, and learning.* New York: Macmillan.

Ekman, P. (1964). Body position, facial expression, and verbal behavior during interviews. *Journal of Abnormal and Social Psychology, 68,* 295–301.

Elkind, D. (1982). Parental stresses: Their detrimental effects on the emotional well-being of children. *International Journal of Sociology of the Family, 12,* 275–283.

Emery, R. (1982). Interpersonal conflict and the children of discord and divorce. *Psychological Bulletin, 92,* 310–330.

Epstein, J. L. (1992). School and family partnerships: Leadership roles for school psychologists. In S. Christenson & J. Conoley (Eds.), *Home-school collaboration: Enhancing children's academic and social competence* (pp. 499–515). Silver Springs, MD: National Association of School Psychologists.

Epstein, J. L. (1995). School/family/community partnerships. *Phi Delta Kappan, 76*(9), 701–712.

Espinosa, L., & Shearer, M. (1986). Family support in public school programs. In R. R. Fewell & P. F. Vadasy (Eds.), *Families of handicapped children: Needs and supports across the life-span* (pp. 253–277). Austin, TX: PRO-ED.

ETS Policy Information Center. (1990). *The education reform decade.* Princeton, NJ: Educational Testing Service.

Eyeberg, S. M., & Robinson, E. A. (1982). Parent-child interaction training: Effects on family functioning. *Journal of Clinical Child Psychology, 11*(2), 130–137.

Farber, B. (1968). *Mental retardation: Its social context and social consequences.* Boston: Houghton Mifflin.

Fast, J. (1971). *Body language.* New York: Pocket.

Featherstone, H. (1980). *A difference in the family: Living with a disabled child.* New York: Penguin.

Fewell, R. (1986). A handicapped child in the family. In R. R. Fewell & P. F. Vadasy (Eds.), *Families of handicapped children: Needs and supports across the life span* (pp. 3–34). Austin, TX: PRO-ED.

Fewell, R. R., & Vadasy, P. F. (1986). *Families of handicapped children.* Austin, TX: PRO-ED.

Fiedler, C. (1991). Preparing parents to participate: Advocacy and education. In M. J. Fine (Ed.), *Collaboration with parents of exceptional children* (pp. 313–333). Brandon, VT: Clinical Psychology Publishing.

Fiedler, C. R. (1986). Enhancing parent-school personnel partnerships. *Focus on Autistic Behavior, 1*(4), 1–8.

Fine, M. (1979). *Parents vs. children: Making the relationship work.* Englewood Cliffs, NJ: Prentice-Hall.

Fine, M. J. (1989). (Ed.). *The second handbook on parent education.* San Diego, CA: Academic.

Fine, M. J. (1990). Facilitating home-school relationships: A family-oriented approach to collaborative consultation. *Journal of Educational and Psychological Consultation, 1*(2), 169–187.

Fine, M. J. (1991). The handicapped child and the family: Implications for professionals. In M.J. Fine (Ed.), *Collaboration with parents of exceptional children* (pp. 3–24). Brandon, VT: Clincial Psychology Publishing.

Fish, M. C. (1991). Exceptional children in nontraditional families. In M. J. Fine (Ed.), *Collaboration with parents of exceptional children* (pp. 45–59). Brandon, VT: Clinical Psychology Publishing.

Fisher, R., & Brown, S. (1989). *Getting together: Building relationships as we negotiate*. New York: Penguin Books.

Fisher, R. J. (1994). Generic principles for resolving intergroup conflict. *Journal of Social Issues, 50*(1), 47–66.

Flaskerud, J. H., & Nguyen, T. A. (1988). Mental health needs of Vietnamese refugees. *Hospital and Community Psychiatry, 39*(4), 435–437.

Forer, L. G. (1970). *No one will listen: How our legal system brutalizes the youthful poor*. New York: Day.

Forness, S. (1988). Planning for the needs of children with serious emotional disturbance: The National Special Education and Mental Health Coalition. *Behavioral Disorders, 13*(2), 127–139.

Fox, J., & Savelle, S. (1987). Social interaction research and families of behaviorally disordered children: A critical review and forward look. *Behavioral Disorders, 12*(4), 276–291.

Fredericks, H. D., Bullis, M., Nishioka-Evans, & Lehman, C. (1993). Community-based vocational training for adolescents with behavioral disorders. *Journal of Vocational Rehabilitation, 3*, 61–71.

Frey, K. S., Fewell, R. R., & Vadasy, P. (1989). Parental adjustment and changes in child outcome among families of young handicapped children. *Topics in Early Childhood Special Education, 8*(4), 38–57.

Friend, M., & Cook, L. (1992). *Interactions: Collaboration skills for school professionals*. New York: Longman.

Friesen, B. J., & Huff, B. (1990). Parents and professionals as advocacy partners. *Preventing School Failure, 34*(3), 31–35.

Frieze, I. H., Parsons, J. E., Johnson, P. B., Ruble, D. N., & Zellman, G. L. (1978). *Women and sex role: A social psychological perspective*. New York: Norton.

Fuchs, L. S., & Deno, S. L. (1994). Must instructionally useful performance assessment be based in the curriculum? *Exceptional Children, 61*, 15–24.

Galagan, J. E. (1985). Psychoeducational testing: Turn out the lights, the party's over. *Exceptional Children, 52*, 288–299.

Galen, H. (1991). Increasing parental involvement in elementary school: The nitty-gritty of one successful program. *Young Children, 14*(2), 18–22.

Gallagher, J., Beckman, P., & Cross, A. (1983). Families of handicapped children: Sources of stress and its amelioration. *Exceptional Children, 50*, 10–19.

Gallup, G. (1979, September). The eleventh annual Gallup Poll of the public's attitudes toward the public schools. *Phi Delta Kappan*, p. 41.

Gautt, S. (1990). Early childhood special education. In E. L. Meyen (Ed.), *Exceptional children in today's schools* (pp. 131–170). Denver: Love.

Gaylord-Ross, R., & Haring, T. (1987). Social interaction research for adolescents with severe handicaps. *Behavioral Disorders, 12*, 264–275.

Ginott, H. G. (1957). Parent education groups in a child guidance clinic. *Mental Hygiene, 41*, 82–86.

Glenn, C. (1989). Just schools for minority children. *Phi Delta Kappan, 70*, 777–779.

Glidden, L. M. (1991). Adopted children with developmental disabilities: Post-placement family functioning. *Children and Youth Services Review, 13*, 363–377.

Goldenberg, I., & Goldenberg, H. (1980). *Family therapy: An overview.* Belmont, CA: Brooks/Cole.

Goldstein, H., Arkell, C., Ashcroft, S., Hurley, O., & Lilly, S. (1975). Schools. In N. Hobbs (Ed.), *Issues in the classification of children* (Vol. 2, pp. 4–61). San Francisco: Jossey-Bass.

Goldstein, S., Strickland, B., Turnbull, A., & Curry, L. (1980). An observational analysis of the IEP conference. *Exceptional Children, 46*(4), 278–286.

Goode, W. J. (1971). World revolution and family patterns. *Journal of Marriage and Family, 33*, 624–635.

Goodman, J. F., Cecil, H. S., & Barker, W. F. (1984). Early intervention with retarded children: Some encouraging results. *Developmental Medicine and Child Neurology, 26*, 47–55.

Gordon, I. J. (1971). *A home learning center approach to early stimulation.* Gainesville, FL: Institute for Development of Human Resources.

Gordon, T. (1970). *Parent effectiveness training.* New York: Wyden.

Gordon, T. (1978). *PET in action.* New York: Bantam.

Gordon, T. (1980). Parent effectiveness training: A prevention program and its effects on families. In M. J. Fine (Ed.), *Handbook on parent education* (pp. 101–121). New York: Academic.

Gorham, K. A. (1975). A lost generation of parents. *Exceptional Children, 41*(8), 521–525.

Gorham, K. A., Jardins, C. D., Page, R., Pettis, E., & Scheiber, B. (1975). Effect on parents. In N. Hobbs (Ed.), *Issues in the classification of children* (Vol. 2, pp. 154–188). San Francisco: Jossey-Bass.

Graliker, E. V., Fishler, K., & Koch, R. (1962). Teenage reaction to a mentally retarded sibling. *American Journal of Mental Deficiency, 66*, 838–843.

Gray, S., & Klaus, R. (1965). Experimental preschool program for culturally deprived children. *Child Development, 36*, 887–898.

Green, J. W. (1982). *Cultural awareness in the human services.* Englewood Cliffs, NJ: Prentice-Hall.

Green, L. (1988). The parent-teacher partnership. *Academic Therapy, 24*(1), 89–94.

Greenwood, C., Delquadri, J., & Hall, R.V. (1984). Opportunity to respond and student academic performance. In W. L. Heward, T. E. Heron, D. S. Hill, & J. Trap-Porter (Eds.), *Focus on behavior analysis in education* (pp. 55–88). Columbus, OH: Merrill.

Greenwood, C., Whorton, D., & Delquadri, J. (1984). Tutoring methods: Increasing students' opportunity to respond and achieve. *Direct Instruction News, 3*(3), 47–51.

Greer, B. G. (1975). On being the parent of a handicapped child. *Exceptional Children, 41*(8), 519.

Gregory, D. (1964). *Nigger.* New York: Pocket.

Grosenick, J. K., George, M. P., & George, N. L. (1987). A profile of school programs for the behaviorally disordered: Twenty years after Morse, Cutler and Fink. *Behavioral Disorders, 12,* 159–168.

Grossman, F. K. (1972). *Brothers and sisters of retarded children: An exploratory study.* Syracuse, NY: Syracuse University Press.

Grossman, H. (1991). Special education in a diverse society: Improving services for minority and working-class students. *Preventing School Failure, 36,* 19–27.

Groze, V. K., & Rosenthal, J. A. (1991). Single parents and their adopted children: A psychological analysis. *Families in Society, 72,* 67–77.

Guralnick, M. J., & Bennett, F. C. (1987). *The effectiveness of early intervention for at-risk and handicapped children.* New York: Academic.

Haberman, M. (1993). Visions of equal educational opportunity: The top 10 fantasies of school reformers. *Phi Delta Kappan, 75*(9), 689–692.

Hacker, A. (1983). *U/S: A statistical portrait of the American people.* New York: Viking.

Hall, R. V. (1970). *Behavior modification: The measurement of behavior.* Merriam, KS: H & H Enterprises.

Hall, R. V. (1976). *Parent training: A preventive mental health program* (National Institute of Mental Health Grant T31-HH14543). Washington, DC: Department of Health, Education and Welfare.

Halpern, R. (1990). Fragile families, fragile solutions: An essay review. *Social Service Review, 64,* 637–648.

Hammill, D. (1987). *Assessing the abilities and instructional needs of students.* Austin, TX: PRO-ED.

Hammond, D. C., Hepworth, D. H., & Smith, V. G. (1977). *Improving therapeutic communication.* San Francisco: Jossey-Bass.

Hancock, K., Wilgosh, L., & McDonald, L. (1990). Parenting a visually impaired child: The mother's perspective. *Journal of Visual Impairment and Blindness, 22,* 411–413.

Hanson, M., & Lynch, E. W. (1992). Family diversity: Implications for policy and practice. *Topics in Early Childhood Special Education, 12*(3), 283–306.

Hardin, D. M., & Littlejohn, W. (1995). Family school collaboration: Elements of effectiveness and program models. *Preventing School Failure, 39*(1), 4–8.

Hardman, M., Drew, C., & Egan, M. (1984). *Human exceptionality.* Boston: Allyn & Bacon.

Haring, N. G., & Phillips, E. L. (1962). *Educating emotionally disturbed children.* New York: McGraw-Hill.

Harlow, H. F. (1958). The nature of love. *American Psychologist, 13,* 673–685.

Harrison, R. (1974). *Beyond words.* Englewood Cliffs, NJ: Prentice-Hall.

Harry, B., Allen, N., & McLaughlin, M. (1995). Communication versus compliance: African-American parents' involvement in special education. *Exceptional Children, 61*(4), 364–377.

Hausman, B., & Hammen, C. (1993). Parenting in homeless families: The double crisis. *American Journal of Orthopsychiatry, 63*(3), 358–369.

Hawkins, R. P., Peterson, R. F., Schweid, E., & Bijou, S. W. (1966). Behavior therapy in the home: Amelioration of problem parent-child relations with the parent in a therapeutic role. *Journal of Experimental Child Psychology, 4,* 99–107.

Hayden, A. (1976). A center-based parent training model. In D. Lillie & P. L. Trohanis (Eds.), *Teaching parents to teach* (pp. 89–105). New York: Walker.

Hayden, A. H. (1979). Handicapped children, birth to age 3. *Exceptional Children, 45,* 510–516.

Hayden, A. H., & McGinness, G. D..(1977). Bases for early intervention with handicapped infants. In E. Sontag, J. Smith, & N. Certo (Eds.), *Educational programming for the severely and profoundly handicapped* (pp. 118–145). Reston, VA: Council for Exceptional Children.

Heron, T. E., & Harris, K. C. (1993). *The educational consultant: Helping professionals, parents, and mainstreamed students.* Austin, TX: PRO-ED.

Herzog, E., & Sudia, C. E. (1973). Children in fatherless families. In B. M. Caldress & H. N. Ricciuti (Eds.), *Review of child development research* (Vol. 3, pp. 117–138). Chicago: University of Chicago Press.

Hetherington, E. M., Arnett, J., & Hollier, A. (1985). The effects of remarriage on children and families. In P. Karoly & S. Wolchik (Eds.), *Family transition* (pp. 71–97). New York: Garland.

Hetherington, E. M., & Cox, M. (1985). Long-term effects of divorce and remarriage on the adjustment of children. *Journal of the American Academy of Child Psychiatry, 24,* 518–530.

Hetherington, E. M., Cox, M., & Cox, R. (1982). Effects of divorce on parents and children. In M. Lamb (Ed.), *Nontraditional families* (pp. 223–288). Hillsdale, NJ: Erlbaum.

Hetherington, E. M., & Martin, B. (1972). Family interaction. In H. C. Quay & J. S. Werry (Eds.), *Psychopathological disorders of childhood* (pp. 194–218). New York: Wiley.

Hobbs, N. (1975a). *The futures of children.* San Francisco: Jossey-Bass.

Hobbs, N. (1975b). *Issues in the classification of children.* San Francisco: Jossey-Bass.

Hobbs, N. (1978). Classification options: A conversation with Nicholas Hobbs on exceptional child education. *Exceptional Children, 44*(7), 494–497.

Hodgkinson, H. (1991). Reform versus reality. *Phi Delta Kappan, 73*, 9–15.

Hodgkinson, H. (1992). *A demographic look at tomorrow.* Washington, DC: Institute for Educational Leadership.

Hodgkinson, H. (1993). American education: The good, the bad, and the task. *Phi Delta Kappan, 74*(8), 619–623.

Hoffman, A. (1980). The family life cycle and discontinuous change. In E. Carter & M. McGoldrich (Eds.), *The family life cycle: A framework for family therapy* (pp. 53–68). New York: Gardner.

Hoffman, L. W., & Nye, F. I. (1974). *Working mothers.* San Francisco: Jossey-Bass.

Holmes, G., Simpson, R., & Brittain, L. (1979). Effect of an infant stimulation program on children with developmental disabilities. *Educational Considerations, 7*(1), 22–26.

Homme, L. H. (1969). *How to use contingency contracting in the classroom.* Champaign, IL: Research Press.

Honig, S. (1975). *Parent involvement in early childhood education.* Washington, DC: National Association for the Education of Young Children.

Hoover, J. J. (1993). Helping parents develop a home-based study skills program. *Intervention in School and Clinic, 28*(4), 238–245.

Hoover-Dempsey, K. V., Bassler, O. C., & Brissie, J. S. (1992). Exploration in parent-school relations. *Journal of Educational Research, 85,* 287–294.

Huxman, J. (1976). *Rights and responsibilities of parents under the Education for All Handicapped Children Act (P.L. 94-142).* Unpublished manuscript, University of Kansas, Lawrence.

Idol, L., Paolucci-Whitcomb, P., & Nevin, A. (1986). *Collaborative consultation.* Austin, TX: PRO-ED.

Idstein, P., Gizzi, P., Ferrero, K., & Miller, S. (1994). There are others in the mainstream. *Phi Delta Kappan, 75*(9), 718–720.

Innocenti, M. S., Huh, K., & Boyce, G. C. (1992). Families of children with disabilities: Normative data and other considerations on parenting stress. *Topics in Early Childhood Special Education, 12*(3), 403–427.

Isakson, R. L. (1979, September). Whatever happened to the Waltons? *Instructor,* pp. 77–79.

Ivey, A., & Authier, J. (1978). *Microcounseling.* Springfield, IL: Thomas.

Ivey, A., Ivey, M., & Simek-Downing, L. (1987). *Counseling and psychotherapy: Integrating skills, theory, and practice.* Englewood Cliffs, NJ: Prentice-Hall.

Ivey, A. E., Normington, C. J., Miller, D. C., Morrill, W. H., & Hease, R. F. (1968). Microcounseling and attending behavior: An approach to prepracticum counselor training. *Journal of Counseling Psychology, Monograph Supplement* 15(5, Pt. 2).

Jago, J. L., Jago, A. G., & Hart, M. (1984). An evaluation of the total communication approach for teaching language to developmentally delayed preschool children. *Education and Training of the Mentally Retarded, 19,* 175–182.

James, M., & Jongeward, D. (1971). *Born to win.* Reading, MA: Addison-Wesley.

Jaramillo, M. (1974). Cultural conflict curriculum and the exceptional child. *Exceptional Children, 40,* 585–587.

Jencks, C. (1966). Education, the racial gap. *New Republic, 155,* 21–26.

Johnson, H. L. (1993). Stressful family experiences and young children: How the classroom teacher can help. *Intervention in School and Clinic, 28*(3), 165–171.

Johnson, J. L. (1969). Special education and the inner city: A challenge for the future or another means for cooling the mark out? *Journal of Special Education, 3,* 241–251.

Johnson, J. L. (1976). Mainstreaming Black children. In R. L. Jones (Ed.), *Mainstreaming and the minority child* (pp. 159–180). Reston, VA: Council for Exceptional Children.

Johnson, S. M., & Lobitz, G. R. (1974). The personal and marital status of parents as related to observed child deviance and parenting behaviors. *Journal of Abnormal Child Psychology, 3,* 193–208.

Johnson, W. (1956). *Your most enchanted listener.* New York: Harper Brothers.

Jones, R. L., & Wilderson, F. B. (1976). Mainstreaming and the minority child: An overview of issues and a perspective. In R. L. Jones (Ed.), *Mainstreaming and the minority child* (pp. 1–13). Reston, VA: Council for Exceptional Children.

Jourard, S. M. (1966). *Personal adjustment.* New York: Macmillan.

Justice, R. S., O'Connor, G., & Warren, N. (1971). Problems reported by parents of mentally retarded children—Who helps? *American Journal of Mental Deficiency, 75*(6), 685–691.

Kahne, J., & Westheimer, J. (1993). Building school communities: An experience based model. *Phi Delta Kappan, 75*(4), 324–329.

Kanner, L. (1957). Parents' feelings about retarded children. In C. Stacey (Ed.), *Counseling and psychotherapy with the mentally retarded* (pp. 61–78). Glencoe, IL: Free Press.

Karnes, M. B., & Lee, R. C. (1978). *Early childhood: What research and experience say to the teacher of exceptional children.* Reston, VA: Council for Exceptional Children.

Karnes, M., & Lee, R. (1980). Involving parents in the education of handicapped children. In M. J. Fine (Ed.), *Handbook on parent education* (pp. 201–225). New York: Academic.

Karnes, M., Teska, J., Hodgins, A., & Badger, E. (1970). Educational intervention at home by mothers of disadvantaged infants. *Child Development, 41,* 925–935.

Karnes, M. B., & Zehrbach, R. R. (1972). Flexibility in getting parents involved in the school. *Teaching Exceptional Children, 5,* 6–9.

Karpowitz, D. H. (1980). A conceptualization of the American family. In M. J. Fine (Ed.), *Handbook on parent education* (pp. 27–50). New York: Academic.

Kauffman, J. (1977). *Characteristics of children's behavior disorders*. Columbus, OH: Merrill.

Kauffman, J. M. (1993). How we might achieve the radical reform of special education. *Exceptional Children, 60*(1), 6–16.

Kauffman, J. M., & Hallahan, D. P. (1995). *The illusion of full inclusion*. Austin, TX: PRO-ED.

Keele, R., & Harrison, G. (1971, September). *A comparison of the effectiveness of structured tutoring techniques as used by parents and paid student tutors in teaching basic reading skills*. Paper presented at the annual meeting of the California Educational Research Association, San Diego.

Kelly, E. J. (1974). *Parent-teacher interaction: A special educational perspective*. Seattle: Special Child.

Kelly, J. B. (1993). Current research on children's postdivorce adjustment: No simple answers. *Family and Conciliation Courts Review, 31*(1), 29–49.

Kelly, J. B., & Wallerstein, J. S. (1976). The effects of parental divorce: Experiences of the child in early latency. *American Journal of Orthopsychiatry, 46*(1), 20–32.

Kentowitz, L. A., Gallagher, J., & Edgar, E. (1977). Generic services for the severely handicapped and their families: What's available? In E. Sontag, J. Smith, & N. Certo (Eds.), *Educational programming for the severely profoundly handicapped* (pp. 61–83). Reston, VA: Council for Exceptional Children.

Kerr, M. M., & Nelson, C. M. (1983). *Strategies for managing behavior problems in the classroom*. Columbus, OH: Merrill.

Keystone View. (1971). *Keystone Visual Screening Tests*. Davenport, IA: Author.

Klein, S. D. (1972). Brother to sister: Sister to brother. *Exceptional Parent, 2*, 10–15.

Kliewer, W., & Sandler, I. (1993). Social competence and coping among children of divorce. *American Journal of Orthopsychiatry, 63*(3), 432–440.

Knitzer, J., Steinberg, Z., & Fleisch, B. (1990). *At the schoolhouse door: An examination of programs and policies for children with behavior and emotional problems*. New York: Bank Street College of Education.

Kohl, H. (1967). *36 children*. New York: New American Library.

Kosa, J. (1975). The nature of poverty. In J. Kosa & I. K. Zola (Eds.), *Poverty and health: A sociological analysis* (pp. 18–27). Cambridge, MA: Harvard University Press.

Kozol, J. (1991). *Savage inequalities: Children in America's schools*. New York: Crown.

Kronick, D. (1975). *What about me?* San Rafael, CA: Academic Therapy.

Kroth, R. L. (1980). *Strategies for effective parent-teacher interaction*. Albuquerque: University of New Mexico, Institute for Parent Involvement.

Kroth, R. L. (1981). Involvement with parents of behaviorally disordered adolescents. In G. Brown, R. L. McDowell, & J. Smith (Eds.), *Educating adolescents with behavior disorders* (pp. 123–139). Columbus, OH: Merrill.

Kroth, R. L. (1985). *Communicating with parents of exceptional children*. Denver: Love.

Kroth, R. L., Whelan, R. J., & Stables, J. M. (1970). Teacher application of behavior principles in home and classroom environments. *Focus on Exceptional Children, 3*, 1–10.

Kroth, R. L., & Simpson, R. L. (1977). *Parent conferences as a teaching strategies*. Denver: Love.

Kübler-Ross, E. (1969). *On death and dying*. New York: Macmillan.

Kupper, L. (1993). Parenting a child with special needs: A guide to readings and resources. *NICHCY News Digest, 3*(1), 1–25.

Kysela, G. M., McDonald, L., Reddon, J., & Gobeil-Dwyer, F. (1988). Stress and supports to families with a handicapped child. In K. Marfo (Ed.), *Parent-child interaction and developmental disabilities* (pp. 273–289). New York: Praeger.

Lambie, R., & Daniels-Mohring, D. (1993). *Family systems within educational contexts*. Denver: Love.

Langton, G., & Stout, I. W. (1954). *Teacher-parent interviews*. Englewood Cliffs, NJ: Prentice-Hall.

Laosa, L. M. (1977). Nonbiased assessment of children's abilities: Historical antecedents and current issues. In T. Oakland (Ed.), *Psychological and educational assessment of minority children* (pp. 47–69). New York: Brunner/ Mazel.

Larry P. v. Wilson Riles, NOC-71-2270 RFP, U.S. Dist (N.D. Ca. 1972).

Larsen, S., & Poplin, M. (1980). *Methods for educating the handicapped: An individualized education program approach*. Boston: Allyn & Bacon.

Levenstein, P. (1970). Cognitive growth in preschoolers through verbal interaction with mothers. *American Journal of Orthopsychiatry, 40*, 426–432.

Lewin, K. A. (1935). *A dynamic theory of personality*. New York: McGraw-Hill.

Lewis, D. K. (1977). A response to inequality: Black women, racism, and sexism. *Journal of Women in Culture and Society, 3*(2), 339–361.

Lieberman, L.M. (1992). Preserving special education . . . For those who need it. In W. Stainback & S. Stainback (Eds.), *Controversial issues confronting special education* (pp. 13–25). Boston: Allyn & Bacon.

Lindsley, O. R. (1966). An experiment with parents handling behavior at home. *Johnstone Bulletin, 9*, 27–36.

Long, A. (1976). Easing the stress of parent-teacher conferences. *Today's Education, 64*, 84.

Love, H. D. (1973). *The mentally retarded child and his family*. Springfield, IL: Thomas.

Lyon, S., & Preis, A. (1983). Working with families of severely handicapped persons. In M. Seligman (Ed.), *The family with a handicapped child* (pp. 203–232). New York: Grune & Stratton.

MacMillan, D., & Turnbull, A. (1983). Parent involvement with special education: Respecting individual preferences. *Education and Training of the Mentally Retarded, 18*(1), 4–9.

Madden, N. A., & Slavin, R. E. (1983). Mainstreaming students with mild handicaps: Academic and social outcomes. *Review of Educational Research, 53,* 519–569.

Makielski, S. J. (1973). *Beleaguered minorities: Cultural politics in America.* San Francisco: Freeman.

Mannan, G., & Blackwell, J. (1992). Parent involvement: Barriers and opportunities. *The Urban Review, 24,* 219–226.

Martin, B. (1975). Parent-child relations. In F. D. Horowitz (Ed.), *Review of child development research* (Vol. 4, pp. 463–540). Chicago: University of Chicago Press.

Matarazzo, J., & Wiens, A. (1977). Speech behavior as an objective correlate of empathy and outcome in interview and psychotherapy research: A review with implications for behavior modification. *Behavior Modification, 1*(4), 453–480.

McAfee, J. K., & Vergason, G. A. (1979). Parent involvement in the process of special education: Establishing the new partnership. *Focus on Exceptional Children, 11*(2), 1–15.

McCord, W., McCord, J., & Thurber, E. (1962). Some effects of paternal absence on male children. *Journal of Abnormal and Social Psychology, 64,* 361–369.

McDaniels, G. (1977). Successful programs for young handicapped children. *Educational Horizons, 56*(1), 26–33.

McDonald, E. (1962). *Understanding those feelings.* Pittsburgh, PA: Stanwix House.

McDowell, R. L. (1976). Parent counseling: The state of the act. *Journal of Learning Disabilities, 9*(10), 6–11.

McDowell, R. L. (1981). Adolescence. In G. Brown, R. L. McDowell, & J. Smith (Eds.), *Educating adolescents with behavior disorders* (pp. 10–29). Columbus, OH: Merrill.

McGill, D., & Pearce, J. K. (1982). British families. In M. Goldrick, J. K. Pearce, & J. Giordano (Eds.), *Ethnicity in family therapy* (pp. 3–30). New York: Guilford.

McLanahan, S. (1983). Family structure and stress: A longitudinal comparison of two-parent and female-headed families. *Journal of Marriage and the Family, 45,* 347–357.

McLoughlin, J. A., & Lewis, R. B. (1986). *Assessing special students.* Columbus, OH: Merrill.

McNaughton, D. (1994). Measuring parent satisfaction with early childhood intervention programs: Current practice, problems, and future perspectives. *Topics in Early Childhood Special Education, 14*(10), 26–48.

McWhirter, E. H., McWhirter, J. J., McWhirter, B. T., & McWhirter, A. M. (1993). Family counseling interventions: Understanding family systems and the referral process. *Intervention in School and Clinic, 28*(4), 231–237.

Mead, M. (1928). *Coming of age in Samoa.* New York: Morrow.

Melville, K. (1977). *Marriage and family today.* New York: Random House.

Mercer, J. R. (1970). Sociological perspectives on mild mental retardation. In H. C. Haywood (Ed.), *Social-cultural aspects of mental retardation* (pp. 161–188). New York: Appleton-Century-Crofts.

Mercer, J. R. (1971). The meaning of mental retardation. In R. Koch & J. C. Dobson (Eds.), *The mentally retarded child and his family* (pp. 112–139). New York: Brunner/Mazel.

Mercer, J. R. (1973). *Labeling the mentally retarded*. Berkeley: University of California Press.

Mercer, J. R. (1975). Psychological assessment of the rights of children. In N. Hobbs (Ed.), *Issues in the classification of children* (Vol. 1, pp. 130–158). San Francisco: Jossey-Bass.

Messineo, L., & Sleeman, P. J. (1977). A parents guide to special education. *International Journal of Instructional Media, 4*(4), 364–368.

Meyen, E. L. (1978a). An introductory perspective. In E. L. Meyen (Ed.), *Exceptional children and youth: An introduction* (pp. 1–33). Denver: Love.

Meyen, E. L. (1978b). *Exceptional children and youth: An introduction*. Denver: Love.

Millenson, J. R. (1967). *Principles of behavior analysis*. New York: Macmillan.

Miller, S. P., & Hudson, P. (1994). Using structured parent groups to provide parental support. *Intervention in School and Clinic, 29*(3), (pp. 151–155).

Mills v. Board of Education of the District of Columbia, 348 F. Supp. 866 (1972).

Minke, K. M., & Scott, M. M. (1994). The development of Individualized Family Service Plans: Roles for parent and staff. *Journal of Special Education, 27*(1), 82–106.

Mintz, S., & Kellogg, S. (1988). *Domestic revolutions: A social history of American family life*. New York: Free Press.

Minuchin, S. (1974). *Families and family therapy*. Cambridge: Harvard University Press.

Mira, M. (1970). Results of a behavior modification training program for parents and teachers. *Behavior Research and Therapy, 8*, 309–311.

Moeller, C. (1986). The effect of professionals on the family of a handicapped child. In R. R. Fewell & P. F. Vadasy (Eds.), *Families of handicapped children* (pp. 149–166). Austin, TX: PRO-ED.

Moxley-Haegert, L., & Serbin, L. A. (1983). Development education for parents of delayed infants: Effects on parental motivation and children's development. *Child Development, 54*, 1324–1331.

Mullins, J. B. (1987). Authentic voices from parents of exceptional children. *Family Relations, 36*, 30–33.

Mundschenk, N. A., & Foley, R. M. (1995). Collaborative relationships between school and home: Implications for service delivery. *Preventing School Failure, 39*(1), 16–20.

Muss, R. E. (1976). The implications of social learning theory for an understanding of adolescent development. *Adolescence, 11*, 61–85.

Nahmias, M. L. (1995). Communication and collaboration between home and school for students with ADD. *Intervention in School and Clinic, 30*(4), 241–247.

National Assessment of Educational Progress. (1988). *Computer competence: The first national assessment.* Princeton, NJ: Educational Testing Service.

National Association for Retarded Citizens. (1973). *The right to choose.* Arlington, TX: Author.

National Council on Disability. (1989). *The education of students with disabilities: Where do we stand?* Washington, DC: Author.

National Education Association. (1978). *Education for all handicapped children: Consensus, conflict, and challenge.* Washington, DC: Author.

Needle, R. H., Griffin, T., Svendsen, R., & Berney, C. (1980). Teacher stress: Sources and consequences. *Journal of School Health, 50*(2), 96–99.

Neel, R., Meadows, N., Levine, P., & Edgar, E. (1988). What happens after special education: A statewide follow-up study of secondary students who have behavioral disorders. *Behavioral Disorders, 13*(3), 209–216.

Nelson, C. M., & Polsgrove, L. (1981). The etiology of adolescent behavior disorders. In G. Brown, R. L. McDowell, & J. Smith (Eds.), *Educating adolescents with behavior disorders* (pp. 30–59). Columbus, OH: Merrill.

Newland, K. (1979). *The sisterhood of man.* New York: Norton.

Nuttall, E. V., Landurand, P. M., & Goldman, P. (1984). A critical look at testing and evaluation from a cross-cultural perspective. In P. C. Chinn (Ed.), *Education of culturally and linguistically different exceptional children* (pp. 42–62). Reston, VA: Council for Exceptional Children.

Oakland, T. D. (1973). Assessing minority group children: Challenges for school psychologists. In T. D. Oakland & B. N. Phillips (Eds.), *Assessing minority group children* (pp. 71–95). New York: Behavioral Publications.

Obiakor, F. E., Algozzine, B., & Ford, B. (1993). Urban education, the general education initiative, and service delivery to African-American students. *Urban Education, 28*(3), 313–327.

O'Dell, S. (1974). Training parents in behavior modification: A review. *Psychological Bulletin, 81,* 418–433.

O'Leary, K. D., O'Leary, S., & Becker, W. C. (1967). Modification of deviant sibling interaction patterns in the home. *Behavior Research and Therapy, 5,* 113–120.

Olshansky, S. (1966a). Chronic sorrow: A response to having a mentally defective child. In R. Noland (Ed.), *Counseling parents of the mentally retarded* (pp. 21–38). Springfield, IL: Thomas.

Olshansky, S. (1966b). Parent responses to a mentally defective child. *Mental Retardation, 4,* 21–23.

Olson, D., Russell, C., & Sprenkle, D. (1980). Marital and family therapy: A decade review. *Journal of Marriage and the Family, 42*(4), 973–993.

O'Neil, J. (1995). Can inclusion work? A conversation with Jim Kauffman and Mara Sapon-Shevin. *Educational Leadership, 52*(4), 7–11.

Parents Campaign for Handicapped Children and Youth. (1977). *Closer look.* Washington, DC: Author.

Patterson, G. R. (1965). A learning theory approach to the treatment of the school phobic child. In L. P. Ullman & L. Krasner (Eds.), *Case studies in behavior modification* (pp. 223–249). New York: Holt, Rinehart & Winston.

Patterson, G. R., Cobb, J. A., & Ray, R. S. (1972). A social engineering technology for restraining aggressive boys. In H. Adams & L. Unikel (Eds.), *Georgia Symposium in Experimental Clinical Psychology* (Vol. 2, pp. 42–66). Springfield, IL: Thomas.

Paul, J., & Epanchin, B. (1991). *Educating emotionally disturbed children and youth: Theories and practices for teachers.* New York: Macmillan.

Paul, J. L., & Simeonsson, R. J. (1993). *Children with special needs.* Ft. Worth, TX: Harcourt Brace Jovanovich.

Pennsylvania Association for Retarded Children (PARC) v. Commonwealth of Pennsylvania, 343 F. Supp. 279 (E.D. Pa. 1972).

Pepper, F. (1976). Teaching the American Indian child in mainstreaming settings. In R. L. Jones (Ed.), *Mainstreaming and the minority child* (pp. 133–158). Minneapolis: Special Education Leadership Training Institute.

Perry, W. G. (1976). On the relation of psychotherapy to counseling. In G. S. Belkin (Ed.), *Counseling: Direction in theory and practice* (pp. 198–223). Dubuque, IA: Kendall/Hunt.

Perske, R. (1973). *New directions for parents of persons who are retarded.* Nashville: Abingdon.

Peterson, N. L. (1987). *Early intervention for handicapped and at-risk children: An introduction to early childhood special education.* Denver: Love.

Phillips, E. (1985). Parents as partners: Developing parent support groups. In M. K. Zabel (Ed.), *Teaching behaviorally disordered students.* Reston, VA: Council for Exceptional Children.

Phillips, L. W. (1978). The soft underbelly of behavior therapy: Pop behavior mod. *Journal of Behavior Therapy and Experimental Psychiatry, 2,* 139–140.

Piaget, J. (1952). *The origins of intelligence in children.* New York: International Universities Press.

Polloway, E. A., & Smith, J. D. (1983). Changes in mild mental retardation: Populations, programs, and perspectives. *Exceptional Children, 50,* 149–159.

Polsgrove, L. (1991). *Reducing undesirable behavior.* Reston, VA: Council for Exceptional Children.

Popkin, M. (1983). *Active parenting handbook.* Atlanta, GA: Active Parenting.

Powell, T., & Ogle, P. (1985). *Brothers and sisters—A special part of exceptional families.* Baltimore: Brookes.

Price, J. P. (1991). Effective communication: A key to successful collaboration. *Preventing School Failure, 35*(4), 25–28.

Quay, H. C., & Werry, J. S. (1972). *Psychopathological disorders of childhood*. New York: Wiley.

Rabbitt, J. A. (1978). The parent-teacher conference: Trauma or teamwork? *Phi Delta Kappan, 52,* 471–472.

Ramos, K. (1995). Advocacy: Friend or foe? *Preventing School Failure, 39*(1), 37–40.

Rappaport, J. (1984). Studies in empowerment: Introduction to the issues. In J. Rappaport, C. Swift, & R. Hess (Eds.), *Studies in empowerment: Steps towards understanding and action* (pp. 1–7). New York: Haworth.

Raths, L. E., Harmin, M., & Simon, S. B. (1966). *Values and teaching: Working with values in the classroom*. Columbus, OH: Merrill.

Redl, F., & Wattenberg, W. W. (1959). *Mental hygiene in teaching*. New York: Harcourt, Brace & World.

Reed, S., & Sautter, R. C. (1990). Children of poverty: Kappan special report. *Phi Delta Kappan, 71,* 1–12.

Reilly, T. F. (1991). Cultural bias: The albatross of assessing behavior-disordered children and youth. *Preventing School Failure, 36,* 50–53.

Reiss, I. L. (1971). *The family system in America*. New York: Holt, Rinehart & Winston.

Reith, H. J., & Hall, R. V. (1974). *Responsive teaching model readings in applied behavior analysis*. Lawrence, KS: H & H Enterprises.

Reusen, A. K., Bos, C. S., Schumaker, J. B., & Deshler, D. D. (1994). *The self-advocacy strategy*. Lawrence, KS: Edge Enterprises.

Reynolds, M. C., Wang, M. C., & Walberg, H. J. (1987). The necessary restructuring of special and regular education. *Exceptional Children, 53,* 391–398.

Risley, T. R., & Wolf, M. M. (1966). Experimental manipulation of autistic behaviors and generalization into the home. In R. Ulrich, T. Stachnik, & J. Mabry (Eds.), *Control of human behavior* (pp. 112–144). Chicago: Scott, Foresman.

Roberts, M. (1986). Three mothers: Life-span experiences. In R. R. Fewell & P. F. Vadasy (Eds.), *Families of handicapped children* (pp. 193–220). Austin, TX: PRO-ED.

Robinson, E., & Fine, M. J. (1995). Developing collaborative home-school relationships. *Preventing School Failure, 39*(1), 9–15.

Robinson, H. B., & Robinson, N. M. (1965). *The mentally retarded child*. New York: McGraw-Hill.

Robinson, R. (1970). Don't speak to us of living death. In R. Noland (Ed.), *Counseling parents of the mentally retarded* (pp. 61–837). Springfield, IL: Thomas.

Rogers, C. (1942). *Counseling and psychotherapy*. Boston: Houghton Mifflin.

Rogers, C. R. (1951). *Client-centered therapy*. Boston: Houghton Mifflin.

Rogers, C. R. (1961). *On becoming a person*. Boston: Houghton Mifflin.

Rogers, C. R. (1962). The interpersonal relationship: The core of guidance. *Harvard Educational Review, 32*(4), 416–429.

Rogers, C. R. (1969). *Freedom to learn*. Columbus, OH: Merrill.

Rogers, H., & Saklofske, D. H. (1985). Self-concepts, locus of control and performance expectations of learning disabled children. *Journal of Learning Disabilities, 18*, 273–278.

Ronnau, J., & Poertner, J. (1993). Identification and the use of strengths: A family system approach. *Children Today, 22*(2), 20–23.

Roos, P. (1978). Parents of mentally retarded children—Misunderstood and mistreated. In A. P. Turnbull & H. R. Turnbull (Eds.), *Parents speak out: Views from the other side of the two-way mirror* (pp. 12–27). Columbus, OH: Merrill.

Roos, P. A. (1977). Parents' view of what public school education should accomplish. In E. Sontag, J. Smith, & N. Certo (Eds.), *Educational programming for the severely handicapped* (pp. 72–83). Reston, VA: Council for Exceptional Children.

Rose, S. (1969). A behavioral approach to group treatment of parents. *Social Work, 14*, 21–29.

Rosenthal, J. A., & Groze, Y. (1991). Behavioral problems of special needs adopted children. *Children and Youth Services Review, 13*, 343–361.

Ross, A. O. (1972). Behavioral therapy. In B. B. Wolman (Ed.), *Manual of child psychopathology* (pp. 282–318). New York: McGraw-Hill.

Ross, A. O. (1974). *The exceptional child in the family*. New York: Grune & Stratton.

Rotheram, M. J. (1989). The family and the school. In L. Combrinck-Graham (Ed.), *Children in family contexts: Perspectives on treatment* (pp. 347–368). New York: Guilford.

Rubin, J. Z. (1994). Models of conflict management. *Journal of Social Issues, 50*(1), 33–45.

Rudor, M. H., & Santangelo, N. (1979). *Health status of minorities and low-income groups*. Washington, DC: U.S. Department of Health, Education and Welfare, Public Health Service.

Ruma, E. H. (1976). Counseling the single parent. In G. S. Belkin (Ed.), *Counseling: Directions in theory and practice* (pp. 308–317). Dubuque, IA: Kendall/Hunt.

Rusch, F., Destefano, J., & Szymanski, E. (1992). *Transition from school to adult life: Models, linkages and policy*. Sycamore, IL: Sycamore.

Rusch, F., & Phelps, A. (1987). Secondary special education and transition from school to work: A national priority. *Exceptional Children, 53*(6), 487–492.

Rutherford, R. B., & Edgar, E. (1979). *Teachers and parents: A guide to interaction and cooperation*. Boston: Allyn & Bacon.

Rutter, M. (1971). Parent-child separation: Psychological effects on the children. *Journal of Child Psychology and Psychiatry, 12*, 233–260.

Safford, P. L., & Arbitman, D. C. (1975). *Developmental intervention with young physically handicapped children*. Springfield, IL: Thomas.

Sailor, W. (1991). Special education in the restructured school. *Remedial and Special Education, 12*(6), 8–22.

Sailor, W., Anderson, J., Halvorsen, A.T., Doering, K., Filler, J., & Goetz, L. (1989). *The comprehensive local school: Regular education for all students with disabilities.* Baltimore: Brookes.

Salend, S., & Taylor, L. (1993). Working with families: A cross-cultural perspective. *Remedial and Special Education, 14*, 25–32.

Salvia, J., & Ysseldyke, J. (1985). *Assessment in special and remedial education.* Boston: Houghton Mifflin.

Santrock, J. W. (1975). Father absence, perceived maternal behavior, and moral development in boys. *Child Development, 46*, 753–757.

Sasso, G., Hughes, V., Critchlew, W., Falcon, M., & Delquadri, J. (1980). *The effects of home tutoring procedures on the oral reading rates of learning disabled children.* Unpublished manuscript, Juniper Gardens Children's Project, University of Kansas, Lawrence.

Sasso, G. M., Simpson, R. L., & Novak, C. G. (1985). Procedures for facilitating the integration of autistic children in public school settings. *Analysis and Intervention in Developmental Disabilities, 5*, 233–246.

Satir, V. (1983). *Conjoint family therapy* (3rd ed.). Palo Alto, CA: Science and Behavior Books.

Scherer, M. (1993). On *Savage Inequalities:* A conversation with Jonathan Kozol. *Educational Leadership, 50*(4), 4–9.

Schlesinger, H. S., & Meadow, K. P. (1976). Emotional support for parents. In D. Lillie & P. L. Trohanis (Eds.), *Teaching parents to teach* (pp. 35–49). New York: Walker.

Schorr, L. B. (1989). *Within our reach: Breaking the cycle of disadvantage.* New York: Doubleday.

Schulman, S. (1988). The family of the severely handicapped child: The sibling perspective. *Journal of Family Therapy, 10*, 125–134.

Schulz, J. (1978). The parent-professional conflict. In A. P. Turnbull & H. R. Turnbull (Eds.), *Parents speak out: Views from the other side of the two-way mirror* (pp. 18–36). Columbus, OH: Merrill.

Schultz, J. B. (1987). *Parents and professionals in special education.* Boston: Allyn & Bacon.

Seligman, M., & Darling, R. B. (1989). *Ordinary families, special children: A systems approach to childhood disability.* New York: Guilford.

Shapiro, J. P., Loeb, P., & Bowermaster, D. (1993). Separate and unequal. *U.S. News and World Report, 115*(49), 46–60.

Shaw, S., Biklen, D., Conlon, S., Dunn, J., Kramer, J., & DeRoma-Wagner, V. (1990). Special education and school reform. In L. M. Bullock & R. L. Simpson (Eds.), *Critical issues in special education: Implications for personnel preparation* (pp. 12–25). Denton, TX: University of North Texas.

Shea, T., & Bauer, A. (1985). *Parents and teachers of exceptional students: A handbook of involvement*. Boston: Allyn & Bacon.

Shearer, M., & Shearer, D. (1972). The Portage Project: A model for early childhood education. *Exceptional Children, 39*, 210–217.

Shinn, M. (1978). Father absence and children's cognitive development. *Psychological Bulletin, 85*, 295–324.

Sicley, D. (1993). Effective methods of communication: Practical interventions for classroom teachers. *Intervention in School and Clinic, 29*(2), 105–108.

Siegel, E. (1975). *The exceptional child grows up*. New York: Dutton.

Siegel, S., Waxman, M., & Gaylord-Ross, R. (1992). A follow-along study of participants in a longitudinal transition program for youths with mild disabilities. *Exceptional Children, 58*, 346–356.

Siegman, A. W., & Pope, B. (1972). The effects of ambiguity and anxiety on interviewee verbal behavior. In A. W. Siegman and B. Pope (Eds.), *Studies in dyadic communication* (pp. 67–84). New York: Pergamon.

Siladi, M. S. (1980). *A survey of parental preferences in types of involvement, interactions and information in the education of severely handicapped children*. Unpublished master's thesis, University of Kansas, Lawrence.

Silberberg, N. E., & Silberberg, M. C. (1974). *Who speaks for the child?* Springfield, IL: Thomas.

Simeonsson, R. J., & Simeonsson, N. E. (1993). Children, families, and disability: Psychological dimensions. In J. L. Paul & R. J. Simeonsson (Eds.), *Children with special needs* (pp. 25–50). Ft. Worth, TX: Harcourt Brace Jovanovich.

Simmons-Martin, A. (1976). Facilitating positive parent-child interactions. In D. Lillie & P. L. Trohanis (Eds.), *Teaching parents to teach* (pp. 61–82). New York: Walker.

Simon, S. B. (1974). *Meeting yourself halfway*. Niles, IL: Argus.

Simon, S. D., Howe, L. W., & Kirschenbaum, H. (1972). *Values clarification: A handbook of practical strategies for teachers and students*. New York: Hart.

Simpson, R. (1988). Needs of parents and families whose children have learning and behavior problems. *Behavioral Disorders, 14*(1), 40–47.

Simpson, R. (1992). *The Individuals with Disabilities Act: Guidelines for parents*. Unpublished manuscript, University of Kansas Medical Center, Kansas City, KS.

Simpson, R., & Regan, M. (1986). *Management of autistic behavior*. Rockville, MD: Aspen.

Simpson, R., Whelan, R., & Zabel, R. (1993). Special education personnel preparation in the 21st century: Issues and strategies. *Remedial and Special Education, 14*(2), 7–22.

Simpson, R. L., & Carter, W. (1993). Comprehensive, inexpensive, and convenient services for parents and families of students with behavior disorders. *Preventing School Failure, 37*, 21–25.

Simpson, R. L., & Combs, N. N. (1978). *Parenting the exceptional child: A workshop manual* (Developed under federal contract 300-75-0309 with the Bureau of Education for the Handicapped, U.S. Office of Education, Department of Health, Education and Welfare). Lawrence: University of Kansas.

Simpson, R. L., & Fiedler, C. R. (1989). Parent participation in individualized educational program (IEP) conferences: A case for individualization. In M. Fine (Ed.), *The second handbook on parent education: Contemporary perspectives* (pp. 145–171). New York: Academic.

Simpson, R. L., & Poplin, M. S. (1981). Parents as agents of change: A behavioral approach. *School Psychology Review, 10*(1), 15–25.

Simpson, R. L., & Sasso, G. M. (1992). Full inclusion of students with autism in general education settings: Values versus science. *Focus on Autistic Behavior, 7*(3), 1–13.

Simpson, R. L., & Simpson, J. D. (1994). Needs of parents and families of at-risk and disabled students. *Preventing School Failure, 39*(1), 21–25.

Simpson, R. L., & Swenson, C. R. (1978). *Parts I-III: Parenting the exceptional child: Developing and maintaining adaptive behavior* (An audio-visual presentation developed under federal contract 30-75-0309 with the Bureau of Education for the Handicapped, U.S. Office of Education, Department of Health, Education and Welfare). Lawrence: University of Kansas.

Simpson, R. L., & Whorton, D. (1982). Parental involvement. In E. L. Meyen & D. Lehr (Eds.), *Exceptional children in today's schools* (pp. 529–554). Denver: Love.

Simpson, R. L., & Zionts, P. (1992). *Autism: Information and resources for parents, families, and professionals.* Austin, TX: PRO-ED.

Skinner, B. F. (1948). *Walden two.* New York: Macmillan.

Skinner, B. F. (1953). *Science and human behavior.* New York: Macmillan.

Smith, B. (1983). Homophobia: Why bring it up? *Interracial Books for Children, 14*(2), 7–8.

Smith, C. (1993). Cultural sensitivity in working with children and families. In J. L. Paul & R. J. Simeonsson (Eds.), *Children with special needs: Family, culture and society* (pp. 113–121). Ft. Worth, TX: Harcourt Brace Jovanovich.

Smith, D. D., & Luckasson, R. (1992). *Introduction to special education.* Boston: Allyn & Bacon.

Snyder-McLean, L., & McLean, J. (1987). Effectiveness of early intervention for children with language and communication disorders. In M. J. Guralnick & F. C. Bennett (Eds.), *The effectiveness of early intervention for at-risk and handicapped children* (pp. 213–274). New York: Academic.

Solnit, A. J., & Stark, M. H. (1961). Mourning the birth of a defective child. *Psychoanalytic Study of the Child, 16,* 523–537.

Sonnek, I. M. (1986). Grandparents and the extended family of handicapped children. In R. R. Fewell & P. F. Vadasy (Eds.), *Families of handicapped children: Needs and support across the life span* (pp. 99–120). Austin, TX: PRO-ED.

Sontag, J. C., & Schacht, R. (1994). An ethnic comparison of parent participation and information needs in early intervention. *Exceptional Children, 60*(5), 422–433.

Stahlecker, J. E., & Cohen, M. C. (1985). Application of the strange situation attachment paradigm to a neurologically impaired population. *Child Development, 56,* 502–507.

Stainback, S., & Stainback, W. (1992a). *Curriculum considerations in inclusive classrooms: Facilitating learning for all students.* Baltimore: Brookes.

Stainback, S., & Stainback, W. (1992b). Schools as inclusive communities. In W. Stainback & S. Stainback (Eds.), *Controversial issues confronting special education* (pp. 113–121). Boston: Allyn & Bacon.

Stainback, S., Stainback, W., & Forest, M. (1989). *Educating all students in the mainstream of regular education.* Baltimore: Brookes.

Stainback, W., & Stainback, S. (1984). A rationale for the merger of regular and special education. *Exceptional Children, 51*(2), 102–111.

Stainback, W., & Stainback, S. (1990). *Support networks for inclusive schooling: Interdependent integrated education.* Baltimore: Brookes.

Stokes, T., & Baer, D. (1977). An implicit technology of generalization. *Journal of Applied Behvavior Analysis, 10,* 349–367.

Strain, P., Cooke, T., & Apolloni, T. (1976). *Teaching exceptional children: Assessing and modifying social behavior.* New York: Academic.

Stuart, J. C. (1986). *Counseling parents of exceptional children.* Columbus, OH: Charles E. Merrill.

Sugai, G., & Tindal, G. (1993). *Effective school consultation.* Pacific Grove, CA: Brooks/Cole.

Sullivan, R. (1976). The role of the parent. In M. A. Thomas (Ed.), *Hey, don't forget about me* (pp. 84–97). Reston, VA: Council for Exceptional Children.

Sulzer-Azaroff, B., & Mayer, G. R. (1977). *Applying behavior analysis procedures with children and youth.* New York: Holt, Rinehart & Winston.

Summers, J. A., Brotherson, M. J., & Turnbull, A. (1988). The impact of handicapped children on families. In E. W. Lynch & R. B. Lewis (Eds.), *Exceptional children and adults* (pp. 504–544). Glenview, IL: Scott, Foresman.

Szymanski, E. M. (1994). Transition: Life-span and life-space considerations for empowerment. *Exceptional Children, 60,* 402–410.

Telford, C. W., & Sawrey, J. M. (1977). *The exceptional individual.* Englewood Cliffs, NJ: Prentice-Hall.

Tew, B., & Laurence, K. (1973). Mothers, brothers, and sisters of patients with spina bifida. *Developmental Medicine and Child Neurology, 15,* 69–76.

Thiessen, I. (1993). The impact of divorce on children. *Early Child Development and Care, 96,* 19–26.

Thomas, C., English, J., & Bickel, A. (1994). School-linked services: A model for change. *Thrust for Educational Leadership, 23*(4), 8–12.

Thurow, L. C. (1987). The new American family. *Technology Review, 90,* 26.

Thurston, L. (1977). *The experimental analysis of a parent-tutoring program to increase reading enjoyment, and oral reading and comprehension skills of urban elementary school children.* Unpublished doctoral dissertation, University of Kansas, Lawrence.

Tooley, K. (1976). Antisocial behavior and social alienation post divorce: The "man of the house" and his mother. *American Journal of Orthopsychiatry, 46*(1), 33–42.

Truax, C. B., & Carkhuff, R. R. (1967). *Toward effective counseling and psychotherapy: Training and practice.* Chicago: Aldine.

Truax, C. B., & Mitchell, K. M. (1971). Research on certain therapist interpersonal skills in relation to process and outcome. In A. E. Bergin & S. L. Garfield (Eds.), *Handbook of psychotherapy and behavior change* (pp. 299–344). New York: Wiley.

Tuchman, J., & Regan, R. A. (1966). Intactness of the home and behavioral problems in children. *Journal of Child Psychology and Psychiatry, 7,* 225–233.

Tuma, J. M. (1989). Mental health services for children: The state of the art. *American Psychologist, 44,* 188–198.

Turnbull, A., & Turnbull, R. (1986). *Families, professionals, and exceptionality.* Columbus, OH: Merrill.

Turnbull, A. P. (1981). Parent-professional interactions. In M. Snell (Ed.), *Curriculum for the moderately and severely retarded* (pp. 201–229). Columbus, OH: Merrill.

Turnbull, A. P., & Strickland, B. (1981). Parents and the educational system. In J. L. Paul (Ed.), *Understanding and working with parents of children with special needs* (pp. 231–263). New York: Holt, Rinehart & Winston.

Turnbull, A. P., Summers, J. A., & Brotherson, M. J. (1983). *Working with families with disabled members: A family systems perspective.* Lawrence, KS: University of Kansas, Research and Training Center on Independent Living.

Turnbull, A. P., & Turnbull, H. R. (1978). *Parents speak out: Views from the other side of the two-way mirror.* Columbus, OH: Merrill.

Turnbull, A. P., & Turnbull, H. R. (1990). *Families, professionals, and exceptionality: A special partnership* (2nd ed.). Columbus, OH: Merrill.

Turnbull, H. R. (1993). *Free appropriate public education.* Denver: Love.

Turnbull, H. R., & Turnbull, A. (1978). *Free appropriate public education: Law and implementation.* Denver: Love.

U.S. Bureau of Labor Statistics. (1991). *Monthly labor review.* Washington, DC: U.S. Department of Labor.

U.S. Bureau of the Census. (1988). *Household and family characteristics.* Washington, DC: U.S. Government Printing Office.

U.S. Bureau of the Census. (1990). *Current population report* (Series P-70#29). Unpublished data.

U.S. Bureau of the Census. (1993). *Current population reports*. Washington, DC: U.S. Government Printing Office.

U.S. Department of Commerce, Bureau of the Census. (1993). *Statistical abstract of the United States*. Washington, DC: U.S. Government Printing Office.

U.S. Department of Education. (1991). *America 2000: An education strategy*. Washington, DC: Author.

U.S. National Center for Health Statistics of the United States. (1995). *Vital statistics of the United States*. Washington, DC: Author.

Vadasy, P. (1986). Single mothers: A social phenomenon and population in need. In R. R. Fewell & P. F. Vadasy (Eds.), *Families of handicapped children* (pp. 221–249). Austin, TX: PRO-ED.

Van Reusen, A. K., Bos, C. S., Schumaker, J. B., & Deshler, D. D. (1994). *The self-advocacy strategy for education and transition planning*. Lawrence, KS: Edge Enterprises.

Visher, E. B., & Visher, J. S. (1979). *Stepfamilies: A guide to working with stepparents and stepchildren*. New York: Brunner/Mazel.

Visher, E. B., & Visher, J. S. (1988). *Old loyalties, new ties: Therapeutic strategies with stepfamilies*. New York: Brunner/Mazel.

Visher, E. B., & Visher, J. S. (1991). *How to win as a stepfamily*. New York: Brunner/Mazel.

Voltz, D. L. (1994). Developing collaborative parent-teacher relationships with culturally diverse parents. *Intervention in School and Clinic, 29*(5), 288–291.

Wagner, M., D'Amico, R., Marder, C., Newman, L., & Blackorby, J. (1992). *What happens next? Trends in postschool outcomes of youth with disabilities*. Menlo Park, CA: SRI International.

Wagonseller, B. R. (1979). *The parent/professional education relationship*. Unpublished manuscript, University of Nevada, Las Vegas.

Wagonseller, B. R., Burnett, M., Salzburg, B., & Burnett, J. (1977). *The art of parenting*. Champaign, IL: Research Press.

Walker, H. M. (1979). *The acting out child: Coping with classroom disruption*. Boston: Allyn & Bacon.

Walker, H. M., & Fabre, T. R. (1987). Assessment of behavior disorders in the school setting: Issues, problems and strategies revisited. In N. Haring (Ed.), *Assessing and managing behavior disorders* (pp. 198–234). Seattle: University of Washington Press.

Wallace, G., & Larsen, S. C. (1978). *Educational assessment of learning problems: Testing for teachers*. Boston: Allyn & Bacon.

Wallerstein, J. (1985). Effects of divorce on children. *Harvard Medical School Mental Health Letter, 2*(3), 1–11.

Wallerstein, J. S., & Blakeslee, S. (1990). *Second chances*. New York: Ticknor & Fields.

Wallerstein, J. S., & Kelly, J. B. (1975). The effects of parental divorce: Experiences of the preschool child. *Journal of the American Academy of Child Psychiatry, 14,* 600–616.

Wallerstein, J. S., & Kelly, J. B. (1976). The effects of parental divorce: Experiences of the child in later latency. *American Journal of Orthopsychiatry, 46*(2), 256–269.

Wang, M. C., Reynolds, M. C., & Walberg, A. J. (1986). Rethinking special education. *Educational Leadership, 44*(1), 26–31.

Warfield, G. J. (1975). Mothers of retarded children review a parent education program. *Exceptional Children, 42,* 559–562.

Warschaw, T. A. (1980). *Winning by negotiation.* New York: McGraw-Hill.

Weber, B. (1974). A parent of a retarded child gives her idea of services needed. *Child Welfare, 53*(2), 98–101.

Weikart, D. (1970). *Longitudinal results of the Ypsilanti Perry preschool project.* Ypsilanti, MI: High-Scope Educational Research Foundation.

Weintraub, M., & Wolf, B. (1983). Effects of stress and social supports on mother-child interactions in single- and two-parent families. *Child Development, 54,* 1297–1311.

Weissbourd, B., & Kagan, S. (1989). Family support programs: Catalysts for change. *American Journal of Orthopsychiatry, 59,* 20–31.

Weitz, S. (1977). *Sex roles.* New York: Oxford University Press.

Werrbach, G. B. (1992). A study of home-based services for families of adolescents. *Child and Adolescent Social Work Journal, 9,* 505–523.

Westinghouse Learning Corporation and Ohio State University. (1969). *The impact of Head Start: An evaluation of the effects of Head Start on children's cognitive and affective development.* Springfield, VA: Clearinghouse for Federal Scientific and Technical Information.

Whelan, R. J. (1988). *Special education procedural due process checklist.* Unpublished manuscript, University of Kansas, Lawrence.

Whiteside, M. F. (1981). A family systems approach with families of remarriage. In I. R. Stewart & L. E. Abt (Eds.), *Children of separation and divorce: Management and treatment* (pp. 319–336). New York: Van Nostrand Reinhold.

Who can help? (1977). Philadelphia: National Learning Resource Center of Pennsylvania.

Wielkiewicz, R. M. (1986). *Behavior management in the schools.* New York: Pergamon.

Wiener, D., & Ehrlich, D. (1960). Values and goals. *American Journal of Psychotherapy, 73,* 615–617.

Will, M. (1984). Let us pause and reflect—But not for long. *Exceptional Children, 51,* 11–16.

Will, M. (1988). Family support: Perspectives on the provision of family support services. *Focal Point, 2*(3), 1–2.

Williams, B. F. (1992). Changing demographics: Challenges for educators. *Intervention in School and Clinic, 27*, 157–163.

Williams, C. D. (1959). The elimination of tantrum behavior by extinction procedures. *Journal of Abnormal and Social Psychology, 59*, 269.

Wilmore, E. L. (1995). When your child is special. *Educational Leadership, 52*(4), 60–62.

Winston, P. (1986). Effective strategies for involving families in intervention efforts. *Focus on Exceptional Children, 19*(2), 1–12.

Wolchik, S., West, S., Westover, S., & Sandler, I. (1993). The children of divorce parenting intervention: Outcome evaluation of an empirically based program. *American Journal of Community Psychology, 21*(3), 293–331.

Wolf, J. S. (1982). Parents as partners in exceptional education. *Theory into Practice, 21*, 77–81.

Wood, F. H. (1990). Issues in the education of behaviorally disordered students. In M. C. Wang, M. C. Reynolds, & H. J. Walberg (Eds.), *Special education research and practice: Synthesis of findings* (pp. 101–118). New York: Pergamon.

Wright, L. S., Matlock, K. S., & Matlock, D. T. (1985). Parents of handicapped children: Their self-ratings, life satisfaction and parental adequacy. *Exceptional Children, 32*, 37–40.

Wyckoff, J. L. (1980). Parent education programs: Ready, set, go! In M. J. Fine (Ed.), *Handbook on parent education* (pp. 140–163). New York: Academic Therapy.

Yaffe, E. (1994). Not just cupcakes anymore: A study of community involvement. *Phi Delta Kappan, 75*(9), 697–704.

Yell, M. (1989). Honig v. Doe: The Supreme Court addresses the suspension and expulsion of elementary school age children. *Exceptional Children, 56*, 60–69.

Yorburg, B. (1983). *Families and societies.* New York: Columbia University Press.

Yoshida, R., & Gottlieb, J. (1977). Model of parental participation in the pupil planning process. *Mental Retardation, 15*, 17–20.

Ysseldyke, J. E., Algozzine, B., & Thurlow, M. L. (1992). *Critical issues in special education.* Boston: Houghton Mifflin.

Ysseldyke, J. E., & Thurlow, M. L. (1984). Assessment practices in special education: Adequacy and appropriateness. *Educational Psychologist, 9*(3), 123–136.

Zeilberger, J., Sampen, S. E., & Sloane, H. M. (1968). Modification of a child's problem behavior in the home with the mother as therapist. *Journal of Applied Behavior Analysis, 1*, 47–53.

Zill, N., & Nord, C. W. (1994). *Running in place: How American families are faring in a changing economy and an individualized society.* Washington, DC: Child Trends.

Zionts, P., & Simpson, R. (1988). *Understanding children and youth with emotional and behavioral problems.* Austin, TX: PRO-ED.

Ziskin, L. Z. (1978). The story of Jennie. In A. P. Turnbull & H. R. Turnbull (Eds.), *Parents speak out: Views from the other side of the two-way mirror* (pp. 70–80). Columbus, OH: Merrill.

Zolko, M. E. (1991). Counseling parents of children with disabilities: A review of the literature and implications for practice. *Journal of Rehabilitation, 57*(2), 29–34.

Index